AGRICULTURAL AND FOOD POLICY

Second Edition

Ronald D. Knutson
Texas A&M University

J. B. Penn
Sparks Commodities, Inc.

William T. Boehm
The Kroger Co.

PRENTICE HALL, Englewood Cliffs, New Jersey 07632

Library of Congress Cataloging-in-Publication Data

KNUTSON, RONALD D.
    Agricultural and food policy / Ron Knutson, J.B. Penn, William T.
Boehm. — 2nd ed.
        p.   cm.
    Includes index.
    ISBN 0-13-018789-5
    1. Agriculture and state—United States. 2. Food supply–
–Government policy—United States. 3. United States—Commercial
policy. 4. United States—Economic policy—1981–   I. Penn, J. B.
II. Boehm, William T. III. Title.
HD1761.K65 1990
338.1′873—dc19   89-3761
                                CIP

Editorial/production supervision
  and interior design: *Carol L. Atkins*
Cover design: *20/20 Services, Inc.*
Manufacturing buyer: *Laura Crossland*

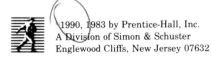

Printed in the United States of America
10 9 8 7 6 5 4 3 2 1

ISBN   0-13-018789-5

Prentice-Hall International (UK) Limited, *London*
Prentice-Hall of Australia Pty. Limited, *Sydney*
Prentice-Hall Canada Inc., *Toronto*
Prentice-Hall Hispanoamericana, S.A., *Mexico*
Prentice-Hall of India Private Limited, *New Delhi*
Prentice-Hall of Japan, Inc., *Tokyo*
Simon & Schuster Asia Pte. Ltd., *Singapore*
Editora Prentice-Hall do Brasil, Ltda., *Rio de Janeiro*

Contents

Preface

This book is designed and written primarily as an undergraduate textbook on agricultural and food policy. It recognizes that policy formulation involves a blending of economics and politics. It also recognizes that the government policies and programs that are uniquely important to agriculture today are more than the traditional domestic farm programs. In fact, as one looks back on the past two decades, the policy decisions having the greatest impact on agriculture may arguably have been in the international, consumer, and general economic policy arenas.

Understanding contemporary domestic farm policy decisions requires knowledge of the process of policy formulation, the macroeconomics of agriculture, the international agricultural economic and policy environment, and the fundamental economic relationships and principles that affect today's agriculture. These topics, therefore, are treated before discussions of more traditional policy instruments such as target prices, loan rates, grain reserves, and production controls. Subsequent chapters describe and analyze contemporary issues such as the structure of agriculture, price controls, nutrition policy, food safety, farm labor, and the use of finite resources.

The issues are treated in a current context intended to capture the interest of students. The book does not prescribe solutions to problems. Instead, it emphasizes developing an understanding of the problems, policy alternatives, and their consequences.

Recognition is given to the fact that the nature of agricultural and food problems changes over time. This is due to the inherent volatility of agriculture, food production, and the domestic and international factors affecting the politics of food. While policymakers in the 1970s worried about production deficits, their attention in the 1980s returned to surpluses and low prices that have tended to characterize agriculture since the first major farm programs of the 1930s.

The problems of agriculture, or their symptoms, have a tendency to reappear periodically. Agricultural and food policy goals shift as the nature of the problem and related priorities change. These apparent policy cycles underscore the need to review the lessons of past policy experience. Yet agricultural policy tools, over time, evolve as old programs and are modified to fit changing agricultural circumstances and demands of policymakers.

This second edition reflects that shifting nature of the farm and food problems. It places greater emphasis on the long-run tendency of agriculture to overproduce. The food deficits of the 1970s had profound impacts on domestic and international agriculture. Additional resources were attracted into food production by abnormally high prices and incomes, but expanding export markets were choked off by world recession, huge debt for developing countries and emphasis on self-sufficiency by many nations. Contractional U.S. macroeconomic policies contributed to these world economic problems and reduced competitiveness of U.S. agricultural products in world markets. Agriculture entered its worst recession since the Great Depression as commodity prices, net farm income, and asset values tumbled. Government attempts to protect farmers from the adverse economic conditions became exceedingly costly and increasingly controversial, both at home and abroad.

This edition adds a chapter to Part II (macroeconomics of agriculture), which reflects the increasing importance of general economic policies on the agriculture sector. These shifting conditions also necessitated major revisions in Part III to explain the changing nature of the farm problem and government's attempts to deal with adversities in agriculture. In Part IV, the two chapters on consumer policy have been reorganized, with one covering food price issues and the other nutrition, food safety, and quality issues. Resource issues are contained in Part IV as a reflection of the public interest in policy regarding resources and the environment. A new chapter has been added on the impact of agricultural and food policy on agribusiness.

Economic principles are introduced throughout the book where they are particularly relevant to analyzing a particular problem, policy, program, or consequence. This is done to develop an understanding of how the tools of analysis can be used to provide insight into the economic impact of particular policies. Ultimately, our goal is to provide students with a framework and the tools to evaluate policies on which they, as the leaders of the future, will have to make decisions.

Many people at Purdue University, the University of Minnesota, Pennsylvania State University, Texas A&M University, and in the U.S. Department of Agriculture had a unique influence on the content of this book through their contributions to the education of the authors. Primary among these were Don Paarlberg, G. Edward Schuh, George Brandow, J. C. Bottum, Willard W. Cochrane, and James W. Richardson. The first edition benefited from the detailed comments of B. L. Flinchbaugh, William H. Meyer, and G. Edward Schuh. Dr. Flinchbaugh deserves special credit for his tenacious admonitions to remove personal prejudices, biases, and value judgments from the book.

This second edition benefited from the many comments from students and professors who used the first edition. Three word processors, Dawne Hicks, Donna Muras, and Vicki McClain, produced several versions of the manuscript. Joe Outlaw was in charge of graphics production. Sharron Knutson assisted in editing and proofreading several drafts of the manuscript. All are to be credited for their effort and patience with the authors.

Ronald D. Knutson
J. B. Penn
William T. Boehm

Part I

Process

Economic policy is a course of action pursued by the government in the management of national economic affairs. It is a product of both economics and politics. It is implemented by government programs enacted into law by elected political representatives on behalf of the citizenry—or special-interest segments of the population.

Farm policy is sectoral economic policy that deals with agriculture and food. Understanding farm policy requires a knowledge of both the political process by which laws are enacted and administered and the economic origin and consequences of those laws. Developing an appreciation for the process of policy development is the purpose of Part I.

Chapter 1 is designed to provide insight into the factors influencing people's attitudes or feelings about policies relating to agriculture. Why are people willing to spend up to $30 billion in tax revenues on farm programs?

Chapter 2 provides a condensed overview of the problems agricultural and food policies are designed to address. These problems are discussed in greater depth later in the book.

Chapter 3 describes how policy is made. It is a minicourse in how government makes decisions regarding farm and food programs. Emphasis is placed on the political actors.

Chapter 4 explains how agricultural and food policy interest groups organize to affect the policy outcome. Specific information is provided on the typical policy positions taken by the major farm, agribusiness, and public interest groups that influence farm and food policy decisions.

Chapter 1

The Policy Setting

*The translation of values into public
policy is what politics is about.*

Willard Graylin

The constitution of the United States stipulates that government exists to ensure domestic tranquility, provide for the common defense, establish justice, protect individual liberties, and promote the general welfare. Historically, one of the major policy issues has been the expanding size and role of government, particularly as it relates to the function of promoting the general welfare. A wide philosophical gap separates public opinions regarding the extent to which the powers of government should be utilized in solving economic and social problems. This is particularly true of agriculture, where the extent of government involvement continues to be a major controversial issue.

What should government do to treat a problem of low farm prices and low farm incomes? Some believe that government should not get involved. The free market will solve the problem. Low farm prices, they suggest, are a consequence of excess supplies. Low farm prices will, if allowed to exist, provide the incentive for reduced production and expanded consumption. Less production will bring higher prices and higher farm incomes. The problem, therefore, is self-correcting if the market is allowed to operate.

Others suggest that such a market remedy is too harsh, that food production is too important for a laissez-faire approach, and that without assistance, only the largest and most efficient farms will survive. Government, they suggest, should provide a level of assistance that allows all farmers an opportunity to survive, compete, and earn an income comparable to their nonfarm counterparts.

POLICY

Policy is a course of action or guiding principle pursued by the government. It influences or determines the actions and decisions of government.

Economic policy involves principles or actions related to the management of the national economy. Free trade in international markets is an economic policy. An administration that embraces a free-trade policy is opposed to restrictions on product imports and to subsidies for export. It actively pursues international actions that will reduce barriers to trade.

Agricultural and food policy is economic policy that deals with the production, marketing, and consumption of food. Production is defined broadly enough to include the resources used in the production process. Marketing includes both the domestic and international aspects of the agricultural economy. Consumption encompasses the retail price, distribution, nutrition, and safety aspects of food.

Agricultural policy involves numerous interrelated and highly controversial issues. In the Smithsonian Museum of Science and Industry sits a tractor that was driven from the wheat-producing areas of the Texas High Plains to Washington, D.C., by protesting farmers in the 1970s. In the 1980s, farm foreclosure sales were stopped by farmers who protested government policies regarding farm prices and credit, just as had occurred 50 years earlier. Such protests are by no means limited to the United States. Both European and Japanese governments have been restrained from reducing economic assistance to farmers by demonstrations against government.

Yet farmers are not of one mind regarding appropriate policies for food and agriculture. A 1984 survey of farmers in 17 states revealed nearly equal numbers favored the voluntary commodity programs requiring farmers to reduce production and eliminating all government programs.[1] A slim majority (54 percent) of the wheat producers who voted favored mandatory production controls in a poll mandated by the 1985 farm bill.[2]

[1] Harold D. Guither, Bob F. Jones, Marshall A. Martin, and Robert G. F. Spitze, *U.S. Farmers' Views on Agricultural and Food Policy*, N.C. 227 (Urbana, Ill.: University of Illinois, December 1984), p. 15.

[2] USDA Press Release, *USDA Releases Wheat Poll Results* (Washington, D.C.: Office of Information, August 15, 1986).

FACTS, BELIEFS, VALUES, AND GOALS

The role of and interaction among facts, beliefs, values, and goals are important to understanding how individuals, firms, or organizations as well as government officials come to develop and hold specific policy positions. *A* **policy position** *indicates a conclusion as to what the role of government ought to be with respect to a particular problem or a set of circumstances.* Policy positions are derived from the interaction of facts, beliefs, values, and goals that are held by individuals (Fig. 1.1). In a firm or organization, differences among individuals in facts, beliefs, values, and goals must be discussed and rationalized before a policy position can be developed. This generally involves a process of education and compromise. It is important to recognize that all policy positions are legitimate—based on compromise among individuals with respect to their interpretation of the facts, beliefs, values, and goals.

Facts

A **fact** *is something known with certainty.* It can be objectively verified, and rational people will tend to agree on a fact. Facts describe what is. In physical or biological sciences, facts are more readily determined and agreed upon than in the social sciences. Facts are more nebulous in social sciences such as economics. The definition of farm income is an example. When comparing incomes of farmers and nonfarmers, should farm income include income earned from an off-farm job? Should it include changes in the value of the farmer's land and other assets?

Causal relationships are also more definitive in the physical and

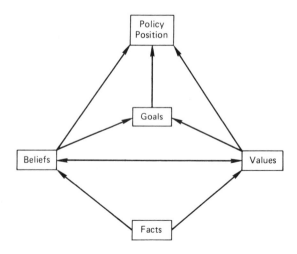

Figure 1.1 Factors influencing one's policy position.

biological sciences. A specific herbicide kills certain weeds. Causal relationships in social sciences are less precise, less measurable, less readily agreed upon, and almost always subject to qualification. For example, economists disagree over whether government support of farm prices and incomes aids the survival of the family farm or hastens its demise. They also disagree over whether the inheritance tax exemption helps to preserve the family farm from generation to generation, simply attracts outside investors, or both.

The inability to be definitive does not mean that economics is useless, that there are no observable facts, or that economic explanations are useless. It does mean that a need exists to identify, analyze, weigh, and evaluate economic facts and relationships. Different perspectives on facts need to be understood and evaluated in analyzing a policy issue. In addition, factual knowledge is important to objectivity in making policy decisions. As a result, a considerable amount of time is spent in this book on clarifying facts and explaining them from different perspectives.

Beliefs

Beliefs *describe what people think is reality*. A belief involves mental conviction, acceptance, confidence, or faith that a proposition is true. Beliefs are not dependent on the intrinsic, objective truth of the proposition. There are true beliefs, partially true beliefs, and false beliefs. Beliefs may, therefore, be based on fact, partially based on fact, or have no basis in fact. It is generally possible to sort out beliefs that have a factual basis from those that do not.

Many policy disagreements arise when beliefs are based only partially on facts. Such beliefs are not only a source of disagreement, but they can also be deceptive. Averages frequently fall in this category. For example, during the 1970s, the income of the farm population from all sources averaged 90.2 percent of nonfarmers' income. But in two of those years, farm income was higher than nonfarm income. In the mid-1980s, farm income once again fell substantially below nonfarm income. Yet farmers who gross over $100,000 in sales had consistently higher average incomes than the nonfarm population.

Policy disagreements frequently have their roots in mythology or notions that are based more on tradition, values, or convenience than on fact. For example, many farmers ascribe to the myth that land is the source of all wealth. This myth has its roots in eighteenth-century economic thought developed by the physiocrats. It fails to recognize that land is only one economic factor—the others generally being labor, capital, management, and water, which are as important to productivity as the land. Extensions of this physiocratic doctrine led to other myths, such as the notion that recessions or depressions in agriculture lead to recessions or depressions in the overall economy. Reality suggests that agriculture's impact on the economy is no greater than its share of overall economic activity.

Values

Values *are conceptions of what should be.* They provide an image of what is good and right and thus specify that some things are better than others. Values indicate what is desirable. They provide justification for proposed or actual behavior.

Values are influenced by beliefs and by facts. Values also influence beliefs. For example, farmers value individual initiative. This value arises in part from the belief that individuals are responsible for their own fate through their own initiative or lack thereof. Thus farmers frequently believe that many people receiving public assistance could earn a living if they were willing to work.

Historically, many of the values attributed to farmers are associated with the concept of Jeffersonian agrarianism. The **agrarian ideology** has three basic tenets:

- Agriculture is the basic occupation of humankind.
- Rural life is morally superior to urban life.
- A nation of small independent farmers is the proper basis for a democratic society.[3]

The agrarian ideology with its declaration of moral superiority and its blueprint for democracy was highly acceptable to the American people of the nineteenth and early twentieth centuries. Out of this ideology grew a body of rhetoric, known as the *agricultural creed*, that has garnered widespread support for farm programs. The articles of the agricultural creed as explained by Paarlberg include:

- Farmers are good citizens, and a high percentage of the population should be on farms.
- Farming is not only a business but a way of life.
- Farming should be a family enterprise.
- The land should be owned by the person who tills it.
- It is good to make two blades of grass grow where one grew before.
- Anyone who wants to farm should be able to do so.
- A farmer should be his own boss.[4]

[3]Edward W. Hassinger, *The Rural Component of American Society* (Danville, Ill.: The Interstate Printers and Publishers, Inc., 1978), pp. 83–85.

[4]Don Paarlberg, *American Farm Policy* (New York: John Wiley & Sons, Inc., 1964), p. 3.

Even today, despite the advanced development of U.S. society, it would be a mistake to suggest that the agrarian ideology and its associated agricultural creed are dead. Its application can still be seen in political campaign rhetoric extolling the family farm and lauding the farmer as the backbone of democracy and in the tendency to view farmers as a homogeneous body having similar problems, justifying the need for a single national farm policy. Agrarianism thus continues to serve as one of the justifications for farm programs. Closely related, agrarianism serves as the foundation for many of the values still held by farmers and their organizations.[5]

Despite such campaign rhetoric and organizational dogma, substantial disagreement exists over whether rural–urban differences in values any longer exist. One school of thought holds that they do. These proponents point to studies that suggest values held in high esteem by farmers include:

- Quality education is viewed as the means to occupational achievement and success. Technology, being a product of education and research, has traditionally been looked upon favorably by farmers and ranchers.
- Work and proficiency in one's job is a key to success. The work ethic is generally believed to be held in stronger esteem by farmers than by urban people.
- Puritan ethical standards are stronger in rural America. Farmers are, in general, more religious and express greater opposition to divorce, premarital sex, abortion and consumption of alcoholic beverages.
- Personal freedom, patriotism, and support of the democratic system are strongly held values that are consistent with the agrarian ideal.

The high value placed on personal freedom can be associated with the desires of farmers and ranchers to be their own bosses. However, studies also have shown a tendency for farmers to conform to typical patterns of behavior and commonly held beliefs and values in rural America.[6] Despite this trend toward conformity, no consensus exists among farmers on any value, related belief, or behavior. This lack of agreement on values could be a source of disagreement on policy remedies to problems.[7]

While farmers desire an equal status for themselves in society,

[5]Hassinger, *Rural Component*, p. 95.

[6]Olaf F. Larson, "Values and Beliefs of Rural People," in *Rural U.S.A.: Persistence and Change*, T. R. Ford, ed. (Ames, Iowa: Iowa State University Press, 1978), p. 93.

[7]Ibid., p. 111.

studies have consistently shown a very conservative attitude toward movements giving equal rights to racial minorities and women. These attitudes are consistent with findings of farmers' willingness to lend a helping hand in time of need, tempered by considerably less support for food stamp programs, which ironically increase the demand for farm products. It appears that farmers attribute many of the problems of minorities and the poor to a lack of willingness to work.[8]

The opposing school of thought holds that rural and urban values have changed and blended over time so that they are now so similar that significant differences no longer exist. Copp, for example, notes that "rural society as we used to know it is virtually nonexistent."[9] Even Larson, a proponent of the existence of value differences, admits that studies

---

NEW YORK CITY OR LUBBOCK: WHICH IS WHICH?

While there [New York City] I stumbled upon a "country-western" bar where—to my sincere surprise—I witnessed students from CCNY doing a passable rendition of a country dance called the cotton-eyed Joe. They drank Pearl and Lone Star Beer and vigorously applauded star-spangled cowboy musicians who played the latest Willie Nelson hits. They wore cowboy hats, boots, and belts with buckles as big as bulls. Meanwhile, in Lubbock [Texas] the "city" fathers were bemoaning problems previously associated with urbanism—the local drug crisis and the finding of two bodies in the trunk of an abandoned car. And, to the astonishment of many, the once fogyish *Texas Tech University Daily* rather matter-of-factly reported that daughters of farmers from across the South Texas plains were posing nude for *Playboy* magazine. At the same time, the "kickers" at Coldwater—a local cowboy watering hole—did the same dances displayed in New York City; they also drink the same beer, listen to the same kinds of music, and ride the same mechanical bulls with the same gusto that might be seen at any tavern in any community of any size across the United States. Simply put, after a beer or three in either a Lubbock or New York bar, even the most sensitive anthropologist could become confused about his or her geographical whereabouts.

Thomas K. Pinhey, "Two Chickens: A Response to Bealer's Question," *The Rural Sociologist*, Vol. 1 (January 1981), p. 26.

---

[8] Ibid., pp. 98–99.

[9] Paul McKay, "Modern America Brings Changes to Rural Life," *The Bryan–College Station Eagle* (Bryan, Tex.), November 4, 1981, p. 10D; and William P. Kuvlesky and James H. Copp, "Rural America: The Present Realities and Future Prospects," in *Toward an American Rural Renaissance*, unpublished manuscript (College Station, Tex.: Texas A&M University, 1982), pp. 16–25.

show a surprising uniform ranking of values between rural and urban people.[10] The major motivating forces facilitating this change have been increased mobility, school consolidation, television, improved education, and increased off-farm employment.

Whether significant differences in rural–urban values, in fact, exist has become a major source of controversy among sociologists. Pinhey charges that the existence of value differences is assumed, not real.[11] Bealer wants to believe that such differences exist but admits that the evidence supporting them suggests the need for considerable caution.[12] Their verification, Bealer argues, must await detailed study of values held by the operators of different sizes and types of farms.

If farmers' values are no different from those of the general population, it removes the agrarian arguments for preserving the family farm. It does not mean that farm programs are no longer justified. It does, however, shift the burden for justification of domestic farm policy primarily to economic differences between farm and nonfarm sectors as opposed to a combination of economic differences and preserving the ideals of Jeffersonian agrarianism and the agricultural creed.

Agriculture's ability to secure public support and legislation favorable to it is influenced by the beliefs and values of the urban and suburban majority toward farm people. The image of rural people held by their city cousins is very favorable. Rural people are considered friendlier, healthier, more honest and hard-working, as getting more enjoyment out of life, and as having fewer tensions and fewer pressures. While rural areas were viewed as the best place to raise children, they were considered to offer the least opportunity for a young person.[13] Available evidence suggests that the general population has a very favorable image of farmers. A survey of a random sample of U.S. adults concerning their attitudes toward agriculture, farming, and farmers indicates strong support for farming as a way of life, for family farms, and for maintaining an agriculture where farmers can make economic decisions independently (Table 1.1).

This favorable image of farmers leads to widespread public support for government programs that support farm prices and incomes. For example, a public opinion poll conducted early in 1985 revealed that only 24 percent of the voting population favored cutting government farm subsidies and crop controls as a means of reducing the federal deficit.[14] The

[10]Larson, "Values and Beliefs," p. 94.

[11]Thomas K. Pinhey, "Two Chickens: A Response to Bealer's Question," *Rural Sociol.* (January 1981), pp. 26–30.

[12]Robert C. Bealer, "On Policy Matters and Rural–Urban Differences," *Rural Sociol.* (January 1981), pp. 19–25.

[13]Ibid., pp. 93–94.

[14]*Public Opinion* (February–March), p. 19.

TABLE 1.1 Beliefs of U.S. Adults Concerning Agriculture, Farming, and Farmers (Percent)

	Agree	Undecided	Disagree
Agriculture is the most basic occupation in our society, and almost all other occupations depend on it.	80.0	11.6	8.4
Farming involves understanding and working with nature; therefore, it's a much more satisfying occupation than others.	57.4	22.4	20.1
We hear so much about crime and corruption today because our nation is becoming so urbanized.	53.6	25.2	21.1
Farming should be an occupation where farmers can make their economic decisions independently.	76.8	18.1	5.1
Farmers ought to appreciate farming as a good way of life and be less concerned about their cash income.	14.3	11.8	74.0
The family farm must be preserved because it is a vital part of our heritage.	82.1	8.6	9.3
Government should have a special policy to ensure that family farms survive.	67.3	19.3	13.5
Obtaining greater efficiency in food production is more important than preserving the family farm.	22.3	22.4	55.4
Most consumers would be willing to have food prices raised to help preserve the family farm.	24.1	23.1	52.8
Corporate farms should pay more taxes than family farms.	66.8	16.6	16.6

Source: Brenda Jordan and Luther Tweeten, *Public Perceptions of Farm Problems,* Res. Rep. P-894 (Stillwater, Okla.: Oklahoma Agricultural Experiment Station, June 1987), p. 3.

vast majority, 71 percent, favored cutting the deficit by some other means, while only 5 percent were not sure. A higher proportion (38 percent) of the voting population favored cutting food stamps, although a clear majority (58 percent) still favored finding some other way. Farm and food stamp programs enjoyed considerably more support than loans to college students (which 56 percent favored ending) but less support than social security, where only 12 percent favored canceling cost-of-living adjustments.

In June 1987, when the government was spending over $25 billion on farm subsidies, 40 percent said that the government should be spending more to help farmers.[15] Interestingly, urban people appear to be more willing to support farm subsidies than rural people. While 51 percent of the people polled in cities of over 500,000 population said spending on farm programs should rise, only 41 percent of those in rural areas supported higher subsidies.[16] (*Note*: All of these surveys were done at a time when the financial crisis in rural America regularly made the news.)

The findings of reasonably uniform rural and urban values and a favorable urban image of farmers are consistent with a consumer perspective of farmers as not being the main source of problems such as rising food prices and food safety. Instead, consumer activists have tended to focus their criticisms on bad decisions by government, suppliers of inputs to farmers, or the excessive market concentration in food processing and distribution.

Goals

Goals *are desired ultimate end results or objectives.* A goal is the purpose toward which an endeavor is directed. Goals are long term in nature. The inability of groups of individuals to achieve their goals may lead to visible dissatisfaction, agitation, and eventually turning to government for assistance.

The choice of goals is influenced by a person's values and beliefs. Whether the inability to achieve a goal becomes a public issue depends on the importance attached to it, the influence of the group identifying with the goal, and the extent to which the goal is not being achieved under current government and private initiatives. Farmers hold a wide variety of goals. Some more important ones include:

- Self-preservation and survival are goals of every human being. While the values of many farmers favor individual as opposed to government initiative to solve problems, they usually turn to government when farm prices and incomes plummet and their survival is threatened. They are not, however, as likely to turn to government for a solution to incremental problems or less visible action

[15]Kenneth E. John, "Top Priorities," *The Washington Post National Weekly Edition,* June 8, 1987, p. 38.

[16]*U.S. News and World Report,* March 24, 1986, p. 82.

that could, in the long term, lead to their self-destruction. For example, the political pressures for government assistance accelerated sharply in the 1980s as an increasingly large number of farmers faced financial failure and bankruptcy. Sociological studies revealed that conditions of severe financial and/or mental stress were evident in much of rural America.[17] In contrast, most farmers have never become sufficiently disturbed by progressive trends toward large-scale farming and corporate-integrated production marketing systems to advocate policy steps that effectively curb these trends. The unwillingness of family farmers to support policies that would inhibit encroachment by corporate and nonfarm interests is cited by Breimyer as a case where the self-preservation instinct has not prevailed.[18]

• Raising the level of living has traditionally been a goal of farming and public policy toward farming. The traditional standard used for this goal has been the attainment of the same level of income, housing, and personal possessions as the nonfarm population. Once this standard is achieved, there is no evidence that the goal of continuous increases in the level of living is any less important.

• Ownership of farmland satisfies farmers' values favoring freedom and independence. Farmland is so closely tied to agriculture that its ownership becomes a natural status symbol and key to raising the level of living and long-term survival.

• Progress, efficiency, and productivity goals are consistent with farmers' faith in the work ethic as a key to survival. Since farmers as individuals or even groups have little or no influence on price, improved efficiency and productivity have become the key to progress. This helps to explain their traditional strong support for education and research.

• The development of a strong rural educational base has been a major goal of farmers. The initial establishment of the land-grant university system has its roots in agriculture.

Goals of importance to food and agricultural policy are not just those of farmers. The goals of individuals and groups other than farmers have an increasingly important role in policy decisions. Such goals can be characterized as having a public interest orientation. Examples include:

• A desire for an ample supply of food at reasonable prices. This goal has traditionally been a public interest justification for policies subsidizing farm prices and incomes. Farmers from time to time

[17]William D. Heffernan, and Judith Bortner Heffernan, *Rural Sociol.* (May 1982), pp. 110–117.

[18]Harold F. Breimyer, *Farm Policy: 13 Essays* (Ames, Iowa: Iowa State University Press, 1977), pp. 67–78.

characterize this goal as an integral part of a policy designed to ensure consumers low food prices—the so-called cheap food policy.
- The removal of hunger and malnutrition. Although this goal applies
to both American and foreign consumers, it is clear that the domestic priority ranks significantly above foreign priorities.
- A desire to maintain health and reduce health hazards. From this
goal arise policies and programs designed to protect the environment and ensure the safety of the food supply. These policies and
programs frequently have been viewed by farmers as conflicting
with their goals of increased income and values supporting personal
freedom.
- A desire to preserve resources such as land and water for use by future generations. Although the goal of soil conservation has long
been a concern of farmers, it has recently taken on new meaning in
a public interest dimension.

The Importance of Compromise

Persons belonging to the same organization tend to have common
goals, values, and beliefs. However, even within an organization the
goals, values, and beliefs of all individuals are not the same; nor are they
held with the same intensity. To arrive at a cohesive policy position, compromise among the members of a group with respect to goals, values, or
beliefs frequently is necessary. The willingness of the members to compromise is a source of strength.

Without compromise, constant friction among members of the group
is possible. Sufficient friction results in an inability of the group to arrive
at a policy position. This is particularly a problem among farm organizations, where major differences in goals, values, and beliefs frequently exist.

Historically, considerable attention has been focused on differences
that exist among farm groups in their attitudes toward government involvement in agriculture, as well as toward specific policies and programs. These differences appear to have their roots less in goals such as
the need to increase farm prices and incomes than in values favoring personal freedom, opposition to government involvement, and beliefs in the
market system as a means of solving problems.

The Impact of Time

Goals, values, and beliefs change over time. Such changes may result from improved communication, exposure to new ideas, improved education, or a change in the nature of the problem. For example, the decline

in values associated with Jeffersonian agrarianism has been attributed to improved roads, improved schools, the spread of television to rural America, and improved farm incomes.[19]

The goals of policy may also change over time because of the relative importance of individuals or groups influencing policy. For example, increased consumer and environmental activism has made the goals related to conservation, food safety, and nutrition more important in the policy process.

WHY GOVERNMENT BECOMES INVOLVED

The specific reasons for government involvement in agriculture have changed as the nature of the farm problem and the overall political, social, and economic environment within which agriculture operates has changed. Five major reasons currently are given for government involvement in agriculture:

- Low farm income traditionally has been the major justification for programs that support farm prices and incomes. These programs, however, have become increasingly controversial as government costs have risen, farm numbers have declined, and farm size has become more diverse.
- The need to stabilize farm prices and incomes also has provided an important justification for farm programs. Stability is desired both to reduce the incidence of mistakes in production decisions and to reduce economic stress on farm families. Stability has been used as a justification both for raising prices and for lowering them.
- In the early 1970s, the impact of rapidly rising food prices on the general economy was used to justify price controls and embargoes.
- The importance of an adequate supply of food historically has been used to justify government programs that expand farm production, such as irrigation projects, agricultural research, and extension. U.S. agricultural abundance has been seized upon as a source of export earnings and as a diplomatic weapon of foreign policy. Food has thus become recognized as having a value that extends beyond nutrition.
- The safety of the food supply became an important issue once the ability of the U.S. farmer to produce an adequate supply of food was demonstrated. Over time, the safety issue evolved from a concern with sanitation to the contemporary controversy over additives, residues, and nutrition.

[19]McKay, "Changes to Rural Life"; and Kuvlesky and Copp, "Rural America."

- Protecting the capacity of agriculture to produce in future generations has led to programs that conserve the soil. This concern has since spread to improving the quality of groundwater runoff, conservation of limited water supplies, and preservation of prime farmland in populous areas.

ECONOMICS, ECONOMISTS, AND PUBLIC POLICY

Economics plays an important role in the development of agricultural and food policies. The traditional farm problems of surplus production and instability are rooted in economics. Agricultural and food policies, in turn, have a direct impact on the production and marketing decisions of farmers and ranchers. Economic variables have a major impact on the world's ability to satisfy future food needs with limited resources. Many of the contemporary food concerns have a direct impact on food availability, cost of production, and prices. This is not to imply that economics has exclusive jurisdiction over agricultural and food policy issues. Values, beliefs, facts, and goals, as well as individual and group behavior, make sociology and psychology an integral part of policy development and implementation. Policy is determined in the political arena, and policy decisions are fundamentally political decisions.

The Role of Economics

Within this interdisciplinary setting, economics has three main functions:

- It provides insight into the origin of economic problems. This insight can be traced from the aggregate or macro level to the individual firm or micro level. An understanding of the origin of problems is crucial to developing solutions.
- Economics assists in developing policy and program alternatives for solving problems.
- Economics can be used to analyze the consequences of policies. It is an understanding of the consequences, more than anything else, that is critical to informed policy decision making.

The greatest need of the policymaker is for an objective analysis of the consequences of the alternative courses of action available. As a result, economic analysts exist throughout the public and private sectors. Such analysts are employed by interest groups such as farm organizations, businesses, consulting firms, and the government. Interest groups are more effective in getting their policy proposals implemented when they are based on factual economic analysis. Their arguments are more persuasive, and policymakers are more likely to listen to a case based on facts.

Within government, it is not unusual to have two or three separate economic studies of a controversial policy proposal. Such studies may be carried out from the perspective of a member of Congress concerned about being reelected; the secretary of agriculture, concerned about the proposal's impact on farm income and on U.S. Department of Agriculture (USDA) spending; or the president's economic advisers, who are concerned about its impact on inflation and the budget.

All these analyses will bear on the final public policy outcome. In the end, however, the final decision is political. Yet even here, the politician is often faced with a decision that involves weighing the impact of the policy alternatives on his various constituencies—farmers, business firms, consumers, and taxpayers.

The role of economics does not end with the decision of the policymaker. Once a policy or program has been implemented, its economic impact must be evaluated as a means of detecting problems, identifying the magnitude of specific relationships, fine-tuning programs, and as a guide for future decisions.

Some General Economic Principles

Throughout this book, relevant economic principles are introduced and thoroughly discussed. There are, however, three general principles that are of overriding concern to one's understanding of the origin of economic problems in agriculture. Discussion of these economic principles at this point not only helps one to understand subsequent discussions of food and agricultural problems, but also provides readers with an opportunity to review and sharpen their tools of economic analysis.

Supply and demand.   Many agricultural and food policies are designed to overtly influence the supply and demand for farm products. For example, international market development programs are designed to expand demand and, thereby, raise prices. Supply control programs raise prices by restricting production. Other programs are designed to avoid the consequences of shifts in supply or demand. For example, the target price program guarantees farmers a specific return per unit of commodity produced, regardless of market price. The government makes up the difference between the market price and the target price in the form of a direct payment. Farmers make decisions on what to produce based on the target price, not the market price. An understanding of the supply and

demand for farm products and the factors affecting them becomes critical
to understanding policy.

Figure 1.2 contains a representation of typical supply and demand
schedules that are used extensively throughout this book. The demand
schedule slopes downward to the right, indicating that as price falls, consumers will buy more of a product. Every consumer has an individual demand schedule. The market demand (in Fig. 1.2) is the sum of all individual consumer demands. The slope of the demand schedule indicates the
responsiveness of consumers to price changes. Economists refer to this
sensitivity as the elasticity of demand. *The* **elasticity of demand** *relates
the percentage change in quantity demanded resulting from a one percent
change in the price of the product.*

The demand for farm products generally is composed of two segments—from the domestic and export markets. Domestic demand generally is more inelastic than export demand. That is, domestic buyers are
less responsive to increases in U.S. farm prices than are foreign buyers.
This more elastic foreign demand has important policy implications. For
example, U.S. producer returns can be increased by charging a higher
price in the domestic market than in the foreign market—if the two markets can be effectively separated.

Demand elasticities vary from product to product. For example, the
demand for a staple such as flour is less price responsive (more inelastic)
than demand for meat, which has several substitutes. In addition, demand for all foods is more inelastic than it is for any individual food.

The magnitude of the elasticity of demand is very important from a
policy perspective. If the elasticity is less than −1.0, it means that the
income of farmers can be raised by increasing the price. That is, the percentage increase in price is greater than the percentage reduction in
quantity, yielding an increase in revenue to farmers. The more inelastic
the demand, the greater the benefit from a price increase to farmers.

Demand shifts in response to income, population, and consumer

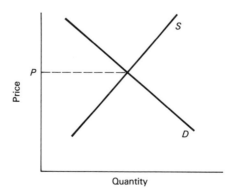

Figure 1.2 Supply and demand schedules.

preferences. When income rises, demand generally increases. The relationship between changes in income and corresponding changes in demand is referred to as the income elasticity of demand. Income elasticities vary from food to food and consumer to consumer. Lower-income consumers generally are more income elastic than high-income consumers, meaning that poorer consumers increase consumption more in response to an income increase than the wealthy. Similarly, export demand is more income elastic than domestic demand; that is, foreign consumers purchase more food products in response in an increase in income than do domestic consumers.

The supply schedule slopes upward and to the right. For an individual farm, its supply schedule is the marginal cost curve (Fig. 1.3). Farmers maximize profit by equating the returns they receive for a unit of the product with the marginal cost. As price per unit increases, the quantity supplied increases. Each farm has its own supply curve, which in the short run is the segment of its marginal cost curve above average variable cost. If the firm cannot cover its average variable cost in the short run, it stops producing. In the long run, the supply schedule is the segment of the marginal cost curve above average cost. The market supply schedule is the sum of all individual farm marginal cost schedules.

For most of an undergraduate student's training in economics, the point at which the supply and demand schedule crosses is the magic competitive equilibrium price. However, for many agricultural commodities, the equilibrium price is not politically acceptable, giving rise to government involvement in agriculture. The policy becomes one of trying to change that price to the benefit of farmers. When government becomes involved, price may no longer be at the competitive equilibrium, P in Fig. 1.2. Getting used to this price not being at equilibrium is a problem for many students studying agricultural and food policy.

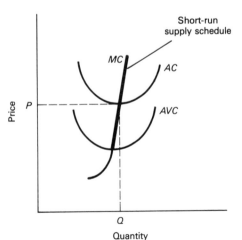

Figure 1.3 Short-run supply schedule for a farm.

Fallacy of composition.   Individuals and firms, by and large, pursue production and consumption decisions that enhance their own welfare, whether measured in terms of profits, wealth, or satisfaction. Yet as a result of pursuit of individual goals, the group as a whole may be worse off. *This inverse relationship between the pursuit of individual goals and group results is referred to as the* **fallacy of composition.**

Many different illustrations of the fallacy of composition exist. One, which also provides the opportunity to introduce the concept of market equilibrium, involves incentives for firms operating in a purely competitive market to increase production. Figure 1.4 provides a representation of a typical farmer's marginal cost (MC) and average cost (AC) of producing different quantities of corn on a given number of acres of land. There are enough of these typical farmers that no single farmer can have a significant influence on the marketplace.

Figure 1.4 also contains a market supply (S_1) and demand (D) schedule. The market price in Fig. 1.4 is P_1, and Q_1 is the quantity supplied. At this price the typical farm in the market produces quantity q_2, at the point where marginal cost is equal to marginal revenue. That is, the extra cost of producing the last unit of output is equal to the extra revenue from selling that unit of output. At this quantity the typical farm's average cost of producing corn is P_2. It is thus making a pure profit of $(P_1 - P_2)q_2$, the shaded area. A pure profit is one which more than covers the farmer's return on capital contributed to the farm operation.

With the farmer in a pure profit position, there is incentive for the typical farmer to plant a larger number of acres of corn and for new producers to begin producing corn. As this occurs, the supply schedule shifts to the right. In pure competition, one farmer can expand the number of acres planted without having a significant price effect. However, if all farmers expand their output, price falls and profits fall. This overall re-

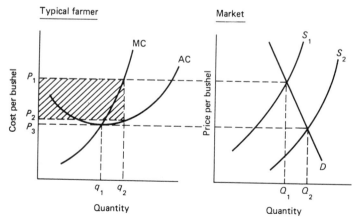

Figure 1.4   Representation of firm and market equilibrium concepts.

duction in profits illustrates the fallacy of composition concept—even though it is profitable for any individual farm to expand production, if all farms expand, profits decline for all farms. Incentives will exist for individual farms to increase production until the supply schedule shifts to S_2. At S_2 the market is in equilibrium. That is, supply and demand are equal at a price (P_3) where only normal profits exist. That is, profits provide no more than a normal return on capital invested.

The fallacy of composition is a source of many errors in agricultural policy decisions. For example, lowering the inheritance taxes has been a major policy objective for many farm organizations. This action is favored when viewed from the perspective of individual family farms. However, when viewed from a broader and longer-term economic perspective, it encourages outside investment in agriculture, raises land prices, and in turn, raises the cost of production. The objective of promoting intergeneration transfer is thus thwarted by the fallacy of composition. To avoid falling into the fallacy of composition trap, policy consequences need to be viewed both from the perspective of the individual farmer and from the perspective of the market as well as from that of the economy as a whole. Closely related, they must be viewed both from a long-run perspective after market forces have worked themselves out as well as from a short-run perspective.

Externalities and market failure.   Many of the government policies and programs that exist today arise from the fact that the free market does not provide the same incentives or rewards for the production or the conservation of certain goods and services that society attaches to their production or conservation. For example, the market provides incentives for farmers to get the highest possible yields from available land resources. However, if land is continuously farmed to get the highest possible yield, its production potential in the future declines. This reduced return, in the longer run, is not reflected in either the short-run costs or returns upon which most farmers make production decisions. In other words, some benefits and costs are external to the market in that they accrue to parties other than the immediate buyer and seller.

Externalities *are benefits or costs accruing to some individuals or groups who are apart from a market transaction.* For example, a farmer experiencing cash flow problems may decide to avoid conservation practices and thus incur higher rates of soil erosion. The result is excessive runoff and pollution of streams. That pollution is an externality to fishermen, cities that utilize surface water for their water supply, and people who simply enjoy clean streams.

Where supply and demand do not accurately reflect *all* the benefits and costs of production, the price system cannot be expected to bring about an allocation of resources which best satisfies the wants of society.

Externalities, thereby, create **market failures**—*the failure of markets to allocate resources in society's interest.*

Many examples can be cited of cases where government has stepped in with services or regulations designed to fill the gap left by the failure of agricultural markets to reflect externalities. Regulations may be enacted that prohibit or limit pollution from livestock farms. Farmers may be required to engage in certain conservation practices in return for government subsidies. Ironically, subsidies encourage more intensive farming, which in the absence of conservation requirements would result in a higher level of erosion.

Externalities do not just involve costs that spill over to other segments of society. There often are external or spillover benefits as well. *Where these benefits are large and the market would not otherwise provide them,* **public goods** result. For example, the land-grant university system was set up because market rewards were not sufficient for either farmers or agribusiness to invest in large-scale programs of agriculture research and education. Similarly, market information, crop and livestock production reports, rural electrification, and farm credit are programs where markets were judged to have failed to provide sufficient services to agriculture and rural America. Government programs filled the void.

Externalities are not, however, limited to the market. Government fails to recognize or overtly ignores externalities when it takes action in the short run without considering the long-run consequences. For example, it frequently prices water or electricity from government projects as if they were nearly free goods and in unlimited supply. It introduces externalities when it continues a set of farm programs while production and market conditions change markedly.

Many of the disagreements that exist over the role of government in agriculture result from questions of whether the market has failed—that is, whether it can be relied on to perform certain functions better than government. The answer could also be expected to change over time as agriculture becomes better (or worse) in managing programs.

Limits of Economics

Although the tools of economic theory are useful in providing insight into the origin of economic problems and the consequences of alternative solutions to those problems, they have a limited usefulness in deciding which alternative is "best." The only case where economists can say that one policy option is "better" than the current policies is where someone or some group is made better off with no one else, including taxpayers, being made worse off. Such changes are referred to as movements in the direction of Pareto optimality. A **Pareto optimum** *exists when it is* *impossible to make anyone better off without making someone else worse off.*

Since such situations are rarely found, the Pareto criteria are not very useful in most policy decisions. As a result, some economists suggest using the **compensation principle** as a basis for policy decisions. *This principle suggests that as long as those who are made better off by a policy change are able to more than compensate those who are made worse off, the change is justified.* Considerable debate exists, however, over the usefulness of the compensation principle. This debate centers on:

- How to measure the magnitude of the costs and benefits
- Whether compensation, in fact, has to be paid to those who are made worse off

Resolving this debate inherently involves making interpersonal comparisons. That is, it assumes that, for example, increased satisfaction to farmers from higher price supports and reduced satisfaction to consumers and taxpayers are directly proportional to dollar costs and revenues involved—that each values the dollar similarly. Such an assumption is, of course, a value judgment. Although economists can be useful in helping to evaluate the trade-off in terms of the magnitude of the economic costs and benefits, politicians, whether elected or appointed, are responsible for making such judgments. If politicians make such value judgments incorrectly a sufficient proportion of the time, the electorate will remove them from office.

SYNOPSIS

Most of the remainder of this book involves explaining the economic conditions that lead to government involvement in agriculture. This includes explaining how specific programs affect agriculture as well as the domestic and world economy. This is accomplished in four major parts or sections:

- Part I recognizes that agricultural and food policy is developed through the political process at the urging of interest groups. Policy is thus more than economics. It is designed to solve the problems of people through the political process. Understanding policy thus requires a knowledge of the overall nature of the problems being solved, the process of policy formulation, and the role of the various interest groups in the process. This is the focus of the first four chapters.

- Part II recognizes the increasingly important role macroeconomics and international policy instruments play in U.S. agriculture. Too often there is a tendency to think about agriculture and food in a narrow state or national context. Chapters 5, 6, and 7 are designed to dispel this tendency—to recognize that U.S. production and policies have world implications, but yet to realize that significant limits exist on America's ability to direct or control agricultural economic events. Chapter 8 then explains the impacts of macroeconomic policies upon agriculture and the relationship to international markets.
- Part III includes three chapters covering the various aspects of domestic farm policy. These chapters stretch beyond traditional farm price and income policies to include discussions of structure policy. In doing so, they recognize what has been learned from the past, the situation that exists today, and the problems, policies, and consequences that could evolve in the future.
- Part IV recognizes that domestic agriculture is more than farms. It includes issues involving consumers, resource use, and agribusiness. These interests are an integral part of developing a national agricultural food policy.

ADDITIONAL READINGS

1. A discussion of the status of value differences between the rural and urban sectors is contained in the January 1981 issue of *The Rural Sociologist*. In particular, see the article by Robert C. Bealer titled "On Policy Matters and Rural–Urban Differences."

2. The most comprehensive discussion of the changing demographic and sociological characteristics of rural society is contained in Thomas R. Ford, ed., *Rural U.S.A.: Persistence and Change* (Ames, Iowa: Iowa State University Press, 1978).

3. An extensive compilation of articles on the philosophical and economic issues surrounding the family farm is contained in Gary Comstock, ed., *Is There a Moral Obligation to Save the Family Farm?* (Ames, Iowa: Iowa State University Press, 1987).

Chapter 2

Policy Problems
of Food and Agriculture

A problem well stated is a problem half solved.

Charles F. Kettering

Food and agricultural policies and programs are intended to solve chronic problems encountered in the production and marketing of agricultural products. These policies and programs evolve gradually over the years as the problems become increasingly apparent and change in character. The nature of the problems confronting both producers and consumers of food has changed substantially in the past 15 years.

In this chapter we provide an overview of the major problems confronting the agricultural and food sector and how they have changed. A more detailed discussion of each problem area is contained in subsequent chapters. This chapter concludes with five different philosophical approaches to dealing with the current and evolving mix of problems.

SYMPTOMS, PROBLEMS, AND POLICIES IN TRANSITION

The agricultural policies and programs that exist today evolved from the problems and policies that existed in the past. This happens because problems and policies change gradually and unevenly. As experience is gained with particular programs, adjustments are made. In addition, people differ in their perceptions of the nature of problems and how they have changed. These differences account for a substantial proportion of the disagreement over the appropriateness of current and evolving policies.

From the 1930s through the 1960s the most pervasive problem confronting agriculture was excess capacity, resulting in low farm prices and incomes. Throughout this period, farm income averaged only 51 percent of nonfarm income. Not until 1965 did average farm income exceed 70 percent of nonfarm income.[1]

The origin of this low price and income problem was excess food and fiber production capacity, combined with too many farmers among which to divide the available income. Agriculture's production capacity expanded more rapidly than effective demand, thus holding prices and income down. Over time, low incomes encouraged farmers and their wives, sons, and daughters to seek employment outside farming. Despite massive migration from the farm to the city, farm incomes remained low relative to nonfarm incomes. Improvement in the situation was slow and gradual over the 40-year period.

The chronic nature of this excess capacity problem led to extensive government involvement in agriculture. Public debate centered on how to achieve higher incomes for farmers. Price supports were employed along with efforts to control production.

The existence of low farm prices and income was by no means limited to the U.S. farmer. Farm product prices throughout most of the world were low. American price support policies frequently resulted in domestic prices being above world prices. Under these conditions, U.S. products were not competitively priced in the world market, and any export sales generally required subsidies. Export subsidies were not only expensive but invited retaliation by other countries which desired to protect their own producers from the effects of low prices. The result was the erection of barriers to trade.

In the mid-1960s, there was increasing recognition that if the United States were to become a competitor in international markets, the domestic price must be reduced. But the political unpopularity of this move would require at least partial compensation for farmers, and direct payments from the government were instituted.

While economic conditions in agriculture improved marginally in the late 1960s, they improved abruptly in the early 1970s, when a confluence of forces brought the biggest boom since early in the twentieth century, often referred to as the "golden years" of agriculture. Adverse weather and disease combined to reduce global crop production just as demand began growing strongly, a result of population growth and rapidly rising incomes. The result was a growing concern over both the immedi-

[1]*Agricultural Statistics* (Washington, D.C.: USDA, various issues).

ate-term and long-run ability of the world to feed itself. The problem was exaggerated by a decision of the Soviet leadership to enter the world markets and purchase large quantities of grain in response to reduced production. Previously, the Soviets had responded to production shortages simply by reducing consumption. With strong demand from other importers, notably the developing countries, world agriculture was suddenly in a boom period.

World food conferences were expressing concern about the capacity of agriculture to meet present and future food needs. Prices for farm products—sometimes almost panic markets—reached record levels, such as $13 per bushel for soybeans in 1973. The mentality of policymakers, so long confronted by chronic surpluses, suddenly shifted to deficits. Farmers were encouraged to expand acreage, to plant from fence row to fence row. They responded and, in the face of strong export demand, were rewarded with higher incomes. They also expanded the size of their farm operations and, in the process, bid land prices far above a level that could be sustained on the basis of past earnings.

These developments created the opportunity for Earl Butz, a market-oriented secretary of agriculture, to take substantial steps reducing government's role in agriculture. New market-oriented farm policies were implemented that placed greater reliance on supply and demand forces to determine prices. At the same time, policy inconsistencies became more apparent, notably export embargoes to control domestic farm prices and/or to obtain foreign political concessions.

Disagreement arose over whether the new-found prosperity of the 1970s represented a permanent change toward a much tighter world supply–demand balance or was simply an aberration. The answer was soon forthcoming when burdensome supplies once again developed and prices tumbled in the early 1980s. Assuming, or hoping, that these adversities were only temporary, government once again attempted to support farm prices and income, as well as to control production. U.S. farm products once again became priced out of the world market by high domestic price supports and a strong dollar. This situation persisted until 1986.

In an effort to restore competitiveness in world markets, the 1985 farm bill began to sharply lower support prices while maintaining farm income through direct payments to farmers. In addition, foreign buyers, including the Soviet Union and China, were given subsidies to buy surplus U.S. grain, to the chagrin of exporters competing with the United States, notably Canada, Australia, Argentina, and Thailand. The result was skyrocketing costs of farm programs to $26 billion in 1986.

The events of the 1960s through the 1980s may be viewed as a *policy cycle*—agriculture going from surpluses to deficits and back to surpluses, from bust to boom and back to bust. Agricultural policy has cycled from supporting prices and incomes and controlling production, to market-oriented policies, and then back to supporting prices and incomes and controlling production.

The concept of policy cycles is a useful way to review history. It provides lessons on the mistakes and successes of the past. Yet the concept can easily be oversimplified and overdrawn. The 1970s changed agriculture in several profound ways:

- It made U.S. agriculture export and world market dependent. The agriculture production plant expanded to serve a world market with the production of almost 2 acres of every 5 acres being exported. Reducing production to serve only the domestic market became a much less feasible policy option after the 1970s.
- The fragility of agriculture became more evident. Complacency regarding the importance of an abundant food supply was removed by the 1970s experience. Similarly, in the 1980s, complacency about the durability of agriculture was shaken as the price of farm real estate plummeted, many banks failed, and the cooperative Farm Credit System required federal assistance to remain solvent.
- Public interest in agriculture and its policies accelerated sharply. Consumer interests extended beyond the price of food to the safety, nutritional content, and quality of the food supply. Foreign policy interests in agriculture mounted as food once again became an international negotiating tool. Conservationists became more interested in agriculture's impact on the quality of water, wildlife habitat, and the future productive capacity of the soil resource.
- The face of agriculture itself changed as large farms became more predominant, and moderate-size farms began to disappear. The inevitability of a bimodal small farm/large farm distribution of farm sizes began to gain general acceptance. The efficiency and resilience of moderate-size family farms were placed in doubt.

TODAY'S FOOD AND AGRICULTURAL PROBLEMS

Food and agricultural problems can no longer be characterized in simple terms such as low prices and incomes. Today, there are several problems, including:

- The world food problem,
- The farm problem,
- The consumer food problem,
- The resource problem.

These problems are interrelated and have overlapping dimensions (Fig. 2.1). Their importance shifts over time with the emergence of specific issues. All dimensions of the problems affect farmers and the conditions under which food is produced, marketed and consumed.

Major dimensions of each of the problems are briefly reviewed here. More detailed discussion is presented later.

The World Food Problem

The world food problem is perhaps the most complex of the major problems. This is true not only because its solution involves satisfying the nutritional needs of over 4 billion people, but because governmental systems, policies, and programs of the many nations of the world must be rationalized. It has at least three major dimensions:

- **Distribution.** Reducing the most acute hunger and malnutrition is primarily a distribution problem. Properly distributed, there is enough food to feed the approximately 500 million malnourished people in the world. This was true even during the world food crisis of the 1970s. The cause of the distribution problem is low incomes— a lack of economic growth and development. The solution frequently lies with trade. Open trade channels facilitate economic growth and development. With higher incomes, food assistance or aid is a less frequent need. Yet massive food assistance programs are sometimes necessary to avoid widespread starvation and malnutrition (e.g., sub-Saharan Africa in the 1980s).

- **Trade.** Keeping trade channels open has been a perpetual problem. While the benefits of free trade to society as a whole are abundantly evident, from the perspective of an individual farmer—a milk producer in Wisconsin or a cattleman in Texas—the benefits of protectionism are equally clear. It is generally believed that U.S. agriculture stands to gain more from free trade than it would lose.

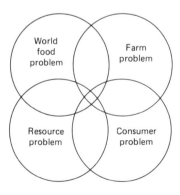

Figure 2.1 Food and agricultural policy problems are interrelated.

This explains why the United States typically is a strong advocate of reduced trade barriers. Yet, while advocating free trade, many U.S. farm policies actually are protectionist, as are those of many other countries. Policies designed to encourage domestic production frequently mean domestic prices above world prices, requiring competitive imports to be restricted. Some countries have policies that discourage farm production by placing ceilings on prices at which products may be sold, to the benefit of consumers. Open trade channels would ameliorate many of these problems, albeit at the expense of some producers and/or countries.

- **Capacity.** The adequacy of global production capacity was the subject of several studies during the 1970s.[2] The conclusions of these studies since have proven to be overly conservative. In the late 1980s, capacity concerns were expressed once again by greenhouse effect advocates due to a warming of the earth's atmosphere. Given favorable weather, agriculture has tremendous capacity to respond to market needs, but that response is to economic incentives. Agriculture's resource base extends beyond farming to agribusiness and public support for agricultural research and education, as well as public investments in the infrastructure that serves agriculture, including irrigation systems and roads.

Expanding production is dependent on the existence of incentives or rewards to producers. In market-oriented economies, these incentives are higher prices and profits and appreciation of asset values. Farmers respond to profit incentives. Richard Lyng, secretary of agriculture for President Reagan, put it this way: "When farm prices rise to profitable levels, even the roosters begin to lay eggs."[3]

It would be a mistake to leave the impression that the world food problem is simply a matter of supply and demand for food. It is, in fact, much more complex. Many of the complexities result from governments whose decision makers respond to immediate political pressures. Decisions of governments around the world affect American farmers, related businesses, and consumers. For example, assurance of an adequate food supply at reasonable prices is such a high priority that most countries have policies to encourage domestic production, manage exports and imports, and regulate food prices.

[2]See particularly the *World Food and Nutrition Study* (Washington, D.C.: National Academy of Science, 1977), and *The Global 2000 Report to the President* (Washington, D.C.: Council on Environmental Quality and Department of State, 1981).

[3]Richard Lyng, speech presented at the 1980 Agricultural Outlook Conference (Washington, D.C.: USDA, November 19, 1980).

The Farm Problem

The farm problem, like the world food problem, is also multidimensional, making it difficult to treat from a policy perspective. Its primary dimensions include:

- **Instability.** Agricultural production is inherently unstable, largely because of weather conditions, pests, and diseases. This instability not only leads to variation in domestic production, but also to abrupt changes in export demand as weather affects output in other countries. Export demand also is affected by changes in the value of the dollar or policies of importing countries. The supply and demand for farm products is sufficiently inelastic that changes in either can result in proportionately larger changes in prices. Unless buffered by government programs, farmers typically face a high degree of price and income risk.
- **Excess capacity.** Agriculture tends to have chronic excess capacity in the United States and some other countries. The U.S. excess capacity in the mid-1980s was about 10 percent. That excess capacity results primarily from government farm programs which, attempting to protect farmers in times of declining prices, impede the outflow of the unneeded resources.
- **Low incomes.** Agriculture experiences periodically low prices and net farm income, a result of excess capacity in the short run and sustained productivity growth in the long run. Farm income generally has averaged below nonfarm income, but was on par during the 1970s.
- **Fixed resources.** Resources are slow to adjust out of agriculture because many production costs tend to be fixed. Production thus continues as long as variable costs are recovered and there is some residual contribution to fixed costs. Also, agricultural labor and management skills are not well adapted to move into other occupations.
- **Diversity.** Farms are highly diverse in terms of size and financial conditions. This results in great diversity in net farm income, cash flow, and the ability to withstand financial stress. Some 40 percent of all farms have no debt and generally are able to generate substantial net income.[4] On the other hand, some farms in times of declining prices have such high debt that their cash flow will not even cover

[4]Marvin Duncan and David H. Harrington, "Farm Financial Stress: Extent and Causes," in *The Farm Credit Crisis: Policy Options and Consequences* (College Station, Tex.: Texas Agricultural Experiment Station, 1986).

current expenses. In addition to this diversity, farms vary by regions of the country and commodities produced. Incomes for producers of some commodities can be high in one year while producers of other commodities have low incomes that same year. For example, when grain prices are high, livestock producers' incomes typically are low. Such diversity leads to widely different net farm income and farmers' prospects for survival.

- **Program changes.**   Government policies themselves can be a major source of problems in agriculture. Sharp changes in policy, such as imposition of an embargo on exports, can have devastating effects on farm prices. Sharp changes in farm program spending make it difficult for farmers to plan their investment and output. This is true not only for the United States but also for agriculture throughout the world.[5]

- **Family farm survival.**   For decades, the family farm was the basic production unit in American agriculture. Most of the labor and management were supplied by the family and at least a portion of the land was owned. In the early 1980s, less than half of the value of farm production fits this family farm pattern of production.[6] The issue of family farm survival is part of a larger issue known as the structure of agriculture. This issue is concerned with the trends toward large-scale integrated agriculture, the potential development of a landholding class, the decline of rural communities, and the impact of a wide range of government programs on the organization and control of agriculture.

Government's role in domestic agriculture is directly related to its role in international agriculture. Increased commitment to the export market fosters increased instability in agriculture. Farm programs designed to deal with price and income instability affect the structure of agriculture. These impacts have been neither adequately understood nor taken into account when designing farm programs. Doing this requires an in-depth knowledge of both the economics of the problem and the programs.

[5]D. Gale Johnson, "The World Food Situation: Recent and Prospective Developments," in *The Role of Markets in the World Food Economy* (Boulder, Colo.: Westview Press, Inc., 1983), pp. 1–33.

[6]Harold F. Breimyer, "Perspectives on a Time to Choose, the USDA Report on Structure of Agriculture," in *Structure of Agriculture* (Washington, D.C.: Subcommittee on Forests, Family Farms, and Energy, Committee on Agriculture, U.S. House of Representatives, February 27, 1981), pp. 123–126.

The Consumer Food Problem

Historically, the influence of consumers on food and agricultural policy has ebbed and flowed. From 1900 through 1970, the major emphasis of consumer interest was limited largely to assurance that food was processed under sanitary conditions and protection against food poisoning or outbreaks of diseases. This complacency changed abruptly in the early 1970s when the consumer interest expanded to major food and farm policy issues such as food prices and certain commodity support programs.

Contemporary consumer concerns with respect to food and agriculture stretch far beyond the extensive USDA nutrition programs. Increasing concern exists with the adequacy of the food supply, food price, food safety, the relation between diet and health, and the level of government spending on farm programs. Consumer advocates also have joined forces with public interest groups to support environmental, conservation, and even animal rights causes. Yet in the 1980s, the political influence of consumers in agricultural and food policy decisions declined perceptibly.

Today, the primary dimensions of consumer food issues include:

- **Nutrition.** Contemporary consumer involvement in food issues likely had its roots in the concern about poverty in America that emerged in the early 1960s, and out of which emerged the food stamp program. It and related nutrition programs have since expanded to include over 20 million people at a cost of over $20 billion despite Republican administration efforts to reduce the scope and costs of the program.

  With the population increasing at an annual rate of less than 1 percent and one-third of the farm production exported, the ability of the United States to feed *itself* is not an issue. There is a danger that in a particular year, however, foreign demand will be so strong that unrestricted exports could lead to rapid increases in food prices. Such a situation occurred in 1974, when soybean prices became sufficiently high that an export embargo was imposed.

- **Price.** The combination of sharply increased world demand for food and general inflationary pressures increased the proportion of income spent on food in the United States from a low 16.2 percent in 1973 to 16.8 percent in 1980.[7] That proportion since has declined to less than 15 percent. While the proportion of income spent on food in

[7]Data from the Bureau of Labor Statistics (Washington, D.C.: U.S. Dept. of Commerce, 1981) and from Julie Kurland, "Food Spending and Income," *Nat. Food Rev.* (Washington, D.C.: ERS, USDA, Winter 1986), p. 30.

the United States is lower than in most other countries in the world, real increases in food expenditures relative to income place visible pressure on consumers' budgets. Thus, despite a low share of income spent on food, questions arise as to what can be done to reduce the price of food.

• **Safety.** In an age of highly processed and fabricated food, the issue of food safety has expanded far beyond the question of sanitation, to residues and additives that could potentially cause disease or mal- nutrition. To date, attention has been primarily on chemical agents that potentially cause cancer. The Delaney clause of the federal Food, Drug and Cosmetic Act of 1938 specifies that any agent found to cause cancer in either human beings or animals must be removed from the food supply. Controversy exists over (1) the zero-tolerance requirement of this law; (2) the use of extremely high dosages of the suspected agent in laboratory animals to establish the existence of a cause–effect relationship; and (3) the assumption that if the agent causes cancer in animals, it also will cause cancer in human beings.

• **Nutrition.** Consumer concern about the relation between diet and health was highlighted by the activities of the Senate Select Com- mittee on Health and Human Needs in the early 1970s. This com- mittee eventually developed dietary goals and guidelines which en- couraged moderation in the consumption of salt, sugar, and products high in cholesterol, such as beef, milkfat, and eggs. The most contro- versial of these guidelines relates to cholesterol. The basis for this guideline lies primarily in the relationship between cholesterol and heart disease. In the 1980s, high-fat foods were also all linked to cer- tain cancers.

• **Food lobby.** With the wide range of important food policy issues, it seems clear that consumer advocates will remain important par- ticipants in the policy process. Consumers are the largest single taxpaying body. While poor people have a vested interest in pro- grams such as food stamps, consumers as taxpayers are also con- cerned about the need to control federal spending. In addition, there is growing realization of the need to weigh the costs of increased reg- ulation in terms of higher food prices and reduced freedom of choice against the benefits.

   The existence of the food lobby is disconcerting to the producer. Producers contend that while they are called on to increase produc- tion to satisfy world food needs and hold down food prices, they face increased restrictions on the use of growth stimulants, pesticides, and antibiotics. Pork, beef, milk, and egg producers express concern about the potential for substantially reduced consumption and prices on the release of studies establishing links between diet and health. Farmers find their farm programs in competition with food-oriented programs for the USDA budget—an agency they feel was designed primarily to help producers. Regardless of their merits, producers' feelings on these issues run deep and are likely to continue to be a major source of controversy.

The Resource Problem

Until the 1970s, the supply of natural resources—land, energy, and water—generally was not recognized as a factor limiting agriculture's productive potential. Except for the largely unnoticed and unheeded rumblings of a few early environmentalists, religious groups, and individuals having a more global perspective, the general assumption existed that the problem was one of overabundance, or at least overuse, of agriculture's productive capacity, not a scarcity of productive resources. The 1970s created an awareness of the fragility of agriculture's productive capacity.

U.S. agriculture has been based on extensive cultivation of large land areas, cheap energy, and plentiful water supplies. The dust bowl conditions that developed in the 1930s have been largely forgotten. Concern about soil conservation has lessened. Farm equipment, fertilization, use of farm chemicals, and irrigation practices have been geared to low-cost energy. Water irrigation has been developed and, more important, used as if it were an unlimited resource.

For the individual farmer pursuing a policy of year-to-year profit maximization, the use of resources in this manner was quite rational. For the United States as a whole, it had potentially long-term devastating effects. More significant is the fact that public policies in certain respects encouraged these resource-depleting developments.

Soil conservation programs developed in the 1930s failed to adjust to changing needs and received reduced public support and attention. This occurred at the time when the demands on agriculture increased sharply. The result was predictable—more intensive farming and more soil erosion. Not until the 1985 farm law was the issue of soil erosion once again seriously addressed.

Water was made available to agriculture free or at a price far below either its cost of generation or the level needed to maintain its longer-term availability. In many respects, water was treated as a free good. Only increasing energy prices, resulting in increased cost of irrigation, have introduced a degree of rationality into cropping patterns in irrigated areas.

Strong resistance developed within agriculture to initiatives to reduce agriculture's contribution to environmental problems such as water and air pollution. Highways, as well as expanding urban and industrial developments, required increasing quantities of prime farmland, with little thought given to its eventual exhaustion.

In the 1980s, questions again arose about the consistency of research and extension programs designed to discover and disseminate new technology while surpluses accumulated. At the same time, questions arose regarding the competitiveness of U.S. farmers in world markets with no apparent recognition of a link to research and extension programs.

PHILOSOPHIES OF PROBLEM SOLVING

As noted in Chapter 1, one's attitude toward policy is influenced by facts, values, beliefs, and goals. That is, facts, values, beliefs, and goals influence one's conclusions concerning the perception of the problem, the economic relationships that relate to solving problems, the appropriate role of government in agriculture, and the effectiveness of government in solving problems.

Specific combinations of facts, values, beliefs, and goals lead to identifiable philosophies toward government's role in agriculture. Five such philosophical approaches are discussed here:

- The free market
- The production stimulator
- The agricultural fundamentalist
- The stabilizer
- The planner

These approaches are discussed in their pure form. Individuals may prefer combinations or variations from the pure form because of differences in the values or beliefs they hold. No attempt is made to evaluate the merits of any of the philosophical approaches.

The Free Market

In the **free-market** approach, *the forces of supply and demand determine product prices as well as allocate and ration available supplies.* This approach normally places a high value on the role of profits, private enterprise, initiative, and hard work; little confidence is placed in the ability of government to solve or even ameliorate problems.

To the free-market advocate, agriculture would be better off if government programs—particularly price and income programs—were eliminated. At most, the role of government should be limited to research, education, provision of production and market information, and actions to reduce barriers to free trade in foreign markets. Even here, however, an increased role for private-sector research, information, and analyses is seen.

Many Republicans, in recent years, ranging from President Nixon's secretary of agriculture, Earl Butz, to President Reagan's agriculture secretaries, Block and Lyng, have been strong advocates of the free-market approach in agriculture. Their tolerance of farm programs has been more a matter of political pragmatism than a belief that these programs solve problems.

The Production Stimulator

The **production stimulator** believes that *the major agricultural problem is to adequately feed an ever-expanding world population.* Government's role in this context is to provide the basis for increased production.

Government policies consistent with the philosophy of a production stimulator include substantially expanded agricultural research and education, increased foreign food aid and development assistance, producer income supplements to provide continuous production incentives in the event of low farm prices, and government-held stocks of grain to guard against a production shortfall.

The production stimulators also have a basic belief in the right to food. The **right-to-food resolution** adopted by the 1974 World Food Conference *holds that every person in the world has a right to an adequate diet.* Associated with this right are government programs designed to encourage production and get it to those who are in the greatest need.

Religious groups such as the Interreligious Task Force on U.S. Food Policy can be directly associated with the production stimulation philosophy. Reports of the National Academy of Sciences, environmentalists, and greenhouse effect advocates also tend to support this point of view.[8]

The Agricultural Fundamentalist

The **agricultural fundamentalist** believes that the *root of all wealth lies in agriculture and the soil, that agriculture has "moral properties—the capacity to engender in human beings an elevated behavior,"*[9] and

[8]*World Food and Nutrition Study.*

[9]Harold F. Breimyer, *Farm Policy: 13 Essays* (Ames, Iowa: Iowa State University Press, 1977), p. 6.

that it creates values in human beings that are generally recognized as being good. The USDA was created with a fundamentalist philosophy. Its seal is inscribed: "Agriculture is the foundation of manufacture and commerce."

The policy prescription of the fundamentalist is to maintain agriculture's economic health and thereby maintain the economy's health. High farm prices give farmers more money to spend in rural communities, which in turn works its way through the whole economy by stimulating employment and investment in new plants and equipment. The fundamentalist philosophy also holds that high farm prices are necessary to preserve the values that are instilled in farm people.

The basic policy prescription of the fundamentalist is government establishment of price floors for agricultural commodities at parity price levels. The parity price gives a commodity the same purchasing power that it had in 1910–1914, an especially prosperous time for agriculture.

The American Agriculture Movement and to a lesser extent the National Farmers Union have this fundamentalist philosophy. Both have had parity prices as a basic policy position. These organizations and their values and beliefs are discussed more fully in Chapter 4.

The Stabilizer

The **stabilization** philosophy holds that *the major problem in agriculture is instability.* Instability, it is suggested, undermines the family farm structure, results in errors in production and marketing decisions, and fosters inflation. Government policy to the stabilizer should ensure that farm prices move over a relatively narrow range and that supplies are always available. This can be accomplished through government control of a portion of the grain stocks and through the establishment of floor prices. The Carter–Bergland administration pursued a stabilization philosophy. Its innovation for accomplishing price and supply stabilization was the farmer-owned grain reserve.

The Planner

The **planner** believes that the *marketplace alone cannot be relied on to influence food consumption and production decisions.* Planners contend that the market is too unstable and its participants are too slow to adjust. The result is chronic problems, ranging from consumers not eating a nutritious diet to producers not producing the proper combination of foods in the right quantities.

The most ardent agricultural planner in the 1960s was Willard Cochrane. As agricultural economic policy adviser to President Kennedy, Cochrane suggested that the way to deal with the problem of excessive capacity in agriculture was to establish programs that effectively control production. That is, government should estimate food and fiber needs and implement programs consistent with those needs.[10]

The 1970s version of Willard Cochrane was Carol Foreman, an assistant secretary of agriculture under President Carter. Her concept of agricultural policy included a government influence on both consumer and producer decisions. This plan included government identification of the nutritional needs of consumers, educational and income supplement programs to influence what was consumed, and production incentives consistent with consumer needs.[11]

In the 1980s, Senator Tom Harkin (Dem.-Iowa) and Texas State Agriculture Commissioner, Jim Hightower, have been strong advocates of the planning approach, proposing strict controls on farm production. Their constituency included primarily farmers especially hard hit by declining land prices.

THE SINGLE-PROBLEM TRAP

It is all too easy to fall into the trap of treating each of the four agricultural and food problem areas separately. Policymakers do this regularly by responding only to the issues of the moment. Reality suggests that the four areas are not mutually exclusive, but, in fact, are interrelated. Increasing world food demand affects the price received by farmers, the cost and availability to consumers, and the availability of resources for future food production. These interrelationships must always be kept in mind. In other words, students of policy must be looking continuously at causes and effects that extend beyond the immediate problem or policy alternative. That is the approach taken in this book.

ADDITIONAL READINGS

1. An excellent discussion of the farm problem and policy issues as they existed in the 1960s is contained in Willard W. Cochrane, *A City Man's Guide to the Farm Problem* (Minneapolis, Minn.: University of Minnesota Press, 1965), pp. 110–123.

2. Cochrane's analysis of the farm problem as it existed in the 1960s can be contrasted with the paper of Howard Hjort, "Economic Setting for Agriculture in

[10]Interestingly, Cochrane's perspective on farm policy shifted to a materially reduced government role in the 1980s.

[11]Carol Tucker Foreman, "Toward a U.S. Food Policy," in *1978 Food and Agricultural Outlook* (Washington D.C.: Committee on Agriculture, Nutrition, and Forestry, U.S. Senate, December 19, 1977), pp. 10–20.

the Eighties," in *1981 Agricultural Outlook* (Washington, D.C.: Committee on Agriculture, Nutrition, and Forestry, U.S. Senate, January 1981).

3. Harold Breimyer's *Farm Policy: 13 Essays* (Ames, Iowa: Iowa State University Press, 1977) contains an extensive discussion of the nature of fundamentalist thought toward agriculture that continues to have substantial impact on opinions about policy and the policy problem in rural America.

4. Carol Foreman's views on the farm problem and government's role are contained in two articles. The first, "Toward a U.S. Food Policy," in *1978 Food and Agricultural Outlook* (Washington, D.C.: Committee on Agriculture, Nutrition, and Forestry, U.S. Senate, December 19, 1977), pp. 10–20, was developed near the beginning of the Carter presidency. The second, "Food and Agricultural Policy in the Eighties," in *1981 Agricultural Outlook* (Washington, D.C.: Committee on Agriculture, Nutrition, and Forestry, U.S. Senate, January 1981), was written after the election of Ronald Reagan.

5. For an excellent pre-1985 farm bill perspective on the farm problem and related policy issues, see Gordon C. Rauser and Kenneth R. Farrell, eds., *Alternative Agricultural and Food Policies and the 1985 Farm Bill* (Washington, D.C.: National Center for Food and Agricultural Policy, 1986).

Chapter 3

The Policy Process

*Congress is so strange. A man gets up to speak
and says nothing. Nobody listens—and then
everybody disagrees.*

Boris Marskaloa

Implementing a cohesive agricultural and food policy requires the establishment of a broad base of support in the Congress as well as in the executive branch of government. Establishing such support depends upon more than just numbers. Strength is in organization, coupled with knowledge of how government works, how decisions are made, and how to mobilize broad support for specific causes.

The essence of the policy process is politics. Politics has been defined as the art of the possible, the art of compromise, and the art of determining who gets what. The policy formulation process is itself often a key determinant of the content of policy. Thus it is important to have an understanding of the nature of the policy process and the central actors who attempt to influence the direction and substance of policies for food and agriculture.

In this chapter we describe the structure of the federal policy process in terms of how the various branches and agencies of government interact to develop and implement food and agricultural policies and programs. An attempt is also made to provide some insight into the dynamics of the policy process. In the next chapter we examine the role of special-interest groups in influencing food and agricultural policy.

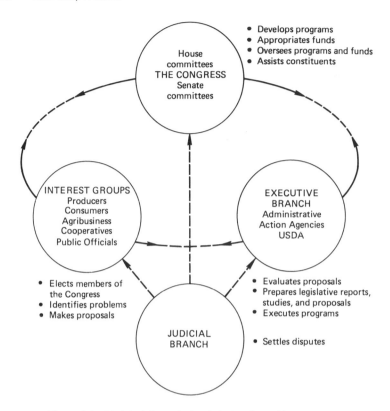

Figure 3.1   Model of the agricultural food policymaking process.

The American democratic form of government is intended to be reflective of the will of the people governed—government of the people, by the people, and for the people. In a representative government, those charged with making laws, determining national policies, and those responsible for the execution of laws and carrying out policy are selected primarily through popular elections. Although many of the people involved in the policy process are appointed, elected persons usually appoint the top decision makers and ultimately are responsible for decisions regardless of who makes them.

The framers of the Constitution embodied in the American system of government the principle of "separation of powers" by establishing three equal branches of government: the legislative, executive, and judicial. The three branches provide a system of checks and balances whereby no branch becomes clearly dominant. It is through the interaction of these branches of government that policies and programs are proposed, developed, adopted, and carried out (Fig. 3.1).

THE LEGISLATIVE BRANCH

The very first provision of the Constitution (Article 1, Section 1) creates the legislative branch by providing that "all legislative powers herein created shall be vested in a Congress of the United States, which shall consist of a Senate and a House of Representatives."

The Senate is composed of 100 members: two from each state, irrespective of population or area. The six-year term of office is arranged so that it does not terminate for both senators from a particular state at the same time.

The House of Representatives is composed of 435 members elected every two years from among the 50 states, apportioned according to their total population.[1] The membership of the House is reapportioned among and within the states every 10 years to reflect changes in population. This has proved important to agricultural policy because population has shifted over time from rural to urban areas. As a result, farm and rural groups have experienced a decline in their power and influence. The number of rural districts and farm-oriented representatives has gradually declined. The change in the composition of congressional districts in the last 30 years is indicated in Table 3.1.

The Constitution stipulates that the Congress assemble at least once every year, beginning at noon on the third day of January. A Congress lasts for two years, commencing in January of the year following the biennial election of members.

The chief function of the Congress is making laws. Definite lines of jurisdiction exist between the House and Senate on certain matters. For example, only the Senate may "advise and consent" on treaties and certain nominations by the president. The House initiates revenue bills (taxes) and usually takes the leadership on appropriation of funds to carry out the functions of government.

Leadership Control[2]

The leadership of the Congress is vested in the party steering committees in both the House and Senate. These committees, made up of ranking leaders of each party, formulate party rules, develop strategies,

[1]In addition to the representatives from the 50 states, there is a resident commissioner from the Commonwealth of Puerto Rico and one delegate each from American Samoa, the District of Columbia, Guam, and the Virgin Islands. They have most of the prerogatives of representatives, with the important exception of the right to vote on matters before the House.

[2]This section draws heavily on B. L. Flinchbaugh and Mark A. Edelman, "The Changing Politics of the Farm and Food Systems," in *The Farm and Food System in Transition* (East Lansing, Mich.: Michigan State University, 1984).

TABLE 3.1 Makeup of U.S. House of Representatives
and Districts by Residence of Population, 1968, 1973, and 1985

	1968	1973	1985	Percent Change 1966–1988
Urban and suburban	280	305	347	+ 23
Rural	155	130	88	− 43
Total	435	435	435	

and make committee assignments. The majority party's committee also nominates the chair of the committees and proposes rules to govern committee and floor action.

All members of each house belong to their respective party caucuses, which approve major rules proposed by the steering committees. Since the majority party controls each chamber, its rules usually govern committee and floor action. The composition of each committee reflects the proportionate party membership of each chamber. Thus a majority of each committee is from the majority party. This is why a united majority party can have a high degree of control over actions of the Congress. It is also why a president whose party also controls the Congress tends to be particularly powerful.

Committee power center.   Committees are centers of power for determining the fate of particular pieces of legislation, and the person chairing usually is the focal point for power within the committee. The Senate has 15 standing committees, and the House has 22. Each committee has jurisdiction over legislation in specific areas, and all measures affecting a particular area of law are referred to that committee. The rules provide for more than 190 different classifications of measures which are to be referred to the respective committees in the House and more than 180 in the Senate. For example, proposed sugar legislation containing provisions for a tariff on imported sugar would be referred to the House Ways and Means Committee, which has jurisdiction over all revenue bills. Sugar legislation without such a provision, focusing on only a domestic price support program for growers, would be referred to the agriculture committee.[3] A proposal containing both provisions would be referred to both committees.

Senators and representatives usually seek membership on a committee that has jurisdiction in a field most relevant to their constituents or in which they are most qualified and interested. The committees still operate largely by the seniority system, although this was substantially

[3]The term "agriculture committee" refers to both the Senate Committee on Agriculture, Nutrition and Forestry and the House Committee on Agriculture. Both committees have essentially the same jurisdiction.

modified by the reform-minded 93rd Congress of 1974. Members rank in seniority according to the order of their appointment to the committee. The ranking member of the committee from the majority party is usually elected chair.

Most of the committees have two or more subcommittees that have initial jurisdiction in the consideration of bills in particular subject areas. Subcommittee chairs also are members of the majority party. Each committee is provided a professional and clerical staff to assist in the consideration of bills. The professional and clerical staff is appointed by the chairman on a permanent basis without regard, in theory, to political affiliations and then must be agreed to by majority vote of the committee.

The Policymaking Process

Generally, the broad national policies of this country are embodied in statutes enacted by the Congress. The policymaking process, thus, is a major component of the formal legislative process. This is especially true for food and agriculture policy, where the major legislation is the omnibus "farm bill," which expires and is reconsidered by the Congress every four or five years. The term "farm bill," however, is really a misnomer. In recent times, **farm bills** have become truly omnibus, *encompassing not only the traditional farm programs, but also the domestic food assistance, foreign aid (P.L. 480), rural development, research and extension, and various other program authorizations.* The rationale for such a omnibus bill is to *broaden the base of support* for farm legislation.

Sources of legislation.   The sources of ideas for legislation are unlimited, and draft bills originate in many diverse quarters. The first is from members of Congress who may have campaigned for election on the promise of introducing specific legislation. Constituents—either as individuals or groups such as bar associations, labor unions, farm organizations, and the like—may suggest proposals and present draft bills to members.

Proposed legislation may also emanate from the executive branch through "executive communication." In recent years, this has become a prolific source of proposals, usually in the form of a letter from the president, a member of the president's cabinet, or the head of an independent agency transmitting a draft of a proposed bill to Congress. Such bills may be introduced by a member of the president's party.

However, getting unpopular bills introduced is not always easy. For example, President Reagan's proposed 1985 farm bill to withdraw government from agriculture was sufficiently unpopular that no member of the Senate wanted to be associated with it. Finally, Senator Helms, chair-

Presidential signature or veto.   Once an enrolled bill is delivered to the White House, the president has 10 days (excepting Sundays) to take action on it. The enrolled bill is handled by the Office of Management and Budget (OMB) in the Executive Office of the President. OMB circulates the bill to all concerned agencies, asking for their views and recommendations to the president as to whether the bill should be signed or vetoed. These statements are then summarized and included in an "enrolled bill memorandum," which is sent to the president for final decision.

The options available to the chief executive are:

- Accept the legislation by signing the bill.
- Do nothing when the Congress is in session. The bill becomes law after the tenth day if no action is taken. This is sometimes done to indicate a negative view of the bill when it is politically untenable to embrace it, or it is sometimes done when serious constitutional questions may surround the legality of the bill.
- Do nothing when the Congress is not in session. This "pocket veto" can occur when the president fails to act on the bill after adjournment at the end of the second session.
- Veto the bill, returning it to the Congress with a "veto message" citing reasons for the veto. A vetoed bill can still become law if two-thirds of the members of both houses vote to override the veto.

The Budget Process

Budget concerns now play an increasingly important role in farm policy development and implementation. Cost considerations are important in framing provisions of a farm bill, and once enacted, the funds must be appropriated to operate the programs.

The basic provisions of a farm bill, such as price supports and direct farmer payments, are known as *entitlements*. An **entitlement** *means that any farmer who qualifies for the program is entitled to the authorized benefits.* About the only time that Congress has control over entitlement expenditures is when the legislation is enacted.[7] Other provisions, however, such as soil conservation and research and extension programs, require direct annual appropriations to implement. The budget process is composed of four basic steps: a proposed budget by the president, a congressional budget resolution and reconciliation, the appropriation process, and revenue raising.

---

[7]An exception to this rule occurred under the Gramm–Rudman–Hollings balanced budget initiative when entitlement price supports and direct payment were reduced the legally required percentage. Such occurrences have been rare.

Presidential budget proposal. The president is required by the Budget and Accounting Act of 1921 to prepare and submit a budget to the Congress. This process, centralized in the Office of Management and Budget, begins almost two years before the fiscal year begins. In the spring of each year, executive agencies begin preparing their budget requests under some instructions from OMB. Informal within-department hearings are held, with OMB generally in attendance. These initial hearings are for the departments to determine their priorities and the overall amount of their requests.

Adjustments for specific programs and total requests frequently are requested by OMB. When serious disagreements exist between OMB and departments, the settlement is left to the president. The proposed budget is put into final form in the fall and winter and presented to the Congress in the president's annual budget message each January within 15 days after Congress assembles.

Budget resolution and reconciliation process. Over time, Congress has become increasingly concerned about the size and complexity of federal spending activities, the growing importance of federal spending in relation to national income, and the amount of relatively "uncontrollable" spending.[8] In the 1970s, concern about the ability of Congress to control spending culminated in passage of the 1974 Budget and Impoundment Act, which gave the Congress a means to establish and enforce spending and debt ceilings and revenue floors.

The 1974 Budget and Impoundment Act created two new budget committees[9] and a staff office, the Congressional Budget Office, to support the process. These tools enable the Congress to develop and manage national economic and fiscal policy through actions taken by joint resolutions, and thus not subject to veto by the president. The act links both the authorization and appropriation processes to the budget.

Almost a full year before a new fiscal year begins, the president must provide the budget committees with an estimate of the cost of current programs for the next fiscal year. Then the president's proposed budget is required 15 days after the Congress convenes. The appropriations committees begin work on appropriation bills, authorizing committees begin work on proposals coming before them, and budget committees begin work on the first concurrent budget resolution.

---

[8]One of the major factors resulting in spending being "uncontrollable" has been the enactment of entitlement programs, which, for example, tie welfare benefits to specified eligibility standards and changes in the consumer price index or agricultural subsidies to changes in the costs of production and market prices.

[9]The creation of the budget committees actually was triggered by confrontations between the Congress and President Nixon over whether monies appropriated could be impounded by the president and not spent.

The budget process contains two closely related steps:

- **Budget resolution** sets a ceiling on the level of spending and on revenue estimates overall and for individual government programs.
- **Budget reconciliation** is the process by which the Congress stays within the spending ceiling as new legislation is enacted and appropriations are made.

Budget resolution and reconciliation activities proceed on a very tight schedule. All authorizing committees, including the agriculture committees, must present recommendations to the budget committees by March 15. By April 15, the budget committees must report a budget resolution to the floor. By May 15, the authorizing committees must report any bills that include spending authority for the upcoming fiscal year, and the Congress must complete work on the first budget resolution for the coming fiscal year.

Once the first budget resolution is complete and adopted, spending ceilings are then known to the appropriations committees. Any new spending authorized by newly reported bills is estimated. To the extent that the revenue floors and the spending ceilings in the first resolution are within total spending proposals, the process is virtually complete. Only modifications caused by changing economic conditions must be provided for in the second and final budget resolution, which must be completed in September before the beginning of the new fiscal year in October.

In the event that proposed spending exceeds the amount in the budget resolution, the authorizing committees are directed to submit legislation to reconcile spending, revenues, or debts. The Congress must complete action on reconciliation bills by September 25. Although these dates are somewhat flexible, the steps in the process are specified and adhered to by the Congress. If spending threatens to exceed the budget resolution, either spending programs must be scaled back or the resolution itself must be changed with necessary supplemental appropriations.

The budget process has had the important impact of constraining spending in both the 1981 and 1985 farm bills. Budget committee-imposed ceilings were used by congressional leadership and the administration to bring the bills' costs within the guidelines. For example, budget ceilings were used as a bargaining lever in the 1985 farm bill to lower target prices for the late 1980s and 1990.

Appropriations process.   The functions of the congressional committees related to the budget are distinctly separated as to authorizations, budget, and appropriations. The subject matter committees, such as agriculture, are **authorizing committees**. That is, laws authorize expenditures of funds for specific purposes. The **budget committees** *set limits on how much can be spent.* *The actual appropriation of funds for carrying out the legislation is the function of the* **appropriations committees** in the House and Senate. Since the appropriations committees must approve funds for agriculture and related programs, most of which are administered by the USDA, they are very influential in determining the content of policy and the execution of programs.

Within the House and Senate appropriations committees exist the highly influential subcommittees for agriculture. The Subcommittee on Agriculture and Related Agencies of the House Committee on Appropriations has been chaired by Representative Jamie L. Whitten (Dem.-Miss.) since January 1949, except for 1953 and 1954, when the Republicans were the majority party in the House. He became chairman of the House Committee on Appropriations in 1978 while retaining chairmanship of the Subcommittee on Agriculture and Related Agencies. By virtue of very nearly controlling the budget of the USDA, he has been one of the most influential people in determining USDA decisions on agricultural policy and, in fact, has frequently been referred to as the "permanent secretary of agriculture."

Revenue raising process. Revenue decisions are made by **tax committees**, namely the Senate Finance Committee and the House Ways and Means Committee. In the 1990s, the willingness of Congress to appropriate money for domestic programs such as agriculture will be determined, in part, by the national attitude toward taxation and the will to bring the budget deficit under control. Taxes, as one of the most enduring political issues, create constant pressure to hold down federal spending. In the first half of the 1980s, political pressures focused on reducing federal expenditures, including farm program costs, to avoid raising taxes. But as the budget deficit has become larger and more burdensome, increased taxes once again became a national political issue.

THE EXECUTIVE BRANCH

While the role of the Congress is to enact legislation that represents the broad will of the people, the role of the executive branch is implementation and administration of these laws. This means carrying out programs to effectuate the intent of the laws. The president, of course, has a political agenda which he attempts to have the Congress enact. The executive branch influences legislation through its proposals to the Congress, support of or opposition to bills, lobbying efforts, and use of the veto.

The executive branch is broadly structured with the chief executive and staff, operating within the Executive Office of the President (EOP), and cabinet departments charged with specific areas of responsibility. In modern times, the structure of the executive branch has become increasingly complex, with the addition of several offices within the Executive Office of the President as well as several new cabinet departments.

The Executive Office of the President

A general distinction is made between the White House—the president, vice president, and their personal staffs and advisors—and the agencies comprising the Executive Office of the President (EOP). The White House staff generally encompasses the staff of the president and vice president, those having responsibility for personally advising the president on political, economic, national defense, and other matters. Although each president operates somewhat differently, the EOP includes the following agencies that influence food and agricultural policy issues:

The *Office of Management and Budget (OMB)* is responsible for development of budget proposals and oversight of executive branch expenditures as appropriated by the Congress. In addition, OMB supervises executive branch development of legislative reports and coordinates policy and procedures for all executive branch procurement.

The *Council of Economic Advisers (CEA)* is responsible for assessing economic conditions and reporting annually to the Congress. The three-member council also advises the president and assists in development of the administration's national economic policy.

The *National Security Council (NSC)* integrates domestic, foreign, and military policy relating to national security. The NSC also advises the president on development of foreign policy and coordinates foreign policy development and execution.

The *Central Intelligence Agency (CIA)* is responsible for foreign intelligence and counterintelligence activities outside the United States. The CIA director has cabinet rank.

The *Office of the Special Trade Representative (STR)* advises the president on trade matters, coordinates executive branch trade policy, and is responsible for directing U.S. participation in trade negotiations.

The *Office of Science and Technology Policy (OSTP)* is responsible for advising the president on matters relating to science policy. It is involved in analysis of all areas of national concern in which policy will have scientific implications.

The *Council on Environmental Quality (CEQ)* advises the president on environmental matters and assists in policy development.

The growing complexity and interdependence of a modern society means that virtually any public concern today cuts across the assigned responsibilities of several of the cabinet departments and interdependent regulatory agencies. A major function of the EOP entities is then the assimilation and coordination of actions and decisions of the many departments, agencies, and offices to ensure a coherent national policy. For example, the Council of Economic Advisors reviews proposed USDA actions to ensure their consistency with the president's overall national economic policy, while OMB assesses USDA actions to make sure that they conform with administration budget policy.

The appropriate role of the EOP versus that of the cabinet departments in determining policy long has been a point of contention, but an especially visible one in the past few administrations. Increasing concern has developed that officials in the EOP, such as the director of OMB, might be making the critical decisions on farm policy about which he knows little. Although this concerns farmers, it is argued that OMB and other agency involvement is necessary to develop a consistent national policy.

The essential nature of the problem is that as the executive branch has grown more vast and complex, increasingly greater coordination is required to harmonize the policies and programs of each cabinet department with the overall philosophy and broad national policies emanating from the chief executive. There are numerous examples of cabinet departments catering to constituent interests and striking off in policy directions at odds with the broad policies enunciated by the White House. The bureaucratic infighting between departments, including USDA and the White House, has at such times been intense.[10]

The issue of cabinet autonomy has been particularly controversial, with much attention given to reported discord and conflict between the secretaries of agriculture and the EOP and the White House over the past decade. A degree of disorder and disharmony in the executive branch policy decision process for food and agriculture has always existed. This is inevitable to some extent; it quite naturally arises that the favored policy course of USDA is often inconsistent with broader national policy objectives being pursued by the administration as overseen by the EOP. However, an adversarial element to USDA–EOP relations, properly harnessed, is generally regarded as important and useful to reaching better decisions by ensuring close scrutiny and broad consideration of the many aspects of an issue.

One of the factors contributing to USDA–EOP conflict has been increased interest by other cabinet agencies, such as the Treasury and State departments, in agriculture and food issues. The linkages of agriculture to other departments became stronger as agriculture's contribu-

[10]An excellent discussion of White House–cabinet pressure is contained in Joseph Califano, Jr., *Governing America: An Insider's Report from the White House and the Cabinet* (New York: Simon & Schuster, Inc., 1981). David A. Stockman's *The Triumph of Politics* (New York: Harper & Row, Publishers, Inc., 1986) also provides an excellent OMB perspective on the political aspects of economic decisions.

MIXING ORANGES AND ORANGES

If there was any thin sliver of the welfare state where the Reagan Administration might have raised the free enterprise and anti-spending banner, it was against the socialistic enterprises of U.S. Agriculture. But by 1984 we had accommodated to the political facts of life here, too. As I contemplated the task of formulating a strategy to deal with the nation's massive deficit after the election, two White House episodes regarding agriculture stood out in my mind vividly. They were the smoking gun which proved that the White House couldn't even tackle the fabulous excesses of the farm pork barrel, and that was the very bottom of the whole spending barrel.

The first episode had occurred in the summer of 1982. The issue was agriculture marketing orders, an out-and-out socialist relic from the New Deal that tells every California orange and lemon grower how many of these little fruits can be marketed each week.

The established growers like this kind of lemon socialism because it keeps prices up, supplies down, and new competition out of the market. . . .

So I'd located some photographs of this lemon socialism at work. They showed gargantuan mountains—bigger than the White House—of California oranges rotting in the field. The reason for all this deliberate garbage creation was that the USDA orange commissar had cut back the weekly marketing quota, fearing that a bumper crop would drop the price and give consumers too good a deal on oranges.

Since we'd also just talked about a free food program for the homeless, my pictures did seem to suggest something rather ludicrous, and everyone around the cabinet table began to laugh. But then the California politicians swung into action.

Dick Lyng, an old California Reaganaut and Under Secretary of Agriculture, said I was fibbing. "The USDA had nothing to do with this. The growers elect their own committees to stabilize the market."

"You remember, Mr. President," he added, "that a lot of our friends out there depend on these marketing orders."

Well, okay. Some of our friends are members of the Navel Orange Growers Soviet. It wasn't a compelling argument. . . .

I asked him how about year-round Florida oranges that come right off the free market, with no supply control by a Florida Orange Grower Soviet at all. He said my point wasn't valid because I was mixing oranges and oranges.

Jim Lake, the Reagan campaign press secretary and paid lobbyist in the off season, had another point. He just went up to the Hill and got a law passed making it illegal for the director of OMB even to read the marketing orders before they were stamped by USDA. That was that for free enterprise in California. Needless to say, there remained equally compelling cases for other variations of Big Government in the other forty-nine states.

tion to the economy's balance of trade increased through large exports, as rising food prices put inflationary pressures on the economy, as commodity subsidies and food aid programs resulted in large budget outlays, and as trade and aid agreements became tools of foreign diplomacy. These changes have created problems for the agricultural establishment in controlling its farm and food policy agenda.

The U.S. Department of Agriculture

Shortly after its creation in 1862, President Lincoln stated his intention for the Department of Agriculture: "It is precisely the people's department, in which they feel more directly concerned than any other."[11] Although the mission and focus of USDA is a source of continuing controversy, the scope and responsibilities of the department have significantly expanded over time.

USDA normally has 15 to 20 agencies; the number varies from time to time as each new administration makes largely cosmetic reorganizations. It employs over 80,000 people, making it one of the largest cabinet departments. Organizationally, USDA's functions are grouped into broad categories with an assistant or undersecretary having direct responsibility for the agencies carrying out programs in closely related areas (Fig. 3.2). USDA programs extend to virtually every aspect of food and agriculture, the full scope generally being indicated by the following brief descriptions of the various agencies.

Commodity and international programs.   The *Agriculture Stabilization and Conservation Service (ASCS)* administers most of the farm price and income programs. A successor to the initial Agricultural Adjustment Administration, once familiar to millions of farmers as the "Triple A Office," ASCS maintains offices in most of the agricultural counties of the country. There, farmers annually enroll in farm programs, report acreages cropped, specific crops grown, yields, and so on, in order to receive program benefits. Each state and county has a politically appointed committee of farmers that serves as a "grass roots" input into ASCS policy.

The *Foreign Agriculture Service (FAS)* has as its principal mission expansion of the foreign markets for U.S. farm products. It stations over 150 attachés and counselors in American embassies in major food-producing and consuming countries around the world to monitor conditions and facilitate market development and sales.

    [11]Abraham Lincoln, *Fourth Annual Message to the Congress*, Washington, D.C., December 6, 1864.

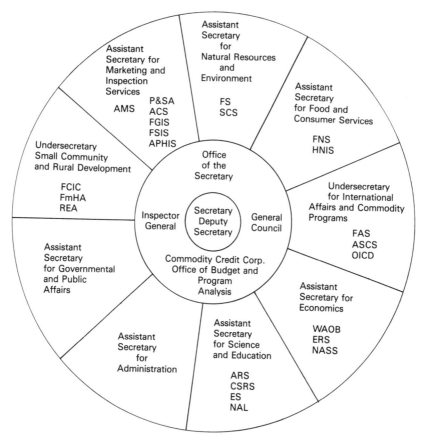

Figure 3.2 Organization of USDA by functional areas and agencies.

The *Organization for International Cooperation and Development (OICD)* conducts training and education programs for foreign nationals and facilitates scientific exchanges and agricultural development activities between the United States and foreign governments.

Marketing programs. The *Agricultural Marketing Service (AMS)* directs the market order programs for fruits, vegetables, and milk; manages product-grading activities; collects and disseminates market news information; and provides oversight of the operations of meat packers and stockyard operations.

The *Animal and Plant Health Inspection Service (APHIS)* is responsible for the inspection and certification of animals and plants moving in interstate and international commerce.

The *Federal Grain Inspection Service (FGIS)* is responsible for determining grades of grain, testing, and quality assurance for grain moving in interstate commerce and international markets.

The *Agricultural Cooperative Service (ACS)* collects statistics, conducts research, and provides technical assistance for farmer cooperatives.

The *Food Safety and Inspection Service (FSIS)* conducts the federal meat and poultry inspection programs.

The *Packers and Stockyards Administration (P&S)* monitors livestock markets for potential unfair trade practices.

Rural development programs. The *Farmers Home Administration (FmHA)* operates numerous credit programs oriented to serving the financial needs of the farmers, rural communities, and rural residents. FmHA is a large lending and grant-making agency whose diverse programs include emergency loans to farmers in areas suffering natural calamities, farm operating and land acquisition loans, loans and grants to rural communities for public facilities such as water and sewer systems, loans for business and industry locating in rural areas, and loans for rural housing.

The *Rural Electrification Administration (REA)* was instrumental in the extension of electric power to remote rural areas of the country and in later years facilitated access to telephones for rural people. It continues to supply electric and telephone cooperatives with large amounts of frequently subsidized credit.

The *Federal Crop Insurance Corporation (FCIC)* directs the operations of the crop insurance program, which was greatly expanded by 1980 all-risk crop insurance legislation. Although a small agency itself, with few of its own agents, it markets its insurance through thousands of private insurance agents.

Resource and environment programs. The *Forest Service (FS)* is responsible for the management of the national forests and federal wilderness lands, encompassing nearly 200 millions acres.

The *Soil Conservation Service (SCS)* administers the several resource-related programs of soil and water conservation, water quality enhancement, and environmental improvement.

Food and consumer service programs. The *Food and Nutrition Service (FNS)* administers food assistance and nutrition programs that account for 40 to 70 percent of the USDA budget, depending on the size of farm program expenditure. The largest of these in terms of people served is the school lunch program, providing almost 24 million students in the nation's schools with subsidized lunches. In 1986, 1 of every 10 Americans (approximately 20 million people) received benefits of the food stamp program—the most expensive of the programs.[12] Many hundred thousands more people are reached through specially targeted programs such as the women's, infants', and children's program, which provides direct commodity distribution and nutrition education.

The *Human Nutrition Information Service (HNIS)* is responsible for the coordination and dissemination of scientific information on the relationship between diet and health. In performing this lead agency function, it works with other departments, such as the Food and Drug Administration and the National Institutes of Health.

Research and education programs. The *Agricultural Research Service (ARS)* conducts problem-oriented biological and related research in its research facilities headquartered in Beltsville, Maryland, and its regional laboratories located throughout the United States.

The *Cooperative State Research Service (CSRS)* coordinates and directs funding for joint federal–state research conducted primarily in agricultural experiment stations located at land-grant universities.

The *Extension Service (ES)* coordinates and directs funding for education programs conducted primarily in state extension services located at land-grant universities.

Economic intelligence programs. The *Economic Research Service (ERS)*, the largest single group of agricultural economists in the world, is the social science research and analysis agency. It monitors the global food and agriculture system and conducts research to enhance understanding of the functioning and performance of the food and agriculture economy.

The *National Agricultural Statistical Service (NASS)* is responsible for the collection of primary data from the nation's farmers and agribusiness firms as a means of improving and monitoring the performance of the farm sector, including markets for farm products.

The *World Agricultural Outlook Board (WAOB)* provides a central USDA clearinghouse for all estimates and data relating to world crop production, consumption, and stock. Top USDA decision makers receive regular briefings from the board on developments affecting the world food situation.

It becomes rather obvious after this brief review that the functions and the programs of USDA are broad in scope. It is equally obvious that this breadth and diversity hold great potential for conflicts within USDA itself and that unanimity on any policy position would be rare indeed. Each of the agencies has a particular clientele and objectives, which from

[12]Masao Matsumoto and Joyce Allen, "Recent Trends in Domestic Food Programs," in *National Food Review* (Washington, D.C.: ERS, USDA, Spring 1986), p. 36.

time to time conflict. Thus, reaching a departmental policy position, let alone an executive branch position, has become increasingly difficult.

Political Appointments

One of the privileges of a president is to appoint a large number of people to decision-making positions within the executive branch. This power of appointment is necessary in order for the president to have trusted individuals of the same political and philosophical persuasion to make and implement decisions consistent with the platform on which the president was elected.

This power of appointment is limited by the civil service laws to persons in "politically sensitive" positions. This involves a large number of people, ranging from the top White House staff and cabinet secretaries such as the secretary of agriculture to most agency heads, and even their personal secretaries.

A new president has the power to make over 5,000 political appointments across all departments of the federal government. In addition, he has the power to move members of the senior executive service, the top government professionals, from one position to another.

Within USDA the president has the power to make an estimated 500 appointments. These appointments include the secretary, deputy secretary, all under and assistant secretaries, and their staffs. The agency heads and their immediate staffs for all agencies, except the research and statistics agencies, are also politically sensitive. In addition, directors of state offices of USDA, such as the state ASCS and FmHA directors, are politically sensitive. Even appointments to committees such as ASCS county and state committees are politically sensitive.

Appointments to these positions realistically involve political consideration as well as people's qualifications. Financial support, work for the campaign, and support from key politicians—particularly from senior members of the agriculture committees—are certainly important factors. The existence of this support may be influenced by the attitudes of special-interest groups, such as farm and agribusiness organizations, toward particular candidates for political appointments. In terms of qualifications, past experience in government plays a role. It is not unusual to see appointments to higher-level positions in the same party from one administration to the next. For example, former Secretary Lyng served as Assistant USDA Secretary in the Nixon administration as did Secretary Yeutter.

It is not difficult to find people who meet these qualifications. The Reagan agriculture transition team alone received and reviewed the résumés of over 5000 individuals who had been suggested for political appointments. Needless to say, the competition for the 500 available positions was keen and highly political.

Organizing for Policy Decisions in USDA

Decision making is handled differently by each secretary of agriculture. The demands on a secretary's time—for public relations and speechmaking and other such functions—in addition to the administrative and management functions are enormous. As a result, there is a tendency for the secretary to rely very heavily on a few people for guidance in decision making. In the Bergland–Carter years that person was the chief economist. For the Block–Reagan years it was the deputy secretary, Richard Lyng, who succeeded Block as agriculture secretary in 1986. Some particularly strong secretaries, such as Earl Butz, have tended to use the undersecretaries and assistant secretaries more as an advisory body, with the secretary being the clear decision focal point.

Economic impacts play an important role in policy decisions. Three centers exist in USDA for economic analysis:

- The economic analysis staff in the office of the assistant secretary for economics handles the daily policy analysis needs of the chief economic advisor to the secretary.
- The policy analysis division of the Economic Research Service (ERS) analyzes longer-term policy issues.
- The agency responsible for the programs in the decision area does its own policy analyses.

For example, a farm program decision involving whether to impose production controls on agriculture will normally be analyzed by ERS and ASCS. The ERS analysis will emphasize the longer-run economic impacts of alternative types and levels of controls. The ASCS analysis will be more program detail oriented. The economic analysis staff would probably become involved only when it became an urgent political issue.

Once these analyses have been completed, they will flow through channels of the chief economist, the undersecretary for international affairs and commodity programs, the deputy secretary, and ultimately the secretary of agriculture. At any one of these levels more analyses may be called for on additional program options.

When the secretary of agriculture has made his decision, it flows to the White House, where it will normally be routed to OMB, the Council of Economic Advisers, and other affected agencies. Once again, there will be analyses of the USDA recommendations, this time largely in terms of their impact on prices and spending as well as their consistency with the overall objective of the president.

The Changing Role of USDA

The Department of Agriculture continues to be the focal point of food and agricultural policymaking, even though it must now share that responsibility with other cabinet and EOP agencies.

The department has at some times been closer to President Lincoln's vision of it as the people's department than at other times. During the depression era of the 1930s, Secretary Henry A. Wallace operated the department as an activist arm of the New Deal social policies. The concern then was not only with supporting prices and incomes, but also with extending public services to rural areas and to the conservation of natural resources and protection of the environment.

After the end of World War II, with the return of surpluses, USDA was returned to a narrow farmer-interest focus. Farmers came to view USDA as "their" department and the secretary of agriculture as "their" spokesman. In the early 1970s, President Nixon proposed a massive reorganization of the executive branch that would have combined USDA with the Department of Interior and other functions into a giant natural resources department. It was at this time that Earl L. Butz was appointed secretary, and many allege that his acceptance of the appointment was made conditional on USDA remaining a separate entity, but that he would not oppose the transfer of some major food assistance programs to other departments.[13]

The Carter administration sought to broaden USDA's concerns for many diverse groups, making it in essence a "department of food" serving farmers, consumers, and people in rural areas. Secretary Bergland, to a considerable extent, was able to achieve this objective. But there was considerable criticism, especially from farm groups, which perceived a diminution of their interests. The appointment of Carol T. Foreman, a vocal consumer advocate, as assistant secretary for consumer affairs was pointed out by farm groups as evidence supporting allegations that consumers were more important than farmers to USDA.

In the 1980 campaign, the Republicans attempted to capitalize politically on this dissatisfaction, indicating they would return USDA to a more narrow farmer-interest role. President Reagan's initial agriculture secretary, John Block, sought to do this by purging USDA of consumer elements and cutting back on consumer programs. These efforts were

[13]See Weldon Barton, "Food, Agriculture, and Administrative Adaptation to Political Change," *Public Admin. Rev.* (March–April 1976), pp. 148–154.

largely unsuccessful, although consumers clearly had a smaller role in USDA under Reagan than under Carter.

The difficulty of narrowly defining the role of USDA in modern times has been evident since the early 1970s, when the economic environment for agriculture changed significantly. As agriculture's importance to the national economy grew, so did the executive branch's interest in its activities. Any agricultural and food policy issue attracts the interest of other agencies, which feel that their responsibilities are affected by the handling of the issue. Today, the Department of State demands a say about food aid going to particular countries as a part of overall foreign policy strategy. The National Security Council and the Department of State are concerned about the negotiation of major bilateral commodity agreements, such as with the USSR. OMB is concerned about the cost of any policy action or program change. The Treasury Department wants USDA programs to prevent or at least not exacerbate inflation, improve the balance of trade, and realistically value the dollar in foreign currency markets. The Interior Department and the Council on Environmental Quality are concerned about the manner of operation of the Forest Service, with its 92 million acres of national forests, and USDA's stance on environmental matters and water policy. The Department of Health and Human Services is concerned about USDA's operation of the nutrition programs, which include the food stamp, school lunch, dietary guidelines, and other programs.

Over time, USDA has acquired responsibility for a broad range of program areas that take it far beyond matters of production agriculture. The extent to which these other functions have assumed importance is reflected in its 1988 budget of about $50 billion (Fig. 3.3). In 1986, the clientele of USDA included farmers (2.3 million), food stamp recipients (20 million), schoolchildren (24 million receiving subsidized lunches), timber companies, commodity exporting companies, food-processing corporations, consumers, environmentalists, and others.

It is obvious that with this diverse clientele, and their frequently conflicting interests, any policy position taken by USDA officials will be controversial. The pressures on USDA are still new and unfamiliar to its traditional agricultural clientele, all further complicating the policy process.

In the final analysis, the secretary of agriculture is not the farmer's representative in Washington. He is the president's man. When he ceases to be the president's man, he becomes an ex-secretary.[14]

[14]B. L. Flinchbaugh, "It's Easy to be Ignored if You Don't Have Your Act Together," speech presented at the National Institute on Cooperative Education, Colorado State University, Fort Collins, Colo., July 28, 1981, p. 1.

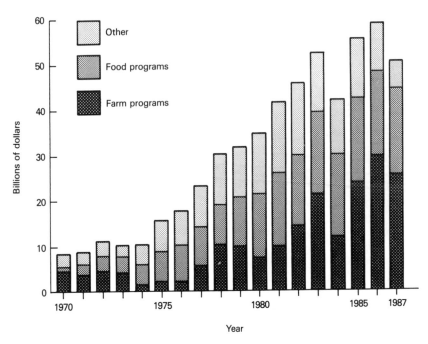

Figure 3.3 USDA outlays by major program category.
Source: Executive Office of the President, *Historical Tables,* Budget of the U.S. Government (Washington, D.C.: OMB, 1988).

THE JUDICIAL BRANCH

The courts have the responsibility for interpreting the Constitution and settling disputes among parties within the framework of existing laws. The Constitution makes the judiciary an equal and coordinate branch of government. American society over the last decade or two has increasingly looked to the courts for resolution of some of its most difficult problems. Courts have been asked, for example, to devise rules for reapportionment of legislatures, integration of schools, protection of the environment, and improving the lot of the poor. Complex as they are, these new challenges have taxed the traditional methods of the courts and promoted substantial controversy.

Although settlement of disputes among individuals, determination of violations of the law, and carrying out legal procedures for settlement of estates, bankruptcies, and so on, still occupy most the court's time, the scope of judicial business has broadened. This broadening has been particularly pronounced in the area of the rights of individuals, groups, and firms to pursue legal remedies against government. The result has been the involvement of courts in decisions that earlier would have been thought unsuited for adjudication. Judicial activity has extended to welfare, prison, and mental hospital administration; to education and employment policy; to road and bridge building; to automotive standards; and to natural resource management.

The impacts have clearly extended to food and agricultural issues. Courts have struck down laws requiring a period of in-state residence as a condition of eligibility for welfare. Federal district courts have laid down elaborate standards for food handling; they have told the Farmers Home Administration to restore a disaster loan program, ordered the Forest Service to stop clear-cutting of timber, and required the Corps of Engineers to maintain the nation's nonnavigable waterways.

What the judges have been doing is new in a special sense. Although no single feature of most of this litigation constitutes an abrupt departure from the past, the aggregate of decisions distinguishes it sharply from the traditional exercise of the judicial function. Many wholly new areas of adjudication have been opened up. In the process, the rights of food stamp recipients, consumers, and farmers have been clarified under the law. To some extent, this judicial activity is a response to invitations from Congress and from state legislatures. By enacting legislation that is broad and vague, the Congress has, in essence, passed many of the problems to the courts. The courts then have to deal with the inevitable litigation to determine the "intent of the Congress," which in some statutes is far from clear. State legislatures have similarly enacted broad, vague legislation with similar results.

To an important extent, increased litigation arises from the realities of increased government regulation and expanded social programs. In this sense, the expansion of judicial activity is a mere concomitant of the growth of government. As governmental activity in general expands, it is very likely that judicial activity will also expand.[15]

USDA, THE ESTABLISHMENT, AND THE FUTURE

In the 1970s, the agricultural establishment began losing control of the farm policy agenda. Food and agricultural policymaking has become more complex and difficult to predict. Although initially the establishment may have thought it was in control, this perception has since given way to the stark reality that:

- Consumers do have an interest in the decisions of USDA.
- The secretary of state may have as big a stake in international food issues as the secretary of agriculture.

[15]Donald L. Horowitz, *The Courts and Social Policy* (Washington, D.C.: The Brookings Institution, 1977).

• The secretary of agriculture cannot consider only farm interests in decisions on agricultural and food policy.

The problem of agriculture being unable to control its agenda becomes most acute when the establishment itself cannot agree on what should be done. That lack of agreement is likely to be most apparent in periods such as the 1970s when conditions in agriculture are favorable and farmers can afford to disagree. In the 1980s, adverse economic conditions pulled farmers together. The establishment was once again successful at getting relief for farmers. Farm program subsidies grew from $7 billion in the late 1970s to $20 billion in the late 1980s. The lesson of the 1970s for the establishment was that the balance of power has changed sufficiently that unity and organization became a key to lobbying success.

Prior to the 1970s, the agricultural establishment was consistently able to manage the political process in its favor. Without being in a position to manage the process any longer, the agricultural establishment is on the defensive. That position is not likely to change in the near future.

ADDITIONAL READINGS

1. For a detailed study of the legislative process, see J. B. Penn, "The Federal Policy Process in Developing the Food and Agriculture Act of 1977," in *Agricultural-Food Policy Review*, AFPR-3 (Washington, D.C.: ESCS, USDA, February 1980), pp. 9–46.

2. An excellent discussion of the relationships between the White House and the cabinet is contained in Joseph Califano, Jr., *Governing America: An Insider's Report from the White House and the Cabinet* (New York: Simon & Schuster, Inc., 1981). Also, see David A. Stockman's *The Triumph of Politics* (New York: Harper & Row, Publishers, Inc., 1986).

Chapter 4

Food and Agricultural Policy
Interest Groups

*No class of Americans, so far as I know,
has ever objected . . . to any amount of
government meddling if it appeared to
benefit that particular class.*

Carl Becker

Interest groups provide the motivating force for the policy process. They identify problems and advance proposals for solving them. They organize to affect the results of elections, influence the position of candidates, and influence appointments to key positions as well as the ultimate votes or decisions on issues that affect their members. Few individuals, acting alone, are in a position to have the influence of an organized interest group.

Food and agricultural policy interest groups include any organization, association, or firm seeking in some way to influence food and agricultural policy decisions of the Congress or the executive branch. Interest groups generally employ lobbyists to represent them directly in the political process and advise them on political strategy.

Interest groups are active at all levels of government decision making. In the executive branch, they may attempt to influence decisions of middle-management career employees who make policy or program recommendations to the secretary of agriculture and ultimately to the president. Interest groups may also directly contact top USDA appointees, the secretary of agriculture, or the president. In the Congress, interest groups actively seek to influence congressional staff, the reports of congressional research and information agencies, and ultimately the position of the senators and representatives.

INFLUENCING EFFECTIVENESS

Substantial differences exist in the effectiveness of interest groups in influencing policy. That effectiveness is largely determined by:

- The priority of the particular policy problem being considered
- The consequences of alternative means of dealing with the problem
- The number of individuals or firms that the interest group represents
- The economic importance and political influence of the individuals or firms represented by the interest group
- The strategies employed by the interest group

Priority of the Problem

The starting point for influencing policymakers' decisions is convincing them that the problem confronting the interest group's members deserves high-enough priority to devote the time required to resolve it. While members of Congress often will introduce a bill proposed by an interest group, substantial time and effort are involved in getting the bill seriously considered by the body and ultimately enacted into law. To command this time and effort, the problem must be substantial, must affect people having political influence, and must not have a solution without creating great hardship in the absence of government action. Economic data frequently are very useful in convincing policymakers that these conditions exist.

Consequences of Alternatives

For the democratic process to work effectively, as much information needs to be brought to bear on a policy decision as possible. Generally, a decision that benefits one segment of the population adversely affects another. One interest group frequently has a different perspective on the merits of a particular policy alternative than another group. Policymakers then are required to balance the merits, views, and impacts of one group's proposals against those of others. Interest groups' effectiveness, therefore, in influencing policy is enhanced by sound and comprehensive analysis of the consequences of each of the policy alternatives.

Number of Individuals or Firms Represented

Power exists in numbers. Numbers represent the votes required to be elected and reelected. Farmers traditionally have relied heavily on numbers to influence political decisions. In former times, they tended to vote as a bloc, and were influenced largely by "pocketbook issues" and their conservative nature. As the farm numbers have declined, farmers' and their interest groups' political power has been affected. Increased consumer interest in food and agricultural policy has at times been an asset to farmers and at other times a liability. For example, the food stamp program has been a factor in holding the interest of many urban members of Congress in support of the farm bill. However, that program also competes with other USDA programs for the increasingly limited federal dollars.

Influence of Individuals or Firms Represented

In the political process, economic importance and political influence are good substitutes for numbers. Agribusiness firms, such as the major grain-exporting companies, derive much of their influence from the economic importance of the business and the political influence of the people who manage and represent them. Their managers generally are politically active, and they frequently have their own lobbyists as well as supporting trade association lobbying activities. They can either be potent political allies or foes to the farm lobby, depending on the issue.

Strategies Employed

The lobbying strategies employed to influence policymakers' decisions cover a wide range. These include communications in the form of letters, newsletters, or telephone calls concerning the organization's position; providing information and undertaking special studies; answering questions; "wining and dining"; making contributions to cooperative or potentially cooperative elected officials; withholding support from uncooperative elected officials; promoting individuals for political appointments; and making elective candidates' voting records or positions on relevant issues known to particular interest groups and population segments. Interest groups, as a general rule, are cautious in taking overt public positions on the election of particular candidates; they realize that, over the long term, they must be able to work with any candidate who is elected.

Interest groups attempt to increase their effectiveness by broadening their base of support and influence through recruiting support from other interest groups. This approach, known as **networking**, involves compromise, horse trading, forming coalitions, and logrolling.

Compromise, in a political setting, is the willingness of each side to make concessions on a particular issue so that a unified position may be reached. The willingness to compromise is an integral part of lobbying. This realization frequently causes opposing parties initially to adopt an extreme position, giving latitude for subsequent compromise. For example, a farm organization may initially support a 30 percent increase in price supports, while actually hoping to obtain at least a 20 percent increase.

Horse trading involves the exchange of support for particular proposals among interest groups as a means of broadening the base of support. A, for example, will support legislation favored by interest group B in return for group B's support for legislation favored by group A. For example, a food service interest group might support a higher milk price support if in return a milk producers' interest group supports increased subsidies for school lunch programs.

Coalitions are alliances of groups or factions formed to attain a particular political end. They frequently result from compromise and horse trading among interest groups. Coalitions frequently are temporary, formed for a particular piece of legislation, but some tend to be enduring. The coalition of greatest importance to farm policy is the National Farm Coalition, a loose but formal alliance of some 30 farm organizations. An even broader informal alliance of farm organizations is referred to as the farm bloc.

Logrolling involves sequentially building congressional support for a particular piece of legislation to the point where it cannot be resisted. Logrolling generally involves compromise and the exchange of political favors—including influence and votes—among legislators to achieve legislation and decisions of interest to one another.

Political action committees (PACs) facilitate the consolidation of political contributions around particular organizations, causes and issues. PAC funds are obtained through ad hoc contributions; donations based on the gross sales of business firms; or in the case of agricultural producers, an amount for each unit of product marketed. In any event, participation in a PAC is voluntary, and decisions on how the funds are used are made by a committee of contributors. Agricultural contributions have become an important factor in the political strategy of the sector. In the 1982 and 1984 elections, agricultural PACs contributed more than $5 million to political candidates.[1] Although certainly not the largest special-interest group, agricultural PACs do rank among the largest—in particular, the dairy cooperative PACs.

[1]"$5 Million in Ag PACS," *Success. Farming*, *'81*, no. 5 (March 1983), p. 13; *Food Fiber Lett.*, June 11, 1984, p. 3.

SUBGOVERNMENTS[2]

The political process is built on power relationships among members of Congress, the administration, and interest groups. *When a congressional committee, administration agency staff, and an interest group become locked in a highly effective, reciprocal, mutually supporting arrangement, it is referred to as a* **subgovernment.** In a subgovernment, all three groups find their particular goals supported by the others, with the result that policy is produced by this tripartite interaction.

Everyone gains from the subgovernment. For the agency, a subgovernment offers congressional support for its program and budget, less harassment in hearings or investigations, regular and predictable daily bureaucratic routine, and friendly relations with the interest group. For committee members, a subgovernment offers the chance to represent the interest of their constituents (the interest groups), campaign contributions, and more immediate attention of bureaucrats in servicing their constituents' interests. The interest group gains a subsidy, favorable administrative rules, and an avenue for direct input into both congressional and administration decisions.

One example of an agricultural subgovernment is the triangle comprised of the Extension Service (in the USDA), the House and Senate Agricultural committees, and the American Farm Bureau Federation. Another is that of the Soil Conservation Service, the agriculture subcommittee of the House appropriations committee, and the National Association of Soil Conservation Districts. Subgovernments exist for even more specialized commodity interests, such as rice, sugar, cotton, wool, and cranberries. National clientele associations are linked with the relevant House agriculture commodity subcommittee and the Agricultural Stabilization and Conservation Service. Other subgovernments have been described for the military–industrial complex, water resource projects, and policy concerning Native Americans.

INTEREST GROUPS

It was indicated in Chapter 3 that the agricultural establishment has less control of food and agricultural policy than in the past. A contributing factor to this loss of control has been splintering of interest groups within

[2]This section on subgovernment draws heavily on the work of Barbara Hinckley, *Stability and Change in Congress* (New York: Harper & Row, Publishers, Inc., 1983), pp. 234–236.

AGRICULTURE'S POLITICAL
POWER BASE IS NOT
DECLINING

Conventional wisdom suggests that declining farm population results in an erosion of agriculture's political power base. Politicians and economists alike have proclaimed the demise of agriculture's power base and the necessity for coalition building with other special interest groups if traditional farm programs are to be maintained. Reality suggests that the decline of agriculture's political power base is more rhetoric than fact.

In the 1980s, a conservative Republican administration spent more in support of the nation's farmers than any previous administration. A myriad of editorials chronicle the massive expenditures of farm subsidies; yet polls reveal general public support for spending even more on farm programs. In fact, polls show that urban dwellers are more sympathetic to farmers' problems than are rural people in rural areas. Yes, farm numbers are declining, but agriculture is continuing to maintain its base of support from both urban and rural politicians and their constituents.

The reasons for this continued support are many:

- Although U.S. agriculture is plagued by surplus production, the American public is constantly reminded, almost nightly, on the six o'clock news of the problems of shortages and famine in various countries around the world.
- Food is one of the basic necessities of life, and with each visit to the grocery store the public is constantly, although perhaps subliminally, reminded of its direct dependence on an efficient agricultural industry. The choice, therefore, is clear.
- To err on the side of surplus food production is more politically attractive in the body politic than the alternative, even with a 20–30 billion dollar price tag.
- It may be that while farm numbers are declining, farmers are becoming much more sophisticated at lobbying. The operators of large farms have enough political muscle to compensate for reduced numbers.
- Consumers, particularly the urban poor, benefit from both food programs and farm programs.

It is not surprising, therefore, that agricultural committees, USDA, and farm organizations capitalize on these strengths. It is also not surprising that the urban members of Congress support farm programs. Agriculture, like defense, sells well whether in New York City or Des Moines.

Edward G. Smith, Department of Agricultural Economics (College Station, Tex.: Texas A&M University, January 1988).

agriculture as well as proliferation of interest groups outside the establishment.[3]

The Producer Lobby

The large number of producer organizations reflects both the geographic scope of U.S. agriculture and the values and beliefs regarding the role of government in agriculture. In general, the producer groups have widely differing views on policy. Yet, despite these differences, the producer lobby has been effective in obtaining support, including substantial government expenditures for farm programs.

The strength of the producer lobby lies in the number of farmers it represents, the importance of food and agriculture to particular states, congressional districts, and the nation; and the level of political activism and influence of farmers and farm organizations. In 1986, the farm population represented 2.2 percent of the total U.S. population.[4] However, in some states, the farm population is a substantially higher percentage of total population. The political power of farmers tends to be augmented by a sizable number of rural residents who maintain close ties to agriculture and, in many instances, are at least indirectly dependent on agriculture for their jobs and economic well-being.

Political power is also augmented by the economic importance of agriculture relative to other sources of economic activity. The counties where agriculture accounts for more than 20 percent of the income of total labor and business income are indicated in Fig. 4.1. It suggests that agriculture's influence is concentrated in the Corn Belt, Great Plains, Northwest, and West.

There should be no doubt that with reduced numbers, farmers' effectiveness as a lobby will increasingly reflect organization, sophistication, unity, political contributions, and the perceived importance of food to the nation. They must learn to practice the politics of the minority.

For lobbying purposes, producers are organized into three major groups: general farm organizations, commodity groups, and cooperatives.

General farm organizations.   *General farm organizations have a producer membership that cuts across commodities.* Their lobbying activities cover a wide range of commodity, agricultural, regulatory, rural, and general economic issues. This diversity of member interests sometimes makes it difficult for these organizations to take positions on certain issues and causes splintering within the group. Conflicts often arise, for ex-

[3]Don Paarlberg, "The Farm Policy Agenda," in *Increasing Understanding of Public Problems and Policies* (Chicago: Farm Foundation, 1975), pp. 94–101.

[4]*Current Population Report Series P27* (Washington, D.C.: U.S. Bureau of Census, August 1986).

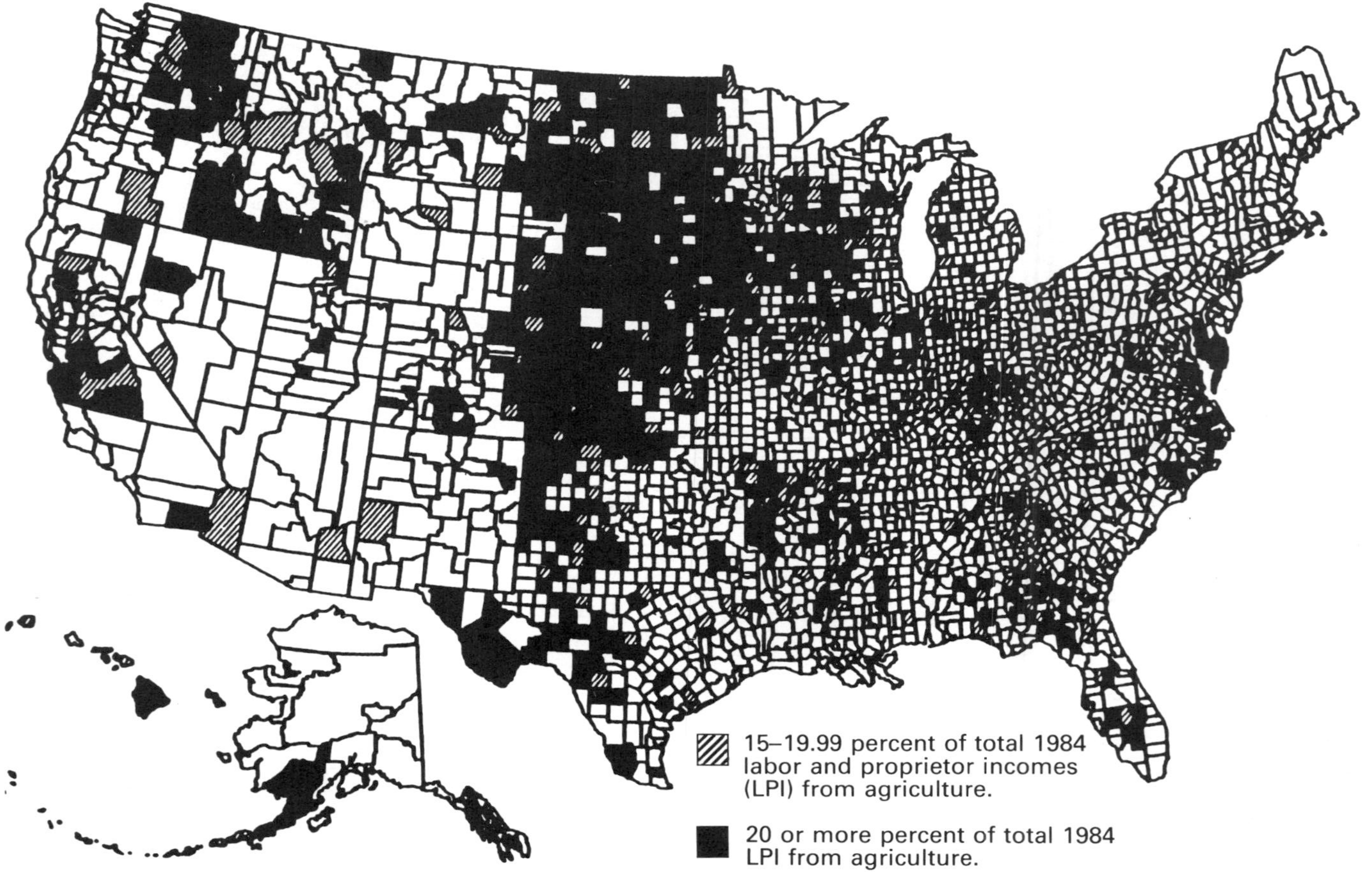

15–19.99 percent of total 1984 labor and proprietor incomes (LPI) from agriculture.

20 or more percent of total 1984 LPI from agriculture.

Figure 4.1 Agriculture counties, 1984.

ample, between livestock and feed grain producers over the appropriate government policies with respect to grain price supports. Feed grain producers want higher price supports, whereas livestock producers prefer lower price supports. Grain producers want to expand exports, whereas beef and dairy producers want to limit imports.

Some of the general farm organizations are also involved in the business of selling insurance and farm supplies. Farm supply sales or farmer product marketings are frequently made through cooperative organizations having a farm organization identity, such as Farm Bureau and Farmers Union. In these instances, farm organization membership is frequently a condition for the purchase of either insurance or supplies. As a result, it is difficult to distinguish between members who join the farm organization because they embrace its policy philosophy or for supply acquisition reasons. Organization membership statistics, therefore, exaggerate the true policy constituency of farm organizations—particularly general farm organizations.

Over time, new farm organizations tend to be formed whenever adverse economic conditions exist in agriculture for an extended period. Only three general farm organizations have survived since the initiation of farm programs in the 1930s. Each of the organizations has distinctly different philosophies on at least some aspects of policy to which a majority of its members subscribe.

The *American Farm Bureau Federation* is the largest of the general farm organizations. Its roots extend to the early 1900s, and its activities were closely aligned with Extension Service educational programs. Their ties were shed eventually at the insistence of USDA, because the Farm Bureau was actively involved in lobbying for farm programs.

The Farm Bureau is generally recognized as being a voice of conservatism and free enterprise in agriculture. It supports market-oriented farm policies, including lower price supports, unrestricted access to markets, opposition to organized farm labor, reduced government regulation, opposition to USDA food programs, and a balanced federal budget. This policy orientation generally has brought the Farm Bureau into close alignment with Republican candidates and officeholders. It is, for example, typical for individuals closely aligned with the Farm Bureau to be on the staff of Republican members of Congress representing rural districts or states, as well as holding high-level positions in USDA during Republican administrations.

Despite its basic conservative nature, substantial regional differences have traditionally existed in the Farm Bureau. For example, Corn Belt farmers have been less willing to accept production control programs than southern cotton, peanut, and tobacco farmers. For years, the center of power in the Farm Bureau was in the Corn Belt states of Illinois, Iowa, and Indiana. In the mid-1970s, the balance of power shifted toward the

South and then in the 1980s, back to the Corn Belt. At its 1987 annual meeting, the Farm Bureau endorsed the Reagan administration's GATT negotiating position to eliminate farm subsidies by the year 2000. Despite such shifts, the basic conservative stance of the Farm Bureau remained.

The *National Farmers Union* represents the liberal side of the farm policy spectrum. Although organized in 30 states, the Farmers Union's strength lies in the Great Plains and upper Midwest, with the largest membership in Oklahoma, North Dakota, and Minnesota.

The Farmers Union has traditionally embraced a goal of government-administered parity prices for farmers, including production control programs in times of surpluses. It supports realistic limitations on direct government payments that give preference to family farms. Preservation of the family farm remains a central goal of its policies.

In contrast to the Farm Bureau's free-trade stance, the Farmers Union has advocated pricing and market-sharing agreements with other grain-exporting countries. It has also, from time to time, suggested that grain export decisions be handled by a government-mandated organization such as a marketing board.

The Farmers Union has a history of joining other liberal causes, including labor union rights, expanded food stamp and child nutrition programs, and increased foreign aid. It has traditionally tended to align itself with Democratic candidates and officeholders.

The *National Grange*, formed in 1867 and once the largest farm organization, is currently the smallest of the three old-line general farm organizations. The Grange is most widely known for leading the fight against the power of railroads and for support of antitrust restraints before the turn of the century. The center of its strength traditionally has been the Northeast and the Northwest.

Among the general farm organizations, the Grange is the voice of moderation and unity in agricultural policy. As such, it has traditionally supported government policies that provide farmers with returns equivalent to those in the nonfarm sector, price supports based on cost of production, elimination of tax incentives for investment in agriculture, increased foreign agricultural aid, and moderation in the regulation of pesticides. It supports smaller family farms by calling for reduced farm program benefits as farm size increases.[5]

The *National Farmers Organization (NFO)* grew out of depressed commodity prices and farm incomes in the mid-1950s. The initial theme of the NFO was collective bargaining. To accomplish its objective of raising farm prices, members signed contracts pledging to market their pro-

[5]Douglas E. Bowers, "The Setting for New Food and Agricultural Legislation," in *Agricultural Food Policy Review*, AFPR-4 (Washington, D.C.: ESS, USDA, April 1981), p. 128.

duction under NFO direction. The NFO, in turn, attempted to sign supply contracts with both corporate and cooperative processing and marketing firms. These actions met strong resistance from processing and marketing firms. The NFO, attempting to strengthen its bargaining position, initiated holding actions against processors and marketing firms in the 1960s, including dumping milk, burning grain, and killing hogs and cattle. Attempts to prevent marketing by farmers and truckers unsympathetic to the NFO resulted in isolated incidences of violence.

In the early 1970s, support declined for its militant bargaining strategies. It then augmented its bargaining activities by marketing milk and grain through cooperatives either newly organized by NFO members or by gaining control of existing cooperatives. At this time, NFO also assumed an active role as Washington lobbyist on behalf of its members. In this role, it typically has taken positions on issues between the Farm Bureau and the Farmers Union. In 1980, the NFO favored the expanded all-risk crop insurance program. The Farmers Union and Farm Bureau may have been less supportive of expanded federal crop insurance because they were already in the business of selling insurance, whereas NFO was not. The NFO continues to press for favorable marketing arrangements on behalf of its members by signing supply contracts with processors.

The *American Agriculture Movement (AAM)* was organized in the mid-1970s when farm prices fell sharply from their 1973 peak. In contrast with the NFO, its center of power was in the Great Plains (Texas, Colorado, Kansas, and North and South Dakota) and in Georgia. AAM membership appeared primarily to be disenchanted NFO and Farmers Union members. Many of its leaders were younger farmers, often Vietnam veterans, who had come on rough times after expanding their farm operations and indebtedness during the relatively prosperous years 1972–1975. When the cost–price squeeze became severe in the mid-1970s, these farmers turned to Washington for relief.

AAM's main early tactic for attracting the attention of lawmakers was driving tractors to Washington, D.C., disrupting traffic, and camping out for several weeks on the Capitol Mall until the Congress acted to raise price supports above levels in the 1977 farm bill. During the demonstrations, goats were turned loose in the Capitol and Secretary Bergland took sanctuary in the White House after his office was invaded by irate AAM members.[6] During this time, extensive discussions occurred be-

---

[6]During this time, Secretary Bergland took time to read a substantial volume of literature published by the USDA and the land-grant universities on the nature of the farm problem. This study led the secretary to identify the changing structure of agriculture and the associated rise of large-scale farms as a central farm policy issue and a source of continuing conflict. Subsequently, major research initiatives and hearings were held on the structure issues. This issue is discussed in Chapter 11.

tween USDA employees and farmers concerning the nature of the farm problem. For many USDA bureaucrats, this may have been their first time to see or talk to a farmer! The AAM also became known for placing substantial pressure on rural businesses to support and contribute financially to support their cause. But such tactics cost the AAM much political support in rural and urban America.

The initial goal of the AAM in Washington was to obtain parity price supports. This was most vigorously pursued in special legislative action following enactment of the 1977 farm bill. However, the price support goals subsequently were reduced substantially. By the debate on the 1985 farm bill, AAM advocated price supports at 70 percent of parity. As farm economic conditions further deteriorated, the AAM backed a legislation proposal by Senator Tom Harkin (Dem.-IA) and Congressman Richard Gephardt (Dem.-MO) to set price supports at 70 percent of parity with escalation to 80 percent, achieved by mandatory production controls and a cartel of grain exporting nations.

The AAM has received substantial support in rural America, even though its specific price goals and related programs generally were recognized as being unattainable. Its strength and influence in policy development varies. For example, in the 1980 presidential election, it ironically supported the Reagan candidacy, even though its policy proposals were directly contradictory to Reagan's free-market proclamations. In the mid-1980s, the AAM strongly supported Texas Commissioner of Agriculture Jim Hightower, a Democrat. Close alignment with Democratic Senators and members of Congress such as Harkin and Gephardt appears to exist in several other states. While still having radical elements among its membership, the AAM now appears much more inclined to work within the political process to achieve its goals.

The *action of agricultural women* and the *family farm lobby* warrant discussion as relatively new general farm organization movements influencing policy. Until the mid-1970s, a wife's place in agriculture was generally one of raising children, helping with the farm work, and keeping records. Women were not generally involved in agricultural interests outside the home farm. The women's rights movement changed this situation for many farm families. Nearly as many farm wives as nonfarm wives now have off-farm jobs.

Farm women's groups have sprung up throughout the major agricultural regions of the United States. Examples include American Agri-Women (AAW), Women Involved in Farm Economics (WIFE), Concerned Farm Wives, Partners in Action for Agriculture, and California Women for Agriculture. Women's organizations generally support maintaining conditions favorable to family farm survival, increased appropriations for research and extension, work incentives for food stamp recipients, increased ease of estate transfers, less government regulation, expanded export markets, and higher price and income supports.

Two major organizations having important religious ties are part of the family farm lobby. One is the National Catholic Rural Life Conference (NCRLC). Another is the Interreligious Task Force on U.S. Food Policy, a coalition of 27 denominations and interfaith groups. Although also concerned with hunger-related issues, the Interreligious Task Force has consistently supported farm programs designed to maintain an economically sound family farm structure. These religious groups have a definite agricultural fundamentalist orientation. They see the decline of family farms as directly influencing rural church membership, the size of the collection plate, and the health of rural communities. Ties to the more liberal farm organizations such as the Farmers Union, AAM, and NFO are evident.

Commodity organizations.   Commodity organizations represent producers of specific agricultural products. They are frequently more effective than the general farm organizations on specific commodity-oriented issues for three major reasons:

- As agricultural production has become more highly specialized, farmers identify more closely with a commodity organization.
- Commodity organizations frequently can speak with a clearer voice on commodity issues. Conflicts among producers of different products, such as feed grain and livestock farmers, that arise in general farm organizations are not as apparent in commodity organizations.
- While once underfinanced, most commodity organizations now have access to federal and/or state-mandated producer check-off funds. A check-off program deducts a small amount per unit or a small percent of the value of product marketed. Although these funds are intended primarily for research and promotion, commodity groups are strengthened financially by the resulting flow of funds and visibility. Federal and state check-off programs now exist for most major commodities as well as for many specialty crops.[7]

There are at least 20 commodity organizations engaged in food and agricultural lobbying in Washington, D.C. The most influential of the organizations representing the major commodities include the following:

The *National Association of Wheat Growers (NAWG)* is one of the largest and most influential of the producer commodity organizations. It

[7]R. M. Morrison, *Generic Advertising of Farm Products* (Washington, D.C.: ERS, USDA, September 1984).

has traditionally been a leader in overall strategy in farm program development. Since over 65 percent of the wheat produced is normally exported, NAWG has a strong interest in export market development and the impact of government policies on the export market. It has also traditionally supported farm programs that provide producers with income support while maintaining the competitive position of wheat in the export market. Since much of the wheat is produced in areas having substantial risk of drought, disaster protection has also been of direct interest. In the 1985 farm bill debate, NAWG's effectiveness was reduced somewhat by conflict between producers who wanted higher price supports and mandatory controls and those favoring lower price supports to improve competitiveness in world markets.

The *National Milk Producers Federation (NMPF)* is a potent lobby on behalf of dairy farmers. Since its members are regional cooperatives, NMPF could also be classified as a cooperative lobby. The NMPF's major objectives include maintaining milk price supports as high as is politically feasible, maintaining quotas restricting imports of dairy products, protecting the federal milk marketing order system against attack, and maintaining the high use of subsidized milk products in domestic and foreign food assistance programs. The NMPF has been very successful in pursuing these objectives. Its success results largely from the number of producers it represents, which account for over 75 percent of total U.S. milk production, strong financial support from its member cooperatives (also politically active), and a substantial number of political action committees associated with its cooperative members.

The *National Cattlemen's Association (NCA)* is recognized as being a highly effective lobbyist for cattlemen and cattle feeders. The NCA's objectives include limiting government involvement in its members' operations, limiting beef imports, controlling natural predators, encouraging low-cost grazing on public lands, and supporting government policies that encourage greater beef consumption. Considerable conflict has developed between the NCA and public interest advocates over dietary guidelines that suggest moderation in beef consumption, reduced cholesterol, and the use of hormones in cattle feeding.

Traditionally, NCA has shown relatively little interest in policy development for commodities other than beef. However, when the 1983 dairy diversion program resulted in many additional milk cows being slaughtered, beef producers became concerned about the resulting adverse effect on beef prices. They lobbied unsuccessfully against the dairy termination (buyout) program in 1985 and then brought legal action against the secretary of agriculture, alleging that he failed to regulate the flow to market of slaughtered dairy cows. This flurry of political/legal activity may foretell a broader role for NCA in commodity program development.

The *American Soybean Association (ASA)*, together with the NCA, is probably among the most conservative of the producer organizations. In fact, the conservatism and export orientation of ASA reflect the combination of producer and agribusiness interests that comprises its membership. Many of the efforts of the ASA have been in support of domestic and foreign market development programs and in opposition to government interferences in export markets. The ASA has been active in promoting the use of soybean meat extenders in the school lunch program.

Not until 1985 did the ASA seek government programs supporting direct payments to soybean producers. In 1985, it sought direct government payments of $50 per acre for soybeans, and in 1987, it sought a marketing loan program similar to that for rice and cotton which would have provided direct income support to its members. The trend appears to be for ASA to support more actively the types of programs that exist for other major crops.

The *National Corn Growers Association (NCGA)*, although not as strong politically as some other commodity organizations, represents producers of a crop that, in volume, is nearly four times as large as wheat. Although formerly quite conservative, NCGA appears to have become more liberal over time. It has supported substantially higher price and

---

SHOOTING YOURSELF IN THE FOOT

For years, sugar producer lobbyists have pressed for high price supports for sugar, maintained by controlling sugar imports. An unforeseen side effect of this policy has been development of a large corn sweetener industry. High-fructose corn sweetener (HFCS) developed in this protected market environment. Its lower cost allowed it increasingly to substitute for sugar, to the extent that it has garnered over half of the total domestic caloric sweetener market. As HFCS consumption and domestic sugar production has increased (both due to high price supports), the sugar import quota has been reduced, and in the late 1980s was approaching zero. Reductions in import quotas have caused sugar producers in developing countries such as the Philippines to complain loudly.

As HFCS consumption has increased (and sugar consumption declines), corn producers, prodded by HFCS manufacturers, have become more overtly supportive of high sugar price supports. But the alliance among sugar producers, corn producers, and HFCS manufacturers could end soon. As U.S. sugar production approaches self-sufficiency, further reductions in sugar consumption will come at the expense of sugar producers, not foreign import quota holders. Sugar producers may have shot themselves in the foot! Corn producers helped them take aim!

income supports, the grain reserve, subsidized loans to build storage facilities, and efforts to control production. It also supports subsidies for ethanol production (used to increase the octane in gasoline) and high sugar price supports (see the box on p. 83).

Cooperatives. Cooperatives are developing one of the more effective producer lobbying forces in agriculture. While concerned mainly with protecting their members' special organizational privileges, cooperatives were an original advocate of the export-oriented marketing loan concept.[8] Their lobbying strategies take advantage of the combination of the producer numbers they represent, their effectiveness in communicating their needs, and their organization of political action committees. PAC contributions to political candidates by cooperatives accounted for about 75 percent of all producer-organization PAC contributions in 1982.[9]

For some cooperative organizations, lobbying activities relate largely to their legal status. Other cooperatives combine protection of their legal status with intensive commodity-oriented farm program lobbying. Associated Milk Producers, Inc.; Dairymen, Inc.; and Mid-America Dairymen provide examples of cooperative commodity lobbying activities by regional milk cooperatives. Aligned with each of these three organizations is one or more PAC. In the 1982 and 1984 elections, these PACs contributed about $3 million to congressional candidates—about 60 percent of all contributions by producer-organization PACs.[10] These contributions also helped to fortify the lobbying activities of the National Milk Producers Federation.

Another example of cooperative activity in commodity lobbying is rice, where Riceland Foods, Inc.; Farmers Rice Cooperative; and the Rice Growers Association of California attempt directly to maintain a policy environment that facilitates exports while providing producer income protection in the highly volatile rice market.

In addition to such commodity-oriented cooperative lobbying activity, two national cooperative organizations have extensive political activities:

The *National Council of Farmer Cooperatives (NCFC)* is a lobbying organization whose membership is basically large regional cooperatives. It commits a major share of its resources to defending marketing cooperatives' antitrust exemption provided by the Capper–Volstead Act, main-

[8]The marketing loan is a modified version of the price support loan, which allows the producer to pay back the loan at the market price. The loan does not, therefore, become a barrier to exports.
[9]$"5 Million in Ag PACs," p. 3.
[10]Ibid.

taining the tax-exempt status of cooperatives and defending market order legislation.[11] In addition, the NCFC directs substantial attention to agricultural chemical and pest control regulations of the Environmental Protection Agency, agricultural transportation issues, and energy problems. In the 1985 farm bill, it actively lobbied for the marketing loan concept to be applied to agricultural commodities.

The *National Rural Electric Cooperative Association (NRECA)* is one of the most powerful, yet least noticed, producer lobbying group. Electrification of rural America occurred to an important degree through the help of the government. One agency of USDA—the Rural Electrification Administration—is devoted almost exclusively to extending credit to rural electric cooperatives. Much of this credit has been heavily subsidized. Ending or substantially reducing such subsidized credits has been an objective of the Reagan and Bush administrations.

In a time when budget cutting is a high national political priority, a major share of the NRECA's lobbying resources is devoted to defending its existing subsidized credit sources. Other projects include protecting the tax-exempt status of cooperatives, assisting in approval for the location of power plants and transmission lines, and discouraging taxes on energy sources.

The Agribusiness Lobby

Agribusiness firms have a large number of food and agricultural lobbyists in Washington and are among the most powerful. Their political clout results from a combination of their knowledge of Capitol Hill; ability to work with members of Congress and their staffs; knowledge of how decisions are made in the executive branch; attention to detail; knowledge of the substance of the issues; and their political contributions through both PACs and as individuals. Their effectiveness is enhanced by the fact that they do their job typically with little public attention.

It is not at all unusual for a person lobbying for the agribusiness sector to move into a high-level post in USDA. For example, Secretary Lyng previously served as the president of the American Meat Institute. Later, that person might move back to a firm in the same industry. *This process of changing jobs between private industry and government generally is referred to as the* **revolving-door syndrome**.

---

[11]Farmer cooperatives have the benefit of a host of exemptions not available to other business firms. Among these are the right to merge with one another and engage in joint pricing activities as long as predatory activity is not involved. Marketing orders help to fortify the effectiveness of these activities that are designed to raise farm prices and incomes. These cooperative benefits are discussed in Chapter 12.

Agribusiness firms clearly feel a need to be represented in the political process. They want to protect a market system of privately owned business firms against government encroachment. They have traditionally opposed tax and antitrust exemptions for cooperatives. They recognize the role that government plays in promoting economic and market stability. They also recognize government as a major purchaser of processed farm products through the school lunch program, as a storer of grain, as a provider of export credit, as a partner in promoting export sales, and as a provider of economic stability to farmers and of credit for rural development.

Agribusiness and producer interests may well diverge over matters of farm policy. Agribusiness generally favors government programs designed to expand farm production and opposes programs that restrict production. However, the interests of all agribusiness firms are not the same. Those producing farm supplies have a greater stake in farm profitability than do marketing firms. Farm machinery, chemical, and fertilizer sales are lower when farm incomes are reduced. The ability of farmers to pay off farm loans also decreases with income reductions. Lobbyists representing farm supply firms, therefore, are more likely to come to the aid of farmers in times of depressed farm prices and incomes than are marketing firm lobbyists. Yet this aid would tend to be more in the form of support for subsidies rather than production controls. Farm input sales are made in almost direct proportion to the number of acres farmed.

Agribusiness lobbyists may be placed in three groups: (1) general organizations, (2) commodity organizations, and (3) Washington representatives of individual firms. General agribusiness organizations represent both input supply and marketing firms. Commodity organizations focus on an individual input or commodity. Washington representatives of agribusiness either may be employees of a firm or a law firm or public relations firm hired to represent them in Washington. Some large agribusiness firms may be represented by general organizations, commodity organizations, and have their own Washington representatives as well.

General agribusiness organizations.   General agribusiness lobbyists have substantial involvement in a wide range of food and agricultural policy issues. The *U.S. Chamber of Commerce*, a conservative business-oriented organization, represents the business community before both the Congress and the executive branch. Its members include most major agribusiness firms. Its food and agriculture committee focuses on policy and program issues of concern to agribusiness members. The Chamber traditionally has supported policy approaches that encourage reliance on the market system, expand export markets, and reduce trade barriers. Interestingly, one analyst has observed that the Chamber's position on major farm commodity policy has not been much different from the Farm Bureau's position.[12]

The *Grocery Manufacturers of America (GMA)* represents most major processors and manufacturers of consumer food products in the United States. Its major policy concerns relate to regulation of nutrition, food safety and quality, advertising policy, packaging and labeling, antitrust regulation, evaluations of industry performance, import restrictions, and consumer protection policies. Although generally not directly concerned with farm program issues, the GMA regularly joins other groups on commodity-specific issues such as sugar user organizations to oppose price supports and reduced sugar imports.

The *Food Marketing Institute (FMI)* represents a large proportion of firms engaged in retail and wholesale distribution of food. On behalf of its supermarket chain members, FMI traditionally has supported the food stamp program—in part, because it expands grocery sales. It has also traditionally taken a keen interest in antitrust regulations and related concerns about competitiveness of the food industry. It has opposed regulations that would require stamping prices on individual grocery items. Since FMI's members handle the products of the GMA and many food retailers are also some of the largest manufacturers of groceries, the FMI has many of the same interests as the GMA.

The *American Frozen Food Institute* represents frozen-food manufacturers across the commodity spectrum. While having major interests in regulations relating to preparation and labeling of frozen foods, similar to those of GMA, a primary concern of the Frozen Food Institute has been encouraging expanded sale of frozen prepared foods through the school lunch program. In particular, it has been a strong supporter of providing schools with cash instead of surplus commodities acquired through the farm commodity programs. The schools then would be free to purchase fully prepared meals, of which a substantial share likely would be frozen.

Commodity agribusiness organizations.   The *National Grain and Feed Association (NGFA)* represents grain marketing firms at all levels of the market channel from country elevator to exporter. The policy positions of the NGFA reflect the market orientation of its major grain-exporting members, unimpeded market operations, and the members' interest in the use of grain as a feed. Although the NGFA favors price supports for farmers, it advocates maintaining them at low levels so as not to interfere unduly with domestic and export uses. Its support for

[12]Harold D. Guither, *The Food Lobbyists* (Lexington, Mass.: Lexington Books, 1980), p. 55.

grain reserves reflects the involvement of many of its members in grain storage. It strongly opposes production controls.

The *American Feed Manufacturers Association (AFMA)* has many interests and members in common with the NGFA. It, for example, not only favors a market-oriented farm policy, but also favors grain reserves to stabilize feed prices. However, its policy emphasis tends more toward issues of importance to feed production for livestock and poultry, such as government regulation of the use of antibiotics, growth stimulants, and residues transmitted from feed to meat, milk, and eggs. It is also directly concerned with protecting the rights of its members to become more involved in livestock and poultry production through various forward integration strategies.

The *North American Grain Export Association (NAGEA)* has as its major purpose the expansion of grain exports. Its members include virtually all of the grain-exporting firms operating in the United States. It has a direct interest in farm, trade, foreign, and general economic policies as they affect exports. It is probably the most conservative and free-market-oriented of the agribusiness lobbyists, generally opposed to higher price supports, production controls, higher inspection standards, embargoes, and use of grain as a tool of foreign policy. In addition, NAGEA has advocated reduced import restrictions on dairy products and beef because such restrictions are inconsistent with greater market access for its products. It also strongly supports U.S. efforts to negotiate reduced global trade barriers through both bilateral means and international forums such as GATT.

The *American Bakers Association*, as an important grain buyer, at times may have conflicting interests with other agribusiness grain lobbying interests. Although it shares the market-oriented farm program philosophy, when wheat prices began to rise sharply in the mid-1970s, it asked the secretary of agriculture for relief in terms of either a price freeze or embargo of exports.

The Bakers Association's overall goal is securing policies that hold food price inflation low and encourage full production. Accordingly, it has advocated low price supports not only for grain but also for sugar and dairy products, all main ingredients in the products of its members. The Association also believes that USDA is too producer oriented in its decisions.[13]

The *National Cotton Council* is a unique organization in that it attempts to represent the policy interests of the entire cotton industry. Its members include producers, shippers, merchants, exporters, and textile mills. Its policy positions are more closely aligned with agribusiness than producers. Over time, it has increasingly supported a market- and export-

[13]Guither, *Food Lobbyists*, p. 56.

oriented farm policy. In the mid-1980s, it was prominently opposed to mandatory production controls.

The *American Meat Institute (AMI)* represents meat packers throughout the United States. Its major concerns are increased government regulation of the meat industry and defending against the impact of curing additives such as sodium nitrite on health. AMI has had a continuing interest in the contribution of meat to food price increases. In this regard it has been concerned about studies of the Small Business Committee linking a high market share of the industry's largest packers and packer ownership of feedlots to meat price increases. Its interest in this issue increased in the mid-1980s when the market share of the largest meat packers rose sharply due to several mergers and acquisitions.

The *Milk Industry Foundation (MIF)* represents milk processors and is especially concerned with government regulation of the milk industry. Its activities cover three major areas: (1) government regulation of producer prices under the milk price support and federal marketing order system, (2) regulatory standards for the composition of milk and ice cream products promulgated by the Food and Drug Administration, and (3) government action that influences prices and availability of ingredients such as sugar and casein in products such as ice cream.

In its lobbying activities, the MIF has tended to emphasize studies of alternative methods of solving particular milk pricing problems as a means of fostering industry dialogue and providing Congress with information relevant to policy issues. It has been particularly effective in organizing coalitions of user groups for issues relating to milk and sugar. However, the MIF has found the milk producer cooperative lobby to be a formidable foe and considerable compromise to be required on dairy policy issues.

The *Sweetener Users Association* is a coalition of food firms for which sugar and other sweeteners are an important ingredient. Its major objectives concern the sugar program and the elimination of price supports and quotas which raise the price to its members. Its members include soft-drink bottlers, bakers, ice cream manufacturers, and confectioners.

The *Tobacco Institute* has been described by one health advocate as "one of the most lethal trade associations going."[14] In recent years, a large proportion of its efforts have been directed toward defending against the mounting evidence linking smoking and health problems, fighting restrictions on smoking in public places, and supporting studies of methods of reducing potentially harmful substances in tobacco smoke. To accomplish its lobbying objectives, it has employed two former representatives, a former senator, and a former governor.

---

[14]Guither, *Food Lobbyists*, p. 68.

The *Fertilizer Institute* is the association of firms engaged both in manufacture and distribution of fertilizers. The Institute traditionally has supported programs that improve farm prosperity. It has joined with the American Feed Manufacturers and the National Council of Farmer Cooperatives to express concern about the impact of railroad deregulation on rail abandonment and rural communities. It has also traditionally had a special interest in USDA soil conservation programs and has been a supporter of research and education. Since fertilizer sales occur in proportion to acres farmed, the Fertilizer Institute has been an active opponent of programs that remove farmland from production, especially proposals for mandatory production controls.

The *American Bankers Association (ABA)*, agricultural bankers division, protects the interests of bankers in government agricultural lending programs. Although concerned about expanded credit through the Farmers Home Administration and the Small Business Administration, public agencies such as the ABA have generally been supportive of expanded government-guaranteed loans. When the Cooperative Farm Credit System required an infusion of federal capital, ABA was mainly concerned with maintaining a level playing field for its banks by means such as securing a secondary market for farm mortgages.

The ABA traditionally has supported government programs that reduce risk in agriculture such as crop insurance, disaster payments, and, in some instances, target prices. Support also has, from time to time, been expressed for higher price and/or income supports on the grounds that it would increase deposits and allow farmers to repay some questionably solvent loans. However, it has consistently opposed government subsidies on interest rates for any type of loan. ABA applauded suggestions of the Reagan and Bush administrations to reduce subsidies on Rural Electrification Administration loans and limiting the functions of the Farmers Home Administration to guaranteeing loans.

The "Public Interest" Lobby

It is a prime responsibility of the Congress, the president, and the courts to see that decisions are made in the public interest. The **public interest** *means to benefit society as a whole as opposed to a particular segment of society.* Other than the special interests of producers and agribusiness firms, there exists a large number of people who are affected by food and agricultural policy and program decisions. These people are generally known as the public. Their interest in policy covers a wide range of values, beliefs, goals, and factual knowledge. There are, therefore, many different organizations and concerns expressed by them. Those groups that attempt to reflect interests other than the special interests of producers and agribusiness groups are generally known as **public interest groups**.

Why would the public interest in agricultural and food programs differ from the farmer interest or the agribusiness interest? Differences arise because the groups may be affected differently by agricultural policies, and those most advantageous to farmers may be perceived as adversely affecting others who may not be well organized to protect their interests. Some of the differences derive from the following:

- Food is a necessity of life. An adequate supply of food, therefore, is a necessity. Individuals deprived of food suffer serious mental and physiological consequences. Society bears a moral obligation to prevent such consequences. Although all may agree on this point, questions arise over whose budget should be cut to cover the cost of eliminating hunger and malnutrition.
- Food has costs. While the average consumer spends about 15 percent of disposable income on food, lower-income consumers spend considerably more. All consumers are affected by a change in the price of food and commodity prices do affect retail prices. Also, farm programs can affect farm and food prices. While farmers and economists may argue over the existence of a "cheap food policy," public interest in the price of food is legitimate and can be expected to continue.
- Citizens may be affected by externalities originating from agricultural production such as stream pollution from runoff, soil erosion, pesticide residues, chemicals in the soil and water, and an adverse effect on wildlife.
- Consumers want to be assured of a safe food supply and that farmers, processors, retailers, and the government are protecting it from contamination. Yet even the mention of a safety problem with a particular product has extremely adverse effects on sales, prices, profits, and even the survival of particular firms.
- Public interest groups represent taxpayers. When reducing the federal budget deficit is a national priority, taxpayers have a legitimate interest in farm program costs, just like the cost of all other government programs.

The question is raised from time to time by producer and agribusiness groups as to the extent to which public interest groups truly represent the public. Each public interest organization does represent a specific set of concerns other than the primary concerns of producers and agribusiness. The Congress and the executive branch have to gauge the extent of the support of all groups in reaching decisions on various issues.

How well they perform this function is determined by the public in subsequent elections.

During the 1970s a sharp increase occurred in the number of public interest organizations involved in food and agricultural lobbying. The level of their activity and its effectiveness likely peaked during the Carter presidency when a substantial flow of public funds supported these groups. The Reagan administration moved quickly to reduce these funds, both because of their Democratic political alignment and as part of overall efforts to trim federal spending. Despite their relatively small funding, these interest groups frequently are effective in presenting their concerns. They primarily focus on four major areas: consumer concerns, nutrition, hunger, and the environment. A few public interest organizations work in more than one of these areas and are mentioned below more than once.

The consumer food lobby.   The consumer food lobby is led by the Community Nutrition Institute, the Consumer Federation of America, the Consumers Union, Congress Watch, Public Voice for Food and Health Policy, and the Center for Budget and Policy Priorities. These and other public interest organizations frequently form coalitions for specific issues to provide a united consumer lobby.

The *Community Nutrition Institute (CNI)* has emerged as the major consumer force for specific food and agricultural policy issues. The CNI is a nonprofit advocacy agency whose goal is assuring all people an adequate, safe, nutritious, and affordable diet. It is, to an important extent, a consumer research and lobbying agency, treating a broad scope of domestic consumer concerns. Its activities include studies that largely are supported by contracts with government agencies. Many of its projects also involve assembling experts on particular topics for workshops, seminars, and conferences. CNI publishes a newsletter, the *CNI Weekly Report*, which provides an excellent summary of current issues and legislative activity related to food.

CNI has been a leading advocate for a more consumer-oriented USDA. CNI has been deeply involved in efforts to accomplish a reevaluation of the marketing order program. It was active in the 1973 meat boycott and has been involved in all farm bills since 1973. It effectively led opposition to Reagan administration proposed cuts in nutrition programs.

The *Consumer Federation of America (CFA)* represents consumers on a wide range of issues, including food and agricultural issues. CFA has a membership composed of credit unions, electric cooperatives, labor unions, state and city consumer associations, and somewhat surprisingly, the National Farmers Union.

CFA once supported changing USDA to a Department of Food responsive to the needs of all affected by the food system. One of its former presidents, Carol T. Foreman, served as assistant secretary of agriculture for food and nutrition programs in the Carter administration.

Since its organization in 1968, CFA has been an important factor in enacting stronger federal meat and poultry inspection requirements, eliminating the food stamp purchase requirement, encouraging direct farmer marketing programs, and opposing sugar and milk price support increases.

The CFA has not always been opposed to farm interests. In fact, it joined several farm organizations in support of the Emergency Farm Act of 1975 to raise target prices and loan rates. This legislation was eventually vetoed by President Ford.

Congress Watch, the lobbying arm of Ralph Nader's Public Citizen organization, provides oversight on a wide range of public issues before the Congress. Congress Watch regularly testifies before the agriculture committees on farm programs as well as consumer issues. It also monitors voting records of members of Congress and their relation to lobbyists that support them with political contributions. For example, it has been critical of large contributions made by dairy cooperatives to members serving on the agriculture committees.

It is noteworthy that Ralph Nader previously has been associated with several projects that looked critically at agricultural firms and lobbyists. For example, the Agriculture Accountability Project sponsored a study that was critical of ties among the land-grant universities, large farmers, and agribusiness firms.[15] Another one of its studies charged that most large cooperatives were controlled by their management rather than by their producer members.[16] Both studies, although extensively criticized, contained elements of truth and had considerable impact. Some suggest that is why they were criticized so extensively.

Consumers Union also has published several studies critical of farm programs, government regulation of food industries, and the products of food firms. Its main enterprise, however, traditionally has been evaluating quality and performance of particular products, including food products. After the early 1970s, it also became an active advocate for particular causes related to food, especially regulations directly affecting food prices, such as marketing orders, and the safety of the food supply.

The *Public Voice for Food and Health Policy* engages in a wide range of agricultural and food policy issues on behalf of consumers. Its participation in farm policy development is built on the formation of coalitions

---

[15]Jim Hightower, *Hard Tomatoes, Hard Times* (Cambridge, Mass.: Schenkman Publishing Company, Inc., 1973).

[16]Linda Kravitz, *Who's Minding the Coops?* (Washington, D.C.: Agriculture Accountability Project, 1976).

among consumer, nutrition, and environmental groups. Ellen Haas, its executive director, has devoted her professional life to representing the public in agricultural and food issues.

The *Center on Budget and Policy Priorities (CBPP)* was founded by Robert Greenstein, the administrator of USDA's Food and Nutrition Service during the Carter administration. CBPP was organized to do analytical work on Reagan food policy. Its success in serving the policy analysis needs of both Republicans and Democrats is based on the accuracy of its numbers, timeliness, and objectivity.

Labor unions, including the AFL-CIO, United Food and Commercial Workers, United Autoworkers, Aerospace and Agricultural Implement Workers, and the National Association of Farm Worker Organizations, have been active in promoting consumer causes. They have surfaced concerns of their members in consumer advocacy groups as well as in the Congress. Equally important, they have provided a critical base of financial support for the consumer movement. The major labor union concerns generally can be classified as being those of middle-class Americans, the cost of food, assurances that the food supply is safe, ease of shopping, and in the 1970s, the eligibility of strikers for food stamps.

The center of the agriculture labor movement for many years was in California under the leadership of Cesar Chavez. The major thrust of the movement to organize farm labor occurred among grape and lettuce workers. These efforts were actively supported by nonfarm unions. Their success is illustrated by California's becoming the first state to establish an agricultural labor practices law (discussed in greater detail in Chapter 14).

The nutrition, safety, and quality lobby.   The nutrition, safety, and quality lobby is concerned primarily with the impact of diet on health, including nutrients in food and safety, and quality as well. The relationships among health, diet-nutrition, and the safety of the food supply have spawned some of the most direct conflicts between public interest advocates and producers. Issues such as the establishment of nutrition guidelines, the linkage of cholesterol to coronary disease, the relationship of nitrites to cancer, and the use of growth stimulants in cattle feeding create highly emotional reactions. The nutrition, food safety, and food quality lobby has been a strong supporter of research to examine the nature and extent of the causal effect of diet on health. As a result, it should not be surprising that the major interest groups involved in this area have an applied scientific orientation. The Community Nutrition Institute once again plays a key role in the study of the issue as well as an advocacy role in the Congress, the executive, and the courts.

The *Center for Science in the Public Interest* is a consumer activist organization that investigates food, nutrition, consumer, and environmental concerns. The Center has become a focal point for specific issues that are closely related to new scientific evidence. Its activities are closely coordinated with those of other consumer, hunger, and environmental groups. Its monthly magazine, *Nutrition Action,* has become a guiding force for focusing on nutrition and food problems in the United States and other countries.

In addition to its major concerns about the relationship of food to health, the Center has spoken out on such diverse issues as low-nutrient processed foods, corporate investment in agriculture, food prices, and conflicts of interest between industry and government. In one of its lighter but yet serious moments, it raised questions concerning the nutritional example set by President Reagan's Jelly Belly (a jelly bean candy) consumption. More recently, it has become an advocate against the use of biotechnology products in agriculture and their potential introduction into the food supply and environment.

The *Health Research Group* is another Ralph Nader organization related to Public Citizen and Congress Watch. It has been concerned primarily with the safety of food additives, being extremely critical of existing food safety regulations and of the scientific staff in both the Food and Drug Administration and USDA.

Health Research has advocated a policy of considering all "generally recognized as safe (GRAS)" substances as potentially dangerous unless scientifically proven otherwise. It has also suggested that new food additives not be permitted in food unless their benefit is demonstrated to be more than cosmetic and better than an existing additive. It has proposed all safety-related testing of additives be shifted from industry to academic centers. Needless to say, the food industry has become very concerned with such suggestions.

The *Society of Nutrition Education* is an organization of professionals in nutrition education and related fields. Its major mission has been to increase the effectiveness of nutrition education. Within its ranks, the society has developed new leadership in nutrition education, advocating a more activist role in educating consumers and influencing policy on the relationships between diet and health. Specific concerns include support for the issuance of food consumption guidelines, dietary goals, increased nutrition research, and educational activity on the dangers of additives and highly processed foods. The society has been a major factor in shifting the thinking of nutrition educators from the basic food groups to those ideals embedded in the dietary goals and guidelines.

The hunger lobby.   The **hunger lobby** is *concerned with issues related to hunger, malnutrition, and the adequacy of the food supply worldwide.* Concern about hunger in America rose to a national policy issue in the early 1960s. Prior to that, hunger in America was viewed largely as a problem for the church and local communities rather than government. The concern of the hunger lobby switched from the United States to the world when the hunger problem was substantially reduced in the United States. Thus in the early 1970s, the combination of hunger, worldwide food shortages, and recurring famines led to the formation of new organizations and a renewed commitment on the part of existing organizations to address the problems of hunger and malnutrition.

These organizations are active in influencing foreign agricultural development assistance and foreign aid policies, as well as related dimensions of foreign policy and food assistance programs in the United States. They also actively attempt to increase the level of awareness and concern by the American people for problems of world hunger and malnutrition. The leadership and the conscience for the hunger lobby lie largely in church-related organizations.

Bread for the World is a nondenominational Christian public interest movement concerned about adequacy of food for the poor in the United States and the rest of the world. It advocates a greater U.S. commitment to problems of hunger, food, and agricultural development policy. Specifically, it has been a strong proponent of domestic and international grain reserves, domestic food programs for those in the greatest need, and appropriate combinations of foreign food aid and development aid. It has expressed concern about U.S. emphasis on surplus disposal and the accomplishment of foreign policy objectives, as opposed to increasing foreign food production, eliminating hunger, and increasing development aid. Bread for the World coordinates its activities with the relief mission-oriented programs of Church World Service, Lutheran World Relief, and Catholic Relief Services.

The *World Watch Institute* raised to national attention the adequacy of the world food supply and associated resource problems. Its founder, Lester Brown, is a prolific author and has exhibited a unique ability to sense the emergence of problems and to draw together facts and concerns in a timely manner. World Watch is frequently the first to address evolving policy issues involving the use of the world's limited resources.

The *Food Research and Action Center (FRAC)* is a nonprofit law firm and advocacy center working to end malnutrition in the United States. FRAC has sought to expand the coverage of food assistance programs through both advocacy and litigation. Cases won by FRAC include requirements to issue food stamps retroactively to eligible recipients and a requirement that USDA increase its efforts to inform potential food stamp recipients. Former Congressman Wampler, then senior minority member of the House Agriculture Committee, once expressed frustration with FRAC for "frustrating the whole process with lawsuits."[17] Interest-

[17]*The Food Stamp Program* (Washington, D.C.: Committee on Agriculture, U.S. House of Representatives, April 17, 1977), p. 349.

ingly, FRAC has received a large share of its financial aid from the federal government, against whom the lawsuits are filed.[18]

The resource and environment lobby.   Controversies involving resource use and the environment rival those in nutrition and food safety for creating conflict among producers, agribusiness, and the public interest lobby. The concerns cover a wide range, from pesticide use to the organizational rights of farm labor. The lobbyists are well organized, enjoy stronger financial support than many other public interest groups, and in many instances, raise issues with longer-term implications for the ability to produce an adequate supply of food at reasonable prices.

The *Sierra Club* is one of the oldest, largest, and most effective organizations working to protect and conserve natural resources. Its major concerns include wilderness preservation, air and water pollution, soil conservation, energy conservation, wildlife preservation, elimination of toxic substances, population, and land use planning. Specific concerns involving food and agriculture include availability of water for irrigation, use of public lands for grazing, existence of toxic substances in the food supply, ability to feed future populations, and humane treatment of livestock.[19] Sierra Club proposals for dealing with these issues generally would increase production costs and reduce the level of production. Under the 1985 farm bill, the Sierra Club was an active supporter of removing erosive land from production, requiring approved soil conservation plans in return for farm program benefits, and prohibiting newly broken out farmland or wetlands from receiving farm program benefits.

The *Environmental Defense Fund* in many respects serves as the scientific backstop for the environmentalists. As such, its mission is finding scientifically sound solutions to environmental problems. Its support comes from a combination of membership dues, contributions, and grants from foundations for specific studies. The fund has done extensive research on the causes of cancer, chemicals in food, integrated pest management, and the impact of Environmental Protection Agency (EPA) policies on the environment. It has been a strong advocate of tighter EPA regulation.

Friends of the Earth is an environmental lobby based in the United States, but having affiliations in several foreign countries. It was founded in 1969 when its president moved from the Sierra Club. Its agricultural concerns relate primarily to pesticide issues. It favors less pesticide use and would restrict U.S. corporations from selling or using pesticides internationally that are not approved for use in the United States. It would

---

[18]Many of the Reagan administration efforts to trim the federal budget severely restricted or eliminated federal funds available to groups such as FRAC.

[19]Kathryn Ann Utrup, "How Sierra Club Members See Environmental Issues," *Sierra* (March–April 1979), pp. 14–18.

also place increased restrictions on pesticide use by households and has expressed concern about what it considers to be excess profits earned by the chemical companies.

The *National Association of Farm Worker Organizations (NAFO)* is the central lobbyist for over 50 migrant and seasonal farm worker organizations. It provides services and training to farm workers, but its main agenda includes unionization rights for migrant and seasonal farm labor, improved living conditions, access to food assistance programs, access to education, and effects of working conditions, including pesticides, on the health of farm workers.

The *Humane Society of the United States, Animal Protection Institute of America* and *Friends of Animals* are a few of the several public interest groups concerned with animal welfare and animal rights. These groups see modern livestock and poultry production methods as cruelty to animals. Caged layers, confinement hog production, and raising veal calves in crates are particular concerns, in addition to traditional issues involving slaughter techniques and the use of animals in research.

INTEREST GROUP STRATEGIES AND THE FUTURE

The days of the agriculture establishment having complete control over the agricultural policy agenda are clearly past. Three major reasons account for this:

- New public interest groups, recognizing the impact of food and agricultural policy on the people and interests they represent, are continuously injecting new ideas into legislative and executive decision processes. More frequently, they are willing to challenge adverse decisions in the courts.
- The members of the agriculture committees of the Congress are no longer responsive only to the agriculture establishment. The new interest groups have members on these committees who not only hear them out but either plead their case directly or give them opportunity to plead their case.
- USDA is no longer in full control of the food and agriculture policy decisions in the executive branch, if it ever was. These decisions are viewed as too important to be left to USDA. They may have important foreign policy, budget, balance-of-trade, or food price implications. On specific issues, the secretary of state, director of the Office of Management and Budget, or the secretary of the treasury may be more influential in a policy decision than the secretary of agriculture.

The new public interest groups will not go away. The agriculture committees of the Congress will continue to have members responsive to the appeals of public interest groups, and food and agriculture decisions will probably increase in importance in the executive branch.

Coalitions will be more important in determining the outcome of policy and program decisions. Attempts by the agriculture establishment to organize a broad-based coalition have been less than a resounding success. The National Farm Coalition is an informal alliance of over 30 general commodity and cooperative farm organizations. But only the National Grange, of the general farm organizations, participates. The Farm Bureau and Farmers Union contend that they do not need to be part of the Farm Coalition since they represent a cross section of all farmers.

Agribusiness lobbyists appear much more effective than producers at organizing coalitions. The Food Group, agribusiness organizations having an interest in food issues, meets regularly to coordinate positions on farm and food policy. The Agricultural Round Table has been organized as a combination of agribusiness organizations and commodity groups to promote solid opposition to government programs involving mandatory production controls. Numerous other coalitions are formed for brief periods to address issues of interest.

Farm organizations continue to be tremendously successful in getting farm bills enacted, while economists and politicians have been suggesting the farmers' influence had declined. The 1981 and 1985 farm bills are vivid examples. Bills that provide farmer subsidies of over $25 billion in one year and more than $60 billion over four- or five-year periods can hardly be considered the result of ineffective or splintered lobbying!

What counts is relative influence at the time the bill is being developed. Relatively, in the 1980s, farmers have proved more powerful than consumers—although both groups received their share of benefits from the two recent farm bills. The farm lobby success of the 1980s could prove to be the last as farm numbers grow smaller and smaller. *But there is little evidence of it yet!* Political power may increase as farm numbers decline because farmers have become more astute regarding the requirements for effective lobbying.

The farm lobby is most effective when its position is compatible with agribusiness. The Harkin bill favoring mandatory production controls died quickly in Washington because of agribusiness opposition. *Networking* (mutual support among organizations) has enabled some groups, notably consumers, to become stronger. When farm organizations truly have their backs to the wall, they may be forced to develop such networks as well.

To remain politically effective in the next two decades, agriculture may have to practice the politics of the minority. This involves:

- Finding allies and building coalitions issue by issue rather than by philosophy. Agricultural interest groups too often may depend on philosophical niceties and folklore.
- Looking for common ground and compromise. Getting a small increase in government support is better than getting nothing.
- Deescalating arguments with adversaries. An adversary on one issue may be an ally on another. Be positive by playing down small differences, playing up mutual interests, and working within the system.
- Basing policy positions on facts. Political contests not based on fact and solid analysis generally will be lost.
- Avoiding identification with either political party. To succeed, agriculture needs the support of both political parties.[20]

ADDITIONAL READINGS

1. This chapter drew heavily from an excellent study of lobbying in food and agriculture by Harold D. Guither, *The Food Lobbyists* (Lexington, Mass.: Lexington Books, 1980).
2. A detailed discussion of public interest lobbyists is contained in Jeffery M. Berry, *Lobbying for the People, The Political Behavior of Public Interest Groups* (Princeton, N.J.: Princeton University Press, 1977).
3. *The Policy Studies Journal* (Urbana, Ill.: University of Illinois, Summer 1978) published an excellent series of articles on the topics of political change in American institutions and issues on the new agricultural agenda. Alex McCalla's article, "The Politics of the U.S. Agricultural Research Establishment," is particularly enlightening.
4. The original article by Don Paarlberg titled "The Farm Policy Agenda," in *Increasing Understanding of Public Policy Problems and Policies* (Chicago: Farm Foundation, 1975), pp. 94–101, is a classic.
5. Jim Hightower's *Hard Tomatoes, Hard Times* (Cambridge, Mass.: Schenkman Publishing Company, Inc. 1973) is a classic. It is essential reading for those interested in agricultural policy. Its public interest message is as relevant today as when it was written.

[20]B. L. Flinchbaugh, "Its Easy to Be Ignored if You Don't Have Your Act Together," speech presented at the National Institute on Cooperative Education, Colorado State University, Fort Collins, Colo., July 28, 1981, p. 1.

Part II

International Trade
and Macroeconomic Policy

The world economy is highly interdependent. Agriculture operates in a world economic environment that can be insulated neither from events in the U.S. economy nor in the world economy. Domestic policies cannot be evaluated in terms of either their effects or their effectiveness without a basic understanding of the interrelationships among the U.S. economy, the world economy, and agriculture. The next four chapters are designed to provide that understanding.

Chapter 5 will describe the world food problem. Emphasis will be placed on the factors influencing the international demand for and supply of food. Conclusions will be drawn regarding the world supply–demand balance.

Chapter 6 discusses the role of trade domestically and internationally. It develops the theory of trade and barriers to trade. The competitive position of the United States in international markets is evaluated.

Chapter 7 explains the major policy issues and tools relating to trade. The impacts on U.S. agriculture as well as on other countries are explained.

Chapter 8 explains the economic interrelationships between the U.S. economy and agriculture. Linkages, thereby, are provided between the international economy, the domestic economy, and the agricultural economy. Emphasis is placed on those general economic variables that most directly affect the agricultural economy. Then the general macroeconomic tools that are used to influence those variables are described.

Chapter 5

The World Food Problems

The gap in our economy is between what we have and what we think we ought to have—and that is a moral problem, not an economic one.

Paul Heyne

In the 1970s the American farmer was overtly, as a matter of public policy, thrust into the world agricultural economy. Foreign demand became the major determinant of farm prices and incomes. Expanding foreign demand for American farm products had multiple objectives:

- Agricultural exports were seen as a means of reducing the need for government subsidies and controls.
- Agricultural exports had the potential for becoming a major source of export earnings and bolstering the value of the dollar.
- Agricultural exports held the potential for dealing with major world issues, including hunger and malnutrition, economic and political instability, and the deteriorating position of the United States as a world power.

In reality, American farmers and U.S. policymakers had little choice in making U.S. agriculture part of the world economy. World food supplies were becoming visibly tighter in the late 1960s. The American economy badly needed new sources of export earnings to offset the rising cost of imported oil. Vivid television portrayals of the plight of the hungry and starving engendered the concern about future food supplies and the need to help among the American people. The interaction of factors such as these led to the realization that whereas at one time it may have been possible for U.S. agriculture to ignore the rest of the world, it was no longer.

In the 1970s, farmers in the United States and throughout the world geared up to meet world demand. Importing countries questioned whether, in a turbulent world economic and political environment, they could rely on farmers located in other countries to satisfy their food needs. Many established goals of self-sufficiency in food production. Farmers throughout the world brought new lands into production and planted fencerow to fencerow.

The boom conditions of the 1970s went nearly as fast as they came. But once a part of the world economy, U.S. farmers and policymakers had to live with its consequences—unstable export demand, farm prices, and incomes. During the decade crop output had increased by nearly 47 percent. Most of the increase went to the export market.

When the bust came in the 1980s, agricultural policymakers throughout the world had to make a choice of whether to protect their farmers against the vagaries of international markets. Many have chosen to provide that protection—leading to protectionist trade policies.

The purpose of this chapter is to put the world food supply–demand balance into perspective.

THE 1970s: AN ABERRATION?

The world supply–demand balance for agricultural products is the most important determinant of the agricultural economic environment. Since the mid-1800s, except for World War II and in the early 1970s, the long-run trend has been toward lower real farm prices. In 1972 and 1973 many predicted that the trend would reverse—that golden years were ahead for farmers and ranchers. A major government study of future economic trends requested by President Carter fortified the prediction. The resulting report, *Global 2000*, painted a bright economic outlook for farmers and a bleak picture of their ability to satisfy world food needs. The report concluded: "After decades of generally falling prices, the real price of food is projected to increase 95 percent over the 1970–2000 period."[1] Absent a series of unforeseen events in the 1990s, that projection appears to have been wrong.

---

[1]Gerald O. Barney, *The Global 2000 Report to the President* (New York: Penguin Books, 1982), p. 17.

THE WORLD SUPPLY–DEMAND BALANCE

Thomas Malthus published his famous essay, titled *An Essay on the Principle of Population, As It Affects the Future Improvement of Society*,[2] in 1798. The essay attacked theories of eternal human progress by arguing that the standard of living cannot be indefinitely improved because the growth of the population will exceed the capacity of the earth to produce. Malthus asserted that population, unchecked by war, disease, or famine, increases geometrically, whereas food production increases only arithmetically. He contended that the implication of his argument was a clear need to restrain global population growth.

As the end of the second century since these predictions were made approaches, it is generally concluded that Malthus has been proven wrong.[3] The reasons generally cited include Malthus's failure to recognize that population growth slows with increases in per capita real income, with increases in population density, with improved health and nutrition, and with the realization that less food is available per capita. Further, Malthus did not foresee the advances in food production that have enabled the food supply to grow faster than arithmetically. Increased food production has not only come from increases in cultivated acres but also from technological innovation, the substitution of capital for labor, and from the very fact that in a market economy when demand increases relative to supply, it creates a reward for increased productivity.

Although such denials of the Malthusian theory represent the clear majority of contemporary thought, there are those who still predict eventual exhaustion of the world's resources and a decline in the standard of living. For example, in 1972 a widely publicized study of the implications of continued worldwide economic and population growth embraced the concept of exponential population growth.[4] It then asserted the need for planning of both population growth and resource use at levels consistent with the earth's carrying capacity. In addition, world population has from time to time been checked by war, disease, and famine, as Malthus predicted. The world food crises of the early 1970s was as much of an aberration in the sequence of world economic events as was World War II.

What went wrong? D. Gale Johnson,[5] a U.S. expert on international

[2]D. V. Glass, *Introduction to Malthus* (London: C. A. Watts & Co. Ltd., 1953).

[3]Kenneth Smith, *The Malthusian Controversy* (London: Routledge & Kegan Paul Ltd., 1951).

[4]Donella H. Meadows et al., *The Limits of Growth* (New York: Universe Books, 1972).

[5]D. Gale Johnson, "The World Food Situation: Recent and Prospective Developments," in *The Role of Markets in the World Economy*, D. Gale Johnson and G. Edward Schuh, eds. (Boulder, Colo.: Westview Press, Inc., 1983) pp. 1–33.

economics, makes five crucial points regarding why the projections of long-term prosperity in agriculture failed to materialize:

- Over optimism was prevalent regarding the demand for grains to be used for feeding livestock. Developed countries' feed use has not grown significantly since the early 1970s. Annual growth in feed use by middle-income developing countries generally has been in the 7 percent range, but overall supplies have grown more rapidly than demand. The ability of developing countries to upgrade diets has been limited by sluggish domestic economic growth and the inability to generate required hard currency for imports.
- Experts underestimated the potential supply of cropland. Despite interstate highways, suburban growth, and industry development, the United States now has about the same arable acreage that it had in 1950. The amount of arable land in developing market economies increased by 5.8 percent during the 1970s. Substantial potential exists for further development of agricultural land in South America, Africa, and Southeast Asia. In addition, the potential adverse impacts of soil erosion on crop production were overestimated.
- Experts overestimated the impact of high energy prices, energy shortages, and the potential for using agricultural products as a source of energy. While energy prices tripled from 1970 through 1982, the adverse impact on farm output was not as apparent as had been predicted. Energy shortages were overcome by conservation, increased domestic production, and the eventual ineffectiveness of OPEC. The potential for agriculture becoming a major source of energy was a hoax.
- The adverse impact of water shortages on crop production was overestimated. While water has generally been underpriced relative to its cost to the government, predictions of water shortages jeopardizing the food supply have been grossly overstated.
- The ability of highly populated countries to feed themselves and generate exports was underestimated. Classic examples include China and India.

RECENT ASSESSMENTS OF THE SUPPLY–DEMAND BALANCE

The failure of predictions during the 1970s resulted in a number of assessments of the world food supply–demand balance. *These assessments support the basic conclusion that the 1970s were an aberration in the long-*

run trend toward lower real commodity and food prices. The 1980s have been a painful readjustment to the optimism that pervaded the 1970s.

Johnson Study (1982)

In a comprehensive review of world supply and demand developments, D. Gale Johnson concludes: "It is reasonable to expect that international prices of grains and vegetable oils will remain at historically low and perhaps declining levels for the next one or two decades."[6] Johnson emphasized the absence of conditions that would void basic pervasive trends in supply and demand since the early 1900s. In addition, Johnson concludes that "Resources are available that would permit increasing the rate of growth of per capita food production in developing countries."[7] This conclusion casts substantial gloom over U.S. agriculture's ability to regain a posture of sustained export growth to developing countries.

In reviewing past events that resulted in price changes, Johnson observes that one of the major sources of world price instability is government intervention.[8] *When governments attempt to stabilize domestic prices or farm income, they contribute to international price instability.* Johnson's rank ordering of commodities in terms of the degree of international price instability from least stable to most stable is sugar, wheat, corn, and cotton. This ordering exactly coincides with studies of the degree of government price and income interference. *In other words, efforts to achieve price stability in domestic markets often translate into instability in world markets as supplies are added to the world market at subsidized prices or demand is curtailed by import restrictions.*

Resources for the Future (1983)

The Resources for the Future (RFF) study[9] agrees with Johnson's assessment of the world food situation in that it predicts a general downward trend in the level of real prices for farm products. But RFF appeared to project a somewhat tighter supply–demand balance than did Johnson.

The RFF conclusion was based on a comprehensive analysis of global demand (using both population and income projections), the extent to which individual countries could meet its needs, and the resulting implications for international trade. The study foresaw reduced rates of growth in global demand compared to the 1970s. This slower growth rate

[6]Ibid., p. 2.

[7]Ibid.

[8]Ibid., p. 18.

[9]Fred H. Sanderson, "An Assessment of Global Demand for U.S. Agricultural Products to the Year 2000," *Am. J. Agric. Econ.* (December 1984), pp. 577–584.

can be accounted for by reduced rates of population growth, slower income growth, and declining income elasticities.

After detailed examination of land and water resources and the possibilities of increased yields, the study concludes that increased demand can be met largely from increased domestic production except in sub-Saharan Africa. Even so, RFF projected "increased dependence on grain imports from North America and Australia; oilseeds from the United States, Brazil, and Argentina; and meat from Oceania, Western Europe, and Eastern Europe."[10] Out of these apparently contradictory positions, RFF projected stable to declining real food prices.

The RFF report ended with the caveat that the conclusions reached are based on trend projections. This means, among other things, that the study assumed a constant rate of increase in yields. There was little or no analysis of the potential for an accelerating rate of technological change in the RFF study.

Economic Research Service, USDA (1984 and 1985)

The Economic Research Service (ERS), drawing on the extensive expertise and research of a host of its scientists concludes, after analyzing the world food situation, that moderate world plenty is more likely than scarcity. "Hence, the basic scenario recognizes the gradual downward pressure on prices received by farmers, and the upward pressure on prices paid."[11]

In another report from the ERS study, Edwards and Harrington gave three reasons for a probable long-run decline in real prices received by U.S. farmers:

- First, the trend since 1860 has been in that direction, and nothing in the present situation points to a new and compelling reason for concluding that a change has or is about to take place.
- Second, U.S. agricultural capacity is growing faster than markets are expected to grow. This implies a domestic propensity to produce more than will clear the market at current real prices. This force for decreasing real prices need not be strong, but is in the direction of reinforcing the other two forces.
- Third, world agricultural capacity is growing faster than world markets are growing. If U.S. farmers are to expand their markets by

---

[10]Ibid., p. 581.

[11]Clark Edwards, *U.S. Agriculture's Potential to Supply World Food Markets*, Agric. Econ. Rep. 539 (Washington, D.C.: ERS, USDA, August 1985).

means of exports, their real prices received for exported commodities will have to decrease gradually to remain competitive.[12]

The ERS study is also important because it sees U.S. agriculture becoming increasingly dependent on export markets. The study concludes that U.S. exports will grow at a rate slightly under 3 percent per year in the coming decade, and the capacity to produce will grow by slightly over 3 percent. It cautions against protectionist trade policies that directly or indirectly reduce exports by stating: "If U.S. consumers were the only market for U.S. food products, U.S. agriculture would have surplus capacity, low income, and continued outmigration of people and resources."[13]

Edward's caution appears to represent a substantial understatement. Based on either the Johnson and RFF study, or for that matter the ERS base scenario, *continued excess capacity, low incomes, and outmigration can realistically be predicted for the future* even if export markets remain open. Looking back, surplus capacity, low incomes, and outmigration have been the rule rather than the exception over the past 50 years. *Considering these conditions, tremendous changes would need to occur in U.S. agriculture if American farmers were denied the export markets to which 40 percent of crop production is sold.*

Office of Technology Assessment (1986)

The purpose of the Office of Technology Assessment (OTA) study[14] was to assist the Congress in projecting the impact of technological change on the supply of food and natural fibers. Although not designed to be a study of the future world supply–demand balance, the OTA study adds an important missing dimension to the other studies by analyzing the rate of technological change. It utilized the expertise of leading agricultural scientists to identify major expected technological breakthroughs, their timing, and their potential impact on the production of particular commodities.

The results of the OTA study stand in stark contrast to the mid-1970s, when it was thought that the shelves of new technologies were becoming bare. OTA identified a multitude of new and evolving forms of biotechnology and information technology. The pervasiveness and potential impacts of these new technologies were projected to increase at an increasing rate through the turn of the century. Rapid technological

[12]Clark Edwards and David H. Harrington, "The Future Productive Capacity of U.S. Agriculture: Economic, Technological, Resource, and Institutional Determinants," *Am. J. Agric. Econ.* (December 1984), p. 590.

[13]Edwards, *U.S. Agriculture's Potential*, p. 12.

[14]Office of Technology Assessment, *Technology, Public Policy, and the Changing Structure of Agriculture* (Washington D.C.: U.S. Congress, March 1986).

change was projected to impact animal agriculture sooner than plant agriculture. Despite this lag, the long-range impact on plant agriculture and its crop producers could be equal or even more profound in terms of types of plants grown, cultural practices, yields, and structural changes in farming.

If the OTA study is anywhere near accurate, it renders obsolete the studies of the world supply–demand balance that assume a constant rate of technological change. This is particularly the case as time progresses toward the year 2000 and beyond. The case for declining real farm prices is, thereby, fortified.

Despite all of these studies, it is still possible that a series of adverse political and weather circumstances could once again thrust the world agricultural economy into a situation of food shortages. The late 1980s, for example, demonstrate that two consecutive years of major U.S. drought have the potential for creating severe shortages. Because of that possibility, the governments of most countries prefer to err on the side of abundance and food security. This, of course, contributes to the likelihood of surpluses and protectionist policies.

SHORTAGES IN THE MIDST OF PLENTY: THE DISTRIBUTION PROBLEM

Even in the 1980s, a period when U.S. farm policymakers have been trying to figure out what to do about surpluses and low prices, starving African children have regularly appeared on television. Hunger and malnutrition in the midst of world plenty is a distribution problem. The **distribution problem** *involves getting food to people who cannot produce it and do not have the resources to buy it.*

The distribution problem presents itself in three dimensions:

- A *chronic calorie gap* exists when production in a country persistently falls short of minimum nutrition-based food requirements, and it does not have the financial capability to import commercially. In other words, the country is dependent on food aid to meet the nutritional requirements of its people.

    USDA regularly projects additional cereal grain needs required to eliminate this calorie gap. In recent years this gap has totaled from 15 to 27 million tons.[15] The major areas requiring food aid in recent assessments include North Africa, South Asia, and Southeast Asia.

    The problem in sub-Saharan Africa is particularly acute. In

[15]Economic Research Service, *World Food Needs and Availabilities, 1986/87: Spring Update* (Washington, D.C.: USDA, May 1987).

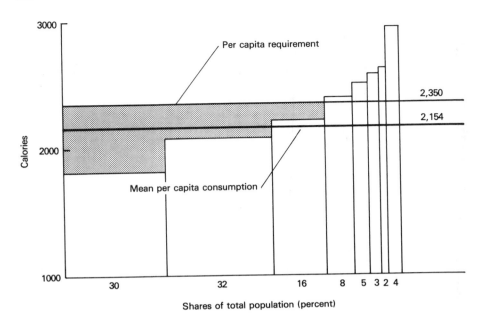

Figure 5.1 Distribution of calorie consumption in Africa.
Source: Shahla Shapouri, Arthur J. Dommen, and Stacey Rosen, *Food Aid and the African Food Crisis*, Foreign Agric. Econ. Rep. 221 (Washington, D.C.: ERS, USDA, June 1986), p. 12.

this region, severe food shortage problems are encountered about once every three years. A calorie gap has existed in the region nearly every year since the 1950s.[16] In 1981–1983 the gap was as wide as 20 percent of food needs and has frequently exceeded 10 percent. The African problem involves complexities of regular droughts, civil wars, rat and insect infestations, poverty conditions, and internal food distribution problems. In addition, agricultural policies frequently depress farm prices, which, of course, discourage production. USDA, in a comprehensive study of the African food crises, concluded: "Nine of 11 low- and medium-income sub-Saharan African countries studied by the authors may face even greater problems feeding their populations if recent trends continue."[17]

- An *income gap* exists when, due to poverty conditions, significant population segments are unable to purchase food through commercial channels. Food aid becomes essential for these population seg-

[16]Lester R. Brown and Edward C. Wolf, *Reversing Africa's Decline*, Worldwatch Paper 65 (Washington, D.C.: Worldwatch Institute, June 1965), p. 9.

[17]Shahla Shapouri, Arthur J. Dommen, and Stacey Rosen, *Food Aid and the African Food Crisis*, Foreign Agric. Econ. Rep. 221 (Washington, D.C.: ERS, USDA, June 1986), p. v.

ments. Figure 5.1 presents the dimensions of the distribution problem graphically for Africa. Only 22 percent of the population consumed more than the per capita nutritional requirement of 2350 calories. Thirty percent of the population averaged 520 calories under the requirement. Because of uneven incomes, the distribution problem has the important dimension of getting the food to those who need it the most in the right amounts. This is a major problem in any food-aid program.

- *Temporary shortages* of food arise almost every year somewhere in the world. Most often they are due to weather, although wars have also been a factor in temporary shortages. The major problem encountered in dealing with temporary shortages is the development of the distribution system itself. Regular commercial channels which are designed for commercial sales and not food aid may be disrupted.

FACTORS AFFECTING THE SUPPLY–DEMAND BALANCE

Economics plays a major role in influencing the supply–demand balance for food. Throughout the world there is increasing realization that economic incentives are critical to food production as well as in rationing the available food supply. Even the Soviet Union and China have placed increased emphasis on using price as an allocator in production and consumption decisions.

The Demand for Food

The total demand for food is determined by price, population, and income. Demand for individual foods is also influenced by tastes and preferences. The demand schedule indicates the relationship between price and the quantity demanded. Population, income, tastes, and preferences are demand shifters.

Price and demand.   The price elasticity of demand for food in the aggregate is **highly inelastic**. *This means that an increase in price will result in a proportionately smaller reduction in demand.* The elasticity of demand for food worldwide is generally considered to be in the range −0.1 to −0.2.[18] That is, a 10 percent increase in price results in only a 1.0 to 2.0 percent reduction in demand.

[18]Anthony Rojko et al., *Alternative Futures for World Food in 1985*, Vol. 1: *World GOL Model Analytical Report*, Foreign Agric. Econ. Rep. 146 (Washington, D.C.: ESCS, USDA, April 1978), pp. 100–101.

It is important to recognize that the aggregate world elasticity of demand for food is more inelastic than the demand for food from a specific exporting country such as the United States.[19] For an individual country, the demand for food is a combination of the domestic and the foreign demand. The foreign demand is more elastic than either the domestic or world demand because importing countries have alternative sources of supply from several exporting countries. When a country raises its support price for a commodity, it must also be wary if other countries will follow. In addition, import demand elasticities vary from commodity to commodity and from country to country.[20] Yet substantial evidence exists that both domestic and export elasticity for major grains are inelastic. Davidson and Arnade found the export demand for U.S. corn and soybeans to be − 0.62 and − 0.30[21] respectively, with all individual countries having an inelastic demand.

It is also important to recognize that demand elasticity differs among commodities. Once again, the *demand for an individual commodity is generally more elastic because there are more substitutes for it than for all food*. At the farm level in the United States, the price elasticity of demand ranges from about − 0.1 for basic foods such as potatoes to − 0.6 for chicken.[22]

It will be seen in the next chapter that an understanding of the concept of elasticity of demand is important for evaluating policy initiatives that raise the price of a particular grain or grains internationally. For example, with supply held constant, a cartel such as OPEC for wheat-exporting countries will raise producer returns only if the world demand for wheat is inelastic, which it is. Further, the more inelastic the demand is, the greater the producer benefits. In the longer run, however, these producer benefits would be dissipated if producers respond to the higher prices by increasing production. This is exactly what has happened to OPEC in oil.

Population and demand.   Changes in regional and world population constitute the fundamental and most important force likely to increase the world demand for food as well as U.S. export demand. Rapid

[19]Maury E. Bredahl, William H. Myers, and Keith J. Collins, "The Elasticity of Foreign Demand for U.S. Agricultural Products: The Importance of the Price Transmission Elasticity," *Am. J. Agric. Econ.* (February 1979), pp. 58–63.

[20]Terry Roe, Mathew Shane, and De Huu Vo, *Price Responsiveness of World Grain Markets*, Tech. Res. Bull. 1720 (Washington, D.C.: ERS, USDA, June 1986).

[21]C. W. Davidson and C. A. Arnade, *Export Demand for U.S. Corn and Soybeans* (Washington, D.C.: ERS, USDA, August 1987).

[22]P. S. George and G. A. King, *Consumer Demand for Food Commodities in the United States with Projections for 1980*, Giannini Foundation Monogr. 26 (Davis, Calif.: University of California, March 1971), p. 66.

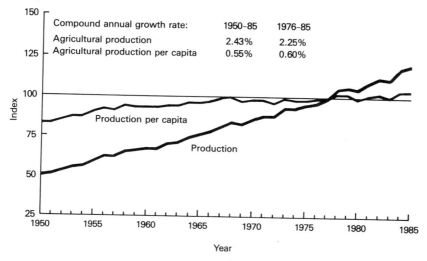

Figure 5.2   World: index of production (1976–1978 = 100).
Source: Economic Research Service, *World Indices of Agricultural and Food Production, 1976–85*, Stat. Bull. 744 (Washington, D.C.: USDA, July 1986), p. 7.

population growth means larger potential markets for exports; but for countries that do not have the resources to buy, it means diminished growth in living standards and dampened demand relative to the potential.

World food production has been increasing at a rate only slightly faster than population (Fig. 5.2). From 1970 to 1985 world population increased by 14 percent while world production increased by 19 percent.[23]

One of the factors aiding increased food production per capita is the decline in the rate of population growth.[24] With the exception of sub-Saharan Africa, every region in the world where the 1970s population growth rates exceeded 1 percent is experiencing declining rates today. Expectations are for much slower growth by the end of the century (Table 5.1). Yet by 2000, there are expected to be 6.2 billion people in the world and by 2200 as many as 8 billion (Fig.5.3).

Population growth creates food supply, space, economic, and political pressures. Over the past two decades, an average of 87 million people have been added annually to the world's population—about one-third of the U.S. population. Population growth is not evenly distributed. Over 90 percent of the increase in population over the next two decades will be in

[23]Economic Research Service, *World Indices of Agricultural and Food Production, 1976–85*, Stat. Bull. 744 (Washington, D.C.: USDA, July 1986), pp. 10, 14.

[24]This section draws heavily on the work of Kenneth R. Farrell, Fred H. Sanderson, and Trang T. Vo, "Feeding a Hungry World," in *Resources* (Washington, D.C.: Resources for the Future, Spring 1984), pp. 1–20.

TABLE 5.1 Historic and Projected Population, Absolute Change, and Growth Rate

Region	1980 Population (millions)	1980–1990 Absolute Change (millions)	1980–1990 Rate of Growth (%)	1990–1995 Absolute Change (millions)	1990–1995 Rate of Growth (%)	1995–2000 Absolute Change (millions)	1995–2000 Rate of Growth (%)	2000 Population (millions)
North Africa–Middle East	243	70	2.56	35	2.12	40	2.22	388
Sub-Saharan Africa	387	141	3.16	95	3.37	105	3.15	727
European Community	270	7	0.26	5	0.34	4	0.30	286
Other Western Europe	79	5	0.62	2	0.54	2	0.46	88
USSR	265	26	0.94	11	0.73	10	0.63	312
Eastern Europe	135	9	0.65	4	0.56	4	0.54	152
South Asia	874	216	2.24	112	1.97	112	1.80	1315
East Asia	459	87	1.75	45	1.59	45	1.47	635
Asia, centrally planned economies	1075	161	1.41	82	1.30	80	1.18	1398
Oceania	23	3	1.23	1	1.10	1	0.99	28
Latin America	359	90	2.26	48	2.03	47	1.83	544
North Africa	252	20	0.73	8	0.60	7	0.50	287
Total world	4421	835	1.75	448	1.65	457	1.55	6160

Source: Kenneth R. Farrell, Fred H. Sanderson, and Trang T. Vo, "Feeding a Hungry World," in *Resources* (Washington, D.C.: Resources for the Future, Spring 1984), p. 4.

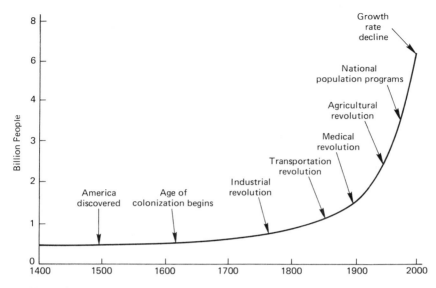

Figure 5.3   World population growth, 1400–2000.
Source: Adapted from L. Jay Atkinson, *World Population Growth*, Foreign Agric. Econ.
Rep. 126 (Washington, D.C.: ERS, USDA, February 1977), p. 3.

the world's six least developed regions. By the year 2000, only 19 percent
of the world's people will live in the six most developed regions. An economic, policy, and distribution system will need to exist that can get food
from where it is produced to where it is consumed.

Income and demand.   Demand for food does not increase strictly
in proportion to population. Income is also a driving force behind demand.
This is particularly the case in developing countries where increases in
demand depend as much or more on the ability to buy as on population
growth. **Effective demand** *exists only when the ability to buy exists.* Such
effective demand corresponds most directly with increases in income.
Without increases in income, demand becomes increasingly dependent on
government food assistance programs as population increases. Without
effective demand in terms of either income growth or government assistance, potential demand dictated by population growth goes unsatisfied.

The diet in much of the world today is grain-based. Increasing incomes enable people to buy more food and different types of food. As incomes increase, more grain is consumed initially. Further income increases lead to shifts in consumption from grain to fruits, vegetables,
meat, milk, and eggs. *The* **income elasticity** *of demand measures the
percent change in demand associated with a 1 percent change in real income.* The income elasticity differs among countries and falls fairly stead-

THE PROCESS
OF POPULATION GROWTH

One of the major determinants of population growth is the relative magnitude of birth rates and death rates. The most rapid population growth occurs when the death rate declines while the birth rate remains relatively high. For example, it is not unusual for the death rate to decline from 30 per thousand to 10 per thousand, while the birth rate remains at a high 45 per thousand. Under these conditions population grows by over 3.5 percent per year, doubling in 20 years.

Fortunately, this decline in the death rate is normally followed by a drop in birth rate from 45 per thousand to 20 per thousand or even lower. The lag separating the drop in the death rate from the drop in birth rate is crucial in determining the rate and magnitude of population growth. For example, with a lag of 45 years, population can multiply fourfold; with a lag of 75 years, it can multiply ninefold.

The relationship between the decline in the death rate and the subsequent decline in the birth rate is referred to as population transition. In the early stages of the transition there is an increased proportion of younger age groups. This is the stage the less developed countries are in now. After the transition is completed, there is a larger proportion of older people. This is the stage of population growth that the United States and Europe are in currently.

Based largely on Nathan Keyfitz, "Population," in *Academic American Encyclopedia*, Vol. 15 (Princeton, N.J.: Arete Publishing Co., Inc., 1980), pp. 433–434.

ily as an economy develops. Thus in the very early stages of development, the income elasticity may be as high as 0.7 to 0.9. This means that a 10 percent increase in real income will result in a 7 to 9 percent increase in demand for food. On the other hand, in developed countries such as the United States, the income elasticity may be as low as 0.1 to 0.5.[25] This decline in income elasticity occurs because as income increases, people's need for additional food declines. A large share of the increased food expenditures also goes to services as income rises.

Shifts in consumption patterns as incomes increase suggest considerable variation in the income elasticity among commodities and among countries at different stages of development. For example, while the in-

[25]Timothy Josling, "World Food Production, Consumption and Trade," in *Food and Agricultural Policy in the 1980's* (Washington, D.C.: American Enterprise Institute, 1981), p. 95; *World Population*, p. 94; and Michael K. Wohlgenant, "Conceptual and Functional Farm Issues in Estimating Demand Elasticities for Food," *Am. J. Agric. Econ.* (May 1984), pp. 211–215.

TABLE 5.2 Income as Measured by GNP per Capita by Country Groups
in Terms of Stage of Economic Development and Population,1985[a]

	GNP/Capita (dollars)	Population (millions)	Percent of Population
Low-income economies	270	2,439.4	55.0
Lower-middle-income economies	820	674.6	15.2
Upper-middle-income economies	1,850	567.4	12.8
High-income oil exporters	9,800	18.4	00.4
Industrial market economies	11,810	737.3	16.6
			100.0

Source: World Bank, *World Development Report 1987* (Washington, D.C.: Oxford University Press, June 1987), pp. 202–203.

[a]USSR and related Communist Bloc countries not included.

come elasticity is 0.15 for U.S. corn exports, it is 0.75 for soybeans.[26] Within the United States, income elasticities vary from 1.1 for fruit juice to −0.4 for rice.[27] The concept of a negative income elasticity for a particular food is not unusual. For example, declines in per capita rice consumption have been experienced in rapidly developing countries such as Taiwan and Japan. Thus, as incomes increase, demand for some food groups increases and for others may actually decrease. Foods that normally increase in demand include meats, fresh fruits, and vegetables. In a developing country, cereal consumption may decline with income increases while chicken and pork consumption is rising.

Income and debt are two constraining forces on the exercise of effective demand.

• Income as measured by GNP per capita ranges from $270 in the lowest-income developing countries, which comprise 55 percent of the world population, to $11,810 per capita in the industrial market economies (Table 5.2). Raising food demand is very much dependent on encouraging economic development in the lowest-income countries.

• High developing-country debt became a major problem in the 1980s. High debt requires that capital which might otherwise be used for economic development and imports, instead be used to pay interest expenses. From 1980 to 1986 developing-country debt increased from $429 billion to $753 billion while the ratio of debt to GNP increased from 21 percent to 35 percent. Reducing developing-country debt to tolerable levels is one of the major challenges to the interna-

[26]Davidson and Arnade, *Export Demand*, pp. 13, 15.

[27]Kuo S. Huang, *U.S. Demand for Food: A Complete System of Price and Income Effects*, Tech. Bull. 1714 (Washington, D.C.: ERS, USDA, December 1985).

tional monetary system and is essential in making progress in solving the world food problem.

The income and debt problems facing developing countries are complex. They will not be solved by any individual country. They will not be solved by countries closing their doors to imports from developing countries. They will not be solved by cutting off agricultural development assistance to these countries. Since developing countries are the fastest-growing market for U.S. farm products and the largest potential market, cooperation in solving their income and debt problems is essential.

The Supply of Food

In the 1970s and the early 1980s, there was great concern that the world's farmers would not be able to keep up with expanding world demand. The legacy of Malthus once again loomed as world food conferences were held and resolutions were debated in legislative halls that would give the poor the "right" to a limited food supply. One person who was less concerned about the potential for long-run food deficits was Don Paarlberg (see the box). He professed confidence that when supplies were short, the market system would create the incentives to expand productive capacity consistent with needs. He aptly warned against either a scarcity syndrome or a surplus syndrome.

The supply of food is dependent, to a point, on the price farmers receive for the commodities produced. At some point, the physical resource constraints come into play—the quantity of land suitable for agriculture, the quantity of water available, and the availability of resources used to produce critical inputs such as chemical fertilizers and pesticides. Beyond these physical limits, further increases in production depend on technological advances, such as improved varieties and alternative methods of pest control.

Price and supply.   In many discussions of world food problems, price is often excluded as a factor influencing the level of production and the world's ability to meet expanding demand. However, many illustrations exist of cases where governments have overtly suppressed rewards to producers for food production. This is done to hold consumer prices down to politically acceptable levels. Such price suppression reduces incentives for domestic production.

Peterson found that the average price received by farmers in the eight highest-priced countries was 4.7 times greater than the average price received by farmers in the eight lowest-priced countries.[28] One of the

---

[28] Willis L. Peterson, "International Farm Prices and the Social Cost of Cheap Food Policies," *Am. J. Agric. Econ.* (February 1979), pp. 12–21.

SURPLUS/SCARCITY
SYNDROMES

There is a new mindset about farm and food matters. For half a century the conventional wisdom was that the farm problem was one of surplus. In the 1970s the perception was that the problem was one of shortage.

The focus of the **surplus syndrome** was that we had excess agricultural capacity and that resources in agriculture could not be voluntarily withdrawn. The visible confirmation of the surplus scenario was the pileup of commodities in government hands and the idling of cropland.

The focus of the **scarcity syndrome** was that agricultural efficiency was tapering off and the land available for agricultural purposes was being lost to urbanization and erosion. The visible confirmation of the scarcity syndrome was low world carry-over stocks, increasing world population, and farm prices four times the 1967 level.

The surplus and the scarcity syndromes seem totally different. But in one respect they are strikingly similar. Both largely ignore the effect of price on the quantity supplied and demanded.

The surplus mindset convinced us that prices were low because of a surplus. Protecting farmers from low prices became the central objective. So we ought to increase prices. With prices supported above market-clearing levels, production was stimulated and demand reduced. The result was that products piled up in government hands. The prospect of surplus, therefore, became self-fulfilling. If a cheap food policy were strongly used and long continued, the result would be to stimulate demand and inhibit production, so that the scarcity mindset would become self-fulfilling. Those who predicted the shortage could then congratulate themselves on their foresight, just as those who, half a century earlier, diagnosed that problem as one of surplus.

The best way to avoid these dangers is to allow the market to price our products, with help from some techniques which improve the functioning of the market. Such a system, coupled with responsible management of money and credit, will encourage the volume of agricultural output suited to our resources and our needs, avoiding both surplus and shortage.

Don Paarlberg, "The Scarcity Syndrome," *Am. J. Agric. Econ.*, vol. 64 (February 1982), pp. 110–114.

best contemporary examples of the impact of government policies that suppress farm prices is the USSR, where producer rewards from production on collective farms are limited by government. But production has flourished outside the collective system on family plots where products are sold in the open market. In fact, as much as 25 percent of Soviet farm production comes from these family plots, which comprise only 3 percent of the farmland.[29] The Soviet government is now implementing a program to increase rewards for production on collective and state-owned farms. A new Soviet law authorizes sales through nonstate markets. In addition, new rules tie pay for all employees in the agro-industrial complex to production results.[30] Each of these changes is designed to provide the production incentives that price provides in market economies.

The **elasticity of supply** *indicates the percentage change in the quantity supplied resulting from a 1 percent change in the price of the commodity.* The supply elasticity changes substantially as the time horizon changes. For example, once a crop is planted, the farmer's ability to change the quantity produced in response to price changes is extremely limited. The supply thus becomes perfectly inelastic—that is, supply is essentially fixed regardless of price. Even over a period of one or two years, the supply elasticity is generally in the range 0.1 to 0.3. Thus a 10 percent increase in price received by farmers leads to a 1 to 3 percent increase in production. In the longer run, however, if incentives exist and time allows for bringing new land and technology into production, the supply elasticity becomes much more elastic and may exceed 1.0.[31]

As in the case of demand, it is important to recognize that supply is more elastic for an individual commodity such as wheat than for all commodities combined. Land can be shifted from production of one commodity to another. Also, the long-run supply is considerably more elastic in a country where land is still available for agricultural development than where all or nearly all the land is being farmed. In the latter case, the only option for increased production is more intensive farming of existing land.

Land and supply.   Since the time of Malthus, there has been a periodic concern with running out of agricultural land. The disappearance of prime farmland and depletion of the soil have become important contemporary policy issues in many countries of the world. During the 1970s, area expansion contributed 25 percent to the production increase, while in the 1980s, land is expected to contribute only 15 percent.[32] The growth rate for land in the 1970s of 0.65 percent annually is expected to fall to 0.27 percent between 1980 and 2000. Most of the additional land will be in Asia, sub-Saharan Africa, and Latin America.

Soil erosion is a continuing problem that if not controlled could become a serious threat to the productivity of the supply of land. Yet there

[29]Shawn Tully, "Mapping the Second Economy," *Fortune*, June 29, 1981, p. 40.

[30]Economic Research Service, *USSR Situation and Outlook Report* (Washington, D.C.: USDA, May 1987), p. 7.

[31]Peterson, "Social Cost of Cheap Food Policies."

[32]Farrell et al., "Feeding a Hungry World," p. 8.

is evidence that the erosion threat is not increasing and may be decreasing.[33]

Water and supply.   Water plays a key role in developing new agricultural land and in intensifying cropping patterns. Although irrigated land comprises only 13 percent of the world's total arable area, irrigation is by far the largest single use of water in the world.[34] In the future, irrigation will continue to be important in expanding production and in reducing year-to-year production variability.

Past studies have viewed water as an important factor limiting crop production.[35] Johnson notes that this conclusion is overdrawn and assumes that governments will not be responsive to increased irrigation needs. For example, only a small proportion of Africa's irrigation potential has been realized,[36] but substantial investments are currently being made in improved irrigation systems.[37] One of the principal economic problems is that water is underpriced. Under these circumstances, waste is inevitable. This policy problem is discussed further in Chapter 14.

Technology and supply.   During the 1970s, three-fourths of the increase in world food production came from increases in yield. Some of this increase was due to irrigation, but most was the result of improved farming practices associated with the use of purchased imports such as fertilizer, pest control, and higher-yielding varieties. From 1970 to 1984, U.S. farm output increased by one-third with no change in the quantity of inputs. All of the increase was due to the quality of inputs embodied in technological change.[38]

Substantial disagreement exists over what yield increases to expect in the future. Current hype over biotechnology might lead one to expect increases in the rate of technological advance. Yet a comprehensive study of the impact of technological change to the year 2000 only showed spectacular increases in yields for milk output per cow.[39] Most studies look for

[33]T. W. Schultz, "The Dynamics of Soil Erosion in the United States," University of Chicago Pap. 82–9 (Chicago: Office of Agricultural Economics Research, March 1982).

[34]John J. Boland et al., "Water Projections," in *The Global 2000 Report to the President: The Technical Report*, Vol. 2 (Washington, D.C.: Council of Environment Quality and Department of State, 1981), pp. 150, 158.

[35]Johnson, "The World Food Situation," p. 27.

[36]Shapouri et al., *Food Aid*, p. 3.

[37]Economic Research Service, *Sub-Saharan Africa Situation and Outlook Report* (Washington, D.C.: USDA, July 1986), p. 12.

[38]Economic Research Service, *Farm Income Data* (Washington, D.C.: USDA, 1986), p. 31.

[39]Michael J. Phillips and Yao-chi Lu, "Impact of Emerging Technologies on Food and Agricultural Productive Capacity," *Amer. J. Agric. Econ.* (December 1986), pp. 448–453.

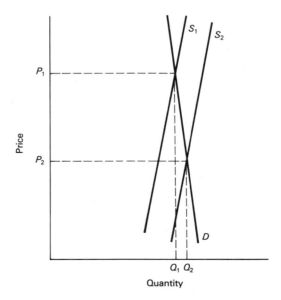

Figure 5.4 Small change in world supply results in larger price change.

reductions in the rate of increase in yields over the next two decades. For example, Resources for Future predicts a decline in the rate of increase in yields from 1.94 percent annually in the 1970s to 1.56 percent from 1980 to 2000.[40] Yet Tweeten finds evidence of a constant rate of increase in output at 1.87 percent annually.[41]

THE SUPPLY–DEMAND BALANCE

It will be recalled that the supply and demand schedules for food are both highly inelastic (Fig. 5.4). It is also evident from Fig. 5.2 that there is substantial year-to-year variation in production. This variation which results in even larger changes in carryover stocks is a major determinant of the price level. *With both an inelastic demand and supply, any change in the world's supply–demand balance results in a proportionately larger change in price.* Thus, for the world as a whole, a 1 percent reduction in supply coupled with a 2 percent expansion in demand can result in a 15 to 20 percent increase in price. As a result of such a price increase, farmers' income increases sharply. The opposite effect, of course, occurs when

[40]Farrell et al., "Feeding a Hungry World," p. 8.

[41]Luther Tweeten, "Excess Supply: Permanent or Transitory?" *Farm Policy Perspectives: Setting the Stage for the 1985 Farm Bill*, Senate Print 98–174 (Washington, D.C.: Committee on Agriculture, Nutrition, and Forestry, U.S. Senate, April 1984), pp. 29–43.

highly favorable weather results in abundant production and sharp price declines.

Year-to-year changes in the supply–demand balance result largely from natural causes such as pests and weather. For example, the corn blight sharply reduced U.S. production, particularly in 1970. Unfavorable weather existed in a number of countries in 1972 and again in 1979. These production declines had worldwide effects on prices in both developed and developing countries. Changes in production levels contributed to large worldwide food price increases. Other factors contributing to the rise in prices included increased reliance on imports by food-deficit countries, a decline in the value of the dollar, and related policy changes.

In the long run, the ability to feed the world's population adequately is determined by the extent to which food production keeps pace with or exceeds consumption. Studies generally conclude that the 1970s were an aberration in the supply–demand balance. They conclude that a relatively slim margin of excess supplies will lead to further declines in the real price of food. This will continue to put pressure on the world's farmers to adjust.

CAN WE BE SATISFIED?

The predictions of a margin of surpluses in production through the year 2000 are based on the presumption that little will be done to eliminate the calorie gap that exists in the world. If this is what happens, the pot of world political and economic stability will continue to boil. Is this a satisfactory situation?

ADDITIONAL READINGS

1. The Economic Research Service publication by Shahla Shapouri, Arthur J. Dommen, and Stacey Rosen, *Food Aid and the African Food Crisis*, Foreign Agric. Econ. Rep. 221 (Washington, D.C.: ERS, USDA, June 1986).
2. Economic Research Service, *World Agriculture Situation and Outlook* reports do an excellent job of keeping up with current supply–demand balance and related country policy issues. It is published quarterly. In addition, ERS regularly issues country reports of current interest.
3. *The Role of Markets in the World Economy*, D. Gale Johnson and G. Edward Schuh, eds., (Boulder, Colo.: Westview Press, Inc., 1983) provides a series of very informative articles on the world food problem.
4. The Office of Technology Assessment Study, *Technology, Public Policy, and the Changing Structure of Agriculture* (Washington, D.C.: U.S. Senate, March 1986) provides a comprehensive treatment of the potential impact of technological change on the agricultural economy.

Chapter 6

The Role of Trade

*Free trade, one of the greatest
blessings which a government can
confer on a people, is in almost
every country unpopular.*

Thomas Babington

U.S. agriculture has become dependent on world markets for its products; the crops from two out of every five cultivated acres are exported. Similarly, many countries of the world have become dependent on American farmers as a principal source of their food supply.

But the growth in agricultural trade has not been a one-way street. American consumers depend on substantial imports of agricultural products from other countries, such as coffee from Brazil. Brazil, in turn, uses a portion of the revenues from coffee to buy wheat from the United States.

Because of increased trade, agricultural economies of the world have become much more interdependent in recent years. This interdependence in trade is not limited to agriculture. Japan uses a portion of its export earnings from automobiles to buy agricultural products from the United States. The United States uses export earnings from grain to help pay for imported oil from the OPEC countries.

The purpose of this chapter is to explain why trade is beneficial to society and, at the same time, why barriers to trade emerge. The characteristics and economic impacts of various types of barriers to trade are also discussed.

TRADE-OFFS IN TRADE

Trade among nations is one of the keys to expanding food supplies and reducing food cost. However, emotions frequently run high when trade issues are discussed. U.S. milk producers fret about the prospects of increased imports of cheese and casein. Feed grain producers want to be able to export more corn, grain sorghum, and soybeans. Ironically, they join beef producers in favoring restrictions on beef imports. Such imports potentially reduce the domestic demand for feed grains and soybeans. The same producers then express concern about restricting imports of Japanese automobiles for fear that Japan will retaliate by curtailing imports of U.S. grain.

Trade restrictions may make sense from the viewpoint of an individual adversely affected by imports. But society as a whole pays the cost of each and every trade restriction in terms of quantity, quality, and price of the goods received—an illustration of the fallacy of composition. The proponents of trade are neither as visible nor as effective as the opponents of trade. There are a number of reasons for this:

- The cost of trade restrictions is hidden in the price of goods, whereas those who lose jobs as a result of imports are visible and get media attention.
- Exports have a price increasing effect; thus the net benefits of trade expansion to the consumer are not as apparent.
- Consumers have been an effective lobbying force only periodically. In addition, a strong free-trade stance may conflict with the goals of organized labor—a supporter of the consumer movement.
- Free-trade concerns have sometimes been overridden by foreign policy concerns, such as Soviet aggression.

WHY TRADE

There are both economic and practical reasons for trade. From a practical perspective, without trade the world could not feed itself nearly as well as it does currently. The distribution of food production in the world is nowhere parallel to the distribution of population (Fig. 6.1). Even though there are vast differences in the quantity and quality of food consumed in different countries, variation in production alone, due to weather, makes trade essential.

From an economic perspective, there are advantages in countries producing those products for which they are best qualified in terms of

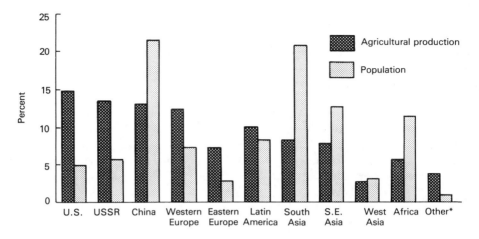

*Includes Australia, Canada, and New Zealand.

Figure 6.1 Share of world agricultural production and population by region, 1983–1985 average.
Source: Economic Research Service, *World Indices of Agricultural and Food Production, 1976–85*, Stat. Bull. 744 (Washington, D.C.: USDA, July 1986), p. 5.

their resource endowment, exporting their excess production, and buying other products which other countries are best qualified to produce. As a result, total world output is increased and resources are allocated to their best use.

Despite reduced agricultural world trade volume in the early 1980s, the longer run trend has been toward increased trade (Fig. 6.2). As might

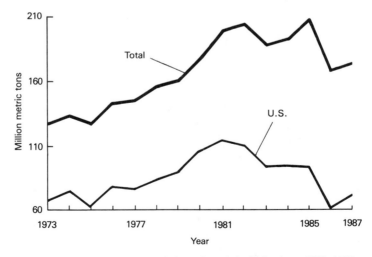

Figure 6.2 Volume of world trade in grain and the U.S. share, 1973–1987.

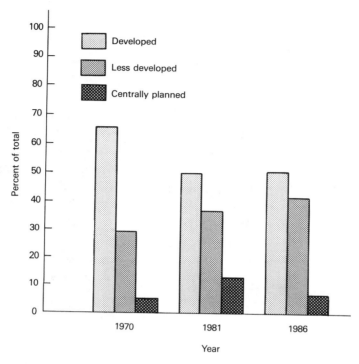

Figure 6.3 U.S. agricultural exports by region, 1970, 1981, and 1986.

be expected from previous discussion of the world food situation and income elasticities, trade with developing countries has increased more than trade with developed countries (Fig. 6.3).

The major products exported by the United States include grains and oilseeds (Fig. 6.4). Significant exports, however, also exist of livestock products, fruits, vegetables, nuts, and cotton. The United States generally exports about half of its wheat, rice, soybean, and cotton production. It exports about 25 percent of its coarse grain production. The U.S. share of the world market is about 60 percent in coarse grains, 50 percent in soybeans, 40 percent in wheat, but only 25 percent in rice and cotton.[1]

Specialization

The benefits of trade arise from advantages of specialization. Production conditions vary from country to country. By each country specializing in producing those commodities in which it has the greatest advan-

[1]*Outlook '88 Charts: 64th Annual Outlook Conference* (Washington, D.C.: ERS, USDA, January 1988), pp. 1–3.

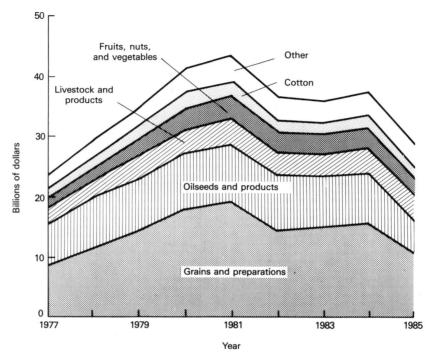

Figure 6.4 Value of U.S. agricultural exports by commodity.
Source: Extension Service, *1986 Agricultural Chartbook*, Agric. Handbook 663 (Washington, D.C.: USDA, November 1987), p. 77.

tage or the least disadvantage, the largest production at the lowest cost results.

It is, for example, widely believed that the United States has a comparative advantage in the production of feed grains and soybeans. Japan, on the other hand, has a comparative advantage in the production of automobiles. It is logical then that Japan would be the United States' largest customer for grains, while the United States is Japan's largest market for automobiles. Both countries are, as a whole, better off because of this trade—even though U.S. automakers and their employees protest Japanese auto imports and Japanese rice farmers protest U.S. grain imports. Social welfare is improved because with a given income level, more automobiles and grain can be enjoyed by more Japanese and American people with trade than in its absence.

The advantages of specialization, although intuitively obvious, lie in two economic principles: absolute advantage and comparative advantage.

Absolute advantage. *A country is said to have an* **absolute advantage** *when it can produce a product at less cost than another country.* Suppose, for example, that the European Economic Community (EC)[2] and the United States have options of growing wheat and corn on 10 million acres of land each. In the United States the yield is 25 bushels per acre of wheat and 130 bushels per acre of corn. In the EC the yield is 20 bushels per acre of wheat and 60 bushels per acre of corn (Table 6.1). If the cost per acre is the same in both the United States and the EC, the United States is said to have an absolute advantage in the production of both wheat and corn.

Suppose that the United States requires a minimum 125 million bushels of wheat and 650 million bushels of corn from the 10 million acres of land. The EC requires a minimum of 100 million bushels of wheat and 300 million bushels of corn. This can be accomplished in each country by using half the land for wheat and half the land for corn (Table 6.1). Total U.S. and EC production of wheat and corn under this self-sufficiency strategy is 1175 million bushels (225 + 950).

Comparative advantage. *The principle of* **comparative advantage** *recognizes that total output can be increased when each country specializes in producing that commodity for which it has the greatest advantage or the least disadvantage.* In the case of Table 6.1, even though the United States has an absolute advantage in the production of both wheat and corn, output can be increased by specialization. This can be seen in Table 6.2. The minimum wheat requirement of 225 million bushels is attained by the EC devoting all its land to wheat and the United States producing wheat on 1 million acres. The remaining 9 million acres of land in the United States are devoted to corn, with a total corn production of 1170 million bushels. The resulting total U.S. and EC production of wheat and corn is 1395 million bushels, 220 million more bushels than without specialization.

Of course, to achieve this higher level of production, it is necessary to specialize and trade. The EC must buy a minimum 300 million bushels of corn from the United States, and the United States must buy a minimum 100 million bushels of wheat from the EC. They both may buy even more because with greater total supplies the price will be lower even after transportation costs are considered.

[2]The EC, frequently also referred to as the Common Market, comprises the 12 countries that have developed a Common Agricultural Policy (CAP), which includes both internal price supports and protectionist trade policies. The 12 EC countries are France, West Germany, Italy, the United Kingdom, the Netherlands, Belgium, Luxembourg, Ireland, Denmark, Greece, Spain, and Portugal.

TABLE 6.1 Production in the EC and the United States from 10 Million Acres of Land Assuming That Each Is Self-Sufficient

Country	Wheat			Corn		
	Yield/Acre (bushels)	Acres (millions)	Production (millions of bushels)	Yield/Acre (bushels)	Acres (millions)	Production (millions of bushels)
United States	25	5	125	130	5	650
EC	20	5	100	60	5	300
Total		10	225		10	950

TABLE 6.2 Production in the EC and the United States from 10 Million Acres of Land Assuming Specialization and Trade

Country	Wheat			Corn		
	Yield/Acre (bushels)	Acres (millions)	Production (millions of bushels)	Yield/Acre (bushels)	Acres (millions)	Production (millions of bushels)
United States	25	1	25	130	9	1170
EC	20	10	200	60	0	0
Total		11	225		9	1170

Differences in costs of production exist among countries because the inherent endowment of natural resources (land, water, and minerals) and other productive resources (labor, capital, management, research, and technology) vary from country to country and because the production of different commodities requires different resources in varying proportions. The advantage of the American farmer in the production of feed grains and soybeans results largely from the favorable soil and climate conditions of the Corn Belt. The EC farmer specializes in producing wheat and barley. Canada produces wheat, barley, and rapeseed. New Zealand is the lowest-cost producer of milk in the world because of soil and climatic conditions that are favorable to roughage, the contentment of cows, and milk production. Over time, a country's resources, and for that matter, the world's resources, are more efficiently and fully utilized when allocated among commodities and industries according to the principle of comparative advantage. This involves specialization and trade.

THE THEORY OF TRADE

Trade occurs because governments, businesses, farmers, and consumers, as buyers or sellers, realize benefits from trade. Trade is beneficial when it allows buyers access to goods that would otherwise be either unavailable or more expensive. *Trade will occur to the point where the costs of goods (including transportation and transaction costs) are equal among countries.*

All people do not benefit equally from trade. Consumers in exporting countries generally pay a higher price for a commodity being exported than they would if it were not being exported. Producers, of course, receive higher prices. On the other hand, consumers in importing countries pay a lower price for the commodity than they would if it were not being imported. Similarly, the importing country's producers receive a lower price.

These complexities are best visualized in a two-country trade model for a single product, in this case wheat.[3] The model is based on conventional economic logic and highlights the interdependence among the agricultural sectors of countries linked by trade. For simplicity, the model consists of two world or "country" segments: exporting countries and importing countries. The model considers only one commodity, wheat. It

[3]The theoretical analysis draws heavily on the following excellent works: Phillip L. Paarlberg, Allan J. Webb, Arthur Morey, and Jerry Sharples, *Impacts of Policy on U.S. Agricultural Trade* (Washington, D.C.: ERS, USDA, December 1984); and Bob F. Jones and Robert L. Thompson, "Interrelationships of Domestic Agricultural Policies and Trade Policies," *Speaking of Trade: Its Effects on Agriculture*, Agric. Ext. Spec. Rep. 72 (St. Paul, Minn.: University of Minnesota, November 1978), pp. 37–57.

is assumed that everything is measured in the same currency and that there are no transportation costs.

Assume initially that there is no trade, a closed economy condition called **autarky**. Prices are determined independently for importing countries and exporting countries utilizing their respective supply and demand curves (Fig. 6.5). The resulting equilibrium is price P_e and quantity Q_e for the "exporting" countries and price P_i and quantity Q_i for the "importing" countries.

Trade is introduced into the two-country trade model by providing for a world market in the middle graph of Fig. 6.6. The quantity available for trade by exporting countries, referred to as excess supply (ES) is the horizontal distance between the supply and demand curve above price P_e. At price P_e, supply equals demand in the exporting country and there is nothing available for export. This provides the intercept in the world market graph.

At prices below P_i, the importing countries have an excess demand (ED) of the difference between their demand and supply schedules. The world market excess demand curve ED, therefore, begins at P_i and slopes downward and to the right.

In the world market graph, at price P_w excess supply and excess demand are identical. Note that in the exporting countries' graph the quantity exported $(S_e - D_e)$ is identical to the quantity imported in the importing countries' graph $(D_i - S_i)$.

Now assess the benefits of trade. The quantity and price received by the exporting countries are increased from the level they would have been under autarky. The quantity consumed by the importing countries is increased at the world price. World production and consumption are increased by trade. But everybody is not better off. Exporting country consumers pay a higher price and importing country producers received a lower price.

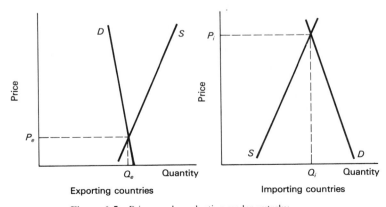

Figure 6.5 Prices and production under autarky.

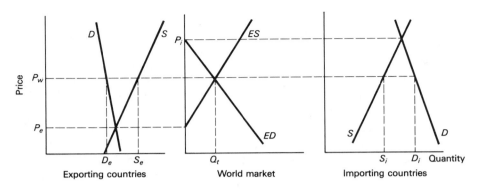

Figure 6.6   Price, production, and quantity traded under free trade.

Barriers to Trade

Despite the benefits of trade, interest groups in both exporting and importing countries may object to trade taking place. Protectionist policies emerge when any group of producers or consumers attains enough political strength to secure barriers to trade that will insulate the group(s) from international competition.

From a national policy perspective a variety of reasons are often advanced to rationalize the pursuit of protectionist policies. The following are leading ones.[4]

- *Protection against painful economic adjustment* probably constitutes the most widely used reason for protectionism. Over time, the comparative advantage of industries changes among countries. As this occurs, substantial economic pressure is placed on producers in the less efficient country. When faced with this situation, the adversely affected industry will tend to first seek protection from government rather than make the adjustments required to adapt to the new economic situation.
- *Maintaining government programs* implemented to achieve specific domestic objectives may require protectionist policies. Suppose, for example, that the EC supports the price of wheat above the world price to improve its farmers' income. Unless protectionist policies exist, EC millers would find it less expensive to import their wheat. EC farmers would then be unable to sell their wheat, and the objective of the price support program would be thwarted. In the United States, Section 22 of the Agricultural Adjustment Act of 1933 pro-

[4]This discussion draws heavily on James P. Houck and Peter K. Pollak, "Basic Concepts of Trade," in *Speaking of Trade: Its Effect on Agriculture*, Minn. Agric. Ext. Serv. Spec. Rep. 72 (St. Paul, Minn.: University of Minnesota, November 1978), pp. 21–35.

vides that import restrictions be imposed by the president whenever imports pose a threat to domestic programs that support farm prices. This legislation is frequently invoked to reduce imports of sugar, milk products, tobacco, and peanuts.

- *Protecting national security* has been a frequently advanced justification for protectionism. For example, Japan has been particularly concerned about maintaining domestic rice production as part of a contingency "food security reserve." In addition, the United States imposed a grain export embargo against the Soviet Union as a punishment for actions in Afghanistan that were said to threaten national security.

- *Protecting infant industries* until they can compete in the world markets is another argument advanced for protectionist policies. Frequently, costs of production are higher in the initial stages of industry development. As the size of the industry expands, costs fall, making the industry competitive in world markets. The problem with this approach to development is weaning the protected industry from the protectionist policies under which it grew up.

- *Protecting national health* leads to outright prohibitions of trade between some countries. For example, the United States will not allow importation of beef from countries having hoof and mouth disease. Also, restrictions are imposed on imports of vegetables containing residues of pesticides banned in the United States.

- *Retaliation against policies* of another country deemed to be unfair sometimes results in the adoption of trade protectionist policies. For example, most countries have policies that protect their industries against another country "dumping" its products on the world market by selling its products below the cost of production. Dumping may be done either to gain access to a market or to get rid of burdensome surpluses. Retaliatory responses have an inherent danger of triggering a worldwide round of trade restrictions, frequently referred to as a *"trend toward protectionism."*

- *Protection against shortages* and increases in domestic prices has been used to justify controls on exports of products. Rather than face the political risk involved in high domestic prices and shortages, governments sometimes resort to export embargoes, thus depriving the world market of the product.

There are nine major types of barriers to trade: import tariffs, import quotas, quality restrictions, export subsidies, export taxes, export embargoes, exchange-rate distortions, state traders, and trade agreements. Each of these barriers to trade is sufficiently important to warrant an explanation of its effect in a two-country trade model context.

Import tariffs.   The classic method of import protection is the tariff, also called an import tax or customs duty. A tariff may be either a fixed charge per unit of product imported (specific tariff), a variable levy per unit of product imported, or a fixed percentage of the value of the product imported (ad valorem tax). In each case, the effect of the tariff is to raise the price of the imported good equal to or above the price of similar domestically produced goods. Tariffs thus make foreign goods economically unattractive to potential importers.

Referring to Fig. 6.7, a tariff of $P_t - P_u$ causes the importing country's price to rise. In effect, the excess demand curve is shifted down by the amount of the tariff from ED to ED_t. At the higher price P_t, the importing countries' producers increase the quantity supplied. Consequently, less is imported ($D_b - S_b$) than would be under free trade. The effect is to drop the world price to P_u. This lower price is reflected to the exporting countries' consumers and producers whose consumption rises to D_s and production falls to S_s. The tariff results in lower overall production (GNP) than under free trade, due to a misallocation of resources.

Variable Levy.   One of the most interesting tariffs is the variable levy, which is used by the EC to provide price support for imported commodities such as corn. To illustrate the variable levy, Fig. 6.8 isolates the EC on the right graph and the rest of the world on the left. Suppose that the level of price support for corn chosen by the EC is P_s. At this price S_e will be produced and D_e demanded with $D_e - S_e$ being imported. The levy results in a world price of P_c, which leads to D_c being demanded in the rest of the world and S_c supplied.

The important feature of the variable levy is that once the price support level is set at P_s under the EC Common Agricultural Policy (CAP), the levy is constantly adjusted to reflect the difference between the P_s and the prevailing world price. Therefore, the EC price is always supported at

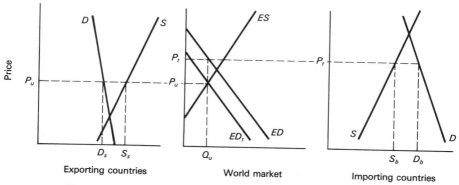

Figure 6.7   Price, production, and quantity traded under an import tariff.

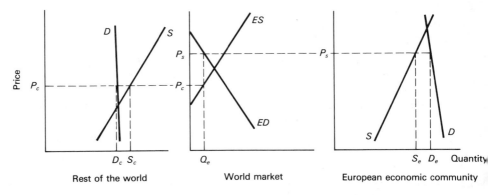

Figure 6.8 Price, production, and quantity traded under EEC common agricultural policy.

P_s and the world price adjusts to yield Q_e imports. All price adjustments are transferred to the world market increasing world price variation. Price variation in the world market is absorbed by adjustments in the variable levy. Changes in supply or demand within the EC are transmitted to the world market through changes in import demand.

Import quotas. An import quota sets an absolute limit on the quantity of a product that can be imported. A zero quota, of course, prohibits all imports. The United States uses quotas to limit imports of beef, dairy products, and sugar. Japan has quotas on beef and poultry imports.

Quotas are easy to analyze in a two-country trade model. Figure 6.9 represents the case of the U.S. quota on beef imports with the United States in the left graph and the rest of the world on the right. If the United States sets the quota at Q_q (or $D_q - S_q$), the excess demand curve is truncated at Q_q, therefore taking the shape of ED_q rather than the

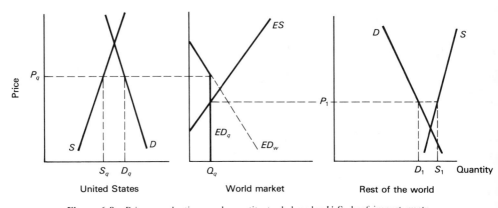

Figure 6.9 Price, production, and quantity traded under U.S. beef import quota.

straight line ED_w. The result is a lower price P_l in the rest of the world than would exist under free trade and a higher price P_q in the United States. The quota, therefore, limits competition to U.S. beef producers. A quota can be set to have the same effect on prices and quantities as an equivalent tariff.

Voluntary import restraints are a subtle form of import quota with the same economic impacts. *They involve agreements negotiated between an importing country and one or more exporting countries to limit their exports to some specified quantity.* The implied "quota" becomes the product of negotiation.

Quotas, whether mandated or voluntarily negotiated restraints, are valuable to both the country that establishes the quota and the quota holder. Quotas are generally divided up among potential suppliers. Since the price received for commodities imported under quota is higher than the world price, quotas are valuable; and giving a country a quota is a political favor. Economists refer to the process of obtaining the *higher price associated with protectionist government policies* as **rent seeking**. The *extra income* associated with a quota is referred to as **quota rent**. Yet, rent seeking activities are by no means limited to quotas. Producers seeking tariffs or other forms of protection are also rent seekers (see the box). For that matter, anyone who seeks competitive protection from the government is a rent seeker.

Quality restrictions.[5]   Quality restrictions include a wide range of measures, such as sanitary regulations, residue standards, product definitions, herbicide and pesticide regulations, grades, and production or processing standards which must be met before products are allowed to enter the importing country. Since such regulations impose costs on the domestic consumers and/or are a threat to consumer health, they must also be applied to imported goods. For example, if certain cancer-causing pesticides, for which there are no effective low-cost substitutes, are banned in the United States, imports of products grown using the cancer-causing pesticides also need to be banned. While such protectionist measures are motivated by legitimate health and safety concerns, quality restrictions may also be very effective barriers to trade.

A recent case from Germany illustrates the nature of the problem. A law dating back to 1516 specifies the ingredients legally permitted in beer. This law, the Reinheitsgebot, stipulates that only yeast, malted barley, hops, and water can be used to brew beer.[6] Recent German legislation

[5]This section draws heavily on the work of E. Wesley, F. Peterson, Guy Henry, and Mechel Paggi, *Implications of Qualitative Restrictions in Agricultural Trade*, Tex. Agric. Exp. Stn. Bull. 1594 (College Station, Tex.: Texas A&M University, February 1987).

[6]*Agra Europe*, Newsletter on the European Economic Community (London), March 13, 1987.

RENT SEEKING IN
INTERNATIONAL TRADE: THE
GREAT TOMATO WAR

The tomato has been the center of many legal and political international trade battles designed to gain rents through both tariff and nontariff barriers. This rent-seeking activity began when vegetable producers got the Tariff Act of 1883 enacted. This Act assessed a 10 percent import duty (tariff) on fresh vegetables but not on fruit. Importers (supermarket buyers of the day) argued that tomatoes were actually a fruit. The Supreme Court ruled that in the common language of the people, tomatoes are vegetables. The Tariff Act of 1938 established duties on vegetables, which for tomatoes and cucumbers were higher in harvest periods.

In the early 1950s, Florida tomato producers' attention turned to creating nontariff barriers to trade. In 1954, Florida Senator Holland got enacted the "golden rule agreement" in marketing orders making imports subject to the same marketing order regulations as domestic fruits and vegetables. The Florida Tomato Committee immediately got a regulation establishing that vine ripe tomatoes marketed from Mexico had to be ¼ inch smaller than mature, green tomatoes marketed from Mexico. This quarter-inch size difference, which would exclude many tomatoes from Mexico, was justified under the golden rule because vine-ripened tomatoes had to grow longer and become larger than mature green tomatoes. This order regulation stood until 1970 when an extended political battle broke out between Arizona–New Mexico interests in imports and Florida producers. Consumer groups got in the fray forcing the issue to hearings. In the hearings it was pointed out that there were only 165 Florida producers who benefited from the regulations, one of which was Gulf and Western Industries, which had one-eighth of the production.

Having lost the marketing order battle, in 1978 three Florida producers filed an antidumping petition with the Department of Treasury, charging that the Mexicans were selling tomatoes at less than their fair value with the intent of destroying the Florida fresh winter vegetable industry. While dumping was never found to exist, extensive negotiations were held at top levels of both governments to obtain voluntary Mexican import restraints.

Abstracted from Maury E. Bredahl, Andrew Schmitz, and Jimmye S. Hillman, "Rent Seeking in International Trade: The Great Tomato War," *Am. J. Agric. Econ.* (February 1987), pp. 1–10.

extended the beer regulation to imported beer. In effect, the old Reinheitsgebot was used to prevent imports of beer from other European countries where additives or other ingredients, such as rice or corn, are used to brew beer. The European Court of Justice ruled that this ban on imports of foreign beers was a barrier to trade aimed at other members of the

European Community (EC). Trade barriers between members of the EC are generally not allowed, and Germany has been instructed to lift its ban on beer imports. The German government had argued that there was a legitimate health concern because Germans drink more beer than others and could be harmed by heavy consumption of the additives used in beers from other countries. The Court did not accept this argument ruling that the law was actually a trade barrier designed to protect German beer producers from foreign competition.[7] These restrictions still prevent most U.S. beers from entering the EC.

Determining whether a quality regulation is a trade barrier or a legitimate measure to protect public health and safety is a complicated problem. Scientific evidence that certain substances are harmful is not always conclusive. Moreover, it is likely that quality differences will be taken into account, in many cases, through the normal functioning of the market. On the other hand, some quality problems are particularly difficult to detect and could be dangerous to human health if left unregulated. For example, salmonella bacteria, a common health hazard arising from unsanitary livestock slaughter and processing procedures, are not visible to the naked eye. However, in many instances it is unclear that quality regulations are necessary to protect human health or safety. To the extent that quality regulations applied to imported goods are trade barriers, they will serve to protect domestic producers and limit the choices available to consumers.

In the two-country trade model context, at their extreme, quality restrictions can lead to autarky (Fig. 6.5). This would happen if the exporting countries' producers were unable able to meet the requirements of the quality restriction. Prices would be determined entirely by domestic supply and demand. A more likely case is where some countries can comply and others cannot. In any case, quality restrictions can distort trade patterns as effectively, or perhaps more effectively, than tariffs or quotas.

Export subsidies.   *An* **export subsidy** *is a government payment per unit of product exported.* Export subsidies and related practices are designed to expand exports by placing products on the world market at prices lower than would exist under competitive conditions. The intent is to reduce the competitive pressures on producers or to dispose of surplus production.

In the two-country trade model, a U.S. export subsidy of $P_z - P_v$ is perceived by the rest of the world as a shift in the excess supply function to the right from ES to ES_s (Fig. 6.10). The subsidy increases the U.S. price and reduces the export price. U.S. exports are increased relative to

---

[7]Ibid.

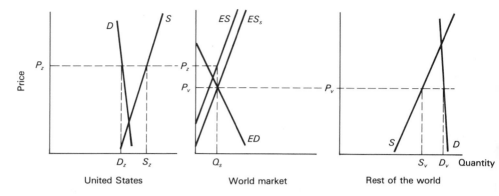

Figure 6.10 Prices, production, and quantity traded under U.S. export subsidy.

free trade, but production in the rest of the world falls. The subsidy produces an economic gain for U.S. producers and foreign consumers. It
causes an economic loss to U.S. consumers, U.S. taxpayers (who pay for
the subsidy), and foreign producers.

Export subsidies come in many forms, some of which are quite subtle. In the 1950s and 60s, the U.S. regularly provided subsidies to foreign
buyers, totaling as high as $822 million in 1964. A 1972 decision to sell
the Soviets grain at a subsidized price was a very controversial decision
preceding the world food crisis years.

Recently, the United States has begun to use *targeted* export subsidies as opposed to the general subsidies provided in the 1950s and 1960s.
The 1972 Soviet subsidy was in a sense a targeted subsidy. A **targeted
subsidy** *is limited to a particular country or sale designed to attract or
regain a customer.* How effective the targeted subsidy is depends on the
longer-run dependability of the buyer as a consumer and on the reaction
of competitors.

It will be seen in Chapter 11 that direct income payments from the
government to farmers are a form of export subsidy—although both domestic and foreign consumers receive the benefits of the resulting lower
price. Under marketing orders, commodities such as almonds are *sold in
the world market at a lower price than in the domestic market.* Such a **two-
price plan** was initially proposed in the 1920s as the *McNary–Haugen
plan,* designed to dispose of surplus commodities on the world market.

The United States is, by no means, the only country that subsidizes
exports. The EC uses export subsidies extensively as a part of its Common Agricultural Policy. For example, price supports on wheat and sugar
are maintained sufficiently high that excess production occurs. These
surpluses can only be sold in the world market at a lower price. This is
accomplished by an export subsidy. This two-price plan results in EC consumers spending a larger share of their income on food.

A much more subtle form of export subsidy involves subsidies on the use of inputs for production. For example, it is common in developing countries to supply farmers with fertilizer and seed at little or no cost. Such subsidies shift the exporting country's supply curve to the right and, in turn, the excess supply curve, resulting in a lower price.

The ultimate export subsidy and two-price plan involves dumping. Technically, **dumping** *means selling on the world market below the cost of production.* Dumping gets its name from an uncontrolled sale on the world market of a quantity of commodity at whatever price it can obtain. Such a commodity is said to be "dumped" on the world market.

Export taxes.   *An* **export tax** *is imposed by the exporting country; it raises the price of goods entering international trade.* Such taxes may serve as a source of revenue for an exporting country. It may also be a means of reducing international demand for a product that is desired for domestic consumption. Export taxes penalize producers and are a source of production shortfalls in developing countries. An implicit export tax occurs when the government puts a ceiling on the producer price as a means of controlling food costs. Consumers benefit from the lower price but may not get enough production to satisfy domestic needs.

Export embargoes.   *An* **embargo** *is a suspension of exports in one or more commodities by a country to one or more countries.* Export embargoes are imposed by government fiat and may be imposed either when supplies of a commodity are very short and prices are extremely high or as part of a foreign policy strategy. The United States, for example, imposed an embargo on the export of soybeans, cottonseed, and related products in June 1973, when the price of soybeans rose above $12 a bushel and concern arose regarding the adequacy of protein feed supplies for poultry and hog production. The domestic price dropped almost immediately after the embargo was imposed to $6 per bushel. The disruption in supplies available to traditional U.S. foreign customers severely strained trading relations with them.[a] The high price of soybeans and the embargo has been correlated with the development of the Brazilian soybean industry, which eroded the dominance of the United States in the world soybean market.

The Soviet grain embargo of 1980 was imposed as a retaliatory reaction to the Soviet invasion of Afghanistan. Virtually every Republican candidate, and some Democrats, have made "political hay" of the Soviet grain embargo. The embargo, from time to time, has been blamed for all of the ills that have beset agriculture since 1980. Interestingly, a comprehensive economic study, mandated by Congress, of the 1980 Soviet grain

---

[a]John T. Dunlop, "Lessons of Food Controls, 1971–74," in *The Lessons of Wage and Price Controls—The Food Sector*, John T. Dunlop and Kenneth J. Fedor, eds. (Cambridge, Mass.: Harvard University Press, 1978), p. 244.

embargo found that it was not effective and had little long-run impact.[9] While not condoning embargoes, the study points up the extent of exaggerated political claims regarding both their effects and effectiveness.

State traders.   One of the most frequently ignored barriers to trade is the state trader. **State traders** *are government or quasi-government monopolistic sellers or buyers of a commodity.* In other words, the government, or a government-authorized agency, sells in the export market on behalf of producers, buys on behalf of consumers.

State traders constitute a significant share of world trade in commodities such as wheat. All centrally planned economies are state traders; most of the less developed countries and several of the major exporters (Canada, Australia, and Argentina) are state traders in wheat. Several of these countries are in a sufficiently strong position to exercise a degree of market power in influencing price and/or quantity traded.[10]

Exchange-rate distortions.   The exchange-rate functions as a relative price between the currencies of different countries. In market economies, changes in exchange rates affect supply and demand for commodities, which, in turn, alter trade levels and flows. As in the case of price changes, exchange rates must be adjusted for inflation in each country to evaluate effects on trade. Also, since countries export and import different goods, it is necessary to calculate a trade weighted exchange rate for those countries actually importing a commodity or group of commodities. Figure 6.11 gives the Federal Reserve trade-weighted-average exchange rate for all exports, for corn, and for cotton.

In a two-country trade model, the exchange rate has the effect of rotating the excess demand function (Fig. 6.12). A real appreciation of the dollar rotates the excess demand function ED downward to ED_a. The downward rotation means that foreign buyers must sell more goods in their currency to purchase a given amount of goods in U.S. dollars. The effect is to restrict export demand to Q_a, as the price to the rest of the world is raised to P_b and the price in the United States is lowered to P_a. When the value of the dollar falls, just the opposite occurs. That is, the excess demand function is rotated upward, indicating that U.S. goods are more favorably priced. Export demand rises, as do U.S. prices.

It can be seen that exchange-rate changes have much the same effect as export taxes and subsidies. When the value of the dollar declined in the 1970s, it took less in foreign currency to buy U.S. commodities. Exports, therefore, expanded rapidly as if there were a large export subsidy.

---

[9]Alex F. McCalla, T. Kelley White, and Kenneth Clayton, *Embargoes, Surplus Disposal and U.S. Agriculture* (Washington, D.C.: ERS, USDA, November 1986).

[10]Paarlberg et al., *Impacts of Policy*, p. 48–49.

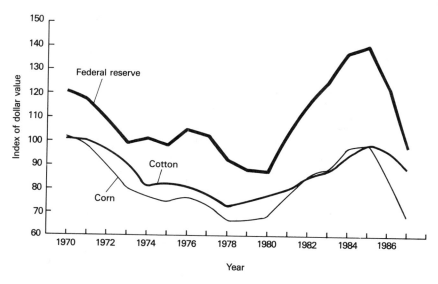

Figure 6.11 Trade-weighted exchange rate of the U.S. dollar 1970–1987.

When the dollar appreciated in the early 1980s, exports plummeted as if they were being taxed. It took more foreign currency to buy a dollar's worth of U.S. wheat, corn, or cotton. A decline in the value of the dollar beginning in 1985 once again increased the competitiveness of U.S. commodities. Instability in exchange rates is translated into instability in commodity markets.

To prevent such adverse consequences, countries will sometimes manage their own exchange rates. Overtly lowering the exchange rate operates like an export subsidy, expands trade, and tends to fuel inflation. Raising the exchange rate operates like an export tax and holds down domestic prices. For example, in the face of high inflation rates, several South American countries overvalued their currencies. This has

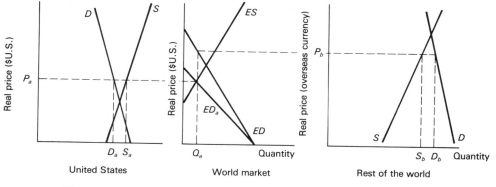

Figure 6.12 Prices, production, and quantity traded under appreciated dollar.

forced their farm prices below world prices. In the early 1980s, Uruguay overvalued its currency to the extent that its cattle prices were less than half the world price.[11]

TRADE WARS AND PROTECTIONISM

This analysis of the impacts of trade barriers on prices, production, and quantities traded assumed that protectionist policies can be pursued without eliciting retaliatory response from exporters. That is seldom the way the real world operates. Countries do not stand idly by when their producers are experiencing lower prices due to an export subsidy. They retaliate with either their own subsidy or with a countervailing duty. A **countervailing duty** is *a tariff imposed to offset the competitive advantage that the export subsidy gives the foreign product.*

In other words, subsidies are matched with subsidies or tariffs. The result is commonly referred to as a trade war or an increase in protectionism. In such periods it is not unusual for discussions to go on in the offices of policymakers as to what it would take in subsidies to break the bank of the EC, for example. At some point, there is the realization that the trade war has gone too far. Policies to reduce trade barriers are discussed in Chapter 7.

LEVELS OF BARRIERS TO TRADE

There are not free traders among the world's agricultural trading countries. Without exception and with varying degrees of comprehensiveness and success, all governments intervene in agriculture.[12]

In a nutshell, these were the findings of a major USDA study designed to quantify the extent of barriers to agricultural trade. Producer subsidy equivalents were calculated based on the combination of government expenditures on subsidies and the difference between the domestic price and the world price. In essence, a **producer subsidy equivalent** *measures the proportion of producers' gross income (including government payments) from government intervention.*

A comparative ranking of the level of producer subsidies is contained in Fig. 6.13. Japan has by far the highest level of subsidies with over 70 percent of producer receipts being a result of government inter-

[11]Lucio G. Reca, "Price Policies in Developing Countries," in *The Role of Markets in the World Food Economy*, D. Gale Johnson and G. Edward Schuh, eds. (Boulder, Colo.: Westview Press, Inc., 1983), p. 124.

[12]Economic Research Service, *Government Intervention in Agriculture: Measurement, Evaluation and Implications for Trade Negotiation*, FAER-229 (Washington, D.C.: USDA, April 1987), p. v.

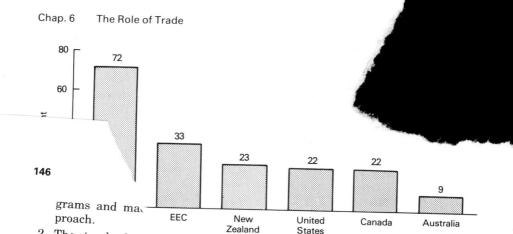

Figure. Levels of government intervention in agriculture, by country, 1982–1984.

146

grams and ma...proach.

2. The standard refei...Spec. Rep. 72 (St. ...University of Mi...

This publica... ranks second, with about one-third of its producer re-ceipts attributable to government. Canada, New Zealand, and the United States each have about 20 percent of their receipts from the government. Australia provides only 9 percent producer benefits.

As a general rule, importing countries provide higher levels of pro-ducer assistance than do exporting countries, reflecting the drive for food security and self-sufficiency. Food grains, dairy products, and sugar were found to be the most highly subsidized. In less developed countries, pro-ducers of some commodities were taxed while others were subsidized.

TRADE POLICY: A WORLD ISSUE

The benefits of free trade are obvious. Yet protectionism is pervasive and has a tendency to become increasingly so. It is driven by a desire to pro-tect an important industry, by the desire to expand economic activity, and by the need for food security. Yet for the world to feed itself effec-tively and efficiently, there must be trade. If world markets degenerate into a dumping ground for surplus production, the world's economic growth potential is stifled. Particularly adversely affected are those de-veloping countries that must depend on trade in agricultural products for their revenue to grow and improve their living conditions. Trade policy, therefore, is a world issue, not just a U.S. issue.

ADDITIONAL READINGS

1. The Economic Research Service staff paper by Philip L. Paarlberg, Alan J. Webb, Arthur Morey, and Jerry A. Sharples, titled *Impacts of Policy on U.S. Agricultural Trade* (Washington, D.C.: USDA, December 1984) provides an excellent review of the theory of trade. It includes an analysis of farm pro-

croeconomic policy using the two-country trade model ap-

ence on trade policy is the publication *Speaking of Trade*, Paul, Minn.: Minnesota Agricultural Extension Service, nnesota, November 1978), edited by Martin K. Christiansen. ion contains a series of outstanding articles on trade policy. While *Speaking of Trade* is getting a bit old, it is still very relevant and well worth reading.

3. The most comprehensive treatment of trade policy issues is by Alex F. McCalla and Timothy E. Josling, *Agricultural Policies and World Markets* (New York: Macmillan Publishing Company, 1985). Although parts of this book are a bit heavy for the novice in economics, other sections are very readable.

Chapter 7

International Trade and Development Policy

Political internationalism without economic internationalism is a house built upon sand. For no nation can reach its fullest development alone.

Wendell L. Wilkie

In the 1970s, the United States made a decision to become an active participant in the world market for agricultural products. It expanded production to take advantage of the high prices and excess profits that were available to crop producers during this period of booming exports. Once in the world market, it has had no choice but to stay.

The purpose of this chapter is to provide the setting for the development of trade policy. The emphasis is on the United States, although the positions of other countries and groups of countries are developed where it is appropriate. The major general policy choices are developed.

IMPORTANCE OF TRADE TO THE UNITED STATES

Beginning in the 1970s, exports soared from less than $6 billion to nearly $44 billion in 1982 and then declined to about $27 billion in 1987. Despite the decline, exports still account for 15 percent of overall farm production, about $30 billion in added gross national product, and a million jobs.

For major crops, the share of production exported is considerably higher. For example, in 1987–1988 about half of the wheat, rice, cotton, and soybeans were exported, while 22 percent of the feed grains were exported. Farm interest groups sometimes assert that if foreign buyers are not willing to pay the cost of production for a commodity, it should not be sold. But if it is not sold, it should not be produced.

The consequence of abandoning the export market would be a reduction in production of about 50 percent in wheat, rice, and soybeans, and 25 percent in feed grains. Production adjustments of this magnitude would send economic reverberations throughout America. The hardest-hit sectors would be the agricultural input industry, which would lose as many as 400,000 jobs, and export-related transportation, storage, merchandising, and port operations, which could lose as many as a million jobs.[1]

COMPETITIVENESS IN TRADE

If U.S. farmers are to be a part of the world market, they must be competitive. Competitiveness has two basic economic requirements:

- The U.S. price must be at a level that allows it to meet or beat the competition to maintain market share.
- The U.S. cost of production must be sufficiently low that its farmers can remain in business at the prevailing world price.

The price requirement must be met in the short run to make any particular sale. The cost requirement must be met in the long run to stay in business. The relevant costs are not only farm costs but also include those costs involved in getting the commodity at least loaded on ships (FOB U.S. port). This concept of costs recognizes the importance of inland transportation, storage, and labor costs as well as production costs.

Public policy plays an important role in both short-run and long-run competitiveness. In the short run, the United States cannot be competitive if it is priced out of the market by any combination of high domestic farm price support, an overvalued dollar, or a requirement to ship in U.S. flagships (cargo preference or cargo reservation).

In the long run, competitiveness is much more a function of the basic endowment of resources, investment in the production and marketing infrastructure, technology, and the growth of demand. Investment, technology, and demand are greatly affected by public policy. Public and private investment in infrastructure, research, and human capital development are critical to competitiveness in the international market. Available evidence clearly shows that many countries are committing

[1]David Harrington, Gerald Schluter, and Patrick O'Brien, *Agriculture's Links to the National Economy: Income and Employment*, Agric. Inf. Bull. 504 (Washington, D.C.: ERS, USDA, October 1986).

COMPETITIVENESS DEPENDS
ON TECHNOLOGY

How can the U.S. farmers be competitive when labor costs are so much lower in other countries and when the costs of inputs are frequently subsidized? This is a question frequently asked by U.S. farmers. The answer to the labor cost advantage lies in superior technology and management as well as in larger-scale farm operations. U.S. agriculture has dealt with the labor cost issue by substituting other inputs, such as machinery and chemicals, for labor. It is always difficult to compete against subsidized inputs. U.S. input subsidies have been limited largely to water, electricity, credit, and the discovery, development, and dissemination of new technology. In many respects, U.S. agriculture competes on the basis of technology. Continued technology investments and accelerated investments in human capital will be the keys to the future competitiveness of U.S. farmers.

---

substantial resources to research designed to create agricultural technological breakthroughs.[2] While technologies are transferrable, the country that is the first to discover, develop, and apply a new technology can gain a critical competitive edge. More important, since technological development and change are long-term processes, the country that has the long-run public and private commitment to invest in research is more likely to be competitive in the long run.

In the past decade, the United States has made some significant public policy changes affecting private-sector agricultural research incentives. The most important of these was the extension of intellectual property rights to discoveries of new life forms and computer software.[3] This change has drawn greatly increased private-sector interest and investment to basic agricultural research.[4] Continued public-sector support for agricultural research combined with new private investment in research holds the potential for improving the competitive position of U.S. agriculture.[5]

[2]Michael J. Phillips and Yao-chi Lu, "Impact of Emerging Technologies on Food and Agricultural Capacity," *Am. J. Agric. Econ.* (May 1987), pp. 448–53.

[3]Robert E. Evenson, "Intellectual Property Rights and Agribusiness Research and Development: Implications for the Public Agricultural Research System," *Am. J. Agric. Econ.* (December 1983), pp. 967–975.

[4]Ronald D. Knutson, "Restructuring Agricultural Economics Extension to Meet Changing Needs," *Am. J. Agric. Econ.* (December 1986), pp. 1297–1306.

[5]James T. Bonnen, "A Century of Science in Agriculture: Lessons to Science Policy," *Am. J. Agric. Econ.* (December 1986), pp. 1065–1080.

Vollrath found that over the period 1961–1984, in wheat, Canada, Argentina, and Australia were generally more competitive than the United States.[6] The study also found that U.S. food grains, feed grains, and oilseeds were more competitive than U.S. agriculture as a whole. The United States was most competitive in oilseeds followed by coarse grains. There were some indications that U.S. agriculture was becoming more competitive over time. This is consistent with changes in domestic farm policies designed to make the United States more price competitive in world markets.

U.S. TRADE POLICY GOALS

From 1970 through at least 1987 the major thrust of U.S. trade policy has been in support of freer trade. For example, the *1986 Economic Report of the President* made the following points with regard to U.S. trade policy goals:

- Government management of trade through protectionism will not solve problems that result from international macroeconomic imbalances.
- The United States has a strong self-interest in advocating and practicing fair trade.
- An important objective of trade policy is to ensure that markets remain open and that competition takes place under internationally agreed upon rules. Countries should be expected to live up to their international commitments regarding market access.
- The United States seeks a major transformation of the world trading system, strengthening GATT discipline and extending it to areas not presently addressed.[7]

Goals of Agricultural Trade Policy

More specific trade policy goals related to agriculture can be specified as:

- Create an environment for trading that facilitates exports.
- Prevent agricultural imports from undermining U.S. government

[6]Thomas Vollrath, "Revealed Competitive Advantage for Wheat," *in U.S. Competitiveness in World Wheat Markets*, unpublished papers (Washington, D.C.: ERS, USDA, June 16, 1986), pp. 23–26.

[7]Council of Economic Advisers, *Economic Report of the President* (Washington, D.C.: Executive Office of the President, February 1987), pp. 123–128.

farm price support policies, from injuring specific producer segments, and from endangering the safety of the U.S. food supply.
- Expand exports of U.S. farm products.
- Promote economic development in countries that are not hostile toward U.S. interests.
- Coordinate trading activities with other countries to assure supplies and promote exports.
- Utilize U.S. agricultural production potential to achieve foreign policy goals.

Such goals espouse lofty ideals, but belie the many conflicts that exist between domestic policy and trade policy as well as the strong political forces favoring greater protectionism. Before discussing these conflicts it is necessary to explain GATT.

General Agreement on Tariffs and Trade (GATT)

GATT is a permanent forum for trade negotiations among nations. It is a multilateral treaty among 92 governments, including the United States. *Its purpose is to liberalize and expand trade through negotiated reductions in trade barriers.*

GATT is a multilateral agreement that lays down rules and guidelines governing world trade. It is also a forum in which countries can discuss and resolve trade problems. GATT covers both agricultural and industrial products. It provides the contractual rights and obligations for contracting parties to formally challenge other members' trading practices. Consultation, conciliation, and dispute settlement are fundamental to GATT's work. GATT serves as the principal international body concerned with negotiating reductions in tariff and nontariff barriers through the Multilateral Trade Negotiations.[8]

The agreement contains a code of principles and provides for a continuing forum for consultation and dispute settlement. GATT has five basic principles:

- Trade must be nondiscriminatory with regard to all GATT parties.
- Domestic industries should receive protection mainly by tariffs as opposed to nontariff barriers.
- Tariff levels agreed upon under GATT bind each country, with provision for compensation to the injured party if violated.

[8]Economic Research Service, *Government Intervention in Agriculture: Measurement, Evaluation, and Implications for Trade Negotiations.* Foreign Agric. Econ. Rep. 229 (Washington, D.C.: USDA, April 1987).

- Consultations are provided by GATT to settle disputes.
- When warranted by economic or trade conditions, GATT procedures may be waived on agreement of the members with provision for compensation.

The most basic objective of these principles is to prevent the development of rounds of retaliatory erection of trade barriers. Adherence to GATT principles keeps trade barriers visible and provides a forum for discussion where in theory, at least, equal knowledge and treatment exist among the contesting parties.

From its inception through 1981, seven major GATT negotiating conferences or "rounds" have been held. Agreements on reduction of agricultural trade barriers have not come easily. More progress has been made in the liberalization of industrial product trade than in agriculture. The following major achievements in GATT negotiations have been of particular significance to U.S. agriculture:

- In the 1960–1961 Dillon Round, the EEC provided assurance of duty-free entry for soybeans, soybean meal, other oilseeds, and cotton. Variable levies on feed and food grains were continued.
- The 1963–1967 Kennedy Round resulted in tariff reductions on a wide range of farm products. These tariff reductions were less than the one-third tariff reductions on industrial products but were still considered to be significant.
- The 1973–1979 Tokyo Round emphasized reduction of nontariff barriers. Codes of conduct were established to discourage the use of export subsidies, discourage the establishment of unique product standards, and remove procedural obstacles to obtaining import licenses. In addition, concessions were obtained which hold the potential for increased exports of beef and citrus fruits. The most substantial U.S. concessions involved an increase in dairy quotas and an agreement not to increase the palm oil import tariff.

In 1987, the United States entered a new round of trade negotiations known as the Uruguay Round. The agreed-upon objectives of this round of trade negotiations include:[9]

- Strenghten GATT rules and disciplines as they apply to agriculture.
- Improve market access through the reduction of import barriers.
- Increase discipline in the use of direct and indirect subsidies.

[9]*Ministerial Declaration on the Uruguay Round.* (Punta del Este, Uruguay: GATT, 1986).

- Minimize the adverse effects of unnecessary health and sanitary regulations on trade.

Conflicts with GATT Objectives

The existence of GATT implies that many countries' trade and agricultural policies conflict with GATT objectives, rules, and guidelines. The key conflicts are among exporting countries, including the variable levy and export subsidies of the European Economic Community, the Japanese protection of its rice and beef markets, and Canadian protection of its dairy and poultry markets.

The United States has several programs that directly affect access to U.S. markets and/or subsidize exports of farm products. Some of these programs are agriculture specific, while others apply to all U.S. businesses and industries:

- **Section 201** *of the Trade Act of 1974 provides temporary protection for import-sensitive industries to facilitate adjustment to the loss of competitiveness internationally.* This statute, and its counterpart in GATT, is known as the "escape clause" because no demonstration of unfair trade practices is necessary to justify temporary protection. Only serious injury or the threat of serious injury must be demonstrated. Devices such as countervailing duties are often used in 201 cases, or more often the dispute may be settled by a voluntary import restraint.

- **Section 301** *of the Trade Act of 1974 prohibits unfair trade practices such as dumping with demonstration of injury to a U.S. industry.* Section 301 might legitimately be referred to as a retaliatory provision allowing the president to impose restrictions on imports with a finding of injury.

- **Section 22** *authorizes the imposition of import restrictions on price-supported commodities if it is found that imports substantially interfere with the operation of the price support program.* Interference is measured by increased imports, resulting in increased purchases of commodities by USDA under the price support program. Under section 22, the president is given the power to either impose tariffs of up to 50 percent of the value of the imported product or impose quotas on up to 50 percent of imports in a representative period.

In recent years, Section 22 has been used extensively to prevent imports of dairy products, peanuts, sugar, and tobacco. Although these import restrictions have been the subject of extensive debate, it is clear that without them, government programs supporting domestic market prices at levels of the past could not be sus-

THE ROOT OF PROTECTIONISM

The root of protectionism lies in domestic farm programs. Every country of the world has decided for one reason or another to protect its farmers from international competition. Trade policy is sometimes an integral part of farm policy. This is the case in the European Economic Community, where the variable levy and export subsidies are used to protect high domestic prices. The United States depends more heavily on direct producer subsidies, which encourage production and reduce world prices.

tained. That is, without import controls, government expenditures on price supports would rise sharply as imported products replace price-supported commodities in domestic markets.

On commodities such as wheat and cotton, where price supports have been reduced to or are below world market levels, Section 22 no longer plays a significant role. The question then becomes one of whether high price support levels can be justified on manufactured dairy products, peanuts, sugar, and tobacco when other countries clearly have a comparative advantage in their production. Answering such questions requires a balancing of the producer, consumer, and taxpayer implications.

- **Section 8e** *of the Agricultural Marketing Agreements Act provides that grade, size, quality, or maturity regulations established for fruits, vegetables, or nuts under a marketing order shall apply equally to imported products.* This regulation, frequently referred to as the "golden rule" of marketing orders, was added to the marketing agreements act in 1954. Prior to its existence, imported products that did not meet order standards could be imported and compete with the products of U.S. producers that were required to meet the order standards. The danger existed that the imported products would capture a substantial market share.

- *Many producer subsidies in domestic farm programs are indirect means of subsidizing the exports of farm products.* In 1987, Canada filed a complaint with GATT that direct farmer payments under the target price program were a violation of GATT rules. The provisions of these domestic programs and their impacts on trade are discussed in Chapter 10.

- *Targeted export assistance and export enhancement provisions of domestic farm policies are designed to recover lost export markets.* The basic export enhancement tool is export payment-in-kind (PIK), which, in essence, is a "buy one, get one free" export subsidy program. (See the market development discussion that follows.)

Each of these programs affecting trade is contentious to the GATT objectives and is thus a subject of discussion in the Multilateral Trade Negotiations. It can readily be seen that trade negotiations cannot be successful unless the domestic farm programs employed by each country are a part of the negotiation. For farm organizations, this should be a very contentious point because the policies and programs that they have successfully lobbied for become the object of international negotiation in GATT.

FOREIGN MARKET DEVELOPMENT POLICY[10]

Expansion of agricultural exports has been a major goal of USDA programs since the 1970s. The lead agency in USDA for foreign market development activities is the Foreign Agriculture Service (FAS). The activities of FAS include assisting in the development of trade policy, supervision of agricultural counselors located in the U.S. embassies of major U.S. trading partners and competitors, analyses of foreign market developments, referral of export opportunities to U.S. exporters, and assisting in and directing foreign market development activities. Because elements of foreign policy, foreign relations, and diplomacy are involved in nearly all of these functions, many FAS activities are conducted jointly with the Department of State and the Office of Trade Representative. One of the prime responsibilities of the agricultural counselors or attachés is to identify markets for U.S. farm products and to assist firms selling U.S. farm products.

The precipitous drop in exports during the 1980s led to new programs designed to expand exports. The following is a summary of the major old and new market enhancement initiatives.

Cooperator Program

The cooperator program combines private and government support to increase the quantity and effectiveness of U.S. market development activities. Under the program FAS works jointly with approximately 50 "market development cooperators." These cooperators are producer-oriented farm groups such as U.S. Wheat Associates, the American Soybean Association, and the Feed Grains Council. They combine the export promotion efforts of producers, processors, handlers, and exporters. Market development activities are planned, implemented, evaluated, and financed jointly by the FAS and the cooperator organizations. Cooperator

[10]This section draws heavily on the excellent description of market development programs contained in Mark Smith, *Increased Role for U.S. Farm Export Programs*, Agric. Inf. Bull. 515 (Washington, D.C.: ERS, USDA, April 1987).

programs emphasize market information and technical assistance in servicing the needs of importing countries to utilize products effectively, enhance buyer awareness and appreciation of U.S. farm products, and assist in conducting consumer education activities in importing countries.

Food Aid

For countries in the early stages of economic development, the first step in establishing a healthy export market may be either through direct food aid or concessional sales. This is accomplished primarily under P.L. 480, the Agricultural Trade Development Act of 1954.

- **Title I** is a concessional program that provides for the sale of agricultural products under long-term dollar credit sales at low interest rates for up to 40 years. Also authorized is sales for local currencies, which had not been used since 1971 but were reauthorized in 1985. Actual sales are made by private U.S. suppliers to foreign government agencies or private trade entities, which, in turn, resell in the recipient countries. Title I country agreements generally contain provisions with regard to how the recipient country uses the proceeds from sales of commodities purchased under Title I.
- **Title II** is the principal U.S. program for responding to emergency food relief needs. Under Title II, food commodities and associated costs are donated to the recipient countries. Such donations are designed to provide commodities directly to specific nutritionally vulnerable groups through child health clinics, school lunch programs, and food-for-work programs. Title II distribution programs are carried out partially by voluntary groups such as CARE and Catholic Relief Services.
- **Title III** is designed to provide the poorest countries with additional encouragement for economic development. Multiyear commodity commitments and loan forgiveness are made in return for agreements to undertake specific development initiatives designed to increase production and improve the lives of the poor.

In the 1950s and 1960s, it was not unusual for concessionary sales under government programs, including P.L. 480, to account for as much as one-third of exports. However, when commercial exports mushroomed in the 1970s, the proportion of P.L. 480 sales declined. In the 1980s, P.L. 480 sales once again became more important, making up about 20 percent of rice, wheat, and vegetable oil exports.

From the foregoing trends it may be observed that P.L. 480 is more than just a food-aid and market development program. It is also used to dispose of surplus farm products. P.L. 480 sales have a pronounced tendency to decline when commercial sales, and thus farm prices, rise. Ironically, this is the time when the need for food aid is the greatest. On the other hand, when farm prices are low, increased political pressures result in more money being appropriated for P.L. 480. It will be seen later that P.L. 480 is also used as a tool of foreign policy and development assistance.

Despite these multiple objectives, P.L. 480 appears to have contributed substantially to export market growth. Japan, South Korea, Taiwan, Brazil, Iran, Peru, Chile, Colombia, and Spain have all graduated from being primarily P.L. 480 customers to being primarily commercial customers. This success is one of the factors that has contributed to its broad-based agricultural support.

Export Credit

A country is in a better position to compete for export sales if an ample supply of competitive credit is available to potential buyers. The extension of credit terms tailored to the needs of particular customers has been important to progressively developing markets from concessional sales to full-cash customers that rely on commercial credit sources.

USDA's Commodity Credit Corporation plays a major role in seeing that credit is available for eligible foreign customers. Each year, 25 to 30 overseas markets are financed by $1 billion to $2 billion of CCC export credit. This has been accomplished under two major programs:

- **Direct short-term credit** programs extend funds provided to CCC by the U.S. government. Loans are normally made on a six-month to three-year basis with interest rates that approach commercial levels.
- **Guaranteed or assured credit** utilizes funds provided by U.S. banks. Loan repayment terms and interest rates are the product of negotiation between the U.S. bank and the foreign buyer. CCC guarantees repayment in the event of a default on the loan. A trend toward primary reliance on commercial credit as opposed to direct government credit shifted export lending toward guaranteed credit in the early 1980s.

Both of these programs depend on annual appropriations from the Congress. As a substitute for these annual appropriations, the 1981 farm bill provided for the establishment of a revolving fund to support USDA export credit programs. Revolving fund credit would be established from a large lump-sum appropriation by the Congress to the CCC for the purpose of either making or guaranteeing loans to export customers. Appropriations for the revolving fund have not, however, been provided. Such a fund would allow the CCC to manage export loans on a longer-term basis, as opposed to unpredictable year-to-year congressional funding. The fund would be self-perpetuating from loans repaid. To the extent that direct loans are made from the fund, accumulated interest would provide a basis for growth of the fund.

Export PIK Subsidies: Export Enhancement Program

At times, due to high price supports or the subsidies of other countries, U.S. export prices simply are not competitive in particular markets. *Under export PIK, USDA provides an in-kind commodity bonus for each regular commercial purchase—a "buy one, get one free" sale.* For example, if a country purchases 1 million metric tons of wheat, it might receive 100,000 tons of export from government stocks as a bonus. The export PIK bonus does not have to be in the commodity purchased. For example, soybean and corn export PIK have been used to subsidize poultry sales.

Development Assistance Programs

U.S. policies to foster economic development are pursued for several reasons:

- Economic development satisfies basic human needs, reduces tension, and fosters political stability. Development policy is thus an integral part of foreign policy.
- Economic development facilitates and encourages trade. Development aid is a means of market development.
- Economic development has humanitarian motives created by a basic desire to improve the lot of people throughout the world. In terms of food, this humanitarian motive is fostered politically by the realization that solving the world food problem requires that people work together to increase production.

A wide range of development strategies has been pursued by the United States. In the process of pursuing these strategies, the United States has learned that an agriculture in the early stages of development cannot be readily transformed into a dynamic capital- and machinery-intensive agriculture in the image of the U.S. farmer.[11] Instead, the development process involves accelerating the rate of growth of agricultural

[11]Vernon W. Ruttan, *Thinking about Agricultural Development*, Texas A&M University Lecture Series (College Station, Tex.: Texas A&M University, October 30, 1975), p. 4.

output and productivity consistent with resources available and the growth of other sectors of the economy. This requires the capacity of research institutions to develop new technical knowledge adapted to country conditions; the capacity of the industry sector to develop, produce, and market the new technical inputs; and the capacity of farmers to acquire new knowledge and effectively use the new inputs.[12]

Although a better knowledge of the development process now exists, that does not mean that uniform rapid progress is being made in moving poorer, developing countries into the "takeoff" stage of growth. Progress remains slow, with political, resource, debt, and social impediments to progress.

U.S. agricultural development assistance is of two basic types: bilateral and multilateral. Bilateral assistance is provided by the United States directly to the recipient country. Multilateral assistance is extended to developing countries in combination with assistance from other countries through organizations such as the World Bank, Inter-American Development Bank, and the United Nations. The operating funds for these institutions are provided predominantly by developed countries. The major tools of development include commodity assistance, institution building and infrastructure development, technical assistance, credit, and research.

Commodity assistance.   U.S. bilateral commodity assistance under P.L. 480 has been one of the most extensively utilized, yet hotly debated forms of development assistance. In addition to its market development role, P.L. 480 has also been used as a tool of development in at least two senses:

- P.L 480 fills the interim food needs of a country, allowing release of labor from subsistence agriculture.
- P.L. 480 assistance normally involves agreements that the recipient country will use funds obtained from the sale of commodities for specified development programs.

The P.L. 480 controversy arises from the potential adverse impact of food aid on farm prices in the recipient country. Economic theory suggests that commodity assistance increases the supply of food available to the recipient country.[13] This, in turn, has the effect of reducing production. These effects have been confirmed in cases where P.L. 480 assis-

---

[12]Ibid., p. 7.

[13]T. W. Schultz, "Value of U.S. Farm Surpluses to Underdeveloped Countries," *J. Farm Econ.* (December 1960), pp. 1019–1030.

tance accounted for a large proportion of the recipient countries' production.[14] However, recent research suggests that the relationship may not be as clear-cut as theory would suggest.[15] The theoretical price-suppressing effect can be offset by developing country policies supporting farm prices.[16]

Institution and infrastructure development.   Institution building involves the development of an infrastructure of those facilities, industries, and agencies that are crucial to development and use of productivity enhancing knowledge and innovation. Examples include the development of irrigation systems, credit agencies, universities, agriculture ministries, statistical collection systems, fertilizer production plants, and marketing systems.

Institution building is costly, requiring substantial credit, and in some instances, direct monetary investments and assistance. The U.S. center for bilateral institution building activities is the Agency for International Development (AID). In terms of multilateral assistance, the United States supports several development lending institutions, of which the World Bank is the largest. Its activities are coordinated with several regional development banks, such as the Inter-American Development Bank.

Technical assistance.   Technical assistance involves providing developing countries with the service of experts in specific need areas. It is, in most instances, a necessary precursor to institution building as well as for the support of effective operation of the institutions. Prior to institution building projects, experts become involved in conceptualizing and conducting feasibility studies. Expert assistance is utilized in initiating smooth operation of institutions and in problem solving when needed.

Experts cover a wide range of knowledge, from advising in setting up specific institutions to helping solve particular problems. For example, the Food and Agriculture Organization (FAO) of the United Nations offers technical assistance in pasture and crop improvement, conservation, water resources, land reform strategies, establishment of cooperatives,

[14]Dale W. Adams, *Public Law 480 and Colombia's Economic Development* (East Lansing, Mich.: Medillin, 1964); and Frank D. Barlow and Susan A. Libbin, *Food Aid and Economic Development*, Foreign Agric. Econ. Rep. 51 (Washington, D.C.: ERS, USDA, 1969).

[15]Brady J. Deaton, "Public Law 480: The Critical Choices," *Am. J. Agric. Econ.* (December 1980), pp. 998–992; and Paul Isenman and H. Singer, *Food Aid: Disincentive Effects and Their Policy Implications*, AID Discussion Pap. 31 (Washington, D.C.: Agency for International Development, 1975).

[16]G. E. Schuh, *Improving the Developmental Effectiveness of Food Aid* (Washington, D.C.: Agency for International Development, September 1979).

price stabilization programs, nutrition improvement projects, and plant and animal disease protection. AID has an equally wide range of technical assistance activities. The expert base for technical assistance activities includes career professionals employed by development assistance agencies as well as consultants from private business, USDA, and universities.

Research.   The development of a strong international agricultural research component to U.S. development activities has occurred only since the 1960s. The U.S. center for international agricultural research is once again in AID. AID-supported agricultural research was given a major boost in 1966 when President Johnson, in his War on Hunger message, emphasized the need to help countries in balancing agricultural productivity with population growth.

As in other development activities, international agricultural research has bilateral and multilateral components. The U.S. component has as its major thrusts conducting research in major problem areas, strengthening research capability in areas where future needs are anticipated, and in training the future scientific manpower from and for developing countries. With leadership and funding from AID, scientists from both USDA and the universities are involved in these activities.

Although at one time the United States was the center for agricultural research, other countries are now seeing the need. In 1980, North America (including Oceania) accounted for only 23 percent of the world's agricultural research (Table 7.1). Research in North America increased no faster than research in the Soviet Union and Eastern Europe. They had the smallest growth rates of any region. The fact that other countries recognized the impact of agricultural research could have long-term impacts on the comparative advantage of these countries.

TABLE 7.1 Agricultural Research Expenditures by Region, 1970 and 1980

Region	Expenditure (millions of dollars) 1970	1980	Percent Increase	Percent of Total in 1980
Western Europe	919	1481	61	20
Eastern Europe and USSR	1282	1493	16	20
North America and Oceania	1485	1722	16	23
Latin America	216	463	114	6
Africa	252	425	69	6
Asia	1205	1797	49	25
World total	5359	7381	38	100

Source: Michael J. Phillips and Yao-chi Lu, "Impact of Emerging Technologies on Food and Agricultural Productive Capacity," *Am. J. Agric. Econ.* (May 1987), p. 452.

The initial scientific breakthroughs that led to the Green Revolution were the product of a combination of country research in the United States and Japan implemented by the international agricultural research system. This system is composed of a number of international agricultural research centers, such as the International Maize and Wheat Improvement Center in Mexico and the International Rice Research Institute in the Philippines. Financial support for these centers comes from a consultative group of international institutions, such as the World Bank, private foundations, and countries.

The multilaterally funded international research centers are generally considered to be excellent research organizations with fine facilities and highly qualified staffs. Their activities are coordinated with basic and applied research conducted in both developed and developing countries. Emphasizing applied research, their direct impact in increasing productivity has been demonstrated.

U.S. Development Support: A Controversy

The impression could be obtained from this discussion of international development that U.S. support for international development activities has been substantial. In one sense this is true; the United States is the largest single contributor to development activities. However, as a proportion of gross national product, the United States is one of the lowest contributors of the developed market economies of the world. Yet the role of the United States is controversial from a producer perspective. The charge is frequently made that U.S. development assistance increases production of commodities that are competitive with U.S. exports. The increased production either reduces the recipient country's imports or, worse yet, ends up on the world market in direct competition with U.S. production.

In the short run, there is a degree of merit to the argument. But in the long run and from a broader perspective, denial of development assistance would be counterproductive. As indicated previously, development begins with agriculture, which generates export earnings and releases people from subsistence to work in other jobs. Agricultural development thus becomes crucial to getting developing economies into the "takeoff phase" of growth. Once in the takeoff phase, the country, more often than not, becomes an importing country, particularly of feed grains and soybeans where U.S. farmers are most competitive.

In addition, development research frequently leads to short-run benefits. For example, cooperative research on soybeans in Brazil led to greater variety in germplasm for the improvement of U.S. varieties. In fact, the primary origins of most crops were in developing countries, where native species have provided genes for dwarf stature; resistance to insects and disease; day-length insensitivity; and high yield potential. For example, semidwarf wheat varieties, grown on two-thirds of the U.S. acreage, contain genes brought from Asia. U.S. agriculture would surely suffer if a decision were made not to participate in international research.

ALTERNATIVE TRADE POLICY OPTIONS, STRATEGIES, AND STRUCTURES

While the current U.S. trade policy favors the free-trade option, this is not the only option available. In addition, there are questions of whether the free-trade option can ever be achieved. The purpose of this section is to discuss the alternative trade policy options, strategies, and structures available to the United States. However, it is first desirable to explain the structure of international markets within which trading takes place.

World Market Structure

The world market is composed of three main components: sellers (exporters), buyers (importers), and market intermediaries (private trading companies). Each is affected by the government policies of the countries in which it is trading. The sellers and buyers may be either state traders or private traders. As noted previously, state traders are government or quasi-government agencies that buy or sell all of a particular commodity for a country. State trading sellers may be either marketing boards, such as the Canadian Wheat Board, which sells all wheat exported from Canada on behalf of its producers, or government agencies, such as China in cotton. State trading buyers may be either a quasi-government-authorized association of firms, such as a flour millers' association, which acts as a buyers' monopoly, or a government agency, such as the Japan Food Agency. Most developing countries and all centrally planned economies are state traders.

Market intermediaries are the middlemen of the grain trade. They are private trading companies that buy and sell grain, hedge, store, ship, insure, handle currency transactions related to sales, or make arrangements for any of the foregoing functions. Private trading companies are generally headquartered in the United States, Western Europe, or Japan. It is generally accepted that a few multinational grain firms account for a large portion of the U.S. exports, and at some point in the marketing process handle well over three-fourths of the world grain trade.[17] Two privately held companies may account for 50 percent of the U.S. trade.

---

[17]Andrew Schmitz, Alex F. McCalla, Donald O. Mitchell, and Colin A. Carter, *Grain Export Cartels* (Cambridge, Mass.: Ballinger Publishing Co., 1981), p. 279.

Private trading companies are involved to some degree in most international commodity trading. However, the degree of involvement varies greatly. For example, for grain originating in the United States, private traders may engage in all of the functions, from country buying through delivery to a foreign port. On the other hand, for transactions between state traders, private trading companies may only arrange for shipping and insurance.

Although differences exist among commodities, the following trends in the relative importance of state and private traders in the grain trade have been identified.[18]

- The proportion of trade that involves *only* private companies is relatively small and appears to be declining. This is clearly the case in wheat trade, where in 1973–1977, sales from private exporters to private importers were less than 5 percent.
- The proportion of trade that involves state traders on at least one side of the market is very high—95 percent in wheat during the period 1973–1977.
- The importance of state trading by exporters depends on the level of exports by the United States and the European Economic Community. In the 1970s the private trader share increased in wheat to about 40 percent. It probably held at about that same level in the 1980s with reduced sales by the United States and increased sales by the European Community.
- Increased importance of state trading buyers is influenced by rising purchases by centrally planned economies and developing countries.
- State trading is less important in feed grains. Australia is not a feed grain state trading exporter; Japan is not a state trading importer; the United States sells a larger share of the world's production and trade; and several importers state trade in food grains but not in feed grains.

U.S. Status under Current Policies

With this background on the structure of international markets, how do U.S. producers fare under current trading arrangements where many barriers to trade are evident? The research on this issue is indecisive. Most research compares the U.S. system with the Canadian Wheat Board. McCalla and Schmitz find strengths in both systems, making it extremely difficult to determine which is "best."[19] Peltier and Anderson

[18]Ibid., pp. 23–48 and 278–279.

[19]A. F. McCalla and A. Schmitz, "Grain Marketing Systems: The Case of the United States versus Canada," *Am. J. Agric. Econ.* (May 1979), pp. 200–212.

indicate that U.S. producer returns have exceeded Canadian returns.[20]

It seems fair to conclude that under the current structure of agricultural policies in the United States, Europe, Japan, Canada, Australia, and New Zealand, the following general observations can be made:

- The total volume of trade is reduced, but not by a large amount. Producer subsidies in the United States and Europe keep grain and cotton production relatively high. Excess production is placed on the world market at low prices. The volume of trade in beef and dairy is probably substantially reduced by current limitations, but this is not necessarily true of grain and cotton.
- World market prices are lowered by producer subsidies. Consumers in countries other than the European Community and Japan benefit from those lower prices.
- Taxpayers bear a major burden of current trade barriers—particularly in the United States.
- The United States holds more than its share of the world stocks of commodities under the current policies. This residual supplier status is, in part, a result of trade policies, but may also be an inevitable consequence of the United States' operating in a world of state traders (see the box).

Freer Trade

One of the major issues is how the United States would fare under a system of substantially freer trade. Note that the emphasis is on *freer trade, not free trade. With state traders as prominent as they are in the world, it is unrealistic to anticipate a world structure that approximates free trade in the classical economic sense.* On a more realistic level, assume that the United States and the EC countries mutually agreed to abolish all producer subsidies and related barriers to trade. What would be the impact?

Economic Research Service analyses indicate that removing subsidies on foodgrains (wheat and rice) and feed grains (corn and barley) would reduce U.S. producer returns by about 19 percent and EC producer returns by 10 percent.[21] World prices for food grains would rise by 10 percent while feed grain prices would rise by 7 percent. Since 43 percent of

[20]K. Peltier and D. E. Anderson, *The Canadian Grain Marketing System*, No. 130 (Fargo; N. Dak.: Department of Agricultural Economics, North Dakota State University, 1978).

[21]Dale J. Leuck, "The Effects of Decoupling Agricultural Subsidies on the United States and the European Economic Community on Budget Expenditures and Producer Surplus," unpublished paper (Washington, D.C.: ERS, USDA, 1988).

U.S. RESIDUAL SUPPLIER: POLICY CHOICE OR INEVITABLE?

A residual supplier holds more than its share of the world stocks of a commodity. The residual supplier tends to be the last country from which commodity supplies are purchased in international trade. The United States is frequently referred to as the world's residual supplier. This characterization has roots in policy but may also be endemic with the U.S. private trading system operating in a world dominated by state traders.

No doubt U.S. policies that support farm prices tend to hold commodities off the world market in government storage. State traders can readily sell their supplies just under the U.S. support price. Private traders are not competitive dealing in U.S. grains, so they concentrate their merchandising activities on the grains or cotton of other exporters.

Even in a freer-trade environment, the United States might still be a residual supplier. The reason lies in the ability of state trading exporters to undercut the U.S. price even in a free market. Private traders set their bid price or tender offer in a potential sale at a price consistent with the cost of acquiring the commodity in the United States plus handling charges. Acquisition costs for the commodity are generally determined from the futures market. A competitive state trading exporter can always underbid the U.S. price because the commodity is not priced to them; they determine the price.

The conclusion is that a state trader can always underbid a sale from the United States regardless of the policy. If their objective is to move the grain, state traders have the advantage. Note that export PIK can be used by the United States to offset some of this advantage. But export PIK gives the United States many of the characteristics of a state trader—the government becomes directly involved in the sale!

The residual supplier issue is discussed further in Maury E. Bredahl and Leonardo Green, "Residual Supplier Model of Coarse Grain Trade," *Am. J. Agric. Econ.* (November 1983), pp. 786–790.

producer returns are a result of government subsidies and 19 percent of U.S. feed grain producer returns come from the government, the rise in price is not sufficient to offset the elimination of subsidies. In order for U.S. producers to be as well off without the program, they would have to be compensated with $7.2 billion annually compared to $10.2 billion under the 1984 farm program. How such a compensation would be paid is referred to as a decoupling policy, discussed in Chapter 10.

The Leuck analysis is not the final answer to the impact of free trade on prices and producer returns. Previous Australian research by Tyers and Anderson indicated that world prices would rise by about 30 percent and U.S. farmers would have been about as well off as under the U.S. farm program.[22] At the other extreme, Josling has reported results that indicate increases in world grain prices of as little as 3 percent.[23]

If the Leuck or Josling studies come anywhere close to reflecting the magnitude of the market price effects of freer trade, producers would be worse off *as long as they were unable to retain current subsidy levels.* With these results, freer trade will not sell well in the United States without either substantial subsidies (an inherent inconsistency) or substantial pain to farmers. Taxpayers and private traders appear to be the main beneficiaries of freer trade.

U.S. Price Leader

It is sometimes asserted by U.S. farmers that the United States sets the world price and everybody else simply follows that price. The sequel to this view is that the United States could raise the world price farm program price support level.

A U.S. **price leader strategy**, *has a naive perspective of the world grain market, the factors influencing it, and the U.S. position in the world market.* Grain producers in the rest of the world would increase production if the U.S. tried to lead price upward. The United States would be in a residual supplier status with a potentially large surplus production.

It is very important to keep in perspective the U.S. position in world agricultural trade and production (Table 7.2). The share of production is important because it provides an indication of the potential for supply response from the rest of the world. U.S. strength is in coarse grains and soybeans. Only in soybeans is the United States clearly dominant. Even

TABLE 7.2 U.S. Share of World Production and Trade, 1987

	Percent of Production	Percent of Trade
Total grain	19	33
Wheat	10	28
Rice	1	21
Coarse grain	30	42
Corn	44	52
Soybeans	56	73
Cotton	14	29

Source: World Outlook and Situation Board, *World Supply–Demand Estimates* (Washington, D.C.: USDA, 1987).

[22]Rod Tyers and Kym Anderson, *Liberalizing OECD Agricultural Policies in the Uruguay Round: Effects on Trade and Welfare.* Working Papers in Trade and Development 87/10 (Canberra, Australia: Australian National University, July 1987).

[23]Timothy E. Josling, "Bilateral Movements toward Harmonization," American Agricultural Economics Association Annual Meeting, East Lansing, Mich., August 3, 1987.

in soybeans, the share of world production and trade is being eroded by expanded acreage, particularly in South America.

Trade Agreements

One of the policy instruments used by exporting countries to secure a share of the market from competitors is trade agreements. **A trade agreement** *is a contract between two countries regarding the quantity of a commodity to be traded within a specified time period.* The principal objectives of trade agreements are supply assurance for the importing country and market assurance for the exporting country. Related objectives may include the normalization of trading agreements and the development of markets. In addition to quantity, trade agreements may contain provisions with respect to product quality, price determination, or the exchange of information on production conditions, available supplies, and needs.

The most widely recognized and discussed trade agreement is between the United States and the USSR. This agreement was signed in 1975 for a five-year period and extended for one additional year in 1981, pending renegotiation. Negotiation for a new long-term agreement was temporarily suspended in 1981, pending the outcome of Soviet intervention in Poland. The original agreement provided that the USSR would purchase at least 6 million metric tons of grain from the United States and could buy up to 8 million metric tons. Larger quantities could be purchased if adequate grain were available but only after government-to-government consultations and agreement on quantity limits.[24] Soviet agreements continue to the present.

The success of the Soviet agreement is subject to considerable question. During the mid-1980s the Soviets refused to live up to the agreement on the grounds that the United States was not price competitive. There was a period of bargaining for U.S. export subsidies, which is always a politically sensitive issue when the Soviets are involved.

Since the development of increased concern about the availability of food supplies in the early 1970s, trade agreements have become increasingly prevalent. They are most common between major developed state trading exporting and importing countries, such as Canada, Australia, the USSR, China, and Japan. Agreements are by no means limited to the United States. Canada and Australia are both actively involved in trade agreement arrangements.

The advantages of trade agreements are limited largely to the two

[24]This section draws heavily on the excellent article by Leo J. Mayer, "The Russian Grain Agreement of 1975 and the Future of United States Food Policy," *Univ. Toledo Law Rev.* (Spring 1976), pp. 1031–1069.

trading partners. The importing country is assured of a source of supply, and the exporting country is assured of a market. In addition, trade agreements have from time to time been considered market development tools in that commitment to trade is increased. They have foreign policy consequences in the sense that they increase cooperation and communication between the parties to the agreement.

Although advantages accrue to the parties to a trade agreement, those without an agreement are potentially disadvantaged. As agreements are extended to a larger number of countries, the potential adverse consequences become apparent: free-market supplies decline with the potential effect of denying countries without agreements access to a commodity and leading to increased price instability. Those countries most likely to be denied the commodity supplies are the developing countries, which are not strong cash customers and are not regularly active buyers of the commodity.

Private traders are skeptical of trade agreements in the sense that they represent departures from traditional open-market concepts and increased government "meddling" in grain marketing. This government interference has, however, been defended on the grounds that trade agreements "preserve intact the American system of private grain trade contracts but at the same time attempt to provide, through a government-to-government agreement, more regularity in future grain exports."[25]

Marketing Boards

A **marketing board** *is a compulsory marketing organization set up under government legislation to perform specific marketing functions.* The board can perform a wide range of specific functions, including the collection and dissemination of market information, product promotion, research, grading, operation, and supervision of selling facilities, collective bargaining, and the purchase, storage, and sale of products.[26]

The functions associated with marketing boards in this discussion include direct participation in the handling, pricing, and marketing of commodities such as grain for export. Such boards have the primary objectives of (1) increasing producer prices and incomes, (2) reducing fluctuation in prices and incomes, and (3) equalizing returns among producers.[27]

[25]Ibid., p. 1032.

[26]Martin E. Abel and Michele M. Veeman, "Marketing Boards," in *Marketing Alternatives for Farmers*, (Washington, D.C.: Committee on Agriculture and Forestry, U.S. Senate, April 7, 1976), pp. 73–81.

[27]C. E. Bray, P. L. Paarlberg, and F. D. Holland, *The Implications of Establishing a U.S. Wheat Board*, Foreign Agric. Rep. 163 (Washington, D.C.: ESS, USDA, April 1981).

Marketing boards are distinguished from competitive marketing systems such as the U.S. grain marketing system, in that with a marketing board:

- There is only one agency responsible for purchasing and/or selling the commodity.
- The board is directly involved in market operations.
- All producers are required to participate.
- All producers receive the same price before adjustment for quality and location.

Board operations.   The best known marketing boards are the Canadian Wheat Board and the Australian Wheat Board. Although these boards differ in detail, the following operational features are common:

- Upon harvest, grain is delivered to a public or privately owned elevator.
- Upon delivery the producer is paid an advance which is a guaranteed price.
- The board sells grain either through direct negotiation with a foreign government or to private grain trading companies that buy grain from the board for resale. There are some indications that boards not only prefer to sell direct to foreign governments but that foreign governments prefer to buy from marketing boards. Private grain trading companies would obviously prefer not to have to deal with marketing boards.
- The board controls the movement of grain from the local elevator to the port elevators.
- Proceeds from the sale of grain are pooled. Costs, including administrative, interest, insurance, and storage costs, are subtracted.
- Producers are paid a uniform average price based on proceeds from sale less cost divided by the total volume of grain sold. Adjustments are made for transportation and grain quality.
- Producers are paid the difference between the pool price and the advance. This final payment may be made more than a year after harvest. If the pool price is less than the advance, the government makes up the difference.[28]

Board impacts.   Marketing boards have been advocated as a means of raising producer returns, stabilizing prices, offsetting the mar-

---

[28]In Australia, a portion of the difference between the pool price and the advance is held back and placed in a "stabilization" fund, which is drawn on when the pool price is below the advance.

ket power of state trading buyers, preventing other exporting countries from undercutting the U.S. price in the world market, facilitating the establishment of a cartel commodity agreement, and rationing available grain supplies. Nearly all of these reasons imply that a marketing board could do a better job of marketing grain at higher and more stable prices than the present U.S. open-market system. The evidence, however, as indicated previously, is inconclusive when the basis for comparison is the U.S. and Canadian systems.

Boards stabilize prices to producers within the year because the producer is paid the pool price. However, the cost of that stability is the opportunity for a farmer to make a higher (or lower) price than the pool price. Most U.S. farmers appear to prefer that opportunity. Whether boards stabilize price from year to year is questionable. A USDA study found that there was no significant difference in year-to-year variation in prices received by producers in the United States, Canada, and Australia.[29]

A marketing board would substantially alter U.S. methods of grain merchandising. Open-market methods of producer price determination would no longer exist. The role of the futures market would be radically changed: It might be changed to a predominantly international device for hedging sales, or it could disappear entirely.[30]

Cooperative and proprietary elevators and exporters would continue to operate but would perform predominantly market intermediary functions such as internal grain storage, handling, operation of port facilities, and arranging for ocean transportation. They would perform sales functions on only that portion of the grain that the Board did not sell directly to another government or purchasing agent.

World Cartel

World cartels of grain-exporting countries are sometimes suggested as a potential solution to the problems of producers in exporting countries. Those who see the need for a cartel not only see the world price as being too low but contend that importers have a sufficiently strong market position to suppress world price. In other words, they believe that the world is a buyers' market with monopsony pricing. This market power originates from state trader activities of large importing countries, such as the Japan Food Agency, Soviet Union, and China. A world cartel, in theory, would offset this market power.

In its pure form, a cartel is designed to increase producer returns through the exercise of market power. That market power would offset the power of monopsonistic buyers; serve as a lever against the use of

[29]Ibid., p. 8

[30]McCalla and Schmitz, "Grain Marketing Systems," p. 206.

tariffs, variable levies, and quotas by importing countries; and potentially extract pure monopoly rents by raising the market price above the competitive equilibrium.

Cartels may have less lofty and more benevolent objectives, such as providing international price stability and/or holding commodity reserves. These more modest objectives will be discussed subsequently under the subheading "international commodity agreement," a form of cartel.

The pure cartel with price enhancement objectives must have a sufficient market share to raise price and, therefore, faces a downward-sloping excess demand function. Figure 7.1 provides a two-country trade model explanation of the operation of a cartel and provides substantial insight into its potential pitfalls. Since the exporting country cartel faces the excess demand curve ED; its marginal revenue curve is MR_{ed}. To maximize profit it equates marginal revenue with marginal cost as represented by ES and changes the demand price P_m for export quantity Q_m or $D_m - S_m$. Note that at price P_m the desire of the exporting cartel countries is to produce S_c, which is greater than the quantity Q_m that can be sold at P_m. Therefore, in a cartel there is always an incentive to sell more than the market will take at the cartel price. Excess production, which has been the principal weakness of OPEC, is inherent in a cartel.

To be effective at raising price over a period of years, a cartel must:

• Be dealing with a commodity that has an inelastic demand. Only with an inelastic demand over the relevant price range does an increase in price result in an increase in revenue.
• Be able to control supplies and entry into production. Without the power to control production, a cartel's policy to raise price will be self-defeating. Production control in a multilateral-country context involves allocation to each country of a quota. Cartel agreements have, therefore, also been referred to as quota arrangements.

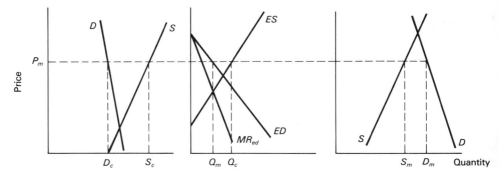

Figure 7.1 Exporting country cartel creates incentive for excess production.

- Be able to prevent substitute products from penetrating the market. For products with close substitutes, to be effective the cartel must control the substitutes.

OPEC has had considerably less than full success in holding its cartel together. It appears that an agricultural product would have greater difficulty for the following reasons:

- Production control programs in agriculture have had few successes. Establishing coordinated production control programs across countries would have an even lower probability of success.
- With price incentives, most agricultural products can be produced in a large number of countries. Price increases on the cartel commodity will tend to attract productive resources from other commodities. This will be particularly likely in countries that are marginal exporters.
- Consumers will, over time, tend to substitute a lower-priced commodity for the higher-priced cartel commodity. With higher prices for wheat, these substitutes will probably become more available.
- Wheat is a renewable resource that is grown each year. Once oil is used, it is gone. More wheat will be available each year.
- A cartel in a commodity such as wheat may draw strong adverse political reactions from Third World countries. This is particularly true in the case of wheat since the major exporting countries, except Argentina, are higher-income, developed countries.

International Commodity Agreements

An **international commodity agreement** *is a multilateral agreement among countries to affect the terms of trade.* The terms of trade directly affected by commodity agreements may include the price at which the commodity is sold, the quantity sold, the quantity of production, or the quantity of the commodity held in reserve stocks. Commodity agreements are cartels with less lofty goals. Legally, commodity agreements are treaties among nations.[31] They have been used and/or proposed to accomplish two primary goals:

- Stabilize the world price within a corridor
- Maintain an international reserve of commodity stocks

[31]Mayer, "Russian Grain Agreement," pp. 1047–1051, contains a very good and interesting discussion of the legal status of international commodity agreements, including the controversy over the authority of the president to enter into and enforce trade commodity agreements without the advice and consent of the Senate.

Corridor commodity agreements *establish a range within which prices are allowed to move.* Provisions requiring participating exporting countries to restrict sales and thus build stocks when prices are low and sell stocks when prices are high frequently accompany these agreements. The result is an attempt to stabilize price within an acceptable range. This may be visualized in Fig. 7.2, where ES_1 and ED are the initial supply and demand schedules in the export market. The price corridor is established within the range P_1 and P_2. That is, the agreement specifies that sales will not be made below P_1 or above P_2.

Corridor agreements encounter problems when supplies increase to ES_2 due to favorable weather and price thus falls below P_1—the commodity agreement minimum. Even with an agreement to accumulate stocks, a clear incentive exists to cut price and undermine the agreement. Even if the minimum price (P_1) were adhered to, at that price surplus production would result. Surplus stocks would undermine the price structure in the next production season.

Corridor commodity agreements tend to break down when the price range specified in the agreement is sufficiently narrow that the market price would be expected to frequently fall outside the specified range. This conclusion is supported by the following observation by Paarlberg on price stabilization attempts in wheat:

> An International Wheat Agreement worked fairly well for a decade or so after its establishment in 1949. This success was due in large measure to the wide latitude for competitive price discovery and to the fact that economic conditions were fairly stable during the period. A subsequent Inter-

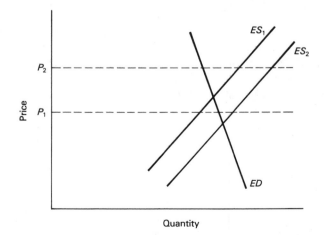

Figure 7.2   Price corridor established by a commodity agreement.

national Wheat Agreement failed when it prescribed a price range less compatible with market conditions.[32]

The agreements to which Paarlberg refers included provisions that guaranteed prices and purchases, recorded transactions, and spelled out enforcement rights and stocks to be established.

Most of the commodity agreements that have been entered into under the United Nation's Conferences on Trade and Development (UNCTAD) establish a price corridor. The United States has participated in several of these agreements, more as a gesture of goodwill and a desire to achieve other foreign policy objectives than as a commitment to the concept. The United States has generally been in a position of advocating a relatively wide corridor within which prices can move to allow relatively free interplay of market forces.

Reserve commodity agreements *are designed primarily to assure supplies.* Proposals for reserve agreements evolved largely out of the world food conference. Specifically, the conference resolutions called for stocks of grain to be maintained in an amount sufficient to provide food security. It recommended a study of the feasibility of establishing an international system of reserves at strategic locations.[33]

International reserves are to be distinguished from domestic reserves held by an individual country. The objectives of domestic reserves are country-specific. The primary objective of an international reserve would be to provide food security for countries that could not afford to purchase commercially.

The primary interest in international reserve agreements comes from developing countries. The 1970s proved that when global strategies occur, widespread hunger and starvation are also a reality. Yet some very difficult issues arise in establishing an international reserve agreement, including the size of the reserve, control over purchase and release decisions, who should supply the grain, and who should pay the costs. These issues proved difficult enough in the 1970s that they were not resolved, and no international reserve agreement has been signed.

THE POLITICAL DIMENSION

This discussion of international trade and development policy has been devoid of international politics. Yet foreign policy obviously plays a very important role in these issues.

[32]Don Paarlberg, *Farm and Food Policy: Issues of the 1980s* (Lincoln, Nebr.: University of Nebraska Press, 1980), p. 248.

[33]Joseph W. Willett et al., *The World Food Situation and Prospects to 1985*. Foreign Agric. Rep. 98 (Washington, D.C.: ERS, USDA, December 1974), p. 90.

The Place of the United States in the World Political Economy

For nearly two decades, the United States has been adjusting to the realities of international politics and its changing economic, military, and political position in the world. Prior to World War II, the United States existed largely outside the mainstream of international policies. The balance of power in the world centered largely in Europe. The United States benefited from its geographic isolation from other world powers, its plentiful resources, and its lack of dependence on world markets.

The United States emerged from World War II as the only clearly dominant world power. It held at least 50 percent of the world's gold, produced 40 percent of the goods and services, possessed 50 percent of the world's effective military manpower, was the world's only nuclear power, and controlled the vote in the United Nations Security Council, the World Bank, and the International Monetary Fund.[34]

In the mid-1960s, this position of dominance began to erode. The number of independent nations multiplied more than threefold. New alliances developed among nations, such as the European Economic Community, the Third World, and OPEC. Multinational corporations and financial institutions began to wield their own power. An increasing number of nations acquired control of nuclear weapons. The will of the United States to fight and win in military conflict was successfully challenged in Vietnam and, some would add, in Cuba and in Iran. The size of the world economy mushroomed, but individual countries became increasingly dependent on foreign sources of food and energy and thus more dependent on trade. The dollar not only declined in value, but it was challenged as the world's prime medium of exchange.

Although America remains a strong force in the world, it has been forced to face the following realities of international politics:

- The United States can no longer dictate or control world political events and economic terms.
- The United States cannot influence all the nations of the world all the time.
- Influencing other nations generally bears a price that frequently requires domestic sacrifice.

These realities have made both the substance and process of international policy significantly different and more complex than domestic policy.

[34]Herbert K. Tillema, "America and the World: 1980," *International Affairs and U.S. Agriculture*, Mo. Agric. Exp. Str. Rep. 259 (Columbia, Mo.: University of Missouri, December 1980), p. 11.

The president is clearly expected to provide leadership on issues of international policy. This power is derived from Article II, Section 2, of the Constitution, conferring on the president the power of the commander in chief, the power to make treaties with two-thirds approval of the Senate, and the power to appoint ambassadors. Although the scope of this power is sometimes disputed, the role of the president as chief diplomat in charge of American foreign policy is widely recognized.

The centralization of power in the president can result in substantial swings in the direction of foreign policy from one administration to the next. President Reagan, for example, was elected on a platform that emphasized reestablishing the United States as a military power, and a perception that President Carter had overextended the pursuit of human rights in foreign policy.

Within the executive branch, at the cabinet and Executive Office of the President level, substantial controversy has developed from time to time over who has prime responsibility for advising the president on decisions having foreign policy implications and for representing the United States in diplomatic exchanges. In food and agriculture, the question of "who is in charge" has generally been a contest between the president's national security adviser, the National Security Council, the secretary of state, the special trade representative, and the secretary of agriculture. Much of this concern has arisen with regard to trade negotiation with the USSR. In these power struggles, the secretary of agriculture has generally played a secondary role in both negotiations and decisions to either the secretary of state, the president's national security advisers, or the trade representative.

The Three Worlds

World economic and political discussions, negotiations, and even conflicts tend to be dominated by three different geopolitical groupings:

The **First World** is composed of the major developed market economies of the world, including the United States and Canada, Western European countries, Japan, Australia, and New Zealand. All are members of the Organization for Economic Cooperation and Development (OECD), which tends to serve as a focal point for international dialogue on their behalf. From a trade perspective, the first world may be divided into two subworlds—the net exporting countries and the net importing countries. This chapter and Chapter 6 have shown that their economic interests are materially different. These differing economic interests have been revealed in the political events of the mid to late 1980s.

The **Second World** includes the centrally planned economies of the Soviet Union, its Eastern European allies, and China. Here the Soviet Union stands as a focal point for international dialogue. Both the Soviet

Union and China are being forced to assess the degree to which economic incentives should be integrated into their systems. Yet tension continues to be the dominant characteristic of relations between the West and the East.

The **Third World** includes the remaining, so-called "nonaligned" nations. The membership of this group includes economic and political diversity ranging from the OPEC countries to low-income developing countries such as Cambodia, Bangladesh, and Ethiopia.

In the 1970s the Third World became the focal point for debate between the predominantly northern, developed countries and the southern, have-not nations—the so-called "North–South" dialogue. The basic contention of the Third World is that past developmental strategies have been insufficient to reduce significantly world inequities in income levels and living standards. These development strategies, by and large, have their roots in the work of Rostow, who theorized that certain preconditions allowing for the accumulation of savings and investment in those areas of greatest comparative advantage set the stage for a takeoff period of accelerating growth.[35] Entering this takeoff phase has been associated with a country experiencing increasing returns to scale; appropriate investments in the country's infrastructure, including transportation systems, utilities, and irrigation projects; and the need to grow progressively from agriculture to manufacturing and ultimately to services.

Third World nations increasingly point out that these development strategies have not solved the many inequalities that exist between the developed nations and the majority of the world's population living in Third World nations. Although several countries, such as South Korea and Taiwan, have entered a phase of rapid economic growth and development, this progress has been too slow to satisfy the Third World nations. They argue that in terms of per capita income, all that has been accomplished is to stabilize the income gap between the people of the developed and developing nations—not reduce it.

The demands of Third World nations have increasingly been revealed in international meetings of nonaligned nations and the UNCTAD. Proposals of the Third World call for the establishment of a **new international economic order**. The basic concepts of establishing such a new order include policy and program proposals such as:

- Revamping the present international credit system by phasing out national currencies and replacing them with a new international currency

[35]Walt W. Rostow, *The Stages of Economic Growth* (New York: Cambridge University Press, 1960).

- Dismantling affluent-nation restrictions on movements of goods, services, and people
- Control by developing countries of primary production, processing, and distribution of their national resources
- Renegotiation of all past leases and contracts given by developing countries to multinational corporations
- Restructuring the United Nations to give it greater operational powers and to increase poor-nation voting strength in the World Bank and International Monetary Fund[36]

Food Diplomacy

Food diplomacy *refers to the use of agricultural exports and development assistance as tools to achieve specific foreign policy goals.* Foreign policy considerations play an important role in many, if not most, international agricultural and food policy decisions.

Food and development assistance may be utilized as a tool of diplomacy with either a positive or a punitive strategy:

- *Positive food diplomacy* refers to efforts to expand exports, provide food aid, or development assistance based on the theory that a government will not bite the hand that feeds it. Positive food diplomacy is pursued on a humanitarian or need basis without regard to the system of government or long-term objectives of the government receiving assistance. It is food assistance without strings attached and with no intention to withdraw food supplied or development assistance in the future. Historically, one of the most ardent advocates of a positive food diplomacy strategy was Hubert Humphrey. He was always a strong supporter of unlimited access to exports, expanded food aid, and expanded agricultural development assistance.[37]
- *Punitive food diplomacy* refers to making access to exports, food aid, or development assistance contingent upon specific action by the recipient government. The most widely recognized example of an effort to utilize food as a tool of diplomacy was the decision by President Carter to partially embargo grain exports to the USSR in January 1980, when the Soviets invaded Afghanistan. Further grain exports to the Soviets were made contingent upon withdrawal of troops. This is not an isolated example. During 1965–1968, the

---

[36]Mahbub ul Haq, *The Third World and the International Economic Order*, Overseas Devel. Counc. Pap. 22 (New York: ODC, September 1976), pp. 9–10.

[37]Emma Rothschild, "Food Politics," *Foreign Affairs* (January 1976), p. 295.

United States unsuccessfully used P.L. 480 food aid to persuade India to support U.S. policies in Southeast Asia.[38] Food aid was used unsuccessfully in 1974 in support of U.S. efforts to achieve military disengagement in the Middle East.[39] Rothschild suggests that U.S. food aid was parceled out in the mid-1970s in return for putting Third World pressure on OPEC countries to discontinue the oil embargo.[40]

Can food be successfully utilized as a tool of diplomacy? The answer to this question probably lies in how it is used and in how success is defined. America's capacity to produce for export, provide for food aid, and assist in agricultural development (positive food diplomacy) alone hopefully builds goodwill. Attaching strings to food aid (punitive food diplomacy) tends to create resentment. For example, in the mid-1960s, U.S. food aid to India was made contingent on the adoption of population control programs. Rothschild observes: "That policy was resented intensely. There would be nothing, I think, more likely to destroy the influence the United States might have over food-importing countries than the possibility of future coercion."[41]

There is also the question of how effective punitive food diplomacy can be in any event. The USSR effectively demonstrated the ability to import grain in the face of the 1980 partial export embargo by shifting world grain flows. The Soviet Union is also often in a position to capitalize on U.S. refusals to provide food aid or development assistance to Third World countries. Equally important, certain forms of food diplomacy, such as embargoes, create adverse political reactions within the United States. Presidential candidate Reagan successfully capitalized on farmer resentment of the Carter-imposed Soviet grain embargo. Once elected, however, Reagan was caught in a dilemma of choosing between fulfilling a campaign promise to lift the embargo and the danger of appearing to take action that conflicts with a hard-line policy toward the Soviets. He eventually opted to lift the embargo. The embargo, however, continued to be blamed for reduced exports of farm products throughout the following years, even through Bush's election.

Despite such dangers and conflicts, the use of food as a tool of diplomacy in both a positive and a punitive sense is likely to continue. Tighter food supplies not only increase the temptation to use food as a tool of diplomacy, but also increase its chances of being effective.

[38]Paarlberg, *Farm and Food Policy*, p. 251.

[39]Ibid.

[40]Rothschild, "Food Policies," pp. 285–307.

[41]Ibid., p. 294

FIGHTING WITH GUNS AND
BUTTER

Drought is a given in her life. It hasn't rained properly here in four years. In that time, her husband hasn't been able to raise a decent crop. Outside her dirt-floor hut, her babies play in a dusty moonscape—rocks, mountains, nothing that is green. But food aid keeps rolling in.

Asked where the food comes from, Kadija replies that it comes from the guerrillas, the Eritrean People's Liberation Front. As Kadija testifies, it doesn't matter much who donated the food. Hearts and minds are won by the people who deliver it.

As long as the EPLF holds these hills and the rebels can truck in food donated by the West and funneled through bordering Sudan, Kadija and her family are famine-proof. As one might suspect, she and her neighbors have only good things to say about the EPLF.

The food weapon is wielded not only by the Eritrean rebels, who want to create an independent nation out of Ethiopia's northernmost region, but by guerrilla fighters in the bordering Tigray region, who want to overthrow Ethiopia's central government, which they describe as a puppet of the Soviet Union.

It also is used by the Ethiopian government, which refuses to negotiate with either rebel organization and repeatedly has mobilized Africa's largest standing army in attempts to crush them.

It is the famine fight, the battle over rights to fill the stomachs of the peasantry. Part of the battle is operational—actually delivering food by airplane, truck and camel. The other half is rhetorical—propaganda attacks on the "enemy" for "playing politics" with food.

"He who controls roads controls food. He who controls food controls the people. This time around, the rebels in Eritrea and in Tigray are prepared to play much harder ball in terms of controlling the people," says Shun Chetty, deputy representative for the U.N. High Commissioner for Refugees in neighboring Sudan.

In the game to control the hungry, the best-known and most powerful player is the Ethiopian government. In the next eight months, the authoritarian Marxist regime in Addis Ababa will supervise distribution of the lion's share of the 1.3 million tons of donated food that the FAO says is needed for Ethiopia's drought victims.

It is outside donors—western governments and private relief agencies—that legitimize the contestants' battle for peasants' hearts and minds by giving away food, trucks and medicines.

This year, according to a western relief official in Sudan, the Eritrean and Tigrayan relief agencies will be given at least 80,000 tons of food. About half of it, the official says, will come from the U.S. government and half from the European Community.

The United States and the EC also are the largest suppliers of relief food for distribution in government-controlled areas.

For both sides, a glut of relief food could upset war strategy. If relief food moved too freely, carefully cultivated loyalties could be lost.

Severed of its political strings, relief food buys no one's allegiance. It just keeps people from dying.

Blaine Harden, "Fighting Guns with Butter: Food Has Become a Weapon in Erithea's Civil War," *The Washington Post Weekly Edition*, January 18–24, 1988, pp. 6–7.

INCREASING POLITICAL
AND ECONOMIC INTERDEPENDENCE

Dealings with international food and trade problems are among the most complex faced by policymakers, in part because they are international in scope. They serve to emphasize the extent and complexity of interdependence that exists in the world. While the Third World makes demands on the developed nations through the North–South dialogue, a contest for political and economic influence exists between First and Second Worlds with respect to the Third World nations. This so-called "East–West" dialogue increases the complexity of international food problems by injecting issues of geopolitical influence and control. These forces frequently take agricultural policy making outside the control of USDA and into the highest levels of government. Agriculture is thus not only affected by world economic events but also by world political events.

Third World pressures will continue to increase. These pressures present particular problems for agriculture because developing countries represent the most significant growth markets for agricultural products. Efforts to increase economic development and stimulate growth, in turn, boost the demand for farm products. At the same time, concern exists among U.S. producers that efforts to help developing countries produce products compete directly with U.S. exports. In addition, Third World countries want higher prices for the products they produce. They look upon OPEC as a model and thus tend to favor cartel strategies for raising the price of the products they export. This places an even broader set of proposals on the international policy agenda.

ADDITIONAL READINGS

1. While recommended at the end of Chapter 6 as an excellent, albeit heavy, reference, Alex F. McCalla and Timothy E. Josling, *Agricultural Policies and World Markets* (New York: Macmillan Publishing Company, 1985) do an excellent job of integrating the economics and politics of trade issues. Particular

attention is called to pages 193–278, which discuss international policy decisions and goals.

2. The book on *Grain Export Cartels*, by Andrew Schmitz, Alex F. McCalla, Donald O. Mitchell, and Colin A. Carter (Cambridge, Mass.: Ballinger Publishing Co., 1981) is a must for anyone interested in understanding world grain markets and policy. It is not necessary to believe in cartels to find this book enjoyable and useful. It is useful to recognize that both of the major authors have a background in Canada.

Chapter 8

The Macroeconomics
of Agriculture

*Practical men, who believe themselves
to be quite exempt from any intellectual
influences, are usually the slaves of
some defunct economist. . . . It is
ideas, not vested interests, which are
dangerous for good or evil.*

John Maynard Keynes

Macroeconomics *is concerned with the economy as a whole and how it
functions.* The **macroeconomics of agriculture** *is concerned with the
relationship between the general U.S. economy and the agricultural economy.* Some economists would prefer to define it even more broadly to include the relationship between the world economy and agriculture. There
is merit in that broader perspective. One of the main effects of
macroeconomic policy is on the value of the dollar, which, as was seen in
Chapter 6, has international trade implications that affect other countries and deflect back on the United States.

The impact of the macroeconomy on agriculture became very apparent in the 1970s and in the 1980s. In 1976, Schuh effectively argued that
changes in macroeconomic and international economic policy had thrust
agriculture into a new era.[1] Subsequently, he asserted that these changes
made contemporary agricultural policies outdated, if not counterproductive.[2] Although these arguments may have been overdrawn to make the
point, it is clear that macroeconomic policy has had and continues to have

[1]G. Edward Schuh, "The New Macroeconomics of Agriculture," *Am. J. Agric. Econ.*
(December 1976), pp. 802–811.

[2]G. Edward Schuh, "U.S. Agricultural Policy in an Open World Economy," testimony
to the Joint Economic Committee (Washington, D.C.: U.S. Congress, May 26, 1983).

a major impact on agriculture. The purpose of this chapter is to (1) describe the place of agriculture in the macroeconomy, (2) explain the impacts of macroeconomic variables on agriculture, and (3) provide a summary of the major macroeconomic policy tools that affect agriculture.

AGRICULTURE IN THE MACROECONOMY

The farm level is by no means the limit of the influence of agriculture on the U.S. economy. Putting food on the table and cotton or wool on people's backs requires many more nonfarmers than farmers. The importance of agriculture in the economy may be viewed either from the perspective of the farm sector or the overall food and fiber system. For every farmer and hired farm worker there are nearly eight additional people employed in the food and fiber system. About 18 percent of the civilian labor force is employed in agriculture.

Farm Sector

The farm sector represents a substantial but generally declining share of the U.S. economy. Measured in terms of share of the gross national product (GNP), the farm sector declined from nearly 7 percent in 1950 to about 2 percent in the mid-1980s (Fig. 8.1). The rest of the econ-

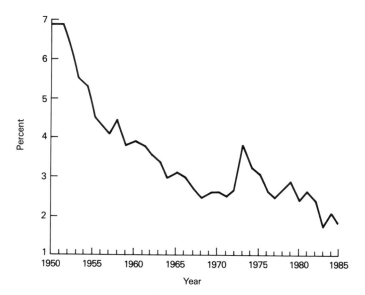

Figure 8.1 Gross farm product share of gross national product.
Source: Extension Service, *1986 Agriculture Chartbook*, Agric. Handbook 663 (Washington, D.C.: USDA, November 1986), p. 12.

omy has grown more rapidly than the farm sector. That should not be surprising. From a domestic perspective, *Engel's law* indicates that as income increases, consumers spend a smaller share of the total on food. Therefore, for farmers' share of GNP to increase, the declining share of domestic consumption would have to be made up for by rapidly expanding exports. While exports experienced a boom in the 1970s, they declined in the 1980s. It will be seen later that this decline was at least partially related to macroeconomic policy changes.

The substitution of technology for labor has made it possible to reduce dramatically the agricultural work force. As a result, farm population has declined considerably (Fig. 8.2). Hence output per farm worker increased more than sixfold from 1950 through the mid-1980s. This has released people from agriculture to produce other goods and services in the nonagricultural economy. While politicians, farmers, and the media bemoan the decline in the number of farmers, the movement of labor from agriculture has facilitated economic progress in the rest of the economy.

A reduced farm work force has been made possible by technological change, as reflected in greater farmer reliance on purchased inputs (Fig. 8.3). Before mechanical power was developed, purchased inputs accounted for less than 50 percent of cash receipts. In the mid-1980s, over 80 percent of cash receipts went to purchased inputs, which made agriculture more subject to inflation and to financial risk. In other words, in earlier years it was easier for farmers to "tighten their belts" and cut

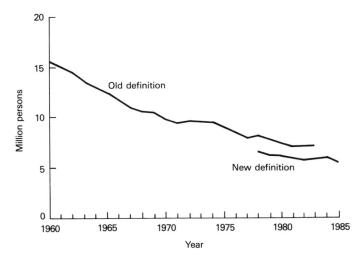

Figure 8.2 Farm population.
Source: Extension Service, *1986 Agriculture Chartbook*, Agric. Handbook 663 (Washington, D.C.: USDA, November 1986), p. 6.

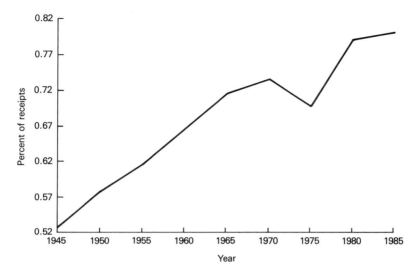

Figure 8.3   Cash expenses account for an ever-increasing share of cash receipts including government payments.
Source: Economic Research Service, *Economic Indicators of the Farm Sector: National Financial Summary* (Washington, D.C.: USDA, 1986).

down on farm expenditures when times got tough. Now there is a smaller margin for belt tightening.

Food and Fiber System

In 1984, the entire food and fiber system accounted for 18 percent of the U.S. total gross national product. Farming is linked to the rest of the food and fiber system, and ultimately to the general economy, through its input purchases and product sales.

Figure 8.4 provides an indication of the linkages between agriculture and the general economy through the gross national product and employment accounts. In 1984, the $648 billion in final consumer and stock demand for farm products was linked to $520 billion in marketing activities beyond the farm, $65 billion on the farm, and $64 billion in import activities before the farm. Total employment in the food and fiber complex was 21.0 million, 16.3 million of which were marketing related, 2.7 million were on the farm, and 2.0 million were in input related activities.

Impact of agricultural prosperity on the rest of the economy. Agricultural fundamentalists in the 1970s and the 1980s have asserted that if agricultural prices were raised by administrative fiat to 100 percent of parity, the whole economy would boom.

DEMAND LINKAGES

Figure 8.4 Agricultural sector GNP and employment linkages, 1984.

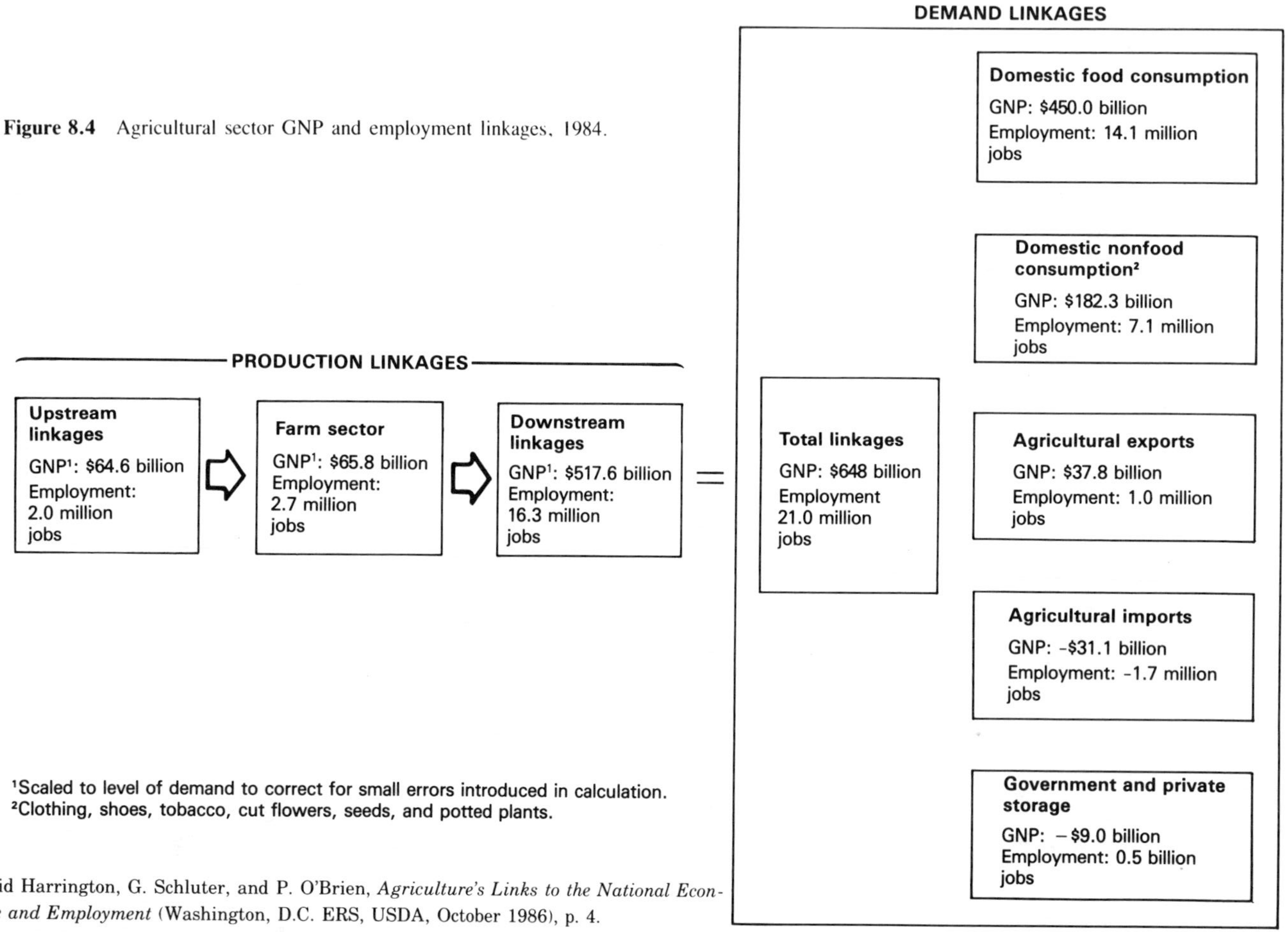

Domestic food consumption

GNP: $450.0 billion
Employment: 14.1 million jobs

Domestic nonfood consumption[2]

GNP: $182.3 billion
Employment: 7.1 million jobs

Agricultural exports

GNP: $37.8 billion
Employment: 1.0 million jobs

Agricultural imports

GNP: −$31.1 billion
Employment: −1.7 million jobs

Government and private storage

GNP: −$9.0 billion
Employment: 0.5 billion jobs

Total linkages

GNP: $648 billion
Employment 21.0 million jobs

PRODUCTION LINKAGES

Upstream linkages

GNP[1]: $64.6 billion
Employment: 2.0 million jobs

Farm sector

GNP[1]: $65.8 billion
Employment: 2.7 million jobs

Downstream linkages

GNP[1]: $517.6 billion
Employment: 16.3 million jobs

[1]Scaled to level of demand to correct for small errors introduced in calculation.
[2]Clothing, shoes, tobacco, cut flowers, seeds, and potted plants.

Source: David Harrington, G. Schluter, and P. O'Brien, *Agriculture's Links to the National Economy: Income and Employment* (Washington, D.C. ERS, USDA, October 1986), p. 4.

They contend that agriculture is the primary determinant of the level of economic activity in the entire nation. This agricultural fundamentalist perspective asserts that the solution to all economic problems is raising agricultural prices and incomes. Farmers will, in turn, spend this income, increasing demand for farm equipment, fertilizer, energy, and other farm inputs, which has a multiplier effect throughout the economy.

In the early days of the American economy there was some merit in this point of view. In fact, throughout the nineteenth-century agriculture directly employed and accounted for a large proportion of the economy's total production. Even in the late 1920s, the farm population accounted for 25 percent of the total U.S. population.[3] Even today for many rural communities and states, the economic health of agriculture is an important factor influencing the level of business activity, employment, and incomes (Fig. 8.5). Yet agriculture is only one link in the total economy. It neither drives nor pulls the whole system. The farm sector cannot unilaterally increase either its output or its prices and expect a proportional increase in economic activity from the rest of the economy. Agriculture can purchase inputs or sell its products only if the demand is there for the final products. But agricultural production usually exceeds demand. The economic system is driven by the combination of output volume and value. Farmers may benefit from increased prices, but many agribusiness segments are hurt by the reduced demand and/or production that goes with it. Thus simply raising farm price does not generate income and employment in the economy as a whole.[4]

Assuming no reduction in output, every $1 billion increase in demand-driven gross farm income generates about $3 billion additional GNP and 30,000 to 35,000 jobs.[5] In agriculture, many of those extra jobs would be created through increased purchases of farm machinery and exports of farm products. Farm income and machinery purchases are closely correlated. The large losses experienced by International Harvester during the 1980s and eventual consolidation into Case was one of the consequences of depressed farm income conditions.

Since exports are a barometer of agricultural prosperity, reduced agricultural exports have impacts that extend throughout the U.S. economy. For example, the decline in exports from $37.8 billion in 1984 to

[3]*Economic Report of the President* (Washington, D.C.: Council of Economic Advisors, 1981), pp. 263, 339.

[4]This section relies heavily on the work of David Harrington, Gerald Schluter, and Patrick O'Brien, *Agriculture's Links to the National Economy*, Agric. Inf. Bull. 504 (Washington, D.C.: ERS, USDA, 1986).

[5]Luther Tweeten, "Sector as Personality: The Case of Farm Protest Movements," unpublished paper, E.T. York Distinguished Lecture Series (Gainesville, Fla.: University of Florida, March 1986).

THE RAW MATERIAL THEORY
OF VALUE

Farm protest movements in the 1970s and the early 1980s embraced the raw material theory of value as their justification for higher farm prices . . . [this theory] constitutes the economic basis for favored treatment of agriculture, and creates frustration when such treatment is not forthcoming. . . .

The central principle of the [raw material] theory [of value] is that raw materials are the sole source of the nation's wealth. Corollaries are that (1) pricing of raw materials at "full" or "honest" parity (never clearly defined but interpreted by many farmers to mean the same ratio of prices received for raw materials to prices paid by producers as prevailed in the 1910–14 period) will restore and sustain the nation's economic health, and (2) that national income is a simple multiple of income from raw materials. . . .

In its simplistic logic, the raw material theory of value is akin to Karl Marx's labor theory of value which gives sole credit to labor rather than to raw materials for creating value. A theory which attributes value solely to labor is as absurd as one which attributes value only to raw materials.

Advocates of the raw material theory of value maintain that 100 percent of parity will make not only agriculture but the entire economy boom. Carl Wilken's leverage principle of $1 of farm income creating $7 of national income grew out of the 1930s when farm receipts happened to be one-seventh of national income. As consumers' income rises, they choose to spend a declining proportion of it for food and fiber ingredients supplied by farmers. The pattern may appear invidious to farmers but is a normal expression of consumers' preferences. It follows that national economic growth reduces the ratio of farm sector income to national income. In 1985, national income was 20 times gross farm income. Are we to believe that raising farm income by $1 will raise national income $20?

Luther Tweeten, "Sector as Personality: The Case of Farm Protest Movements," unpublished paper, E. T. York Distinguished Lecture Series (Gainesville, Fla.: University of Florida, March 1986).

$29.0 billion in 1985 reduced economic activity by about $20 billion and cost over 250,000 jobs.[6] These reduced exports were largely the product of adverse macroeconomic policies and farm programs maintaining U.S. price supports above world market levels.

Of course, when farmers suffer economically the regions most adversely affected are the rural communities and counties that depend on agriculture for a large share of their income (see Fig. 4.1). The people and

[6]Estimated from Gerald Schluter, "Impact of U.S. Agricultural Trade," in *National Food Review* (Washington, D.C.: ERS, USDA, Fall 1983), pp. 2–3.

Percentage of Total Employed Working in
Farming and Agribusiness Industries, 1985

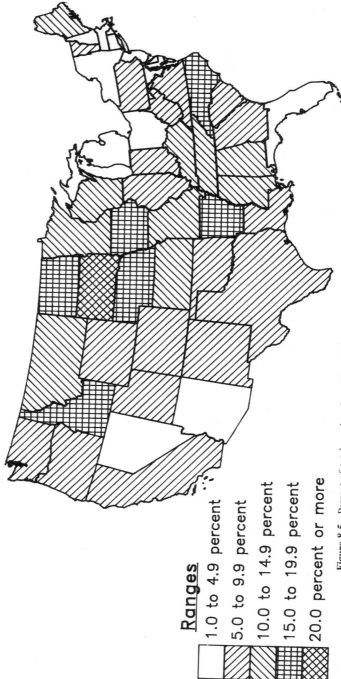

Ranges

1.0 to 4.9 percent

5.0 to 9.9 percent

10.0 to 14.9 percent

15.0 to 19.9 percent

20.0 percent or more

Figure 8.5   Percent of total employed working in farming and agribusiness industries, 1982.
Source: David Harrington and Thomas Carlin, *The U.S. Farm Sector: How Is It Weathering in the 1980s?* Agric. Inf. Bull. 506 (Washington, D.C.: ERS, USDA, April 1987). p. 23.

businesses located in these agriculturally dependent areas along with farm machinery manufacturers, related farm input suppliers, and exporters bore the brunt of the 1980s agricultural recession. These were exactly the same sectors that prospered in the 1970s when agriculture boomed.

The remainder of the food processing and marketing industry was not as adversely affected by the economic bust of the 1980s, nor did it benefit as much from the boom. As a general rule, processing and marketing firms' margins tend to widen when farm prices fall and tighten when they rise—just the reverse of the farmers' situation. In addition, food processors and marketers are as equally, directly affected by the level of general economic activity as by farm conditions. When consumers' real incomes are rising they are willing to buy more of the services that go into today's household food purchases. These relationships are discussed in greater depth in Chapter 12.

MACROECONOMIC VARIABLES AFFECTING AGRICULTURE

While the impacts of agriculture on the macroeconomy are sometimes exaggerated, until recently the effects of the general economy on agriculture have tended to be ignored or at least underrated. Four macroeconomic variables have a particularly pronounced impact on agriculture: (1) income growth, (2) inflation rate, (3) interest rate, and (4) value of the dollar. Each is sufficiently important to warrant separate discussion and comment.

Income Growth

One of the major objectives of macroeconomic policy is to create stable economic growth that fosters low levels of unemployment and persistent increases in real income. The domestic income elasticity of demand for food and beverages is about 0.4. Thus a 10 percent increase in real per capita income will generate about a 4 percent increase in aggregate farm-level demand. With real income trending upward by only about 2 percent annually, food demand trends upward by only 0.8 percent due to income growth and an additional 0.8 percent due to population growth for a total annual growth trend of 1.6 percent annually.[7] However, the demand for several individual foods is quite income elastic. These include processed foods such as canned fruits and vegetables, juices, dried beans and peas, and cheese. Producers of these foods stand to benefit materially from an expanding economy. Some staple commodities such as fluid milk, rice,

[7]Paul T. Prentice and David A. Torgerson, "U.S. Agriculture and the Macroeconomy," in *Agricultural-Food Policy Review: Commodity Program Perspectives* (Washington D.C.: ERS, USDA, July 1985), pp. 9–24.

and flour have a negative income elasticity, meaning that demand declines as income grows.[8]

It was also observed in Chapter 5 that the income elasticity of demand for food in developing countries is more elastic (in the 0.7 to 0.9 range). Not surprisingly, in times of an expanding world economy, developing countries have been a major growth area for exports of agricultural products. The difference in income elasticity between the domestic demand and the income elasticity of developing countries has important implications for U.S. macroeconomic policy. The United States is a major world economic force. It accounts for about 25 percent of the world's economic output.[9] If it conducts its macroeconomic policy in a manner that provides the stimulus for domestic *as well as world* economic growth, U.S. exports of agricultural products stand to benefit. Coordinated macroeconomic policies by developed countries such as the United States, Japan, and West Germany would be even more effective.[10] In addition to favorable macroeconomic policies, this requires maintaining open markets for developing country products as well as increased development assistance.

Inflation

Inflation refers to a general rise in the price of goods and services. Inflation occurs by two primary means:

- Demand-pull when the economy is running near full capacity and the demand for goods and services exceeds the supply
- Cost-push when costs are rising rapidly due to the market power of labor unions, big business, or commodity monopolies such as OPEC.

Of course, macroeconomic policy is the main determinant of the rate of inflation.

In the mid-1980s, it was sometimes said that what agriculture needed was a dose of inflation. Such statements may reflect, more than anything else, the need to stimulate the demand for agricultural products. The impact of inflation on agriculture is the subject of considerable controversy. One argument is that because farm prices are more responsive to changes in supply and demand than prices in the nonfarm sector, farm prices respond more rapidly to unanticipated growth in demand (demand-pull inflation) than prices in the nonfarm sector. Therefore,

[8]Kuo S. Huang, *U.S. Demand for Food: A Complete System of Price and Income Effects* (Washington, D.C.: ERS, USDA, December 1985).

[9]Prentice and Torgerson, "U.S. Agriculture," p. 9.

[10] Alex F. McCalla, "Impact of Macroeconomic Policies upon Agriculture Trade and International Agricultural Development, *Am. J. Agric. Econ.* (December 1982), pp. 861–868.

Starleaf, Myers, and Womack found that farmers have been net beneficiaries of inflation[11] Tweeten, however, has concluded that as inflation rises, prices paid by farmers increase faster than prices received (cost-push inflation).[12] Inflation does allow those in debt to pay it off with lower-valued dollars, but that is the case only if farmers receive higher prices. Inflation does not necessarily mean higher real land prices. The price of land is most closely related to the realization and expectation of higher income to land.[13]

Summing up, farmers quite clearly benefit from inflation during periods of strong demand. But farmers probably benefit most from stable growth in the U.S. and world economies.

Interest Rate

The interest rate is the price of money—the cost of money to a borrower and the return on money to the investor. As such it plays a very important role in the macroeconomy by influencing the level of saving and the value of the dollar. It is the allocator of capital currently and over time.

The interest rate affects agriculture in many different ways. Some of these impacts, such as its effect on interest expenditures, are obvious. A 1 percent change in the real rate of interest leads to about a $2 billion change in interest expenses. The impacts on investment decisions, the price of land, the storage of commodities, or the value of the dollar are considerably more obscure.

As in the case of price and income, the real rate of interest is more important than the nominal rate. The real rate of interest is the nominal rate minus the rate of inflation. The real rate of interest has varied widely over the past two decades (Fig. 8.6). During the period 1973 through 1979, real interest rates were negative for five of seven years. The clear signal during this time was to borrow, to invest, and to expand. Buoyed by high farm prices and incomes, farmers borrowed in a big way. Farm debt rose threefold from $63 billion in 1972 to 181 billion in 1981.[14] Among other things they bought farm machinery and land. The average value of farmland rose from $219 per acre in 1972 to $819 per acre in

[11]Dennis R. Starleaf, William H. Myers, and Abner W. Womack, "The Impact of Inflation on the Real Income of U.S. Farmers," *Am. J. Agric. Econ.* (May 1985), pp. 384–389.

[12]Luther Tweeten, "An Economic Investigation of Inflation Passthrough to the Farm Sector," *West. J. Agric. Econ.*, vol. 5 (1980), pp. 89–106.

[13]J. M. Alston, "Growth of U.S. Land Prices," *Am. J. Agric. Econ.* (February 1986), pp. 1–9; and Oscar R. Burt, "Econometric Modeling of the Capitalization Formula for Land Prices," *Am. J. Agric. Econ.* (February 1986), pp. 10–26.

[14]*Agricultural Statistics* (Washington, D.C.: USDA, 1985); and *Agricultural Finance* (Washington, D.C.: ERS, USDA, March 1986).

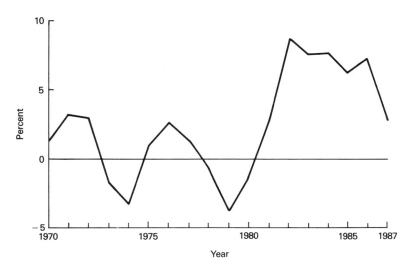

Figure 8.6 Real rate of interest.
Source: Council of Economic Advisers, *Economic Report of the President* (Washington, D.C.: Executive Office of the President, 1988).

1981.[15] A change in macroeconomic policy in 1981 shifted real interest rates to the opposite extreme. The result was a sharp rise to a peak real interest rate of nearly 12 percent. Investment in land and farm machinery tumbled with a corresponding decline in asset values.

Interest rates also affect the willingness of farmers to store commodities. When interest rates rise, the cost of holding commodities in storage likewise rises. The incentive is to sell farm products from the field and pay off money borrowed to buy inputs as opposed to storing commodities in hope of higher prices. Alternatively, farmers will move commodities from private storage into government-financed storage and take advantage of lower interest costs.

Value of the Dollar

In Chapter 6 the impact of exchange rates on the level of exports was discussed. It was noted that while U.S. farm exports benefited from declining dollar values in the 1970s, exports suffered from the high-valued dollar in the early to mid-1980s. It was also noted that macroeconomic policy is one of the prime determinants of the value of the dollar. In a free market, the linkage between the value of the dollar and macroeconomic policy is through the real rate of interest.

[15]John Jones and Charles H. Barnard, *Farm Real Estate: Historical Series Data, 1950–85* (Washington D.C.: ERS, USDA, December 1985).

As the real U.S. interest rate rises relative to other countries, it becomes more attractive for investors to hold dollars as opposed to other currencies. The effect is to bid the price of the dollar up relative to other currencies. In the pre-1972 days of fixed exchange rates, macroeconomic policy received little attention as a factor affecting exports. However, since the advent of floating exchange rates in 1973, macroeconomic policy and related real interest rate and value of the dollar changes have been a center of attention for all segments of agriculture, including policy-makers.

MACROECONOMIC POLICY TOOLS

The objective of macroeconomic policy is to achieve full-employment and stable economic growth without inflation. The tools of macroeconomic policy fall into two general categories: fiscal policy and monetary policy. Fiscal policy deals with the power of government to tax and spend. Spending more than tax revenues leads to deficits that must be financed either by issuing more money or by borrowing. Deficit financing falls in the realm of monetary policy which deals with the power of government to borrow and create money.

Fiscal Policy

Fiscal policy influences the level of aggregate demand for goods and services by changing the level of government spending and taxes.

Government spending has a substantial impact on both the overall level of economic activity and the level of activity in specific sectors, including agriculture. A marked increase in government spending as a proportion of GNP has occurred over time, approaching the level during World War II (Fig. 8.7). Despite efforts by the Reagan administration to reduce the role of government in the macroeconomy, government spending still accounts for about 35 percent of GNP—about the same as in 1975.

Government spending constitutes a direct source of demand for specific goods and services, thus affecting the overall level of production and employment. When government spending lags, total economic growth tends to lag. Surges in spending lead to rapid economic growth and, eventually, inflation.

Spending is politically difficult to control. This is because much spending is based on entitlements, which are indexed to the rate of inflation. Thus, when unemployment rises, more people receive government unemployment benefits. The food stamp and many farm programs fall in the category of entitlement programs.

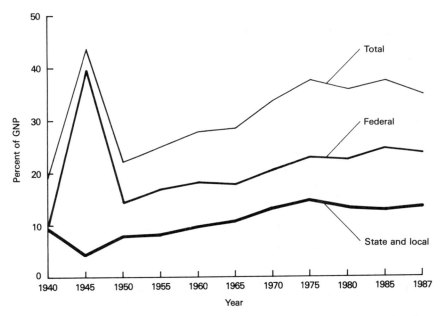

Figure 8.7 Government expenditures as a percent of gross national product, selected years, 1940–1987.
Source: Council of Economic Advisers, *Economic Report of the President* (Washington, D.C.: Executive Office of the President, 1988).

Government spending has become an important variable affecting agriculture in its own right. This is the case because of the sharp increase in farm program expenditures during the 1980s. Since government spending in the 1980s approximates the level of *net* farm income, any reductions in farm programs have a major short-run adverse impact on agriculture. This reality in the face of increased farm bankrupcies made it impossible for the Congress to cut farm program spending effectively in the 1985 farm bill despite Reagan administration and Gramm–Rudman budget-balancing pressure. As a result, the interest in alternative methods of supporting farm income while cutting spending, such as production controls, was heightened.

Taxes are among the most politically sensitive of the macroeconomic policy instruments. Reductions in the level of taxes lead to increased money being available for private-sector spending. As a result, reduced taxes tend to be politically popular. Increased taxes, on the other hand, are difficult for the political process to deal with and normally occur the year after an election.

The composition of taxes may be as important as the level. Tax reform, therefore, has received substantial attention, as it did in the mid-1980s. Under the federal income tax laws, many tax shelters were agriculturally related. Land development, cattle feeding, and purebred breeding stock provide excellent examples. One of the major targets of the 1985 tax reform law was to reduce the incidence of tax shelters while raising corporate taxes and reducing the maximum tax rates for individual income taxes.

Monetary Policy

Monetary policy influences the money supply with the objective of stabilizing output, investment, and the price level. Working through the banking system, the tools of monetary policy include changes in reserve requirements, changes in discounts rates, and open-market operations.

Reserve requirements *specify the proportion of a bank's deposits that must be kept as reserves and, therefore, not loaned.* The money supply expands or contracts by a multiple of the reserve requirement. Thus a change in the reserve requirement has a direct and pronounced impact on the money supply. As a result of this sharp impact, reserve requirement changes are seldom made.

The **discount rate** is *the interest rate that Federal Reserve Banks (FED) charge commercial banks for lending them reserves.* Banks borrow from the FED when they do not have sufficient reserves to expand their loans. Raising the discount rate, of course, has a direct effect on the interest rate that banks charge their customers. Therefore, the discount rate is the most direct means available to the FED for influencing the interest rate.

Open-market operations *involve the purchase and sale of government securities by the FED.* A sale of government securities reduces the supply of money available for banks to lend. With less in free funds available, banks will tend to change a higher interest rate. Being the least harsh monetary policy tool, open-market operations are the most frequently used to influence the money supply.

MONETARY POLICY LINKAGES TO AGRICULTURE

Monetary policy has important linkages to agriculture because interest rates, inflation, and the value of the dollar all directly affect farm income, expenses, and asset values. For purposes of discussing monetary policy linkages to agriculture, two general monetary policy strategies can be distinguished: easy money and tight money.

An **easy money policy** *involves a more rapid rate of money supply growth than is indicated by the growth of the overall economy.* For example, if the GNP is growing at a 2 percent rate, an easy money policy would imply, say, a 6 percent growth in the money supply. This would normally be accomplished either by a reduction in the discount rate or by the purchase of government securities. The effect of each of these policies is to make more money available and thereby lower the real rate of interest, which, in turn, encourages business investment and consumer purchases (particularly of real estate and durables such as automobiles).

Also, with a lower real interest rate, the dollar is a less attractive investment relative to other currencies. As a result, the value of the dollar declines and exports expand. The combination of higher business investment, consumer demand, and export demand leads to a higher rate of GNP growth. This occurs until full employment is reached, at which point an easy money policy translates into inflation.

An easy money policy affects agriculture by reducing interest expenditures, encouraging private-sector farm commodity stock holdings, increasing exports, raising net farm income, and encouraging investment in farm machinery and land. This series of events is typical of the 1970s, although remember that world demand was also strong throughout much of this period due, in part, to adverse weather and foreign policy changes regarding imports of grain by the Soviet Union and China.

A **tight money policy** restricts money supply growth relative to GNP. Tight money may be accomplished by increasing the discount rate, making it less attractive for banks to borrow from the FED, and by selling government securities. These actions increase the real interest rate and, thereby, discourage business investment and consumer purchases, particularly of durables. In addition, with higher real interest rates the dollar is a more attractive investment which increases its value and reduces export demand. The end result is reduced economic growth and low levels of inflation.

This tight money policy scenario was typical of the early to mid-1980s. Its effect on agriculture was to reduce exports of farm products, increase interest expenditures, encourage government farm commodity stock holdings, reduce farm income, and reduce investment in farm machinery and land. But once again remember that this was a period of generally favorable world weather conditions and overproduction—stimulated, in part, by the favorable economic conditions of the 1970s.

Dealing with the Deficit

One of the major problems facing the United States is how to deal with the federal deficit. It should be apparent that this issue has major significance to agriculture. There are two related dimensions to the problem: (1) reducing the deficit and (2) financing it.

As indicated previously, if the deficit is reduced by cutting spending and agriculture took its share of the cuts (or more than its share), there would be substantial adverse short-run effects on farm income as government subsidies declined. These effects would occur unless government subsidies were replaced by strict production controls, in which case consumer food prices would rise and exports decline.

Financing the federal deficit provides two interesting options for agriculture:

- **Increased borrowing** is essentially the tight money policy pursued by the Reagan administration through most of the early to mid-1980s. That is, the deficit has been financed by selling government securities, which has increased real interest rates, kept inflation low by discouraging economic growth, and kept the value of the dollar relatively high. Agriculture suffered under this policy with high interest expenses, low exports, and declining asset values.

- **Monetizing the deficit** is essentially an easy money policy involving lowering the discount rate and purchasing government securities. This policy lowers the interest rate and, thereby, promotes economic growth up to the point of full employment. Agriculture benefits from this policy as long as inflation does not become excessive. Lower real interest rates are accompanied by a lower-valued dollar, which tends to stimulate farm exports. For the Reagan administration an easing of money supply restraints began in 1986 and was accompanied by a decline in the value of the dollar.

OVERCOMING A POTENTIAL WORST-CASE SCENARIO

Events of the 1970s and the 1980s have gotten the world economy into a very difficult, potentially unmanageable situation, with particularly adverse implications for agriculture. The problem is one of getting the world economy back on a growth path as opposed to perpetual stagnation. This problem results from a combination of particularly adverse conditions, including the extremely high Third World developing-country debt, world agricultural surpluses, increased barriers to trade, and the inability to bring the U.S. deficit under control. This combination of conditions makes it extremely difficult to stimulate the world economy sufficiently to overcome its economic problems—particularly those of Third World countries.[16] Unless this combination of conditions is somehow broken, the relatively stagnant economic conditions that began to develop in the mid-1980s could become typical of the future. Such a scenario would make it much more difficult to manage the agricultural economy in the future.

A combination of the following macroeconomic and trade policy

[16]Alex F. McCalla provides an excellent analysis of the linkages between the U.S. macroeconomy and the world in "Impact of Macroeconomic Policies."

strategies would appear to be essential if this worst-case scenario is to be prevented:

- Major developed countries such as the United States, Japan, and West Germany will need to coordinate their macroeconomic policies to stimulate the world economy. Accomplishing this will require an expansionary monetary and fiscal policy.
- Trade negotiations will need to make significant strides in reducing barriers to trade. Successful trade negotiations are critical to opening markets. To stimulate economic development and reduce the burden of Third World debt, it is more important that markets be opened to these countries than to resolve nagging trade problems that exist between developed countries such as the United States and Japan. In the long-run U.S. agricultural trade depends on Third World economic development and growth.
- Reforms will have to be made in the world banking and monetary system to make currencies more fluid and ease the burdens of international financing. In other words, an improved international banking and monetary system will need to be devised. The effect will be to make exchange rates less of a barrier to trade and to reduce the burden on the dollar of serving as both a U.S. and an international currency.

This is an extremely difficult agenda to accomplish, but it is critical to world economic and political stability.

ADDITIONAL READINGS

1. One of the most complete explanations of the linkages between macroeconomic policies and agriculture is contained in Gordon C. Rausser, "Macroeconomics and U.S. Agricultural Policy," in *U.S. Agricultural Policy: The 1985 Farm Legislation*, Bruce L. Gardner, ed. (Washington, D.C.: American Enterprise Institute, 1985).

2. Paul T. Prentice and David A. Torgerson, "U.S. Agriculture and the Macroeconomy," in *Agriculture-Food Policy Review: Commodity Program Perspectives* (Washington, D.C.: ERS, USDA, July 1985), pp. 9–24, do a good job of explaining the state of knowledge regarding the magnitude of the effects of macroeconomic policy.

3. An elementary theoretical explanation of the effect of macroeconomic policy on the general economy and, in turn, on agriculture is contained in John Penson, Rulon Pope, and Michael Cook, *Introduction to Agricultural Economics* (Englewood Cliffs, N.J.: Prentice-Hall, Inc., 1986), pp. 319–421.

Part III

Domestic Farm Policy

Despite the increased relative importance of international policy, macroeconomic policy, resource policy, and food policy, domestic farm policy is the bread and butter of agricultural and food policy. Farm organizations spend the majority of their time and effort lobbying for the type of farm program called for in their policy resolutions. Farmers look to domestic programs to provide protection against low farm prices and incomes. The next three chapters are devoted to an analysis of the domestic farm policy issues.

Chapter 9 is a diagnosis of the farm problem. It distinguishes between the symptoms of the problem, which are frequently the center of discussion, and the root causes. Although the symptoms change over time, the causes are of a more enduring nature.

Chapter 10 explains the major farm program alternatives and their consequences. It also explains how the program has evolved over time from an emphasis on supporting the level of farm prices to supporting farm income.

Chapter 11 involves an analysis of the structure of agriculture issue. It focuses both on the economic forces affecting structure and on the alternative programs for influencing structure. It concludes that while highly emotional issues, such as family farm survival, receive much political ballyhoo, very little has been done explicitly to preserve family farms.

Chapter 9

The Farm Problem

A chicken farmer noticed that one of his
hens was not up to par and was afraid there
might be some disease in the chicken yard.
He decided to have the chicken diagnosed,
wrung the neck and sent it to the county
agent's office. He received a report some
days later which said, "cause of death was
a broken neck."

Maynard Speece

The most crucial step in prescribing policy is correct diagnosis of the problem and its causes. It is easy to fall into the trap of concluding that current conditions are typical of the agricultural economy over the long run. Recall from Chapter 5 that in diagnosing the world food problem, Johnson concluded *in retrospect* that the 1970s were an aberration from a long enduring trend toward lower real farm prices. While hindsight is 20–20, such lessons are important. At the end of Chapter 5, Paarlberg warned against being influenced by current conditions and getting swept up in either a surplus or scarcity syndrome.

The purpose of this chapter is to provide a diagnosis of the farm problem as it exists in the late 1980s and the early 1990s. The hazards of predicting the future are apparent in a review of the agricultural economic history. In the longer run, aberrations due to natural causes or war have been common. Postdepression agriculture through the 1980s will first be briefly reviewed. Out of this review will arise some conclusions concerning long-term trends. The remainder of the chapter is devoted to specific analyses of the symptoms and the causes of the farm problem.

HISTORICAL PERSPECTIVE ON THE FARM PROBLEM

The economic history of depression and postdepression agriculture may be divided into three major periods:

- The 1920–1970 period was the mechanization era, characterized by a rapid transition of labor out of agriculture.
- The 1970s were characterized by booming economic conditions comparable to the golden years of agriculture (1910–1914).
- The 1980s were characterized by deflation of land prices and the transition to an industrialized agriculture.

The Mechanization Era: 1920–1970

The overall problem confronting agriculture during the mechanization era was excess capacity fostered by technological change, fixed resources, and government policy. Agriculture was in a period of constant adjustment to new technology dominated by the trend toward mechanization but compounded by yield-increasing hybrids, expanded use of commercial fertilizer, and the development of chemicals to control weeds and pests. Except for interludes during World War I and World War II, this period was characterized by chronic excess capacity.

The capacity of agriculture to produce increased continuously throughout the mechanization era. From 1920 to 1970 the index of farm output increased by 200, while U.S. population increased by 66 percent.[1] This increase in output was accomplished with virtually no change in total inputs used in agriculture—although the mix and quality of inputs changed dramatically (Fig. 9.1). While total cropland remained amazingly static, the use of mechanical power more than tripled, and the quantity of labor declined by three-fourths. The overall productivity of agriculture doubled, with labor productivity increasing eightfold.

Farm numbers declined from nearly 7 million in 1920 to about 3 million in 1970, while the farm population dropped from 32 million to under 10 million. Agricultural fundamentalists and politicians bemoaned the reduction in farm numbers much as they do today (Fig. 9.2). Yet the release of labor from agriculture contributed materially to the overall development of the economy and the transformation of the United States from an agricultural to an industrial economy.

---

[1]Productivity statistics in this chapter are from the Economic Research Service, *Economic Indicators of the Farm Sector: Production and Efficiency Statistics, 1980*, Stat. Bull. 679 (Washington, D.C.: USDA, January 1982). Population statistics are from Bureau of Labor Statistics, *Census of Population* (Washington, D.C.: U.S. Dept. of Labor, various issues).

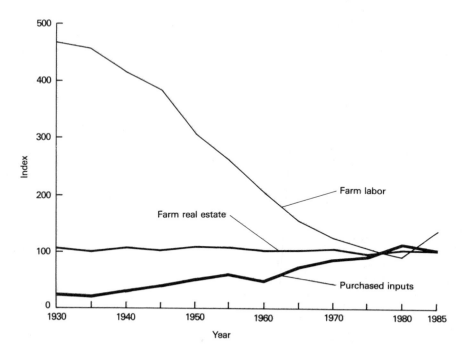

Figure 9.1   Changes in the mix of agricultural inputs measured in index numbers, 1977
base, various years 1930–1985.
Sources: Gary Lucier, Agnes Chesley, and Mary Ahern, *Farm Income Data: A Historical
Perspective*, Stat. Bull. 740 (Washington, D.C.: ERS, USDA, May 1986), p. 31; Council
of Economic Advisers, *Economic Report of the President* (Washington, D.C.: Executive
Office of the President, 1986), p. 363; and Economic Research Service, *Economic Indicators of the Farm Sector: Production and Efficiency Statistics, 1985*, ECIFS 5-5 (Washington, D.C.: USDA, April 1987), pp. 64–65.

With the exception of the war periods, real farm prices during the
period 1920–1970 were generally declining.[2] Even in nominal terms
these were long periods of declining and depressed farm prices. For example, from 1950 to 1970 the price of corn declined from $1.52 per bushel to
$1.33, and the price of wheat fell from $2.00 per bushel to $1.33.[3]

During this period, when there were few direct payments from the
government, low farm prices resulted in low farm incomes. Per capita incomes of persons on farms were frequently less than half of the incomes of
persons not on farms.[4] These conditions fostered considerable unrest in

[2]Gary Lucier, Anges Chesley, and Mary Ahearn, *Farm Income Data: Historical Perspective*, Stat. Bull. 740 (Washington, D.C.: ERS, USDA, May 1986), p. 31.

[3]Douglas E. Bowers, Wayne D. Rasmussen, and Gladys L. Baker, *History of Agricultural Price Support and Adjustment Programs: 1933–84*, Agric. Inf. Bull. 485 (Washington,
D.C.: ERS, USDA, December 1984), p. 45.

[4]*Agricultural Statistics: 1962* (Washington, D.C.: USDA, 1962), p. 570.

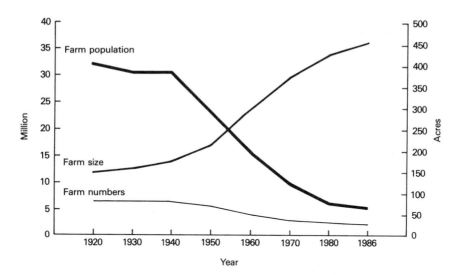

Figure 9.2 Farm population, farm numbers, and farm size, selected years, 1920–1986. *Sources*: USDA, *Agricultural Statistics* (Washington, D.C.: 1962), p. 512; Economic Research Service, *Economic Development in the 1980s* (Washington, D.C.: USDA, July 1987), pp. 4–15. Note that the definition of a farm changed in 1975 to a place that sells at least $1000 in farm products.

rural America. Out of this unrest arose high levels of government intervention in agriculture, which are discussed in Chapter 10.

From the late 1930s through the 1960s there was one bright spot. Farmland prices were on a general upward trend (Fig. 9.3). Land was purchased primarily to expand the size of operation. Land was by far the

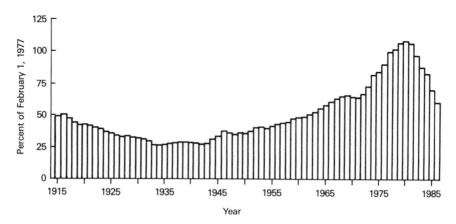

Figure 9.3 Index of real value per acre of U.S. farmland. *Source*: Economic Research Service, *1986 Agricultural Chartbook*, Agric. Handbook 663 (Washington, D.C.: USDA, November 1986), p. 24.

farmer's best and safest investment. The combination of relatively low incomes with the upward progression of land prices led to the frequently used expression that farmers live poor but die rich.

The Golden Years: 1970s

In the late 1960s the progress of constantly increasing output appeared to stall. For three years output remained at the same level. Then in the early 1970s, a confluence of political and national forces combined to change agricultural economic conditions radically. Early frosts and corn blight markedly reduced feed grain production and, in turn, total farm output.[5] In 1972 the Soviet grain sales were made, signaling a major change in policy. Imports as opposed to rationing were used by the Soviets to compensate for production shortfalls. Bad weather in the United States was replicated in several production areas around the world. A floating exchange rate was adopted, while OPEC made oil-producing countries flush with income. Adverse weather, the Soviet policy change, and expansionary economic policies combined with a falling value of the dollar caused exports to surge from $7.3 billion in 1970 to $34.7 billion in 1979 (Fig. 9.4). Crop prices responded to the increased export demand by rocketing 224 percent from 1970 to 1974. Production input prices escalated by 146 percent, still leaving farmers a healthy profit margin.[6]

The result was a 73 percent increase in *real* net cash income per farm from 1970 to 1973, and a 33 percent increase from 1970 to 1979.[7] Farm operator household income rose from 61 percent of the average of U.S. household income in 1960 to 147 percent in 1973 (Fig. 9.5). Higher income meant more money to buy farm machinery and farmland. Farm machinery capital expenditures increased 290 percent from 1970 to 1979.[8] Land values took a sharp upward swing from $196 per acre in 1970 to $737 in 1979—376 percent in a decade![9] The price increase was more than could be justified on the basis of the long-run agricultural income earning potential of land. Even in the short run, an adequate cash flow was frequently impossible.

Back on Trend: The 1980s

As fast as the economics of agriculture improved in the 1970s, it reversed in the 1980s. Actually, the decline in the agricultural economy be-

[5]Economic Research Service, *Economic Indicators of the Farm Sector: Production and Efficiency Statistics, 1985*, ECIFS 5-5 (Washington, D.C.: USDA, April 1987).

[6]Lucier et al., *Farm Income Data*, p. 29.

[7]Ibid., p. 16.

[8]Ibid., p. 29.

[9]John Jones and Charles Barnard, *Farm Real Estate: Historical Series Data: 1950–85*, Stat. Bull. 738 (Washington, D.C.: ERS, USDA, December 1985).

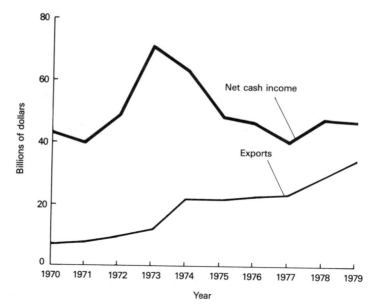

Figure 9.4 Boom in farm exports and net cash income, 1970–1979.
Source: Council of Economic Advisers, *Economic Report of the President* (Washington, D.C.: Executive Office of the President, February 1986), p. 364.

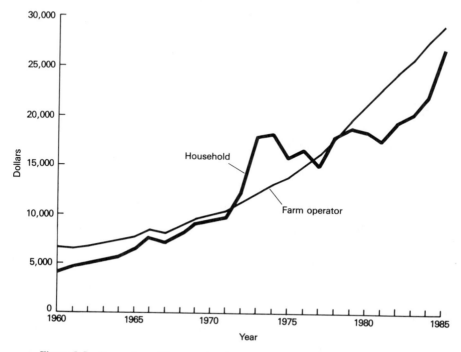

Figure 9.5 Comparison of farm-operator households' income and U.S. households' income, 1960–1985.
Source: David Harrington and Thomas A. Carlin, *The Farm Sector: How Is It Weathering in the 1980s?* Agric. Inf. Bull. 506 (Washington, D.C.: ERS, USDA, April 1987).

gan in the late 1970s, even though exports did not peak until 1983. The significance of the agricultural decline was not realized until land values dropped in the early to mid-1980s.

Crop prices, adjusted for prices paid, declined 43 percent from their 1973 peak to 1985. Most of this drop (34 percent) occurred from 1980 to 1985.[10] Net cash income correspondingly tumbled from a high of $71 billion in 1973 to a low of $38 billion in 1981 and then recovered to $39.5 billion in 1985.[11] In 1985, the government provided $7.7 billion in supplemental direct income payments to farmers and subsequently rose to about $30 billion. From 1985 through 1988 and beyond farm income was supported by government payments. In 1988 the cause was not low income but drought conditions resulting in disaster payments.

Low farm incomes were bad enough in the mid-1980s, but worse was the decline in land values. In 1983, continuous inflation in land values came to an abrupt end, falling 17 percent in three years.[12] For decades farmers and their lenders had banked on increases in land values. The land price decline eroded farmers' equity. The pain was the greatest for those who bought land after 1979 or who borrowed on land to buy farm machinery. Many of these farmers soon faced bankruptcy. For example, in 1985, 3 percent of U.S. farms went out of business, a marked increase from the 1.6 percent average annual rate of decline in the 1970s.

At the same time, agriculture exhibited a surprising amount of resilience during the 1980s. This resilience was primarily a result of substantial off-farm income. Of total cash income available to farmers, more than half comes from off-farm sources (Table 9.1). Moonlighting for farmers and farm wives working off-farm is becoming as common in agriculture as in the nonfarm sector. For many farm families, it is either work off the farm or not survive.

DIAGNOSIS OF THE FARM PROBLEM[13]

Low farm prices, incomes, farmland values, and reduced farm numbers are symptoms of the farm problem. They are what people often identify as the farm problem. But these symptoms are not the cause of the problem.

[10]Council of Economic Advisers, *Economic Report of the President* (Washington D.C.: Executive Office of the President, January 1987), p. 363.

[11]Economic Research Service, *Economic Indicators of the Farm Sector: National Income Summary, 1985* (Washington, D.C.: USDA, November 1986), p. 15; and Lucier et al., *Farm Income Data*, p. 15.

[12]Jones and Barnard, *Farm Real Estate*, p. 3.

[13]This section draws heavily on an excellent paper by Luther Tweeten developed for the Senate Agriculture Committee prior to the 1985 farm bill debate, "Diagnosing and Treating Farm Problems," in *Farm Policy Perspectives: Setting the Stage for 1985 Agricultural Legislation*, S. Prt. 98–174 (Washington, D.C.: Committee on Agriculture, Nutrition, and Forestry, U.S. Senate, April 1984), pp. 75–118.

TABLE 9.1 Farm Numbers, Production, and Income Sources by Sales Class, Including Farm Households, 1985

Item	Noncommercial Farms with Gross Farm Sales of:			Commercial Farms with Gross Farm Sales of:			All Farms
	Less Than $10,000	$10,000–$39,999	$40,000–$99,999	$100,000–$249,999	$250,000–$499,999	$500,000 or More	
Number of farms	1,164,000	473,000	323,000	221,000	66,000	27,000	2,275,000
Percent of farms	51	21	14	10	3	1	100
Percent of Production	3	7	16	25	17	32	100
Net farm income/farm	(1,878)	(1,041)	6,566	36,660	99,661	640,010	13,881
Off-farm income/farm	22,402	16,696	10,347	10,551	11,447	15,448	17,945
Total household income/farm	20,524	15,655	16,913	47,211	111,108	655,458	31,826
Direct government payments	85	1,340	5,193	12,845	21,873	37,499	3,387

Source: Economic Research Service, Economic Indicators of the Farm Sector, National Financial Summary, 1985, ECIFS 5-2 (Washington, D.C.: USDA, November 1986).

211

The purpose of this section is to look at the symptoms in greater depth as a means of providing insight into the *true causes of the problem*. The emphasis here is on the 1980s.

Symptoms of the Farm Problem

Gross numbers and trends such as those presented so far in this chapter fail to reflect the complex nature of the symptoms of the farm problem. This detail makes it clear that there is no easy solution to the problem. Of course, if there were an easy solution, the farm problem would have been solved long ago.

Low farm prices and incomes.   Agriculture is becoming more diverse. Therefore, when diagnosing the farm problem it is essential to look beyond aggregate income levels to the incomes of particular farm segments.

The vast majority of people who live on farms do not depend on farming for their incomes. If a household earns more money from an off-farm job than its net farm income, it can hardly be classified as a farm household. Rather, these workers, are mechanics, carpenters, teachers, truck drivers, assembly line workers, lawyers, or professors. They might be called noncommercial farmers because they do not depend primarily on agriculture for their living. They have also been referred to as non-farm-farmers.

Nearly 2 million (86 percent) of the 2.3 million farms are noncommercial farms (Table 9.1). These farms account for one-fourth of the production. In 1985, the net income of these farms in total was negative. Only noncommercial farms with gross sales of $40,000 to $99,999 earned a profit. But even for these farms, their farm income was only 39 percent of household income.

One can legitimately question whether this noncommercial farm segment is part of the farm problem. No doubt the farm lobby would prefer to claim the numbers as part of its farm constituency. However, it is difficult to justify government farm subsidies to households that do not depend on farming for the majority of their income. Persons in this group may contend that they should be able to earn enough income from farming so that they are not required to work off-farm. But that same argument could be applied to many part-time jobs. Teachers would like to earn enough so they do not have to moonlight.

In 1985, only 314,000 farms were commercial operations in that they depended on agriculture for the majority of their income (Table 9.1). These 13 percent of the total number of farms accounted for three-fourths of the production. Their farm income was 78 percent of total household income. Even the commercial segment is highly diverse, with net farm income ranging from an average of $30,660 for the smaller commercial farms to $640,010 for the large farms. Farms having over $500,000 in sales tend to be concentrated in cotton, vegetables, fruit and nuts, nursery products, poultry, cattle, and fed cattle.[14]

The averages do *not* indicate that these commercial farms have an income problem. Yet without farm program benefits, noncommercial farms with $40,000 to $99,999 in sales would be in poverty and farms with $100,000 to $250,000 in sales would be considerably worse off (Table 9.1). However, such observations are tenuous because it will be seen in Chapter 10 that direct farm program payments lead to lower farm prices and cash income. What farm income would be without direct payments is subject to considerable speculation and, as was seen in Chapter 8, depends on the subsidies of other countries.

Farms in financial stress.   Averages are deceiving. Even though the average income of commercial farmers is reasonably high, there can still be a substantial number of farms experiencing financial stress for which farm programs *might* be justified. These are farms with low income and little equity. Farms that characteristically experience financial stress accumulated substantial debt in the face of declining asset values, which ate away at equity from 1981 through 1986 (Fig. 9.6). In 1987, asset values finally began to reverse the downward trend. The result of lower asset values was a rise in the ratio of debt to assets (Fig. 9.7). High liabilities in the face of high real interest rates made it impossible for farms experiencing these conditions to cash flow.

Farms experiencing severe financial stress are defined as those households with negative cash flow from all sources and with debt/asset ratios of 70 percent or more. These farms are most likely to leave farming for financial reasons. In early 1987, about 6 percent of the farms (130,000) were experiencing financial stress. In terms of numbers, these farms tended to be concentrated in the $40,000 to $250,000 size range (Fig. 9.8). Small farms have less stress because of the availability of off-farm income. It will be seen later that large farms have less stress because they realize higher yields, higher returns from marketing, and lower production costs. Farmers experiencing stress are generally younger, indicating that they entered farming in the past few years.

Decline in farm numbers.   As indicated previously, during the 1980s there was a marked acceleration in the number of farms going out of business. An American Bankers Association survey indicated that the

[14]Donn A. Reimund, Nora L. Brooks, and Paul D. Velde, *The U.S. Farm Sector in the Mid-1980s*, Agric. Econ. Rep. 548 (Washington, D.C.: ERS, USDA, May 1986), p. 14.

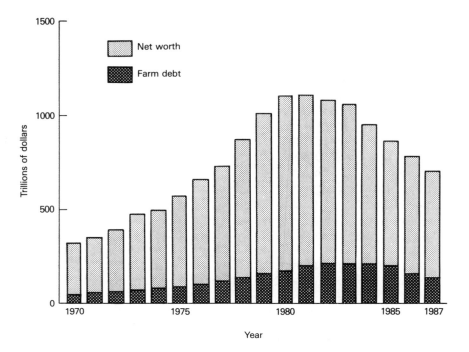

Figure 9.6 U.S. farm balance sheet.
Source: Economic Research Service, *Economic Indicators of the Farm Sector: National Financial Summary* (Washington, D.C.: USDA, various issues).

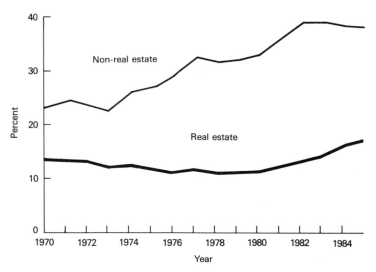

Figure 9.7 Farm debt as percentage of assets.
Source: Economic Research Service, *1986 Agricultural Chartbook*, Agric. Handbook 663 (Washington, D.C.: USDA), p. 13.

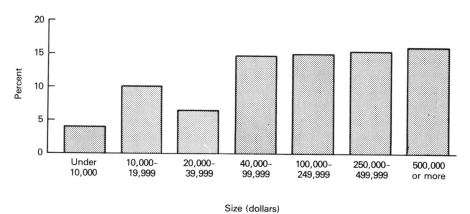

Figure 9.8 Farms experiencing financial stress by size, 1987.
Source: Jim Johnson et al., *Financial Characteristics of U.S. Farms, January 1, 1987,*
Agric. Inf. Bull. 525 (Washington, D.C.: ERS, USDA, August 1987).

number of such farms has increased threefold and the number going
through bankruptcy has increased nearly sixfold (Fig. 9.9).

The financial stress data suggest that the decline in farm numbers
is most extensive among midsize farms having gross sales of $40,000 to
$250,000 (Fig. 9.8). These are farms that are normally characterized as
family farms.[15] The potential demise of family farm agriculture has received extensive media and farm organization attention. The family farm
enjoys strong support from the American public. Recall from Chapter 1
that 82 percent of the public feels that the family farm should be preserved. Two-thirds feel that special policies should be established to see
that it is preserved, and only 22 percent feel that greater efficiency is
more important than preserving the family farm.[16]

Instability.   In a free-market environment, farm prices are inherently unstable because of production and demand changes. These changes,
when combined with the inelastic nature of the supply and demand for
farm products make free-market farm prices highly unstable. The inelasticity of supply and demand will be discussed subsequently as a cause of
the farm problem.

From the 1930s through the 1960s, instability was masked by large
surpluses and government price supports that held domestic prices above
world market levels. During the 1970s, price variability increased mark-

[15]Ibid; and Harrington and Carlin.

[16]Brenda Jordan and Luther Tweeten, *Public Perceptions of Farm Problems*, Res. Rep.
894 (Stillwater, Okla.: Oklahoma State University, June 1987), p. 3.

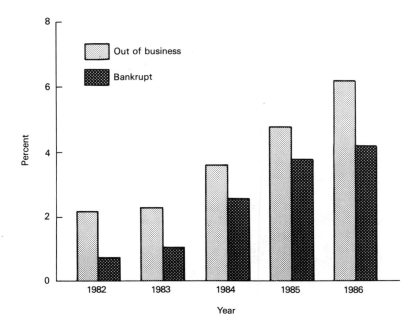

Figure 9.9 Share of farms going out of business, 1982–1986.
Source: David Harrington and Thomas A. Carlin, *The U.S. Farm Sector: How Is It Weathering in the 1980s?* Agric. Inf. Bull. 506 (Washington, D.C.: ERS, USDA, April 1987), p. 17.

edly. An analysis of price and income variability for three time periods is shown in Table 9.2. These data indicate:

- From 1955 to 1963 farm prices and income were extremely stable relative to 1972–1979. Variability in prices for all products increased sixfold, with the variability in crop prices increasing more than livestock prices. The intervening years, 1964–1971, were a transition; crop prices were still relatively stable, while livestock prices were becoming considerably more variable. In the 1980s, price variability once again declined because the government supported prices.
- The variability in farm income was over three times as great in the 1970s as during 1955–1963, then increased again in the 1980s. Income variability in all periods is reduced by government payments and reduced further when income from nonfarm sources is included.
- Nonfarm income received by the farm population was relatively stable in all three periods, primarily reflecting economic conditions in the nonfarm economy.

Overall, these estimates confirm that farm income variability has

TABLE 9.2 Variation in Real Farm Income and
Real Product Prices, Selected Periods, 1955–1985 (Percent)

Item	Coefficient of Variation in:			
	1955–1963	1964–1971	1972–1979	1980–1985
Index of prices received				
All products	2.7	5.5	16.1	3.3
Crops	2.5	3.6	17.0	5.1
Livestock	5.1	10.4	18.7	2.3
Cash receipts				
Crops	9.7	8.4	21.1	3.0
Livestock	7.9	13.5	20.7	2.2
Net farm income				
Net farm income less government payments	9.6	9.1	30.2	39.3
Net farm income including government payments	7.0	7.3	28.9	26.6
Nonfarm income	7.7	5.9	10.0	4.8
Income from all sources	5.9	6.5	26.9	22.8

Sources: Computed from Economic Research Service, *Economic Indicators of the Farm Sector, National Financial Summary 1985* (Washington, D.C.: ERS, USDA, November 1986), pp. 14, 18, 19; Economic Research Service, *Economic Indicators of the Farm Sector, Income and Balance Sheet Statistics, 1980* (Washington, D.C.: ERS, USDA, September 1981), p. 114; *Economic Report of the President*, (Washington D.C.:, U.S. Government Printing Office, 1986), p. 363.

increased for the entire sector in recent years. This variability in income has both favorable and unfavorable aspects. From a favorable perspective, the movement in income reflects changes in supply and demand conditions and is a signal for producers regarding the needs in the marketplace. Yet the price signal is masked by government income payments. When prices become highly unstable, the signals may be misinterpreted and mistakes made in production and marketing decisions. The result frequently is misallocation of resources. In addition, variability in prices and income increases the risk and uncertainly to the farm business. The result is a higher incidence of failure of business firms.

Variability in farm income increased substantially for farms of all sizes in the 1970s over the 1960s (Table 9.3). In the 1980s, income variability, before inventory adjustment, has been reduced, but it is still generally higher than in the 1960s. Variability in net farm income is perceptibly higher for small farms than for larger farms. This probably results from smaller farmers' lack of knowledge of markets and risk management tools. Of course, the small farmer's total income is not more variable than that of large farms because of the stability and importance of nonfarm income.

The implications of economic instability in the farm sector are perhaps more significant today than in previous times, when farm families were thought to be very resilient. In the past, during periods of adverse

TABLE 9.3 Percent Variability in Net Farm Income before Inventory Adjustment per Farm Operation by Size of Farm, Selected Periods, 1960–1985[a]

Sales Class	1960–1969	1970–1979	1980–1985
Less than $40,000	27.1	146.0	87.6
$40,000–99,000	31.6	29.5	37.7
$100,000–499,000	36.1[b]	37.4	20.2
Over $500,000	NA[c]	40.2	13.7
All farms	9.2	24.5	14.3

Source: Computed from Economic Research Service, *Economic Indicators of the Farm Sector, National Financial Sector, 1985* (Washington, D.C.: ERS, USDA, November 1986), p. 43.

[a]Net farm income for different size farms is before inventory adjustment. This explains why all farms variability is greater than net farm income including government payments in Table 9.2.

[b]Includes all farms having over $100,000 in sales.

[c]NA, not available.

economic conditions, family farms would tighten their belts, reduce personal consumption expenditures, and weather the period until conditions improved. They were much less dependent on purchased inputs from the nonfarm sector, and their fixed annual cash obligations were relatively small. Today, however, farmers purchase a high proportion of annual production inputs and may have substantial annual debt repayment obligations for their fixed assets.

The changed situation is evidenced by the ratio of cash production expenses to gross farm income; this ratio has trended upward since World War II (Fig. 9.10). The implications of the ratio of cash production expenses to gross receipts are illustrated in Table 9.4 by the effects of increase in production expenses on net income. The 10 percent increase in production expenses has much more adverse impact on net income the greater the dependence on purchased inputs. Similarly, the higher the proportion of cash production expenses, the more vulnerable farms are to changes in product prices.

The role of government in reducing price variability is an important policy issue. Yet it is difficult to design a set of government programs that will reduce the unnecessary and disruptive aspect of price variability while still allowing the market to provide clear signals to both producers and consumers. How much intervention is optimal is, in fact, the principal point of divergence in the farm policy views of the major political parties and among economists.

Cost of Farm Programs

During the 1980s government expenditures on farm programs reached record levels. For years, government subsidies to farmers had totaled less than $7 billion. Then in 1982 subsidies more than doubled to

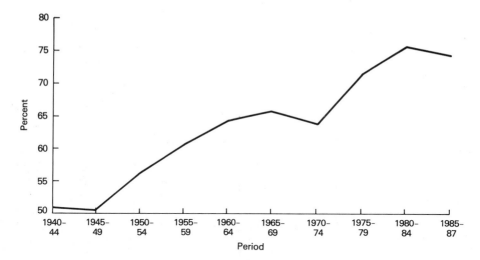

Figure 9.10 Cash production expenses as a percent of cash receipts, 1935–1985.
Source: Economic Research Service, *Economic Indicators of the Farm Sector* (Washington, D.C.: USDA, various issues), p. 14.

over $14 billion; this was followed by a rise to over $21 billion in 1985 and to nearly $30 billion in 1986 (Fig. 9.11). In addition to the high absolute level of spending, questions have arisen regarding the level of payments to large farms and the lack of targeting of expenditures to farmers with the greatest need. The cost dimensions of the farm program and how they arise are discussed in detail in Chapter 10. Suffice it to say that program costs are attracting increasing attention as a dimension of the farm problem.

Causes of the Farm Problem

The farm problem is too complex to have any single cause. The most basic problem facing U.S. agriculture is that of chronic excess capacity.

TABLE 9.4 Sensitivity of Annual
Net Income to Changes in Production Expenses

| Item | Production Expenses (Dollars) as Percentage of Cash Receipts | | | |
	60%	70%	80%	90%
Gross cash receipts	100	100	100	100
Cash production expenses	60	70	80	90
Net cash income	40	30	15	10
10 percent increase in production expenses	66	77	94	99
Net cash income	34	23	6	1
Decrease in net cash income (%)	15	23	60	90

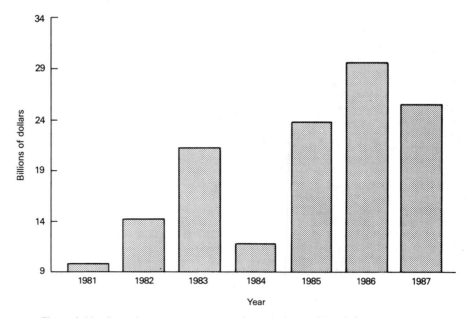

Figure 9.11 Cost of government programs for agriculture, 1981–1987.
Source: Economic Research Service, *National Food Review* (Washington, D.C.: USDA, various issues).

Excess capacity gives rise to surpluses, which, in turn, lead to low farm prices and income. Other significant causes of the farm problem include the inelasticity of supply and demand, economies of farm size, the market position of farmers, and macroeconomic policy.

Excess capacity. **Excess capacity** is defined as the difference between potential supply and commercial demand at prevailing politically acceptable prices, higher than market-clearing prices. Since price is maintained by the government above market-clearing levels, excess capacity results. This excess capacity may be reflected in:

- Increased commodity stocks generally held under government programs
- Commodities given away by the government under both domestic and foreign food-aid programs
- Land removed from production by the government

The extent of excess capacity has been the subject of considerable study. Tweeten estimated that in the early 1980s excess capacity totaled

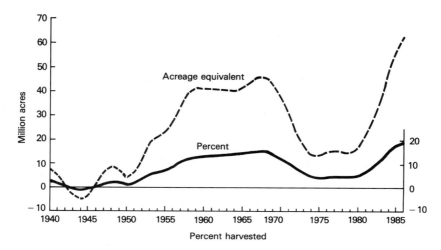

Figure 9.12 Long-run excess capacity in agriculture, 1940–1986.
Source: Dan Dvoskin, *Excess Capacity in Agriculture: An Economic Approach to Measurement*, Agric. Econ. Rep. 580 (Washington, D.C.: ERS., USDA, February 1988), p. 14.

about 11 percent. A substantial proportion of this excess capacity was in the form of land retirement programs that began with the payment-in-kind program in 1983.[17]

The most detailed estimates of excess capacity have been made by Dvoskin in an excellent comprehensive study of the issue.[18] This study found that the long-run excess capacity for the four major crops (wheat, feed grains, cotton, and soybeans) has been *above 20 percent* in 1985 and 1986. In the long run when averaged over all crops, excess capacity was *8 to 9 percent* in the mid-1980s. Dvoskin found that in the mid-1980s, excess capacity was the highest on record (Fig. 9.12). Measured in acreage equivalents, excess capacity averaged over 60 million acres in 1985 and 1986, or 22 percent of harvested acres. Such numbers, however, need to be used with care. During the period 1973–1980, excess capacity spread over all crops averaged only about 2 percent.

Dvoskin did not hold much hope that the level of excess capacity that exists in the mid-1980s would decrease since a large share of the excess capacity is in the form of retired acres, domestic demand is relatively fixed, and the problem is broader than just the United States. This assessment implies a certain set of government programs. It will be seen in

[17]Tweeten, "Diagnosing and Treating Farm Problems," p. 30.

[18]Dan Dvoskin, *Excess Capacity in Agriculture: An Economic Approach to Measurement*, Agric. Econ. Rep. 580 (Washington, D.C.: ERS, USDA, February 1988).

Chapter 10 that the type of program has a major impact on the level, visibility, and form of excess capacity.

An issue not addressed by Dvoskin is the desired level of excess capacity. Clearly, with a commodity as important as food, some excess capacity is needed. That may be a long-run justification for farm programs. Equally clearly, 20 percent excess capacity is too much. The issue is how much excess capacity is desired to deal with risk factors such as weather variability and pests. Private-sector storage decisions are based solely on economic criteria. The public sector may prefer a higher level of food security. Some of this publicly justified excess capacity may be held in the form of stocks to deal with short-run risks, while land may be held in reserve to deal with long-run risks. Despite the importance of such issues, they have not been adequately addressed in terms of either research or public policy.

There are three explanations for the excess capacity that, except during wars and the 1970s, has been a chronic problem in agriculture:

- The **agricultural treadmill theory** notes that new technology constantly flowing into agriculture creates the potential for higher-than-normal profits by the first adopters.[19] As an increased number of farmers adopt new technologies, the supply schedule shifts right and forces down the price. Later adopters, having higher costs, run the risk of falling hopelessly behind. Therefore, farmers are said to be on a treadmill with supply shifting to the right faster than demand; they either adopt or go out of business. The consequence of supply shifting faster than demand is chronic excess capacity.

- The **fixed-asset theory** suggests that once resources enter farming, they tend to be locked in by the fact that they are worth little outside agriculture compared with their cost.[20] In other words, high-cost farm machinery or buildings have a very low salvage value outside agriculture. The fixed-asset theory has been applied to human resources as well as to farm assets. However, with an increasing proportion of farmers being college educated, human capital should be less subject to the fixed-asset theory in the future. Yet, even though human capital leaves, it does not mean that the assets themselves leave. Land tends to be farmed as long as its returns cover the vari-

[19]Willard W. Cochrane, *Farm Prices: Myth and Reality* (Minneapolis, Minn.: University of Minnesota Press, 1958), pp. 85–107.

[20]Glenn L. Johnson, "Supply Functions—Some Facts and Notions," *Agricultural Adjustment Problems in a Growing Economy*, Earl O. Heady et al., eds. (Ames, Iowa: Iowa State University Press, 1958), pp. 74–93. Perhaps the best explanation of Johnson's theory is contained in Dale Hathaway, *Government and Agriculture* (New York: Macmillan Publishing Company, 1963), pp. 110–130.

able costs of production and make some contribution to fixed costs of farming. Of course, in the long run, agricultural resources must earn a normal profit.

- The **government theory** holds that excess capacity is caused by farm programs that prevent markets from clearing. Were it not for high price supports, direct farm subsidies, and barriers to trade, Paarlberg contends that there would be no excess capacity and no surpluses. "Given the price objectives specified in the law, there is undeniably excess production capacity in agriculture. . . . The result of holding farm prices and farm incomes continuously and substantially above equilibrium levels is to create excess capacity."[21]

Inelasticity.   The inelastic nature of *both the supply and demand* curves for farm products is the major cause of instability of farm prices and incomes. As a result of an inelastic supply and demand, a small increase in supply can result in a multiple reduction in price. Thus a 5 percent increase in supply or reduction in demand can easily lead to a 10 to 15 percent drop in price. Demand or supply changes of this magnitude are not at all unusual, with variation in weather being a primary short-run cause, but pests, politics, and macroeconomic policy are also contributing factors.

Price variability increases tremendously under free-market conditions because government is not supporting the price, and stocks are reduced. Thus in the 1970s price variation was at record levels—a direct reflection of a highly inelastic supply and demand (Table 9.2).

Economies of size.   The advantages of large farms in terms of their ability to achieve lower costs and higher net returns are referred to as **economies of size**. These economies are of three types:

- **Technical economies** *exist when an increase in farm size results in a reduction in the average cost of production.* Until the 1980s the preponderance of the evidence supported the hypothesis that the farm having $100,000 to $250,000 in sales was the most efficient. This position has been espoused the most strongly by USDA.[22] More re-

[21]Don Paarlberg, *Farm and Food Policy* (Lincoln, Nebr.: University of Nebraska Press, 1980), pp. 28–30.

[22]J. P. Madden and E. J. Partenheimer. "Evidence of Economies and Diseconomies of Farm Size," in *Size, Structure, and Future of Farms* (Ames, Iowa: Iowa State University Press, 1972), pp. 91–107; T. A. Miller, "Economies of Size and Other Growth Incentives," in *Structure Issues of American Agriculture*, ERS Agric. Econ. Rep. 438 (Washington, D.C.: USDA, 1979); and T. A. Miller, G. Rodewald, and R. G. McElroy, *Economies of Size in United States Field Crop Farming*, ERS Agric. Econ. Rep. 472 (Washington, D.C.: USDA, 1981).

cently, a host of studies have confirmed substantial economies of
size in both crop and livestock production.

The first study contradicting the notion of limited economies of
size was by Matulich. It demonstrated economies of size in California dairies extending to 750 cows, with no evidence of diseconomies
to 3600 cows.[23] Subsequently, Smith et al. found that Texas High
Plains cotton farms to over 4000 acres have lower costs.[24] Based in
part on questions raised by the Smith study concerning the magnitude of economies of size in crop agriculture, OTA commissioned a
major investigation of economies of size in the production of major
crops. The resulting study by Cooke found economies of size extending to 5920 acres in cotton, 1113 acres in corn, and 3909 acres in
wheat. Diseconomies were found in a limited number of production
areas for cotton, corn, and rice.[25] In 1984, Tweeten reported the results of analyses of agricultural census data which indicated economies of size extending far beyond the level indicated in previous
analyses of the same type.[26]

Building on the technique developed by Tweeten, Knutson et
al. utilized census data to evaluate economies of size in each of the
three major states producing wheat, cotton, corn, sorghum, and
rice.[27] Their study indicated economies of size extending throughout
the full range of farm sizes reported by the agricultural census, with
no conclusive evidence of diseconomies. Economies of size were
found to extend to at least 7981 acres in California cotton; 4097
acres in Kansas and Texas wheat; 3769 acres in Nebraska corn;
3992 acres in Kansas sorghum; and 6225 acres in California rice.
The only evidence of diseconomies was in Iowa corn, where the
minimum-cost farm was at 1374 acres.

* **Pecuniary economies** *of size are the advantages gained by larger
firms, resulting in either a lower cost per unit of inputs purchased or*

[23]S. C. Matulich, "Efficiencies in Large-Scale Dairying: Incentives for Future Structural Change," *Am. J. Agric. Econ.* (November 1978), pp. 642–647.

[24]E. G. Smith, R. D. Knutson, and J. W. Richardson, "Input and Marketing Economies: Impact on Structural Change in Cotton Farming on the Texas High Plains," *Am. J.
Agric. Econ.* (November 1986), pp. 716–720.

[25]S. Cooke, "Size Economies and Comparative Advantage in the Production of Corn,
Soybeans, Wheat, Rice, and Cotton in Various Areas of the United States," in *Technology,
Public Policy, and the Changing Structure of American Agriculture*, Vol. II: *Background Pa-
pers* (Washington, D.C.: OTA, May 1986).

[26]Tweeten, "Diagnosing and Treating Farm Problems."

[27]R. D. Knutson, J. W. Richardson, E. G. Smith, M. E. Rister, W. R. Grant, L. A.
Lippke, and C. L. Israelsen, "Economic Impact of Payment Limits," unpublished manuscript
(College Station, Tex.: Department of Agricultural Economics, Texas A&M University,
Texas Agricultural Experiment Station, 1987).

a higher price per unit for the products marketed. Although there has
been considerable speculation on the extent of pecuniary economies
for larger farms, the empirical evidence remains scarce.

Krause and Kyle found that corn farmers having over 2500
acres could purchase inputs, such as fertilizer, for as much as 20 percent less than could smaller farmers.[28] However, they provide little
detail on either the prevalence or methods of determining such
lower-cost inputs. The Smith study suggests that pecuniary economies may be available only to those farmers who are large enough
or have sufficient resources to be integrated (backward) into the
farm supply (input) business.[29] Eighty percent of cotton farmers
operating over 4400 acres of land were found to be integrated into a
source of supply. Such integration resulted in reduced costs of individual inputs of as much as 28 percent, an average of cost reduction
across all inputs of about 16 percent, and an average reduction in
the cost per unit of cotton produced of 5 percent.

Pecuniary marketing economies may also exist for large farms.
But the evidence on prices received as farm size increases is even
more inadequate. The Smith study also found pecuniary economies
of marketing of as much as 10 percent for individual farmers; they
averaged 5 percent for farms having over 1600 acres of cotton. In
contrast with input economies, pecuniary marketing economies did
not appear to be directly related to integration. Instead, it appeared
that farms of over 1600 acres simply had more management and
marketing expertise, thus obtaining a higher price.

Pecuniary economies may substantially alter the shape of the
traditional LAC curve for very large farmers. Average costs may
perceptibly fall at the size where such pecuniary economies become
possible. The average revenue also increases at that point.

- **Technological change economies** *occur when large farms are
  more likely to adopt or gain the benefits of technologies.* Until the
  1980s, it was generally assumed that technology was size neutral;
  that is, all farm sizes were in an equal position to adopt and gain the
  benefits of a new technology.[30] Relatively few studies of the process
  of technology adoption are available. The studies that have been
  done suggest that midsize family farms may be slower than larger-

---

[28]Kenneth R, Krause and Leonard R. Kyle, *Midwestern Corn Farmers: Economic Status and the Potential for Large- and Family-Sized Units,* Agric. Econ. Rep. 216 (Washington,
D.C.: ERS, USDA, November 1971), p. 53.

[29]Smith et al., "Input and Marketing Economies."

[30]F. C. White, "Economic Impact of Agricultural Research and Extension," in *Technology, Public Policy, and the Changing Structure of American Agriculture,* Volume
II—Background Papers* (Washington, D.C.: OTA, May 1986).

scale farms in adopting new technologies. Two recent examples from
dairy can be cited.

In a survey involving 2712 southern dairy farms, Carley and
Fletcher found that size of herd was one of the factors related to
higher output per cow.[31] Size of herd was also positively related to
the use of management practices such as dairy herd improvement
testing, artificial insemination, forage quality testing, and ration
balancing. Each of these factors has been found to have a substantial statistically significant impact on output per cow. The study
concluded by stating that the typical dairy farm operator who would
use several management factors associated with high output per
cow "would tend to have a large herd of cows producing above average, be younger than average, be in a partnership operation, and
have a college education."[32]

In a recent study of milk production costs, Stanton found a positive relationship between herd size and milk output per cow.[33] Increases in milk yields were particularly pronounced for herds of over
200 cows, which had average milk yields of 2120 pounds more than
herds of under 40 cows.

The conclusion drawn from a review of literature regarding economies of size is that prior to the 1980s, the preponderance of the evidence
supported the contention that midsize family farms were the most efficient. Studies in the 1980s, however, have consistently supported the conclusion that economies of size are much larger than had previously been
indicated. There appears to have been progressive expansion in the optimum size of farm over time and, as a result, midsize family farms have
been losing, or have lost, their comparative advantage. This trend is an
integral part of the industrialization process that agriculture is going
through. The result is considerable pressure being placed on farmers to
keep pace with technological change and grow.

Because early adopters of technology earn the highest level of profit
and because most technology increases the optimum size of farm, these
are the farms that are in the best position to grow. They grow by buying
out those farmers who failed to adopt the latest technology. **Economic
cannibalism** *is the process of the large farmers continuously getting*

[31]D. H. Carley and S. M. Fletcher, "An Evaluation of Management Practices Used by
Southern Dairy Farmers," *Dairy Sci.* (1986), pp. 2458–2464.

[32]Ibid., p. 64

[33]B. F. Stanton, *Complexities of Northeast Milk Producers in the National Market*,
Cornell Univ. Agric. Exp. St. 87–5 (Ithaca, N.Y.: Cornell University Department of Agricultural Economies, March 1987).

larger by buying out the smaller farmers.[34] Economic cannibalism is one of the major reasons for the continuous decline in the number of farms as well as for the concern about the long-term ability of family farms to survive.

The implications of size economies and the trend toward large farms are not as clear for consumers:

- In the short run, benefits to consumers from increases in farm size are limited to the extent of technical and pecuniary economies. These appear to vary considerably among crops, geographically, and between crop and animal agriculture.
- In the long run, changes in technology may change the whole shape of the long-run average cost curve. Generally, the effect is to shift the long-run average cost curve downward and to the right, thus benefiting consumers.
- High levels of concentration resulting from increases in farm size could lead to the firms gaining sufficient market power so that the efficiencies would not be reflected in product prices paid by consumers. However, acquisition of such market power will occur at a much higher level of concentration. This point is discussed further in Chapter 11.

Market position.   Perhaps the most neglected potential reason for the farm problem is that farmers are caught in a position without market power between large input suppliers and large marketing firms. Farmers buy inputs from oligopoly sellers and sell to oligopsony buyers. Lanzillothi suggested this structural difference as one of the causes of the farm problem.[35] Market signals to farmers are distorted by market power.

Although it is generally recognized that in most of agriculture, farmers are price takers on both the input and output side of market, there has been little research on the effects of this market position. The best recent discussion of the market position of the farmer is by Schmitz et al. in their analysis of the farmers' position in international grain markets.[36] They postulate a situation where multinational grain companies

[34]Phillip M. Raup, "Some Questions of Value and Scale in American Agriculture," *Am. J. Agric. Econ.* (May 1978), pp. 301–308. A very good description of the relationship between the treadmill theory and economic cannibalism is contained in Willard W. Cochrane, "The Need to Rethink Agricultural Policy and Perform Some Radical Surgery on Commodity Programs in Particular," *Am. J. Agric. Econ.* (December 1985), pp. 1002–1009.

[35]Robert F. Lanzillothi, "Market Power and the Farm Problem," *J. Farm Econ.* (December 1960), pp. 1228–1257.

[36]Andrew Schmitz, Alex F. McCalla, Donald O. Mitchell and Carlin A. Carter, *Grain Export Cartels* (Cambridge, Mass.: Ballinger Publishing Co., 1981), pp. 38–48.

not only have monopsony (buyer) power with regard to producers but also have monopoly (seller) power with regard to importing countries. In this environment it is in the grain companies' best interest, Schmitz et al. contend, to manufacture price instability to create "buy low, sell high" opportunities.

There are only a few instances where farmers have been able to organize sufficiently through cooperatives to offset the market power of buyers and sellers. Generally, cooperative realization of power is accomplished with the aid of marketing orders such as in milk, fruits, and vegetables. However, in major commodities where traditional forms of price and income support exist, cooperative strength has been nil.[37]

Macroeconomic policy.   The impact of macroeconomic policy on agriculture was discussed in Chapter 8. The only purpose here is to recall that the highly expansionary monetary and fiscal policies of the 1970s fueled inflation and undervalued the dollar. The resulting increases in export demand were contributing factors to the overexpansion of output. These conditions also fostered land values that exceeded its income-generating capacity. The macroeconomic policies of the 1980s have been at least equally disastrous—particularly following the policies of the 1970s. Tight money growth fostered high real interest rates, led to an overvalued dollar which choked off export demand, and put debt-burdened farmers in an impossible cash-flow squeeze. In other words, government policies have been an important contributor to the problems of the 1980s but not the only contributor.

A WORD OF CAUTION

Earlier in this chapter and in previous chapters, the reader was cautioned against getting swept up in current events. Agriculture is sufficiently unstable that the minute one gets swept up in conditions of surplus, a production shortfall creates deficits or a military conflict creates uncertainty over food supplies and needs.

The picture painted in this chapter—one of a U.S. food supply–demand balance that lies on the side of surpluses and declining real farm prices—is consistent with long-term trends. Yet, short-run aberrations from that trend are inevitable. Policies must be sufficiently flexible to deal with both the long-run trends and the short-run aberrations. This requires a careful matching of policy solutions with problem causes. This is the subject of Chapter 10.

    [37]R. D. Knutson and W. E. Black, *Cooperative Involvement in Issues of Domestic Farm Policy*, Dep. Agric. Econ. DIR 86–4 (College Station, Tex.: Texas A&M University, 1986).

ADDITIONAL READINGS

1. Willard W. Cochrane's *Farm Prices, Myth and Reality* (St. Paul, Minn.: University of Minnesota Press, 1958) does an excellent job of explaining why agricultural prices are so unstable and how technology combined with agriculture's competitive structure generates surpluses. Although this book was written three decades ago, it is still an excellent reference. Yet in reading *Myth and Reality*, be aware that Cochrane's policy prescription has changed. The reason for this change and his new policy prescription is contained in Willard W. Cochrane, "The Need to Rethink Agricultural Policy in General and to Perform Some Radical Surgery on Commodity Programs in Particular," *Am. J. Agric. Econ.* (December 1985), pp. 1002–1009; and Willard W. Cochrane "Focusing on the Specific Problems of Agriculture: A Fresh Look at an Old Policy Approach," *Am. J. Agric. Econ.* (December 1986), pp. 1102–1108.

2. The major forces influencing U.S. agriculture through the end of the century are summarized in *Forces of Change: Policy Alternatives for the 1980s*, Roy Frederick and Dennis Henderson, eds. (Columbus, Ohio: Department of Agricultural Economy, Ohio State University, 1987).

Chapter 10

Domestic Farm Policy

*Ezra Taft Benson [Secretary of Agriculture, 1953–1961] . . .
announced that he was going to work night and day on farm
problems. The [congressional] protesters requested that he
refrain from night work, since he was doing enough damage to
farmers in a normal day's effort.*

Eugene J. McCarthy

The focus of this chapter is on **farm policy**—*the set of government programs directly influencing agricultural production and marketing decisions.* The economic problems of farmers have occupied public policy attention for over 50 years. Over these years farm policy has evolved slowly. In the process, experience has been gained on what works and what does not work. Yet as indicated early in the text, there is a cyclical nature to policy proposals and even to the policies themselves. Ideas of policy that were discussed and rejected in the 1920s resurfaced in the 1980s. History, therefore, is important in understanding the evolution of policy and its consequences.

Farm policy may be treated either from an historical perspective or by analysis of particular government programs. This chapter tries to do both. Farm policy development is first segmented into five reasonably distinct time periods. The programs or tools of farm policy are then discussed in detail utilizing the following general program categories:

- Price and income support programs
- Commodity reserves
- Production controls

Throughout the discussion an effort is made to provide perspective on how policies were implemented in terms of the specific tools utilized and their consequences.

FARM POLICY GOALS

The changing nature of the farm problem explained in Chapter 9 suggests that the goals of policy have also tended to change over time. Although this is the case in a marginal sense, the goals of policy have been amazingly stable over time. The following goals have played an important continuing role in policy development. These goals have, however, changed in relative importance as well as in the mechanics of implementation.

- **Expanding farm production** to utilize America's bountiful agricultural resources has been an important goal extending over time from the initial land settlement programs to continuous support for the creation of technology and its adoption. Soil conservation programs have been implemented to maintain the productive capacity of agriculture. The beneficiaries of this goal have extended beyond farmers to agribusiness firms and consumers. Programs to expand food production have contributed to the goal of providing an adequate and secure supply of food at reasonable prices. The existence of this goal may be the origin of frequent charges by farm groups of a cheap food policy. At the same time, it can readily be argued that without an adequate supply of food at reasonable prices, the whole complexion of government programs with respect to agriculture would change dramatically—probably involving much higher levels of government involvement and controls.

- **Supporting and stabilizing farm prices and incomes** began in earnest as a policy goal with the depression conditions in the 1930s and has continued through the present. Calls for parity prices permeated legislative debate into the 1980s. Stabilizing farm prices became reemphasized as a policy goal in the 1970s when world economic and political events had a sharp destabilizing effect on American agriculture. Yet the government's role in stabilizing prices remains a controversial issue. Family farm preservation is a driving force behind the price and income policy goal. Interestingly, it will be seen that although nearly all farm bills espouse preservation of the family farm, little has been accomplished. The political attractiveness of appealing to farm audiences with the need to preserve family farm institutions remains.

- **The adjustment of agricultural production to market needs**
  became a major goal of farm policy after World War II. Attempts to
  achieve this goal have covered a myriad of programs, ranging from
  voluntary acreage reduction programs to mandatory production
  controls. An integral part of this goal has involved encouraging the
  transition of excess resources out of agriculture. Reductions in price
  and income support have, at times, been utilized to encourage this
  adjustment process.
- **Expanding agricultural exports** became a goal of domestic farm
  policy in its own right in the 1970s. The pursuit of this goal had a
  major impact on the composition of farm programs in the 1985 farm
  bill and in the debate that has followed.

HISTORICAL PERSPECTIVE ON GOVERNMENT'S ROLE

Farm policy changes are evolutionary not revolutionary. Watershed
changes in policy seldom occur. Yet there are certain points at which major changes in the direction of farm policy, or at least in the tools utilized,
took place. Therefore, the history of American farm policy is divided into
five periods.

The Settlement Period: 1776–1929

Government intervention in the marketplace on behalf of farmers
began with the depression era of the 1930s. Yet government involvement
occurred much earlier in colonial times. Government programs played a
major role in the immigration and settlement of the vast land area of this
country. The federal government at one time owned as much as 1.4 billion of the approximate 1½-billion-acre land area of the country.

*The disposal of these lands in relatively small, widely dispersed par-
cels gave rise to the family farm structure of agriculture.* This structure
became an end in itself. Its perpetuation remains prominent in the rhetoric of public policy to this day.

The scope of government influence extended far beyond land settlement, as is illustrated by a list of some of the major legislation enacted by
the Congress in the nineteenth and early twentieth centuries.

- The Homestead Act of 1862 made vast acreages of federal lands
  widely accessible in small parcels at little or no cost to would-be
  farmers.
- The creation of the United States Department of Agriculture in
  1862 provided a focal point for institutionalization of its constituency and influence in the executive branch.
- The Morrill Act of 1862 created the land-grant college complex by

giving federal lands to the states to endow colleges in the agricultural and mechanical arts.

- The Hatch Act of 1887 provided annual grants to each state for agricultural research, leading to the system of state agricultural experiment stations.
- The land reclamation law of 1902 provided subsidized irrigation water from federally financed projects to family farms up to 160 acres in size.
- The Smith-Lever Act of 1914 created the cooperative federal–state Agricultural Extension Service, completing the system of teaching, research, and extension whereby the benefits of teaching and results of research were extended to farmers.
- The Federal Farm Loan Act of 1916 created the 12 cooperative Federal Land Banks and the beginnings of today's Farm Credit System, the largest lender of short-, intermediate-, and long-term farm credit.
- The Smith–Hughes Act of 1917 provided federal support for the teaching of vocational agriculture in high schools.

While the programs authorized by these statutes aided agriculture and farmers, the government presence did not extend to influencing directly farmers' economic decisions, such as the selection of which crops to plant, how many acres of each to cultivate, and how to market the products. This did not come until the farm depression of the 1920s, which subsequently engulfed the entire economy early in the next decade.

The New Deal Era: 1929–1954

During the 1920s and the 1930s farmers endured the longest period of financial stress in the twentieth century. It began with a precipitous break in farm prices during the crop year 1920–1921 and continued almost uninterrupted throughout the next two decades.[1] During the Great Depression economic conditions went from bad to worse. From 1929 to 1932, the index of farm prices fell by 56 percent, and net farm income fell 70 percent.[2] Radical new answers were sought to the nation's problems. Several ideas were proposed, debated, and rejected.[3]

[1] Harold F. Breimyer, "Conceptualism and Climate for New Deal Farm Laws of the 1930s," *Am. J. Agric. Econ.* (December 1983), pp. 1152–1157.

[2] Don Paarlberg, "Effects of New Deal Farm Programs on the Agricultural Agenda a Half Century Later and Prospects for the Future," *Am. J. Agric. Econ.* (December 1983), pp. 1162–1167.

[3] Douglas E. Bowers, Wayne D. Rasmussen, And Gladys L. Baker, *History of Agricultural Price Support and Adjustment Programs*, Agric. Inf. Bull. 485 (Washington, D.C.: ERS, USDA, December 1984).

Some of these ideas have since surfaced and again debated. One of the more interesting was the McNary–Haugen bill, which if it had not been vetoed by President Coolidge, would have put into place a two-price plan. A "fair price" was to be set in the United States, and a government corporation would sell the rest on the world market—a policy which resembles that used by the EC.

An idea that was adopted in 1929, and failed shortly thereafter, was the Federal Farm Board. A total of $500,000 was appropriated to buy commodities during times of surpluses. The problem was that no shortages developed. This idea was subsequently tried time and again and was generally unsuccessful except during the tight supply period of the 1970s.

Drastic depression conditions called for major reform and a more comprehensive approach that became known as a New Deal farm policy—based on President Roosevelt's campaign promise for a "new deal." The Agricultural Adjustment Act of 1933 and subsequent farm bills enacted during the 1930s set up nearly every farm program institution that exists today.[4] While parts of the initial 1933 bill were declared unconstitutional, the basic farm policy tools remained intact, including:

- The goal of parity price
- The establishment of price support loans through the Commodity Credit Corporation (CCC)
- Provisions for controlling production through diversion payments
- Provisions for commodity storage
- Provisions for crop insurance

Throughout this period the principal objective of the New Deal programs was to raise farm prices. *These initial public policy initiatives were hampered by erroneous diagnosis of the problem.* Instead of correctly diagnosing the problem as being one of too many resources committed to agriculture, low farm prices and incomes were initially incorrectly attributed to reduced demand resulting from the depression conditions of the 1930s.[5] *The public policy tendency was, therefore, to treat the symptoms rather than the problem.* That is, initial policies and programs emphasized inadequate grain storage and price support programs, as opposed to efforts to move resources out of agriculture and curb production. This

[4]Wayne D. Rasmussen, "The New Deal Farm Programs: What They Were and Why They Survived," *Am. J. Agric. Econ.* (December 1983), pp. 1157–1162.

[5]In a review of the post–World War II agricultural economic policy literature, George Brandow [Policy for Commercial Agriculture," in *A Survey of Agricultural Economics Literature* (Minneapolis, Minn.: University of Minnesota Press, 1977)] notes that the first comprehensive diagnosis and description of the farm problem did not occur until 1945 by T. W. Schultz in his book, *Agriculture in an Unstable Economy* (New York: McGraw-Hill Book Company, 1945).

FARM POLICIES BY DEADLINES

The Agriculture Act of 1949 has special significance since it was the last farm bill enacted without an expiration date. Therefore, all subsequent farm bills are amendments to the 1949 law. If a new bill is not enacted before the expiration of the previous one, the provisions of the 1949 law go into effect. This would mean high price supports for farm products and an automatic vote of producers on whether to implement mandatory production controls.

The threat of implementing the provisions of the 1949 law provides the impetus for Congress to vote on a new farm bill before the expiration of the current bill. Since 1954, that threat has been sufficient to get congressional passage and presidential signature before the expiration deadline.

---

problem of incorrect diagnosis continued through the 1949 farm bill (see the box). Policies evolved over the next four decades in response to a growing understanding of the fundamental nature of the farm problem and to the changing economic circumstances. Yet lapses in memory still periodically occur.

Flexible Price Supports: 1954–1970

Until 1954 Congress set the price support level sufficiently high (90 percent of parity or above) that the minimum mandated price became the floor price. Under the urging of Secretary Benson, the 1954 bill gave the secretary discretion in setting the price support level between 75 and 90 percent of parity.

The issue of the degree of flexibility provided the secretary of agriculture has been an item of contention in virtually every subsequent farm bill. For example, in framing the 1981 bill, Secretary Block asked for a bill that would give him maximum flexibility in implementation. The Congress, fearing a swift move toward the free-market policies espoused by President Reagan during the 1980 campaign, passed a bill with little flexibility. Interestingly, in 1985 the administration got what it asked for in 1981—a wide margin of flexibility and discretion.

There were three other important distinguishing attributes of the 1954 legislation:

- It was the first general farm program in that all major grains and cotton were treated in a group or comprehensive program context. Previously each commodity had its own program; raising price supports or controlling production on one commodity would have adverse spillover effects on other commodities.

- The first comprehensive land retirement program was established to address the excess capacity issue openly.
- The export market was recognized as a potential commercial market for farm products through the enactment P.L. 480.

These flexible programs continued essentially intact throughout the 1960s. In the early 1960s, the Kennedy administration attempted to establish mandatory production controls, which were rejected in a producer referendum. In the late 1960s, increased emphasis was placed on direct payments to farmers in return for not producing on certain acreages. This was the first move toward more market-oriented farm programs.

Market-Orientation: 1970s

Prior to the 1970 farm bill, supporting farm prices and incomes were one and the same. However, in 1973, farm price and income support were overtly separated. Price support was provided by conventional CCC loans while income support was provided by direct farmer payments. Throughout the 1970s and the 1980s the size of direct payments increased, giving rise to the government cost problem.

The motivation for increased direct payments was to lower price supports in order to restore competitiveness in the world market. Buoyed by strong foreign demand, exports boomed. With market prices relatively high, income support payments were low. The target price policy, officially established in the 1973 farm bill, appeared to work better than might have been anticipated.

In a time of volatile world demand, government attention turned to storage or reserve programs. A farmer-owned reserve was established as an alternative to government stocks. The reserve was designed to stabilize prices but was used by policymakers as a means of supporting prices. By the end of the decade stocks once again became burdensome.

Reregulation: 1980s

In the early 1980s, prices were once again resting on loan rates for several commodities. The problem was treated as a temporary one. Farmers were paid in the form of commodities (PIK) to remove land from production. Once the surplus was gone, it was thought that the problem would be gone. Yet with high income supports, strong production incentives persisted. Questions began to arise as to whether the 1970s were an aberration.

As the farm financial crisis deepened, neither the Congress nor the administration could come to grips politically with the option of reducing price and income incentives for production. Income supports were maintained while price supports were reduced as a means of restoring competitiveness in world markets. A new program instrument, the marketing loan, removed the price support floor for cotton and rice. Government costs burst through the ceiling.

Mandatory production controls were rejected, but voluntary controls were greatly expanded. From an economic perspective, low market prices left producers no alternative but to participate in the program. Export subsidies reached record levels as the administration tried to recapture lost markets.

Tight money policies and high deficits required that farm programs do more than could be expected of them. Extracting agriculture from this high level of government involvement became the challenge of the late 1980s and early 1990s.

DOMESTIC FARM PROGRAMS

It can readily be seen from this brief historical summary that many different policy tools or programs have been utilized. These tools fall into three general categories: price and income supports, commodity reserves and production controls. Within each of these categories several different individual tools are possible. These tools are generally discussed in the sequential order in which they were tried; at the end of each section some potential new approaches are discussed.

Price and Income Policies

To both the farmer and the politician, the bread and butter of farm programs is price and income policy. There are four major tools that have been used to directly support farm prices and incomes: price support loans and purchases, target prices or direct payments, and marketing loans. One potential new tool will be added, the base buyout.

Price support loans and purchases.   Price support loans and purchase programs set a floor on the market price. Loans and purchase programs provide both price and income support.

The Purchase Program.   Under a purchase program, a price floor is set by the government buying any products offered to it at the support price. This is how the milk price support program operates. The government stands ready to buy cheese, butter, and nonfat dry milk from anyone offering it at the support price.

The Loan Mechanism.   The price support loan is more complex than the government purchase program. At harvest, the government offers the farmer nonrecourse loans where the commodity is the collateral for the loan. The source of funds is the Commodity Credit Corporation (CCC), a government corporation that finances farm programs. Administration of farm programs is by the Agricultural Stabilization and Conservation Service (ASCS), which has federal, state, and county offices.

The farmer receives the loan at the support price for each unit of commodity placed under loan. The farmer pays the cost of storage and is free to sell the commodity at any time but, of course, must immediately pay off the loan plus interest costs. The interest rate normally is set at a somewhat lower level than for commercial credit.

The loan is a **nonrecourse loan** *meaning that if the farmer does not sell the commodity by the due date, the commodity becomes the property of CCC in full payment of the loan.* There is no incentive for the farmer to sell unless the market price rises above the loan rate plus accumulated interest costs. The **loan rate** *becomes a floor on the market price because if the farmer cannot receive a higher price from the market, normally, it will be forfeited to the government.* No market sales will occur at less than the loan rate if producers are rational.

Loan Theory.   The original purpose of the loan was to provide farmers a source of credit to facilitate storage and prevent all of the commodity from being marketed at harvest. With farmers being able to take out nonrecourse loans, they could pay their production bills and market when the price became more favorable later in the year.

In theory, that sounds like it should work. However, the "gut" reaction of any Congress or administration to farmer agitation over low farm prices and income is to raise the loan rates. This reaction has characterized farm policy since the 1930s. If the loan rate is set too high, the market will not clear, and surplus inevitably develops. *The basic dilemma of supporting farm prices and incomes above market-clearing levels is that it inherently leads to increased production, thereby creating the incentives for further government involvement in agriculture through programs that control production.*

Figures 10.1 and 10.2 present two contrasting loan rate situations. Instead of the two-country trade model utilized in Chapter 6, the graph is drawn to reflect only U.S. supply and demand conditions. However, both domestic demand, *DD*, and export demand, *ED*, are reflected in the graph to obtain the total demand, *TD*. Export demand is obtained from the excess demand function in the two-country trade model with the United States in the right graph and the rest of the world on the left (see Fig. 6.10, for example). In Fig. 10.1 export demand is the area between domestic demand, *DD*, and total demand, *TD*. Export demand, therefore, is simply added horizontally to domestic demand.

In Fig. 10.1 the loan rate P_l is below the competitive equilibrium.

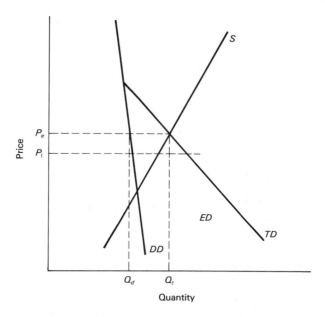

Figure 10.1   Low loan rate has no effect on market price.

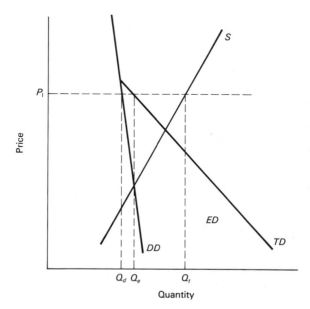

Figure 10.2   High loan rate creates surplus.

The market, therefore, clears at price P_e and quantity Q_t. Quantity Q_d is sold in the domestic market while $Q_t - Q_d$ is exported.

In Fig. 10.2 the loan rate is set above the market-clearing equilibrium at P_e, which becomes the floor price and, therefore, the market price. At this higher price, supply is increased to Q_t while Q_e is the total demand. Quantity $Q_t - Q_e$ is the resulting surplus, which is forfeited to CCC. Note that the export demand falls sharply at the higher price reflecting its greater elasticity. That is, when the U.S. raises its price above the market-clearing equilibrium, export demand suffers, inasmuch as the U.S. price is less competitive in the world market.

The options for handling the surplus include:

• It could be stored. This was frequently done. However, there are limits to the willingness and ability of government to store commodities. Costs of storage are high. In addition, once commodities are purchased by the government, their eventual resale has a depressing effect on market prices. Thus decisions to sell commodities from government storage are highly political.

• The surplus could be purchased and disposed of through nonmarket outlets, such as school lunch or other nutrition programs and foreign food-aid programs. However, such outlets are to a degree competitive with domestic and foreign commercial sales. They therefore also tend to have a price-suppressing effect.

The dilemma thus becomes apparent. *Attempts to support farm prices above market-clearing levels lead to even higher levels of government involvement in farmers' production decisions.*

As noted previously, one of the early guidelines for setting the loan rate was the parity price, which was developed for the original 1933 farm bill. *The* **parity price** *is defined as that price which today gives a unit of the commodity the same purchasing power as it had in 1910–1914.* Paarlberg uses the following illustration: "If a bushel of wheat would buy a pair of overalls in 1910–14, then, to be at parity, a bushel of wheat should be priced so as to buy a pair of overalls today."[6]

The parity concept became the political standard by which to judge the economic position of farmers in the early 1930s and continued to play a major role in setting price support levels through much of the 1960s. The situation of 100 percent of parity was achieved only twice since the turn of the century—in the base period 1910–1914 and during World War II. For the remainder of this century's farm policy history, farmers were forced to accept a price support level specified as some percent of the par-

[6]Don Paarlberg, *Farm and Food Policy: Issues of the 1980s* (Lincoln, Neb.: University of Nebraska Press, 1980), p. 25.

ity price. Any higher price was considered politically unacceptable because of its potential for stimulating even higher levels of surplus production.

Yet parity was worshiped by farmers, their organizations, and by politicians attempting to capture their votes. According to Thomsen and Foote:

> "The concept of parity price has become part of the economic faith of farmers, accepted without question as an objective measure of a fair price. Actually it is merely a mathematical expression of somebody's idea of what is fair. There is no possible objective measure of fairness or equity, which is entirely a subjective concept.'"

Aside from its inherently subjective nature, the parity concept has several more basic flaws:[8]

- Parity assumes that farm commodity price and input costs were in their proper relationship in the 1910–1914 base period. In reality, 1910–1914 was exceedingly favorable to agriculture. This period is frequently referred to as the golden age of agriculture. Farmers were not only exceedingly well off related to costs, they were also well off relative to income in the nonfarm sector.
- Inputs used in production have changed radically since the manpower–horsepower era from which the parity concept arose. New inputs, such as tractors, combines, chemical fertilizers, and pesticides, had to be integrated into the index of prices paid by farmers. This process of determining prices of nonexistent inputs in the base period 1910–1914 was, of course, arbitrary and, in fact, is very difficult statistically.
- Parity fails to take into account the increased productivity of agriculture over time. Increases in efficiency of production have no recognition in the parity concept.
- The parity for an individual commodity such as milk is determined in relation to the index of prices paid for all agricultural inputs, rather than just those inputs used in milk production. Differences in input mix among commodities, therefore, are not considered in the parity price.

[7]F. L. Thomsen and R. J. Foote, *Agricultural Prices* (New York: McGraw-Hill Book Company, 1952), p. 268.

[8]An excellent analysis of the history of the parity concept, the flaws associated with it, and some suggested modifications or alternatives are contained in Lloyd D. Teigen, *Agricultural Parity: Historical Review and Alternative Calculations*, Agric. Econ. Rep. 571 (Washington, D.C.: ERS, USDA, June 1987).

MONUMENT TO THE
AMERICAN COW

Deep beneath the ground here (Independence, Missouri), in more bags, barrels, and boxes than the mind can imagine, the awesome triumphs of the prodigious American milk cow rest enshrined in dark, cool and costly comfort.

What they're keeping here is government-owned milk, butter, and cheese. It keeps piling up, costing the treasury millions upon millions of dollars, and nobody knows what to do with it. . . .

In its subterranean freezers and cooling rooms, CDC (Commercial Distribution Center, Inc.) alone is storing more than 47 million pounds of dairy products that the government has had to buy from U.S. farmers through the controversial dairy price-support program.

But that's only a drop in the bucket. The Department of Agriculture now holds about 1.9 billion pounds of surplus, with only a smidgen of that committed to sales. . . .

About 44 million pounds of cheese (of a 625 million pound inventory) have been identified as moldy. . . .

Dairy product storage and handling comes to about $42.5 million a year, although interest charges on a $2 billion inventory could lift the total daily cost to around $100 million. . . .

Ward Sinclair, "Under Missouri: A Monument to the Output of the American Cow," *The Washington Post* (Washington, D.C.), December 21, 1981, p. A2.

Parity pricing has received sufficient criticism that its use in legislation as a standard for setting price supports has diminished. For example, the 1985 farm bill did not even mention parity. However, permanent legislation, which provides the basis for agricultural programs if a current farm bill expires, relies on parity measures. In addition, price supports for tobacco, honey, wool, and mohair are established on the basis of parity. Marketing orders specify parity as a pricing goal. Suspension of export sales by embargo would result in support prices being set at 90 or 100 percent of parity. Therefore, because of these provisions and the popular appeal of the concept, parity cannot be ignored.

Two related concepts of parity merit mention. **Parity income** *suggests that net farm income per household should be the same in agriculture as in the nonfarm sector.* Parity income is sometimes also related to the base period 1910–1914. **Parity returns** *would give agricultural resources the equivalent returns to what they could earn in the nonfarm sector.* Neither of these concepts has been applied to setting price supports, although they are sometimes confused with parity prices as a farm policy goal.[9]

[9]Ibid., pp. 8–9.

Parity income and returns are considerably more modest policy goals than parity prices.

Target prices.   The **target price** *is the level of returns per unit of commodity guaranteed to farmers who participate in farm programs.* **Target prices** *provide for direct payments to producers of the difference between the target price and the average market price whenever the average market price falls below the target price for a specified time period. The difference between the target price and the average market price is referred to as a* **deficiency payment**. Target prices have been established for all major food grains, feed grains, and cotton as a means of supporting farm income. *Target prices separate price support from income support. Loan rates support price and income. Target prices support only income.*

The Target Price Mechanism.
The target price generally has been set by the Congress. When first authorized in the 1973 farm bill, the target price was set on the basis of what was thought to be the national average cost of production. The 1973 farm bill mandated USDA to make annual average cost of production estimates, presumably as a basis for setting target prices and evaluating the performance of farm programs.

The target price is used to calculate the amount of deficiency payment due producers of a commodity. If the market price is less than the target price, the difference (deficiency payment) is paid to the farmer on his normal level of production. The maximum deficiency payment is the difference between the target price and the loan rate.[10]

Operation of the target price program is illustrated considering three situations (Fig. 10.3):

- The market price P_m is above the target price P_t. This is illustrated in the top left panel of Fig. 10.3, which indicates that no deficiency payments would be made.
- The market price P_m for the specified period is below the target price but substantially above the loan rate (P_l in the top right panel). Deficiency payments would be based on the difference between the target price and the market price times the quantity of eligible production ($P_t - P_m)Q_t$.
- The market price for the specified period is below both the target price and the loan rate (bottom panel). Deficiency payments of ($P_t - P_l)Q_t$ would be made—the maximum payment rate is the differential between the target price and the loan rate. Producers would

---

[10]Since the loan rate should be the market floor price, the deficiency payment should never be any larger than the difference between the target price and the market price. However, later it will be seen that when all producers are not eligible for the loan because they do not participate in the program, market prices below the loan rate can result.

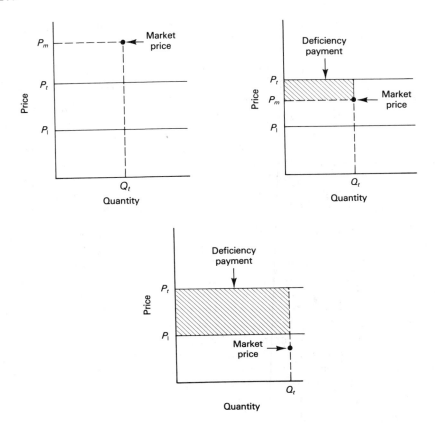

Figure 10.3 Target price/deficiency payment concept.

probably elect to place commodities in the nonrecourse loan program. If unredeemed, the price received for the product would be the loan rate plus the additional deficiency payment, $P_1 + (P_t - P_1)$.

It was noted that the target price is paid only on producers' normal production. Normal production is determined by a farmer's base acreage and farm program yield. The farmer's production history is used to determine both the base acreage and yield. While base acreage is frequently fixed, yields are more regularly updated. Base acreages and yields are used for ease of administration in issuing deficiency payments. Later, it will also be seen that they play a role in production control programs.

Target Price Theory. Since the target price is a guaranteed return to producers having sufficient base and yield, it becomes the marginal revenue upon which production decisions are based. As in the case

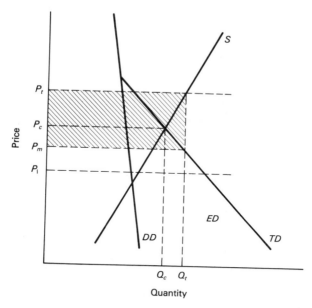

Figure 10.4 Target price depresses market price.

of the loan rate, if the target price is set below the market-clearing price, there is no deficiency payment and no effect on production.[11]

Assuming that the target price P_t is set above the competitive equilibrium price P_c as in Fig. 10.4, it will encourage production Q_t. At this higher level of production the market price has to fall to P_m before the market is cleared. Note that the quantity supplied Q_t is equal to the quantity demanded at price P_m. Therefore, the market is in equilibrium, even though it is not in competitive equilibrium.[12] Note also that the target price does not depress the quantity demanded, as did a loan rate at the same level (Fig. 10.2). Target prices expand the quantity demanded because the market price is depressed. The greatest demand expansion occurs in the export market where the demand is more elastic. The target price can, therefore, also be interpreted as being a form of export subsidy because:

- The quantity of production is expanded, thus artificially adding to the total world supply.

[11]In an unstable real world, production is affected by target prices set below the market price. The target price reduces risk even though it is below the market price.

[12]Recall from Chapter 1 that the reader was cautioned that with government programs, equilibriums exist even though they are not competitive equilibriums. The competitive equilibrium becomes a norm against which other prices are compared.

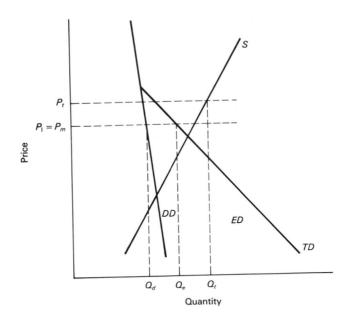

Figure 10.5 High loan rate creates surplus with target price.

- The market price is depressed below the competitive equilibrium.

The difference between the target price and the market price ($P_t - P_m$) is the deficiency payment. It is paid on all units of production.[13] Total government costs, therefore, are $(P_t - P_m)Q_t$, which is the shaded area of Fig. 10.4.

In Fig. 10.4, the loan rate is below the equilibrium market price. Suppose that the loan rate is set higher, at P_1 in Fig. 10.5. Since the loan rate is the price floor, P_1 is also the market price P_m. At P_m, total demand is Q_e, with $Q_e - Q_d$ being exported. The market does not clear as a result of the high loan rate, and $Q_t - Q_e$ is forfeited to the CCC. This is exactly what happened in 1982. That is, a decline in export demand due, in part at least, to tight money policies and the rise in the value of the dollar, shifted the export portion of total demand TD to the right. The loan rate P_t therefore ended up being above the market-clearing price and CCC stocks rose. Not until 1986 was the loan rate lowered sufficiently to make the United States competitive in world markets. By then, CCC stocks were so large in wheat that the market could not be cleared during at least the following two years. It was this condition in cotton and rice that led to the adoption of the marketing loan in the 1985 farm bill.

[13]This assumes that the acreage base and farm program yield are sufficient to cover all units of production.

THE MISSISSIPPI CHRISTMAS
TREE: FARMING THE FARM
PROGRAM

In 1985, a six-member joint venture operated 5841 acres of farmland which the participants in the venture either owned or cash leased from others. The joint venture comprised a father, his four adult sons, and an adult daughter. USDA officials determined that each individual member in the venture qualified as a person for payment limitation purposes under USDA regulations and could receive up to $50,000 in direct support payment subject to the limit.

The joint venture's 1985 farm operations qualified for about $595,000 in payments subject to the limit. The father, since he was operator of much of the land, exceeded the $50,000 on his payment and, as a result, he did not receive about $315,000 that was earned and attributable to his interest in the operation. Each of his five children received about $46,000 as the result of their interests in the 1985 operation.

For 1986, the operation was reorganized by the father and his children into a new joint venture that comprised the same six persons as in 1985 plus 15 new corporations they formed. Each corporation was owned on a 50/50 basis by two individuals, each of whom was a member of the 1985 joint venture. The new joint venture operated 6870 acres of farmland which were either owned or cash leased by its members.

USDA officials determined that each of the six individuals and 15 corporations comprising the 1986 joint venture qualified as a person and could receive up to $50,000 in direct support payments subject to the limit. Their 1986 farm operation earned about $1,050,000 in direct support payments. This resulted in $50,000 to each of the 21 persons comprising the joint venture for payment limitation purposes for a total payment of $1,050,000. This Mississippi Christmas tree organizational structure became subject to the payment limit under the 1988 revised regulations.

Brian P. Crowley, *Farm Reorganizations and Payments to Foreign Owners of U.S. Cropland*, General Accounting Officer testimony before the Committee on Agriculture (Washington, D.C.: U.S. House of Representatives, April 1, 1987), p. 19–20.

Payment Limits.   Before proceeding with a discussion of the marketing loan concept, it should be pointed out that large deficiency payments result in large total payments to large farms. This reality led to limits being placed on payments per farmer. Payment limits were enacted as early as the 1938 farm bill after the first direct payments were made in the 1936 farm bill. Limits were reinstated in 1970. While payment limits could curb some of the production-enhancing tendencies of the target price, farmers have divided their operations among "persons" sufficiently so that the limit has been less than fully effective (see the box).[14] In 1988, an effort was made to tighten the payment limit by preventing the division of farm among more than three persons and by using the farmers' social security number to account for payments.

Generic Payment-in-Kind (PIK). Direct payments to farmers such as deficiency payments do not have to be only in the form of cash. They can also be in the form of commodities; this is referred to as payment-in-kind (PIK). Many people associate PIK with the massive 1983 production control program, when farmers were paid in kind to remove land from production. Generic PIK is another way to use PIK.

Generic PIK pays farmers in the form of negotiable certificates which can be redeemed for commodities. The certificates have a specified face value. Buyers of certificates desire to gain control of a commodity in a specific location without having to pay transportation costs. The commodities purchased with generic certificates are in CCC warehouses. The certificates are generic in the sense that any commodity held by CCC can be purchased with them. Thus a farmer who received a generic PIK on wheat deficiency payments may use it to buy CCC corn.

PIK programs have interesting economic effects that often are not recognized. In the absence of PIK commodities held in CCC storage or under a price support loans, commodities are not readily available to the market. PIK releases commodities to the market, which has a price-depressing impact. As a result, the U.S. commodities become more competitive in world markets. The use of PIK provides another explanation for why market prices may fall below the loan rate.

PIK is only useful in times of surplus when CCC has large stocks. From a short-run accounting perspective, PIK saves the government money because payments do not have to be made in the form of cash, which would be part of current budget expenditures.[15] PIK commodities have already been purchased by CCC, and the government saves storage costs. However, when the government gives commodities away, it is reducing the assets of the CCC, which presumably might have to be replenished some time in the future.

Marketing loans. A **marketing loan** *is a nonrecourse loan which can be paid off by the farmer at the world market price.* The marketing loan effectively removes the floor price set by a loan rate that is "too

[14]General Accounting Office, *Farm Payments: Farm Reorganizations and Their Impact on USDA Program Costs* (Washington D.C.: U.S. Congress, April 1987).

[15]One of the peculiar aspects of government accounting systems involves treating a price support loan as a cash outlay, as opposed to the purchase of an asset. When the loan is repaid, it is treated as a cash receipt. If the commodity is forfeited to the CCC, it is treated as an asset.

high." It was mandated by the 1985 farm bill for rice and cotton and was authorized for wheat and feed grains.

Marketing Loan Mechanism.   At harvest, a farmer receives a loan from the county ASCS office at the loan rate. When the commodity is sold, the loan is repaid but *at the world price*. USDA publishes the world price on a weekly basis. The farmer pockets the difference between the loan rate and the world price, which is referred to as a marketing loan payment. The marketing loan payment is different than the deficiency payment in that the marketing loan is not subject to the payment limit.

The marketing loan was not implemented for wheat and feed grains because of cost considerations and differences of opinion among farmers as to its effects and desirability. However, the 1985 farm bill gave the secretary of agriculture the option of lowering the loan rate by up to 20 percent. This reduction in the loan rate, which was designed to make the prices of these commodities more competitive in the world market, results in a larger direct payment. The new, lower loan rate is often referred to as the Findley loan rate, resulting in a Findley payment, which also is not subject to the payment limit.

Marketing Loan Theory.   As indicated previously, high loan rates have been a major deterrent to allowing the market to clear. Shifting exchange rates, macroeconomic policies, political events, weather, and subsidies make it difficult to set the loan rate high enough to be politically acceptable to producers, while allowing competitive export prices. The marketing loan makes U.S. commodities competitive in export markets by allowing the market price to fall past the loan rate P_l to P_m (Fig. 10.6). At price P_m, the market has cleared with no surplus. Government costs total $(P_l - P_m)Q_t$ and can be divided into a deficiency payment component and a marketing loan payment.

Experience in cotton and rice indicates that the marketing loan is very effective at clearing out government stocks. In cotton, the market price initially fell sharply when the marketing loan went into effect as government stocks were made available to the market. Subsequently, the market price rose as stocks were worked off. Without the marketing loan in cotton and rice, stocks were sufficiently high that there was little hope of market prices rising above loan rates. Research results in cotton suggest that the initial high government costs of the marketing loan may be a long-run option than continuing to carry high stock levels.[16] However,

[16]Dean Chen, Ronald D. Knutson, and Carl Anderson, "Impact of Marketing Loan on Cotton," unpublished manuscript (College Station, Tex.: Department of Agricultural Economics, Texas A&M University, September 1987).

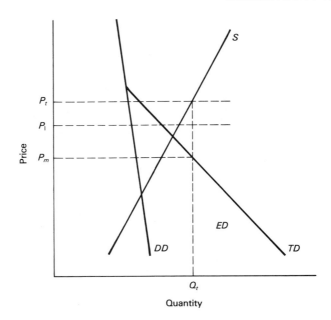

Figure 10.6 Marketing loan allows market to clear despite high loan rate.

other rice- and cotton-exporting countries became quite upset about the short-run price depreciating effect of the marketing loan.

Decoupling.[17]   One of the inherent impacts of the price and income support methods discussed thus far is for production to increase in response to the high target price or loan rate. As a result, either stocks accumulate or exports are subsidized, or it becomes necessary to control production. **Decoupling** *involves the separation of income payments to farmers from prices and production.*

Senator Boschwitz (Rep.-Minn.) has advocated decoupling as a means of reducing government spending, allowing exports to be competitive without subsidies, and reducing or eliminating the need for production controls. Agricultural programs having decoupled payments were proposed by the Reagan administration in GATT as a means of allowing market forces to have greater influence over trade patterns while providing socially desirable income support to farmers.

Decoupling Mechanism.   Boschwitz argues that three conditions are necessary for decoupled payments not to affect production.

[17]This section draws heavily on Dale J. Leuck, "The Effects of Decoupling Agricultural Subsidies on United States and European Community Budgetary Expenditures," unpublished paper (Washington, D.C.: ERS, USDA, February 1988).

- The decoupled payment must be tied to a *fixed base acreage and yield* to avoid additional acreage of crop or yield being increased through the application of more or better quality inputs.
- The payment must be *independent of the quantity planted* in the current year to ensure that planting decisions are based on market prices (as opposed to target prices) equaling marginal costs of production.
- The amount of the *payment must be known in advance* and not tied to fluctuations in market prices or to fluctuations in yields.

If a decoupled program worked as intended, acreage reduction requirements employed during the 1980s would be eliminated.

As originally proposed by Boschwitz and Boren (Dem.-Okla.) a payment per acre planted in an historic period would be guaranteed to farmers regardless of their plantings.[18] No acreage reduction would be required. While the Boschwitz–Boren bill had a phase-out plan, there is no reason this should be a prerequisite to a decoupling plan.

Decoupling Theory.   Profit-maximizing production decisions of farmers are made on the basis of marginal costs and marginal revenues. Just as fixed costs do not enter into a farmer's short-run production decisions, a fixed lump-sum payment would not be expected to affect the production decisions of farmers. This is the theory behind paying farmers a lump-sum income support (say $20,000) regardless of the size of their operation. Such a payment perhaps would be the purest form of decoupling.

Less pure forms, such as those presented by Boschwitz and Boren, build off the current program but contain the basic lump-sum payment concept. For example, Fig. 10.7 provides a simplified comparison of the results under a decoupling plan with a target price. With target price P_t, quantity Q_t would be produced. Under decoupling, *the farmers would be told in advance* that payments of $(P_t - P_m)Q_t$ were guaranteed this year and in future years regardless of their production. With the decoupled payment not being dependent on market prices, yield, or acres planted, the rational profit-maximizing farmer would equate the expected competitive equilibrium price, P_e, with marginal cost (S) and produce quantity (Q_e).[19]

[18]David L. Boren, "Boren, Boschwitz Announce Family Farm Protection and Full Production Act," in *News from U.S. Senator David L. Boren of Oklahoma* (Washington, D.C.: U.S. Congress, April 18, 1985).

[19]The economically astute reader may observe that it would not be necessary to pay farmers $(P_t - P_m)Q_t$ to secure their support for this decoupling plan. By reducing production to Q_e, there are substantial cost savings combined with a higher market price, making a smaller payment possible. A good economic exercise involves determining the breakeven size of lump-sum payment required.

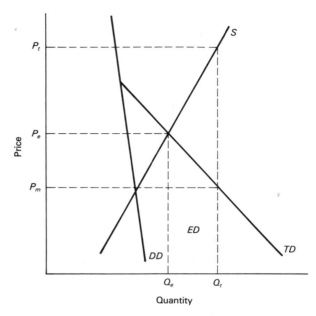

Figure 10.7 Decoupling payments from production and market prices results in lower production and a higher market price.

Decoupling Realities. Decoupling sounds like such a great idea that it should readily be accepted by farmers, their organizations, and policymakers. Four reasons may be cited for the reluctance of farmers and their organizations to accept decoupling:

- Farmers may see decoupling as a means by which government may completely abandon farm price and income supports. The original Boschwitz–Boren bill fortified this concern by completely eliminating payments over a five-year period. For farmers to support decoupling, returns must be guaranteed at a level which at least matches their expectations from traditional farm programs.

- Farmers may treat the block payment as an addition to their marginal revenue and, therefore, expand output. In other words, the payments may be converted to a per unit basis, be added to the market price and then equated to marginal cost, thus resulting in increased output. To economists, such treatment represents perverse economic logic.

- Producers who are profitable in the presence of a lump-sum payment would be economically rational in using this new source of capital to purchase additional land and machinery. This has two effects: (1) it increases the cost of production (land and machinery) for all farmers, and (2) to the extent that yield per acre for the profitable farmers is greater than for less profitable farmers, it increases output.

- A lump-sum payment increases risk to the producer. The risk of market price change is shifted from the government to the farmer. Protection from price risk is one of the major goals of farm programs.
- The base and yield may not be fixed. Over the years, Congress has shown a great propensity to increase farm program bases and/or yields. Political pressure to update farm program bases and yields builds as incentives increase to change cropping patterns and as technological change increases crop yields. The more rapid the pace of change within agriculture, the greater the political pressure to adjust or modernize farm program provisions. If farmers sense a congressional willingness to succumb to political pressure by increasing either bases or yields, they will respond by increasing production.

Insurance.   None of the price and income programs discussed thus far ensures the farmer against crop failure, although the farmer receives deficiency payments on his base acreage and farm program yield regardless of the actual production level. Crop insurance is designed to fill that void.

Since 1938 when federal crop insurance was first established, there have been two main types of programs: federal crop insurance and disaster payments. In addition, there has been discussion and study of the potential for establishing an income insurance program that would substitute for crop insurance, disaster payments, price supports, and income payments.

Federal Crop Insurance.   The objective of this program is to provide crop insurance to farmers who are unable to obtain adequate coverage through commercial channels. While the current program contains a 30 percent federal subsidy, subscription remains low. Problems have been encountered in establishing an actuarially sound rate structure in a political environment.[20] Participation has been the highest in high-risk, nonirrigated, low-rainfall areas. Costs have been too high for farmers in low-risk areas to justify participation. This simply means that the program has not been well run. With a 30 percent federal subsidy on an otherwise actuarially sound program, most farmers should find it advantageous to participate.

---

[20]James W. Richardson, Charles Miller, Gary Helms, and R. D. Knutson, *Comparison of Multi-peril Crop Insurance and Low Yield Disaster Programs* (College Station, Tex.: Agricultural and Food Policy Center, Texas A&M University, February 1988).

Disaster Programs.   During the period 1973–1981, disaster payments provided an alternative to crop insurance as a main line of protection against low yields and prevented plantings. There was no change for disaster protection, although farmers were required to enroll in the farm program.

Payments were generally made when yields fell below two-thirds of normal levels. The level of payment was designed to cover only a producer's variable costs. Yet the disaster program became quite expensive to the Treasury, with payments concentrated in high-risk states such as Texas, Oklahoma, North Dakota, and South Dakota. Aside from this regional bias and high cost considerations, the disaster program was abandoned because of concern that the payments were giving rise to increased production in high-cost, marginally productive cropping areas. Yet whenever a disaster that covers a substantial region occurs, disaster payments are frequently made. This happened with the 1988 drought. The effect of disaster payments is to undermine crop insurance.

Farm Price and Income Insurance.   A potential new approach to reducing the risk of price and income fluctuation in agriculture is price and income insurance for farmers. A price and/or income insurance package could provide farmers with a number of options, each having a different premium cost according to the level of risk. Such packages might include:

- **Price insurance**, giving farmers an option of protecting against price falling below a specified level
- **Income insurance**, giving farmers an option of protecting against income falling below a specified level

Insurance premiums for each package could be contingent on accumulated experience regarding the incidence of potential losses to the insurer. Price insurance premiums would be based on the level of prices to be insured and the probability of the market price falling below the price selected. Income insurance would be based on the level of income insured and the probability of income falling below the selected level.

Income insurance would provide the broadest coverage. It would, in a sense, be equivalent to unemployment compensation available to much of the labor force. It could protect against losses due to crop failure, animal disease, low prices, or the failure of management to make proper production and marketing decisions. Such broad-based protection implies higher premiums than for either crop insurance or price insurance. Some potential problems in establishing an income insurance program include its potential cost, the problem of establishing a sound premium structure when erratic government actions such as embargoes cause large price and income change, and the impact of the quality of management on the level of farm income.

As is presently the case in crop insurance, to be accepted by farmers, price and income insurance would have to be subsidized by the government. One study of income insurance suggests that the required subsidy to encourage adoption and cost of administering the program may be less than the cost of the current target and price support programs.[21]

Income insurance would provide risk protection while not interfering with commodity markets, thus minimizing price and production distortions. Income insurance could also provide producers with a wider range of choice in deferring types and levels of risk.[22]

Stocks Policy, Commodity Reserves

The second major category of domestic farm programs is that of stocks policy. Other than strategic military supplies, the government is more involved in the storage business for agriculture than, perhaps, for any other product. Yet, stocks policy is one of the more difficult and politically sensitive farm policy areas. Government stocks are acquired primarily through the price support loan program. These stocks may either result from CCC loan forfeitures or from the farmer-owned grain reserve.

CCC storage. When a farmer forfeits a commodity from the price support loan program, it becomes the property of the CCC and goes into government storage. This happens primarily when the price support loan rate is set above the market-clearing price (Fig. 10.8). From the initial supply schedule S_1 and target price P_t, quantity Q_t is supplied. With the loan rate set at P_1 only Q_1 is demanded, leaving a surplus of $Q_t - Q_1$ forfeited to the CCC. In the next year, this surplus becomes a part of the supply, shifting the supply schedule to S_2. In the second year, quantity Q_2 is supplied leaving a surplus of $Q_2 - Q_1$. It can readily be seen that as long as the loan rate is kept at P_1, stocks will continue to build. This is, in many respects, the situation that the Reagan administration faced before the enactment of the 1985 farm bill. Loan rates were so high that stocks accumulated year after year. The only choice available was to lower loan rates and/or establish a marketing loan program.

During the 1950s and the 1960s, the government owned a large

[21]James G. Vertrees, *Farm Revenue Insurance: An Alternative Risk Management Option for Crop Farmers* (Washington, D.C.: Congressional Budget Office, August 1983), p. 21.

[22]The income option is discussed more fully in G. Edward Schuh's "U.S. Agriculture in an Interdependent World Economy—Policy Alternatives for the 1980s," in *Food and Agricultural Policy for the 1980s*, D. Gale Johnson, ed. (Washington, D.C.: American Enterprise Institute, 1981), pp. 173–178.

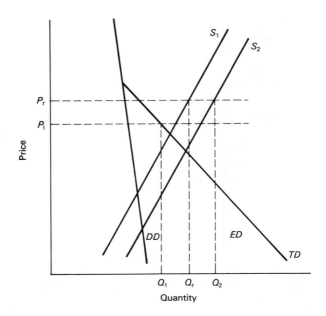

Figure 10.8   High loan rate builds reserve surplus stocks year after year.

amount of storage space. During the 1970s, Secretary Butz sold the then empty bins in the hope that government would never again become involved in the storage business. Such a fate was not to be. While the government never got back into the business of owning and managing grain bins, space is contracted with private warehouses. When commodities are in surplus, these warehouses are full and profitable. Private warehouse owners constitute an interest group that has a special interest in government storage.

The farmer-owned reserve.   The most notable innovation in farm policy in the late 1970s was the development and implementation of the farmer-held grain reserve. The farmer-owned reserve (FOR) was designed to stabilize prices and provide increased supply assurance to domestic and foreign customers. The need for increased management of reserves stock was justified by President Carter and Secretary Bergland on the grounds of greatly increased price instability, higher priorities placed on exports, and adverse producer and foreign customer reaction to shortage- and price-related export embargoes imposed by the Nixon-Ford administrations.

Farmer-Owned Reserve Mechanism.   The **farmer-owned reserve** *is, in essence, an extended loan program covering a period of up to three years.* In return for placing commodities in the FOR, farmers re-

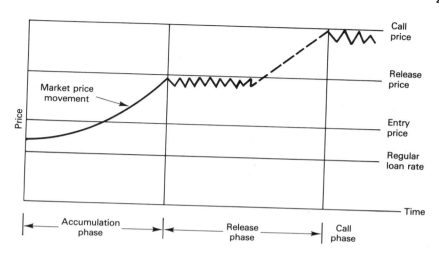

Figure 10.9 Illustration of the operation of the farmer-owned grain reserve.

ceive a higher loan rate (the entry price) than the regular price support loan. During the first year in the FOR, this loan can be interest free. Interest has also, at times, been waived in subsequent years. In addition, a payment approximating the average cost of storage has been provided by USDA. In return for the higher reserve entry price, interest subsidy, and storage payment, the farmers agree not to market the grain until the market price reaches a specified level referred to as the release price. At the release price, the farmers may, but are not required to, sell their FOR grain. Incentives for sale are provided by an ending of interest subsidies and storage payments. In the event that farmers do not remove their grain from the FOR, the secretary has the authority to call or require payment of the loan.[23]

Farmer Owned Reserve Theory.   The farmer-owned reserve has important price impacts (Fig. 10.9).

- When supplies are abundant, commodities are accepted into the reserve at the higher entry price. As grain is placed in the reserve, the free stocks are reduced, and prices rise.
- Once the reserve is established, and if annual production and consumption are at normal levels, the market price fluctuates within

---

[23]From its inception until the enactment of the 1981 farm bill, the FOR also contained a call price. When the market price reached the call price, farmers were required to repay their loans. This action did not necessarily require actual sale but, rather, provided an added incentive for sale. The call provision of the FOR was very unpopular with producers, and USDA, in fact, encountered difficulty getting farmers to pay off their loans when call prices were reached.

the price range bounded by the loan rate and the reserve release price. With sufficient free stocks, the market price would not rise.

- When demand is greater than supply, prices rise to the release price, at which time the reserve stocks may be sold without penalty. Farmers' sales of released grain suppress the price somewhat, as indicated by the jagged market price movement line near the release level.
- If available supplies are relatively small, the price soon rises above the release level. Further price stabilization then becomes dependent on action by the secretary of agriculture to encourage marketing including, potentially, calling the loans.

While the farmer-owned grain reserve was established, in part, to provide increased supply assurance to foreign customers and thus expand exports, this intended effect may not always occur. It will be recalled that one of the principal problems with establishing the loan rate too high is the danger of pricing U.S. grain out of the world market. Suppose, however, that while the regular nonrecourse loan rate is kept low, the reserve entry price is raised substantially. This was done in 1982 to encourage participation in the acreage reduction program. Only those farmers who reduced wheat acreage by 15 percent and feed grain acreage by 10 percent were eligible for the higher loan rate. If a large proportion of the producers participated in the acreage reduction program, the farmer-owned reserve loan rate would, in effect, become the floor and once again price U.S. grain out of the world market.

The FOR also could have the effect of assuring U.S. residual supplier status in the world market. A residual supplier is the supplier of last resort. It holds a disproportionately large share of the world grain stocks. The very willingness of the U.S. government to pay the costs involved in the FOR discourages importing countries such as Japan and the EEC countries from holding stocks. More important, once free U.S. stocks of grain have been used up and the market price begins to rise toward the release price, the FOR is, in effect, supporting the world market price. U.S. grain prices will, under these circumstances, tend to lead world prices and can easily be undersold by state trading exporters such as Canada and Australia. Such potential effects have received little attention.

Production Controls

Early in the history of the domestic price support programs, problems of overproduction and surpluses developed as a direct consequence of supporting prices and incomes above competitive equilibrium (Figs. 10.2 and 10.5). Many different production control methods have been tried with an overall general lack of success. Farmers and policymakers have not desired to regiment themselves to the level of control needed to effectively manage prices and supplies. In this discussion, production control tools are divided into three groups: allotments and quotas, land retirement and set-asides or acreage diversion, and termination or buy-out programs.

Among economists, a great deal of debate has periodically arisen with regard to production control policies.[24] On the one hand, there are those who assert that farmers are one of the few economic segments that do not manage their markets.[25] They contrast agriculture's persistent tendency to overproduce, while other economic segments, such as automobile manufacturers, chemical dealers, and farm equipment manufacturers, tailor production to market needs. These advocates note that the inelasticity of demand for farm products makes agriculture ideally suited for supply management programs. On the other hand, advocates against supply management point to their adverse impacts on exports, their ineffectiveness in controlling production, and their tendency to increase costs of production. An attempt is made below to capture the economic arguments on both sides of the issue without taking a position for or against production controls.

Allotments and quotas.   Acreage allotments and marketing quotas, also referred to as mandatory production controls, trace their origin to the Soil Conservation and Domestic Allotment Act of 1936. These provisions were carried forward and supplemented by the 1938 farm bill and by the 1949 permanent legislation.

Allotment and Quota Mechanisms.   Acreage allotments restricted farmers to planting only a specific number of acres of a specific crop, such as rice, wheat, cotton, peanuts, or tobacco. The peanut and tobacco allotments continue to the present.

A national acreage allotment for a crop was set at a level that would meet anticipated domestic consumption and trade needs. The national allotment was apportioned to individual farms based on their historical plantings of the crop. For many years, planting within the allotment acreage was mandatory with severe civil penalties for violations.

Farmers responded to being restricted to planting on fewer allotted acres by farming the allotment acres more intensely, that is, by applying

---

[24]The main arguments made in a debate on the production control issue are contained in Ronald D. Knutson, "The Case for Mandatory Production Controls," and Bruce Gardner, "The Case against Mandatory Production Controls," both in *Farm Policy Perspectives: Setting the Stage for 1985 Agricultural Legislation* (Washington, D.C.: Committee on Agriculture, Nutrition, and Forestry, U.S. Senate, April 1984), pp. 217–224.

[25]These arguments were initially made most forcefully by Willard W. Cochrane, *Farm Prices: Myth and Reality* (Minneapolis, Minn.: University of Minnesota Press, 1958).

more inputs such as fertilizer, and perhaps by closer management. The result was reduced effectiveness of the allotment, requiring further reductions in the allotment acreage and eventually marketing quotas. Marketing quotas are simply restrictions on the quantity of commodities a farmer is allowed to sell. Quotas are usually used in conjunction with allotments. Marketing quotas have traditionally been implemented only if two-thirds of the producers vote for them in a referendum.

Allotment and Quota Theory.   *Allotments and/or quotas are necessary if the goal of a government program is to raise the price of a commodity above competitive equilibrium.* They may be used either as part of a strategy to raise price over the long run, or to aid in adjustment transition where technological change sharply increases yields, or to compensate for a sharp decline in export demand. For example, it has been suggested that production controls may be needed when the new milk output–enhancing bovine growth hormone is released by the Food and Drug Administration for commercial use.[26]

The effect of imposing allotments is to shift the supply curve to the left. Without a price support program, this has the effect of raising the market price. With a price support program, a surplus can be effectively removed by shifting the supply curve from S_1 to S_2, thereby reducing production from quantity Q_t to Q_p (Fig. 10.10).

In the case of a target price, the analysis is somewhat more complex (Fig. 10.11). Recall from Fig. 10.7 that target price P_t and loan rate P_l result in a surplus of $Q_2 - Q_1$. This surplus can be eliminated by imposing an allotment that shifts the supply curve from S_1 to S_2.

As noted previously, the main problem with allotments is that farmers respond by farming their land more intensely. The effect is to distort the optimum combination of inputs such as fertilizer.[27] Production controls can be made more effective by placing a quota on the quantity that can be marketed.

The theoretical effect of a quota is very direct in that the supply schedule can be treated as being vertical at the level of the quota, Q_q (Fig. 10.12). Since farmers cannot market any more than Q_q, there is no incentive to change the input mix. Distortion in the input mix, therefore, is avoided.

Whether production controls are effective at raising producer income depends on the elasticity of demand. For commodities that are con-

---

[26]See Ronald D. Knutson, "The Case for Mandatory Production Controls in Milk," Barnard F. Stanton, "The Case against Mandatory Production Controls," and Ronald D. Knutson, "Points of Agreement," in *Balanced Dairying* (College Station, Tex.: Texas Agriculture Extension Service, April 1987).

[27]See Chapter 15 for an explanation of this effect and its impacts on agribusiness.

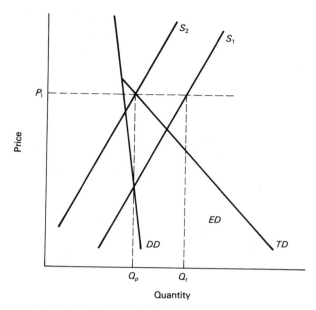

Figure 10.10 Supply reduction required to eliminate surplus with high loan rate.

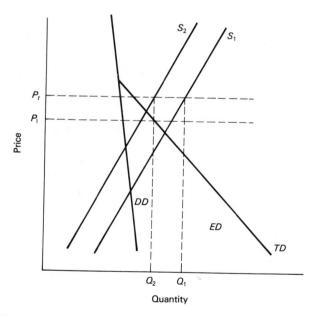

Figure 10.11 Supply reduction required to eliminate surplus with target price and high loan rate.

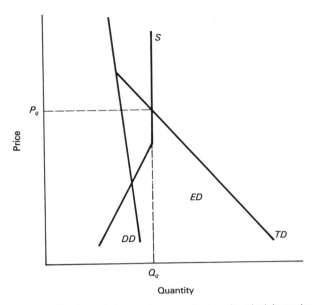

Figure 10.12 A marketing quota makes the supply schedule vertical.

sumed in the domestic market, demand is generally inelastic.[28] The elasticity of export demand varies from commodity to commodity, but it is generally less than −1.0 in the short run, and it may be greater than unity in the long run.[29] The weighted-average elasticity of demand is probably still inelastic, but not nearly as inelastic as it was during the period 1940–1970, when commercial exports were less important for major agricultural commodities.

The argument that mandatory controls destroy the export market has been effective in discouraging policymakers from applying allotments and quotas to major grains and cotton. In reaction, the Harkin bill was introduced in 1986 to set a high domestic price (70 to 80 percent of parity), subsidize exports to maintain market share, and establish marketing quotas to control production. Referendum approval only required a vote of half of the producers to implement. This highly controversial legislation has been the subject of much analysis and controversy. The results of these analyses indicated:[30]

[28] Kuo S. Huang. *U.S. Demand for Food: A Complete System of Price and Income Effects*, Tech. Bull. 1714 (Washington, D.C.: ERS, USDA, December 1985).

[29] Walter H. Gardiner and Praveen M. Dixit, *Price Elasticity of Export Demand: Concepts and Estimates*, Foreign Agric. Econ. Rep. 228 (Washington, D.C.: ERS, USDA, February 1987).

[30] Ronald D. Knutson et al., *Policy Alternatives for Modifying the 1985 Farm Bill*, Texas Agr. Exp. Sta. Bul. B-1561 (College Station, Tex.: Texas A&M University, January

---

WARNING: THE SURGEON GENERAL HAS DETERMINED THE TOBACCO PROGRAM TO BE DANGEROUS TO YOUR HEALTH

Tobacco is one of the most widely criticized farm commodity programs because of its production control features coupled with the inconsistency of government supporting the prices of a product harmful to health.

One million acres of tobacco are grown by 250,000 farmers, an average of 4 acres per farm. Acreage allotments and quotas give farmers the right to grow and market tobacco. The allotments and quotas, being limited in supply, have a capitalized value of $2500 to $3500 per acre. They can be sold or rented but not outside the country. High allotment and quota rental rates (25 to 35 percent of production costs) also reflect the production control policies. Price supports are based on parity. If a lot of tobacco sold at auction fails to receive a bid of 1 cent per pound over the support price, it is bought under a CCC loan by a grower cooperative.

Tobacco interests argue that the program is low in cost, about $32 million on $3 billion in producer income; supports many small rural farmers and related businesses, and garners large public revenues from taxes on cigarettes and the tobacco products.

Opponents argue that: there is no logical basis for government subsidizing production of a harmful product; the program has outlived its original purpose of increasing farm prices and incomes; and the program is far from costless to society as a whole.

- With export subsidies producer returns would rise
- The increase in producer returns would substantially improve the chances of farm survival
- The government costs of subsidies to maintain market share would be at least as large as the current farm program[31]

1987); Daryll E. Ray and Darrell D. Kletke, *Analysis of Selected Farm Program Alternatives for Wheat*, A.E. 8746 (Stillwater, Okla.: Department of Agric. Econ., Oklahoma State University, June 1987); Food and Agricultural Policy Research Institute, *The Commodity Supply Management Program*, FAPRI 2-87 (Columbia, Mo.: University of Missouri, February 1987).

[31]The FAPRI study assumed an international export cartel with market agreements. As a result of the cartel assumption, government costs associated with this version of the Harkin bill were less than under the 1985 farm bill.

USDA officials, free-market advocates, and the agribusiness commodity organizations were irate at the results of these three university studies. Much of their criticism treated only the mandatory controls portion of the bill, ignored the export subsidies, and contended that the domestic market could not be protected against re-import. The latter criticism was a legitimate concern in commodities such as cotton, where re-import would be in the form of textiles whose origin could not be identified.

When production control programs are pursued with the objective of raising the price above the market-clearing level over a substantial time period, the resulting profits are often used by farmers to expand the size of their operation. The more profitable farming is, the more farmers are willing to pay for land or livestock on which production is controlled.

Capitalization is *the process by which farm program benefits are bid into the price of the control instrument.* The instrument may be land or a chicken on which an allotment is held, or a quota which gives the holder a right to market a given quantity product. The value of the quota or allotment is most visible and easily determined if it is freely transferable from one producer to another. For example, marketing quota rights to sell milk from an average cow in Ontario, Canada, cost a potential producer about $3500—considerably more than the cost of an average milk cow.[32] For a new dairy operation, quota costs represent 30 percent of the total initial investment. Under the current allotment program for tobacco, the right to produce and market tobacco sells for as much as $3000 per acre.[33] The capitalization problem is generally played down by mandatory control advocates. Yet the degree of capitalization would be expected to be directly proportional to the vigor with which production control and price enhancement is pursued. One way to estimate the value of an asset that is expected to generate a given level of return to perpetuity is to divide the extra profit earned by the required rate of return.[34] For example, if a quota adds $10 profit per acre at a 10 percent rate of return, the value of the land would increase by $100 per acre ($10/0.10).

The capitalized value of an asset on which there are production controls also depends on the certainty that those returns will be maintained in the future. Recent doubt about the future of the tobacco program mate-

[32]Dan Dvoskin, "Some International Experiences with Mandatory Supply Controls," *Agricultural Outlook*, AO-130 (Washington, D.C.: ERS, USDA, May 1987), p. 32.

[33]Economic Research Service, *Mandatory Production Controls*, Agric. Inf. Bull. 520 (Washington, D.C.: USDA, July 1987).

[34]John B. Penson and David A. Lins, *Agricultural Finance* (Englewood Cliffs, N.J.: Prentice-Hall, Inc., 1980), p. 102.

rially reduced the value of tobacco allotments.[35] Potential depreciation in the value of allotments or quota creates strong producer resistance to modifying the program. Declines in the values of recently acquired quotas or allotments are just as devastating to producers as are falling land values.

Quotas and allotments are not the only source of capitalization. Whenever a farm program generates higher returns, capitalization occurs. In the case of target prices and loan rates, capitalized values are more difficult to detect because they are hidden in land values and changes in the general price level.

Even if all the obstacles associated with political acceptance of mandatory controls could be overcome, questions arise as to whether they would be supported by farmers voting in a referendum. The last official vote on mandatory controls occurred in 1963. The proposal was for a system of penalties for planting wheat in excess of acreage allotments and for marketing quotas based on domestic and export needs. With over a million farmers voting, the referendum was soundly defeated. The 1985 farm bill mandated a poll on whether wheat producers would prefer a system of mandatory production controls. A slim majority voted yes.

Land retirement, diversion programs.   Discontent with the regiment and consequences of mandatory control programs has led to extensive experimentation with voluntary programs to control production. **Land retirement programs** *pay producers to take land out of production.* Payments are based on the productivity of the land being removed from production. From a farmer's perspective, participation is warranted if the payment exceeds the potential earnings from the land to be retired plus the cost of maintaining the retired acres. Since the 1930s, three major land retirement programs have been undertaken—the soil bank, payment-in-kind, and conservation reserve programs.

Soil Bank Programs.   The soil bank, implemented in 1956, was really two different programs. The first, and least effective, involved paying farmers to convert allotment land to conservation uses on an annual basis. This program was discontinued after two years of operation because of high cost. The long-term retirement portion of the Soil Bank put land into a conservation reserve for a 10-year period. Farmers found this program was sufficiently attractive to put nearly 30 million acres in the soil bank by 1960.

Rural communities located in high-participation areas objected to

---

[35]Daniel A. Sumner and Julian M. Alston, *Effects of the Tobacco Program: An Analysis of Deregulation* (Washington D.C.: American Enterprise Institute, 1986).

the whole-farm retirement provisions of the soil bank program.[36] It reduced input purchases and product marketing undermining agribusiness. In some instances the families would simply retire from farming and move. One of the higher levels of participation in the Soil Bank program was in areas of the Southeast where farmers planted trees on the retired land. In the short run, these farmers got soil bank payments and, in the late 1980s, began to receive receipts from harvesting lumber.

The robust economic conditions of the 1970s attracted much of the soil bank land that was not planted to trees back into production. This led to the PIK program in 1983 and a second long-term retirement program in the late 1980s.

Payment-in-Kind.   After the 1982 harvest, grain bins were bulging. Another record harvest in 1983 would have meant the forfeiture of large amounts of grain to the CCC. To prevent this occurrence, USDA announced the PIK program in January 1983.

PIK paid farmers 80 to 95 percent of their farm program yield in return for retiring acreage from production for one year. Farmers' response to the PIK program was stronger than anyone had anticipated. A record 82 million acres of land were removed from production, 25 percent more than any previous production control. [37] This meant that over one-third of the cropland was retired from production.

Exactly how effective PIK was at reducing production is subject to debate. Its effect was confounded with the worst drought since the 1930s.[38] The combination of these events temporarily lowered stocks, raised farm prices, and increased exports. The increase in exports resulted from PIK released commodities being made readily available to the export market at competitive prices.

Conservation Reserve Program (CRP).   The CRP was enacted as part of the 1985 farm bill to remove highly erosive farmland from production. It was thereby designed to accomplish the dual objectives of controlling erosion while reducing overcapacity. Only USDA-designated highly erosive land is eligible to be bid into the program. The 1985 farm bill goal was to retire 40 to 45 million acres of land for a 10 to 15 year period by 1991.

To reduce the consequences for rural communities, the total payments per person could not exceed $50,000 annually. In addition, the amount of land retired in any county could not exceed 25 percent unless it

[36]Bowers et al., *History of Agricultural Price Support*, p. 22.

[37]Economic Research Service, *An Initial Assessment of the Payment-in-Kind Program* (Washington, D.C.: USDA, April 1983).

[38]Bowers et al., *History of Agricultural Price Support*, p. 41.

is determined that there would be no adverse effects on the local economy. Yet there was a strong tendency for CRP retired lands to be concentrated in certain geographic areas such as the southern High Plains, the Southeast pine forest areas, and the southern Iowa/Northern Missouri areas.

Set-aside or acreage reduction programs. Set-aside *requires that a certain percentage of a farmer's cropland be removed from production as a condition for receiving farm program benefits.* Those benefits include deficiency payments and the price support loan.

Set-aside was first introduced in 1970. In the 1981 farm bill the term "acreage reduction" was used in addition to set-aside, although the basic program concept did not change. Aside from its voluntary nature, set-aside had the main advantage of reducing government costs. Not only were payments involved in retiring land avoided by set-aside, but also income support payments were avoided to those farmers who chose not to participate in the program.[39] Of the four general methods of controlling production, set-aside is the least effective. **Slippage** *measures the difference between the size of the set-aside and the actual reduction in production.* Set-aside slippage is high because:

- Not all farmers participate.
- Producers who do participate logically set aside their poorest land.
- The remaining acres are often farmed more intensely.

Experience with the set-aside program suggests that a 15 percent set-aside has resulted in only about a 3 percent decline in production. In other words, there is 80 percent slippage. Higher levels of set-aside are more effective because each additional acre of land set aside tends to be more productive. Thus the PIK program had less slippage because of the large quantity of land removed from production. The conservation reserve would be expected to have more slippage because highly erosive land is being removed from production.

Termination of buyout programs. The 1985 farm bill mandated a new production control concept when it mandated the secretary of agriculture to buy whole dairy farms out of production. Enough farms were to be bought out to equal 7 percent of the nations' milking herd in addition to normal culling. All animals from herds bought out were to be slaughtered over a 17-month period. To help pay for the program, the secretary

---

[39]Large increases in direct payments associated with the 1985 farm bill made participation almost economically mandatory.

deducted $0.40 per hundredweight from the price received during 1986 and $0.25 per hundredweight during 1987.

The buyout program substantially reduced price support purchases of manufactured dairy products during 1986 and 1987. However, farmers not participating in the program continued to increase production, thereby reducing program effectiveness. In addition, some of the producers who were bought out probably would have gone out of production.

Buyout programs have been suggested in other circumstances and for other commodities. For example, the government could buy farmers out of production, including their land, as a means of removing excess capacity and preventing further declines in land prices. Aside from issues of cost, the main deterrent to such a program may be aversion to the government owning large amounts of farmland.

THE PROBLEM OF DISENGAGING

Many people might prefer to get government completely out of agriculture and return to perceptibly freer market policies. The Reagan administration proposed in GATT that all farm subsidies be eliminated by the year 2000. Even if there were a consensus that freer market policies are essential, there are many very real obstacles to achieving this goal.

After the Reagan administration proposal to discontinue subsidies, there were several studies of the impact of such a major policy change on market prices, producer returns, and government costs. Most of these studies indicated that farmers would be worse off than under the current program. For example, a USDA study that employed reasonably realistic assumptions found that producer net returns would decline by about 50 percent.[40] Accompanying this decline in producer returns would be a 60 percent reduction in budget costs and an unmeasured increase in consumer expenditures on food.

Reductions in producer returns under free-trade conditions suggest that farmers are not likely to support the Reagan administration proposal without compensation. In addition, since with a progressive and corporate income tax, those who pay the taxes are not proportionately the same as those who buy the food, consumers (particularly poor consumers) may object to eliminating target price subsidies. Finally, history suggests that lower target prices increase the incentives for higher price supports, which destroys the export market. In summary, there will likely be extensive debate over reducing or decoupling farm program benefits— despite their intuitive appeal.

[40]Leuck, "Effects of Decoupling," p. 15.

ADDITIONAL READINGS

1. An outstanding historical chronology of the development of domestic farm policies and programs is contained in Douglas E. Bowers, Wayne D. Rasmussen, and Gladys L. Baker, *History of Agricultural Price Support and Adjustment Programs*, Agric. Inf. Bull. 485 (Washington, D.C.: ERS, USDA, December 1984). This publication is one of a series issued by the Economic Research Service before the debate began on the 1985 farm bill. In the series are separate publications for each of the major farm program commodities. Each contains a wealth of policy information.

2. After each farm bill is enacted, a summary of its provisions is compiled by the Economic Research Service. The 1985 farm bill edition was by Lewrene K. Glaser, *Provisions of the Food Security Act of 1985*, Agric. Inf. Bull. 498 (Washington, D.C.: ERS, USDA, April 1986).

3. Prior to the enactment of the 1985 farm bill, a seminar was held to review the agenda of issues. The results are published in Gordon C. Ransser and Kenneth R. Farrell, eds., *Alternative Agricultural and Food Policies and the 1985 Farm Bill* (Berkeley, Calif.: Giannini Foundation, 1985).

4. For the more economically literate reader, an excellent reference is Bruce Gardner's, *The Economics of Agricultural Policies* (New York: Macmillan Publishing Company, 1987).

Chapter 11

The Structure of Agriculture

A staunch supporter went up to a political candidate
after a speech and said, "I admire the straightforward
way you dodged those issues."

Maynard Speece

The **structure of agriculture** *refers to the number and size of farms;*
ownership and control of resources; and the managerial, technological,
and capital requirements of farming. The issues of the structure of agriculture are illustrated by such questions as:

- Will the family farm survive?
- Do farm programs help or injure the chances of family farm sur-
  vival?
- Who controls production and marketing decisions at the farm level?
- What is the balance of market power among input suppliers, farm-
  ers, and marketing firms?
- Will U.S. agriculture eventually become industrialized and con-
  trolled by large agribusiness corporations?
- What type of agriculture is wanted in America?

This is not the first time the structure of agriculture has been discussed. In the first chapter, basic agriculture values were associated with
family farm institutions. In the preceding two chapters, questions have
arisen as to whether the benefits of domestic farm policy are too highly

concentrated in the hands of large farmers. The changing structure of agriculture has been highlighted as one of the factors that has led to a questioning of the need to continue the more traditional farm programs involving price and income support which allocate benefits on the basis of volume of production.

In this chapter, after defining a family farm, the sources of economic and social concern about structure are summarized. This is followed by a discussion of alternative structures. The chapter concludes with policies influencing structure including domestic farm policies, marketing policies, and tax policies.

FAMILY FARM DEFINITION

In policy discussions, the term "family farm" is frequently used but seldom defined. In this book, a family farm must meet four requirements:

- A majority of the management and work must be done by the operator and family.
- A close association must exist between the household and the business.
- Managerial control must be exercised by the operator.
- Family farms must obtain the majority of their income from farming.

Thus, as a general rule, part-time farms are not family farms. This is consistent with the earlier discussion of potentially not treating part-time farmers as farmers from a policy perspective. If they are not farmers, they surely cannot be family farmers.

The definition also implies some size limit on what constitutes a family farm, in that the majority of work must be done by the operator and family. For purposes of this chapter, it is assumed that such a farm generally falls in the sales range $100,000 to $250,000 gross. At a maximum, such a farm would have about 750 acres of corn, 1650 acres of wheat, 1550 acres of sorghum, 800 acres of cotton, 500 acres of rice, or 80 dairy cows.

SOURCES OF CONCERN ABOUT STRUCTURE

Concern about the structure of agriculture arises from economic, social, and political sources. The economic concerns relate to the efficiency of production, the level of farm prices, and the cost of inputs. Social concerns relate to the survival of the family farm and the impact on the quality of life in rural America. Political concerns relate to the balance of political power within agriculture and controversy over the role of agriculture in maintaining stability in a democratic system.

Economic Concerns

The economic concerns about the structure of agriculture relate to issues of concentration, efficiency, and integration.

Concentration. **Concentration** *refers to the proportion of production or marketings controlled by the largest firms.* From an economic perspective, concentration is important because the more highly concentrated the market, the greater the potential impact of a firm or group of firms on price. Three dimensions of concentration in agriculture include production, input markets, and product markets.

Concentration of production *in agriculture is generally low but highly variable from commodity to commodity.* Overall decline in farm numbers has been accompanied by growth in the number and size of the largest farms. Concentration of production has occurred to the point where approximately 30,000 farms having sales of over $500,000 (about 1.3 percent of all farms) control over 30 percent of the production and account for over 55 percent of all net farm income. While the image is that large family farms tend to be concentrated in the West and South, over one-third are located in traditional family farming areas of the Midwest and Great Plains.

There is wide variation in the extent of concentration of production from commodity to commodity. For example, in 1986, beef feedlots in the 13 major cattle feeding states with a capacity of over 16,000 head (0.5 percent of the total number of feedlots) produced 51 percent of the fed cattle. The 80 largest of these feedlots produced 31 percent of the fed cattle.[1] The four largest meat packers own about 6 percent of the feedlot capacity.[2] In 1987, the 10 largest broiler producers and contractors controlled about 50 percent of the production. In the vegetable crops such as lettuce and celery, concentration of production and/or control is comparably high.[3]

Such high levels of concentration are limited largely to selected livestock, poultry, and fruit and vegetable products. Concentration is still

[1]National Agricultural Statistics Service, *Cattle on Feed* (Washington, D.C.: USDA, January 1987), p. 10.

[2]Estimate based on data contained in Cheryl Burke, "The Big Four Just Got Bigger," *Nat. Cattlemen* (May 1987), p. 5.

[3]Donald L. Brooke, "Changes in the Structure of Florida Vegetable Farms 1945–1974," in *Farm Structure* (Washington, D.C.: Committee on Agriculture, Nutrition, and Forestry, U.S. Senate, April 1980), pp. 363–379.

very low for most of crop agriculture. In fact, relative to other American industries, where the market share of the four largest manufacturers frequently exceeds 50 percent, concentration in agriculture is quite low. But attention is drawn to agriculture because of the rapidity with which certain industries, such as broilers and fed cattle, have gone from a diffused to a concentrated and integrated structure.

Concern, however, exists that if extended over a period of time, increasing concentration of agriculture production could lead to higher food prices.[4] This would result from increased merchandising and marketing costs, potential unionization of agricultural workers, and the lack of effective competition.[5] The basis for this conclusion is the economic theory of imperfect competition. That is, as an industry progresses toward higher levels of concentration, competition among the remaining firms would be expected to assume higher-cost forms of nonprice competition and increased profit margins. This conclusion assumes that there are relatively few economies to be gained from increased size and from integration of production and marketing functions.

Concentration in purchased inputs *used in agricultural production is generally high in absolute and relative terms.* Concentration in inputs such as machinery, energy, seeds, credit, and chemicals is high at all levels of the market channel, with the four largest firms frequently having over 50 percent market shares.[6] A recent Federal Trade Commission study found concentration of sales in manufacturing that ranges from 35 percent for the four largest fertilizer manufacturers to 83 percent for the four largest combine manufacturers (Table 11.1). At the wholesale level, the absolute number of manufacturers is generally limited, with substantial costly nonprice competition based on brand differentiation.[7] This nonprice competition extends to the producer input market level. At this level, the number of competitors tends to be limited by the distance that a farmer can travel to obtain a better price. Over time this trading area has expanded—particularly for the large farmer who buys in large quantities and can afford to travel substantial distances in search of lower product prices.

[4]Harold F. Breimyer and Wallace Barr, "Issues in Concentration versus Dispersion," in *Who Will Control U.S. Agriculture?* North Central Reg. Ext. Publ. 32 (Urbana, Ill.: University of Illinois, August 1972), pp. 13–22.

[5]James V. Rhodes and Leonard R. Kyle, "A Corporate Agriculture," in *Who Will Control U.S. Agriculture?* North Central Reg. Ext. Publ. 32-3 (Urbana, Ill.: University of Illinois, March 1973).

[6]Dale C. Dahl and Loys L. Mather, "Organization of the Farm Input Industries: Implications for Public Policy," paper presented at the Farm Supply Industry Seminar, Denver, Colo., June 1974.

[7]Dale C. Dahl, "Public Policy Changes Needed to Cope with Changing Structure," *Am. J. Agric. Econ.* (May 1975), p. 210.

TABLE 11.1 Concentration of Manufacturing
Purchased Farm Input Markets

| | Market Share (%) of: | |
Input	Four Largest Firms	Eight Largest Firms[a]
Fertilizer	35	45
Hybrid corn	57	71
Pesticides	57	79
Tractors		
Two-wheel drive	80	NA
Four-wheel drive	68	NA
Combines	83	NA

Source: Robert F. Leibenluft, *Competition in Farm Inputs: An Examination of Four Industries* (Washington, D.C.: Federal Trade Commission, February 1981).
[a]NA, not available.

High levels of input market concentration relative to producer concentration suggest substantial costs associated with advertising and product differentiation as well as the potential for excessive profits. However, there is a lack of evidence of excessive profits. Two reasons may exist for this lack of evidence:

- Cooperatives have experienced substantial success in penetrating farm supply markets. This success may have been a factor in competing away excess profits in inputs such as fertilizer, credit, and chemicals.[8]
- Many of the advances in agricultural technology have been the product of publicly supported research. The results of this research have not only been more generally available for adoption but also continuous infusion of advances has made if difficult to maintain high profits or inputs over the long term. In addition, the Extension Service has generally maintained extensive trial or test plot demonstrations of the effectiveness of a wide range of purchased inputs. This has tended to provide incentives for competition among input suppliers on the basis of product quality and performance.

Recent research policy changes allowing the patenting of new life forms and computer software could change the competitive relationships within the farm input industries. All discoveries involving the products of biotechnology are being rapidly patented, even by the land-grant universities. However, the pace of technological change in biotechnology could be so fast that the danger of a firm capturing a market is minimal.

[8]Ibid., p. 208.

Concentration in farm product markets *also contains substantial evidence of imperfect competition.*[9] An issue involves the extent to which the market power of first handlers (buyers) of farm products may be sufficient to suppress producer prices.

Farmers generally sell in markets where there is a relatively small number of buyers. For example, the market share of the four largest meat packers approaches 80 percent of the steers and heifers slaughtered.[10]

Distance limits the number of alternative outlets available for most grain and cotton producers. Fruit and vegetable producers have long been recognized as facing a highly concentrated buyer market for their products.[11]

The theoretical implications of monopsony pricing are clear (Fig. 11.1). In a competitive market, quantity Q_c would be purchased at price P_c. However, since the monopsonist faces an upward-sloping supply curve, its profit-maximizing quantity purchased falls to Q_m and the price paid producers is reduced to P_m.

Specific economic evidence of the extent of monopsony influence on farm prices is sketchy. Miller and Harris found that buyer concentration was a statistically significant factor having a negative influence on the price of hogs.[12] It has also been found that as the volume of commodities moving through terminal markets declines, prices fall relative to other, higher-volume markets.[13] Although this evidence is far from decisive, it lends support to the general proposition that first handlers of farm products generally have sufficient market power to affect the terms of trade.

Efficiency.   **Efficiency,** as used here, *is defined as minimum cost.* The issue of the most efficient size farm was discussed in Chapter 9 and will not be repeated. Suffice it to say that the least-cost farm size extends far beyond the family-size farm having a maximum of $250,000 in sales.

Table 11.2 provides a rough comparison of the size of a $250,000 gross sales farm with a farm size where most of the economies appear to have been realized during the 1980s. Generally, the efficient farm size is more than twice as large as a family farm.

[9]Marvin L. Hayenga, ed., *Pricing Problems in the Food Industry*, N.C. 117, Monogr. 7 (Madison, Wis.: University of Wisconsin, February 1979).

[10]Burke, "The Big Four," p. 5.

[11]Leon Garoyan, "Thin Markets in the Fruit and Vegetable Industry," in *Pricing Problems in the Food Industry,* Marvin L. Hayenga, ed., N.C. 117, Monogr. 7, (Madison, Wis.: University of Wisconsin, February 1979), pp. 105–114.

[12]Steven E. Miller and Harold M. Harris, "Monopsony Power in Livestock Procurement: The Case of Slaughter Hogs," unpublished manuscript (Clemson, S.C.: Clemson University, October 1981), 26 pp.

[13]William G. Tomek, "Price Behavior on a Declining Terminal Market," *Am. J. Agric. Econ.* (August 1980), pp. 434–444.

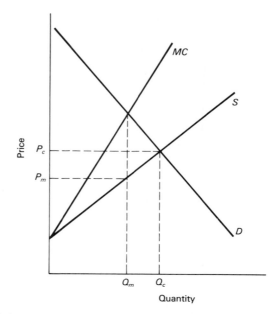

Figure 11.1 A monopsonist reduces the quantity purchased and the price paid producers.

TABLE 11.2 Efficient Farm Size Where Most Economies Have Been Realized Compared with $250,000 Gross Sales Family Farm

Product Produced	$250,000 Size	Efficient Size
Iowa corn	750	1500
Kansas wheat	1650	3300
Kansas sorghum	1550	4000
Texas cotton	800	4000
Arkansas rice	500	1300
New York dairy[a]	80	250 +

Source: Ronald D. Knutson, "Why the Mid-size Family Farm Is Dying," unpublished manuscript (College Station, Tex.: Texas A&M University, August 1987).

[a]Includes the value of forage, feed, and milk production. Based on Office of Technology Assessment, *Technology, Public Policy, and the Changing Structure of Agriculture* (Washington, D.C.: U.S. Congress, March 1986); and B. F. Stanton, *Competitiveness of Northeast Milk Producers in the National Market*, Department of Agricultural Economics, 87-5 (Ithaca, N.Y.: Cornell University, March 1987), p. 13.

Vertical integration. *Firms are* **vertically integrated** *when they control two or more levels of the production-marketing system for a product.* Of particular interest in this chapter is vertical integration, which extends to control of the production and/or marketing decisions of farmers. Such control may be exercised either by contract or by ownership.

Contract integration *exists when a firm establishes a legal commitment that binds the producer to certain production or marketing practices.* At a minimum, contract integration normally requires that the producer sell the product to the buyer. Such a contract is generally referred to as a marketing contract. Additional commitments may bind the producer to specified production practices and sources of inputs. Contracts containing production and marketing commitments are generally referred to as production contracts. While all forms of contract integration have created concern, the greatest controversy exists with production contracts because they control both the production and marketing decisions of producers. In addition, under a production contract, from a legal perspective, the producer may not even own the product being grown.

Contract integration may be undertaken either by a cooperative or by a proprietary (corporate) agribusiness firm. More questions have been raised by farmers and public interest groups about contract integration by corporations than by cooperatives. However, multiyear cooperative contracts in milk have been viewed as a potential violation of antitrust laws by the Department of Justice. In addition, the adoption of a marketing contract by a large Midwestern regional cooperative created a great deal of concern by proprietary grain companies about the potential producer control of markets, even though the probability of such control was minimal.

The extent of contract integration is not well documented. Table 11.3 provides estimates for 1987 based on available historical information and discussions with industry experts. The commodities in Table 11.3 account for 90 percent of all farm sales. When these commodities are weighted according to sales, all forms of contract integration represent 32 percent of farm sales. Overall proprietary contract integration (18 percent) is greater than cooperative contract integration (14 percent). However, the emphasis is on different commodities. In addition, proprietary firms emphasize production contracts, whereas cooperatives emphasize marketing contracts, frequently referred to as marketing agreements. Substantial year-to-year variation may exist in marketing contracts for commodities such as grains and cotton, depending on market price conditions and expectations. With this caveat, the following observations appear to be valid on the extent of contracting:

- Contracting in all forms is more prevalent than is generally recognized. Nearly 32 percent of the commodities listed in Table 11.3 are contract integrated when weighted by sales. These commodities represent 90 percent of all producer sales.
- While contracting was once limited to perishable commodities, it has expanded to virtually all commodities.

TABLE 11.3 Extension of Contract Integration by Commodity, Type of Contract, and Type of Contracting Firm, 1987 (Percent of Total Production)

Commodity	All Contracting[a]	Cooperative Contract Marketing[b]	Cooperative Contract Production	Proprietary Contract Marketing[b]	Proprietary Contract Production	Ownership Integration	Total Integration
Milk	95	65	0	30	0	3	98
Broilers	89	0	12	0	77	10	99
Eggs	52	0	2	0	50	37	89
Turkeys	62	0	18	0	46	28	90
Hogs	10	1	1	0	8	8	18
Fed beef	30	0	0	0	30	6	36
Wheat	5	2	0	3	0	0	5
Rice	67	59	0	8	0	5	72
Feed grains	7	2	0	5	0	0	7
Soybeans	10	3	0	7	0	0	10
Cotton	20	13	0	7	0	10	30
Fresh vegetables	31	7	0	0	24	35	66
Processing vegetables	85	0	20	0	65	15	100
Citrus	72	65	2	5	0	35	95[c]
Other processing fruits and nuts	90	65	0	30	0	5	100
Other fresh fruit	45	40	0	5	0	10	60
Total	31	13	0	6	12	6	38

Source: ERS, USDA statistics used to supplement authors' information.

[a]Does not include production for seed.

[b]Includes call, delayed, or deferred pricing contracts.

[c]Numbers total more than 95 percent because one major packer is a member of a cooperative.

- Some evidence exists that the terms of contracting have a tendency to begin with marketing contracts and expand over time to include production practices.
- Production contracting appears to be associated with commodities where breeding and control of genetic factors play an important role in either productivity determination or quality control.

Ownership integration *exists when single ownership interests extend to two or more levels of the production–marketing system.* The primary interest in this chapter is in vertical ownership interests that involve production of agricultural commodities. Ownership integration may involve either cooperatives or proprietary agribusiness firms.

Proprietary ownership integration (frequently referred to as corporate integration) accounts for about 6 percent of farm sales. Some proprietary agribusiness firms such as Cargill (beef and poultry), CONAGRA (beef, poultry, and hogs), Coca-Cola (oranges and grapefruit), Tysons (broilers and hogs), Tenneco (fruit, vegetables, and nuts), and Ralston Purina (mushrooms) have made substantial investments in agricultural production. In products such as broilers, eggs, turkeys, cotton, vegetables, and citrus, ownership integration is over 10 percent of total U.S. production.

Cooperative ownership integration is much more prevalent than proprietary ownership integration. Overall, cooperative ownership integration accounts for 34 percent of farm sales (Table 11.4). However, in only 13 percent of cooperative integration is there a legal commitment on the part of farmers to market their commodity or purchase inputs from the cooperative in which they have ownership interest. Legal commitments to market products or purchase inputs are established through contracts frequently referred to as marketing and purchase agreements. Cooperative integration of this type accounts for 13 percent of farm sales. While cooperative market shares are significant in all commodities, legal commitments to market do not exist in major commodities such as hogs, beef, grains (except rice), and cotton.

The economic implications of vertical integration are much debated. It has long been recognized that a principal problem in agriculture has been the difficulty of coordinating production with market needs. Vertical integration, to the extent that production is influenced by the integrator, makes substantial contributions to satisfying this need. For example, in broilers and turkeys, vertical integration has contributed to the uniform size and quality of poultry sold in the supermarket and served in restaurants and fast-food outlets.

A more significant contribution of vertical integration has been made to increased efficiency and reduced costs. This is once again seen in broilers, where increased efficiency in feed conversion and reduced costs

TABLE 11.4 Extent of Cooperative Integration by Commodity and
Extent of Producer Commitment (Percent of Total Sales)

Commodity	Cooperative Market Share	Extent of Commitment	
		Marketing or Production Contract[a]	No Marketing or Production Contract
Milk	68	65	3
Broilers	12	12	0
Eggs	2	2	0
Turkeys	18	18	0
Hogs	17	2	15
Fed beef	10	0	10
Wheat	57	2	55
Rice	59	59	0
Feed grains	40	2	38
Soybeans	46	3	43
Cotton	30	13	17
Fresh vegetables	7	7	0
Processing vegetables	20	20	0
Citrus	67	65	2
Other processing fruit	65	65	0
Other fresh fruit	40	40	0
Total	34	13	21

Source: Agriculture Cooperative Service, USDA, statistics used to supplement authors'
information.
[a]This column is the sum of cooperative contracts in Table 11.3.

in real terms have been evident.[14] In addition to technological breakthroughs, vertical integration avoids multiple handling of products and
interstate marketing costs.

Several potentially adverse consequences of integrated agriculture
have been identified. Contract integration with corporations and sometimes cooperatives radically changes the role of the traditional independent farmer. More often than not, the farmer loses control if not legal title
to the commodities grown under a production-integrated arrangement.
Payment to the grower is largely on a per unit of product grown or piece-
wage basis and not necessarily related to product value.

It is frequently suggested that in the long run, market power in integrated agriculture will become sufficiently highly concentrated that

[14]Lee F. Schrader and George B. Rogers, "Vertical Organizations and Coordination in
the Broiler and Egg Subsectors," in *Vertical Organization and Coordination in Selected
Commodity Subsectors,* N.C. 117, W.P. 20 (Madison, Wis.: University of Wisconsin, August
7, 1978); and Ronald D. Knutson, "The Structure of Agriculture: An Evaluation of Conventional Wisdom," in *1980 Agricultural Outlook* (Washington, D.C.: Committee on Agriculture, Nutrition, and Forestry, U.S. Senate, December 23, 1979), pp. 135–143.

the consumer will pay higher prices for food. Although such an idea can be supported by economic theory, most conclusions of this type fail to take into account efficiency gains from integration. Alternatively, it is assumed that such gains could be realized without the development of tightly knit vertical integrated systems. The extent to which this would, in fact, happen can be hotly debated. Would, for example, the highly efficient broiler, fresh mushrooms, or processed fruit and vegetable industries have been possible without the development of integrated production systems?

Social Concerns

Many of the arguments against structural change in agriculture, whether in the form of increased concentration or integration, have been of a social or a socioeconomic nature. These arguments place emphasis on the impact of concentration and integration on the "family farm" institution, rural communities, and rural institutions.

Major concern has been expressed that continuously increasing concentration and integration will lead to the demise of the family farm as an institution. The term "family farm" has been associated with the existence of an independent business and social entity sharing the responsibilities of ownership, management, labor, and financing. The family farm system leads to dispersion of economic power. It has also been associated with the perpetuation of basic American values and the family as an institution. Although the importance of these roles is debated (see Chapter 1), it can be persuasively argued that concentration and integration tend to destroy the family farm institution. Very large farms lose many of the characteristics of the traditional family farm, as the business and hired labor aspects clearly predominate. Contract integration removes many, if not most, of the management functions traditionally associated with the family farm institution. The farmer thus takes on more of the characteristics of a laborer and loses many of the characteristics of a small business owner.

An additional social concern that has been raised is that concentration and ownership integration reduce the number of farms and make the integrator less dependent on the local community. In the process, smaller rural towns and their social institutions decline or vanish. It is further argued that this potentially reduces the cohesiveness of family life. It is also suggested that towns where corporate agriculture dominates have few services, lower-quality education, and less community spirit.[15]

Although these arguments are plausible, they rely on little supporting evidence. The most frequently cited study involves a comparison

[15]*A Time to Choose: Summary Report on the Structure of Agriculture,* Preliminary Report (Washington, D.C.: USDA, January 1981), pp. 38–39.

```
┌─────────────────────────────────────────────────────────────────────┐
│                                                                       │
│                      GOVERNMENT PROGRAMS                              │
│                        WITHOUT POLICY                                 │
│                                                                       │
│   I remember those years now (as a congressman from Minnesota) as one │
│   crisis after another, a seemingly endless debate on agricultural    │
│   bills with little or no discussion of agricultural policy. . . .    │
│       We didn't know who exactly was being helped or who was being    │
│   hurt by the measure before us. The problems were seldom clearly de- │
│   fined. If they were, they were cast as narrow but immediate crises  │
│   that needed patches quickly. Other than a dime a bushel here or a   │
│   few pennies more a pound there, the remedies presented were either  │
│   politically unacceptable or simply made no sense.                   │
│       We thought—we hoped—that if we helped the major commercial      │
│   farmers, who provided most of our food and fiber (and most of the   │
│   political pressure), the benefits would filter down to the          │
│   intermediate-sized and then the smallest producers.                 │
│       I was never convinced we were anywhere near the right track. We │
│   had symbols, slogans and superficialities. We seldom had substance. │
│                                                                       │
│       Bob Bergland, A Time to Choose: Summary Report on the Structure │
│   of Agriculture (Washington, D.C.: USDA, January 1981), pp. 5–6.     │
│                                                                       │
└─────────────────────────────────────────────────────────────────────┘
```

of two California communities, one dominated by corporate ownership integrated agriculture and the other by family farm agriculture. Study of these communities in two different time periods supports the social relationships and hypotheses suggested above.[16] However, studies in contract-integrated agriculture fail to clearly establish these relationships and in some instances, point out distinct contradictions.[17]

Political Concerns

Some of the strongest arguments supporting the maintenance of a decentralized agriculture may be of a political nature. Jefferson visualized the merits of a decentralized political system where power was highly diffused and where every individual had the opportunity for input into public decisions. His agrarian philosophies placed a high value on

[16]Community Service Task Force, *The Family Farm in California,* Report of the Small Farm Viability Project, Berkeley, Calif.; November 1977; and D. MacConnell and Jerry White, "Agricultural Land Ownership and Community Structure in California Central Valley," mimeo (Davis, Calif.: University of California, December 1980).

[17]William D. Heffernan, "Agriculture Structure and the Community," in *Can the Family Farm Survive?* Spec. Rep. 219 (Columbia, Mo.: University of Missouri, 1972), pp. 481–499; and Louis A. Plock, *Social and Family Characteristics of Maine Contract Broiler Growers,* Bull. 569 (Orono, Maine: Me. Agric. Exp. Stn., August 1960)

independent farmers and landowners as a means of maintaining a democratic system of government.

Without question, there has been a marked departure in the United
States from the decentralized power structure ideal visualized by Jefferson. What political influence farmers have today is undoubtedly related
to a combination of numbers, the tendency to vote as a bloc, and a basic
belief in family farming as an institution. Some of the more powerful agricultural political lobbies, such as milk and rice, have come to rely more
on political strategies that are characteristic of the corporate and labor
union sector than of the ideals visualized by Jefferson. As U.S. agriculture continues the trend toward increased industrialization, power relationships will become more highly concentrated. They will increasingly
take on the characteristics of politics in the nonfarm sector. Some will
interpret this trend as progress; others will interpret it as a step backward.

ALTERNATIVE STRUCTURES[18]

The alternative directions that the structure of agriculture might take
are implicit in the concerns. Four basis directions of change exist:

- Dispersed open-market agriculture
- Corporate agriculture
- Cooperative agriculture
- Government-administered agriculture

Dispersed Open-Market Agriculture

The basic features of a **dispersed open-market agriculture** *are
moderate-size farms, operator control over production and marketing decisions, and the existence of an open market.* The trends in agriculture are
contradictory to each of these requirements:

- The most efficient size of farm is constantly increasing. Midsize
  farms continue to decline in numbers while large farms continue to
  increase.
- The trend toward contracting and integration removes from the
  farmer many of the critical production and marketing decisions.
- The trend toward contracting and integration also gradually but

[18]This section draws heavily on a series of articles in the publication *Who Will Control
U.S. Agriculture?* H.D. Guither, ed., North Central Reg. Ext. Publ. 32–1 to 32–6 (Urbana,
Ill.: University of Illinois, August 1972).

progressively eliminates an open market. A farmer cannot sell broilers and an increasing number of other products without a contract.

A dispersed open-market agriculture has been a basic characteristic of the American system of food production. There is no certainty that the independent family farm can compete in today's complex, capital-intensive agriculture.

The arguments for a dispersed open-market agriculture are social and economic. Smaller rural American communities, family farm agriculture, and the dispersed open-market system depend on one another for their existence. A dispersed system avoids the possible pitfalls and costs of operating larger bureaucratic corporate or cooperative firms. Yet the efficiency arguments may be the most debatable and tenuous. Family farmers' willingness to accept a relatively low return on labor, management, and capital contributed by the farm family enhances their chances of being able to compete on an efficiency basis.

Corporate Agriculture

In a **corporate agriculture** *most of the production would be controlled by a small number of very large industrial-type corporations.* Where technology permits, much of the farming would be conducted directly through "factories in the fields" or in large feedlots utilizing hired labor and management. In other instances, production would be controlled by tight production and marketing contracts, as is currently the case in much of the broiler industry.

With corporate agriculture, a dispersed agriculture would virtually disappear. Today's farmers would either sign contracts for production with corporate-controlled food systems, become employees of the corporations, or find jobs outside the food system. Corporate agriculture would enhance the probability of union organization of agricultural workers. It would reduce the government costs that are involved in supporting farm prices and incomes because these programs would, in all probability, be eliminated. The impact on the cost of food requires weighing the effects of increased efficiency of integrated production–marketing systems against the effects of unionization and reduced competition.

Cooperative Agriculture

Under a **cooperative agriculture** *farmers would maintain control of agriculture by entering into tightly organized cooperatives to provide all marketing and inputs used in production.* Cooperatives would interface with existing marketing and input supply firms either through bargaining or through performing marketing and processing functions.

Producers would receive benefits of the cooperative alternative through increased control of production and marketing decisions, higher prices received for products marketed, lower input prices, and savings earned by the cooperative. The producers would, however, have to be willing to accept less freedom in production and marketing decisions than in the open market. The cooperative alternative does not assure lower consumer prices; it does provide increased assurance that farmers who are willing to utilize the cooperative system will survive.

Government-Administered Agriculture

A **government-administered agriculture** *would, in essence, make farming a public utility*. In a public utility, government licenses production, establishes prices, and sets standards for service and performance as well as acceptable profit levels. Government could perform the identical functions in agriculture. Specifically, it could decide who can produce what and how much, it could determine how land is used, provide credit to agriculture, allocate inputs used in production, and specify prices to be charged for inputs and paid for farm products.

The record of governments in other countries performing such functions while maintaining a progressive and efficient agriculture is not particularly good—although there is admittedly considerable variation. Even in the United States, the record on the performance of government in public utility regulation is the subject of considerable debate. It is, however, equally true that the failure of agriculture to perform consistent with what is considered to be in the public interest can readily lead to public policy decisions that constitute significant steps in the direction of a government-administered agriculture.

STRUCTURE POLICY

While numerous farm bills have been enacted to "preserve family farms," no general structure policy can be clearly identified. Instead, there are bits and pieces of policy having influence on structure with the nature of that influence not being well understood.

Domestic Farm Policy

While farm programs were designed to help all farmers overcome the instability, price, and income problems that confront agriculture, it is clear that large farmers receive more total benefits than small farmers. Yet, as a percent of sales, moderate-size farms receive more benefits (Table 11.5). For example, midsize farms with $100,000 to $249,999 sales accounted for 25 percent of the production but received 37 percent of the payments. Farmers with over $500,000 sales accounted for 32 percent of the production but received less than 12 percent of the payments. Some of the lower percentage of payments is accounted for by large farms, such as cattle feeders, not growing program crops. Still, it is not correct to assert that the benefits of farm programs go primarily to large farms, nor disproportionately to large farms.

Research has also indicated that if farm programs were dropped, moderate-size farms would suffer the most. Without government programs, large farms were found to have twice as high a probability of surviving as did moderate-size farms.[19] The reason lies in the greater ability of large farms to manage risk and the economies of size realized by large farms.

Perhaps of greater concern is the inability of government programs to target assistance to those farmers needing it the most. Harrington found that in 1985 the least financially stressed farms (55 percent of the total number of farms) received three-fourths of the farm program benefits. On the other hand, the most stressed farms (45 percent of the total number) received only one-fourth of the benefits.[20] These conditions have caused a former advocate of mandatory production controls (Cochrane) and a congressional research agency (OTA) to argue that farm programs ought to be specifically targeted toward the problems of moderate size farms. The OTA study made the following structure related recommendations.[21]

- Eliminate payments to farms having over $250,000 sales.
- Provide income protection to farms having less than $250,000 in sales through the marketing loan.
- Make nonrecourse loans available only to farms having less than $250,000 in sales. All larger farms would be provided only a recourse loan.

[19]Edward G. Smith, James W. Richardson, and Ronald D. Knutson, "Impacts of Alternative Farm Programs on Different Size Cotton Farms in the Texas Southern High Plains: A Simulator Approach," *West. J. Agric. Econ.* (December 1985), pp. 365–374.

[20]David H. Harrington, *Agricultural Programs: Their Contribution to Rural Development and Economic Well Being, Rural Economic Development in the 1980s* (Washington, D.C.: ERS, USDA, July 1987).

[21]Office of Technology Assessment, *Technology, Public Policy, and the Changing Structure of Agriculture*, OTA-F-285 (Washington, D.C.: U.S. Congress, March 1986), pp. 287–290.

TABLE 11.5 Proportion of Sales and Direct Government
Payments by Farm Size, 1985

Gross Sales	Number of Farms (thousands)	Percent of Farms	Percent of Sales	Percent of Payments
Less than $40,000	1638	72.0	10.3	11.6
$40,000–99,999	323	14.0	15.7	22.5
$100,000–249,999	221	9.7	25.2	37.0
$250,000–499,999	66	2.9	16.6	17.0
$500,000 and over	27	1.2	32.2	11.9

Source: Economic Research Service, *Economic Indicators of the Farm Sector: National Financial Summary, 1985*, ECIFS 5-2 (Washington, D.C.: USDA, November 1986), pp. 42, 45, 46.

- Target educational programs in risk management, futures markets, contracting and cooperative marketing on moderate-size farms.
- Increase testing of new agricultural inputs for their comparative efficiency and intensify extension of results to moderate-size farms.
- Make sure ample credit is available to moderate-size farms.

It is important to note that both the Cochrane and OTA proposals put substantial emphasis on helping family farms become efficient, technologically up-to-date farm managers. Without a set of programs designed to accomplish this objective, the cost of targeting farm program benefits toward moderate size farms is inefficiency. One estimate suggests that a structure of only family size crop farms could increase cost of production by as much as $2.3 billion.[22]

Information Policy

Access to and utilization of information on production, markets, and prices is one of the keys to survival in today's agriculture. Without government assistance, information is available only to large farmers and marketing and input supply firms that have the expertise and can afford to gather it or purchase it. Generally available information makes the

[22]Ronald D. Knutson et al., *Economic Impacts of Farm Program Payment Limits* (College Station, Tex.: Texas Agricultural Experiment Station, Texas A&M University, October 1987).

MAKING THE GAME FAIR

The 400,000 moderate-size family farmers struggling to survive represent a different kind of problem. These farmers have been slow to adopt new managerial, commercial, and technological practices. Hence, they have been slow to get their cost structures down. As a result, they are continually in financial difficulty, except in periods of rapidly rising farm prices. Maintaining the present level of price and income support helps them some, but it helps their large, aggressive neighbors a lot more. And raising the level of price and income support to assist these struggling farmers would create a profit bonanza for the large, aggressive farmers. Either way the support programs provide a price and income shelter under which the large, aggressive farmers can expand the size of their operations by gobbling up their struggling moderate-sized neighbors. And either way a few more of our 400,000 fall by the wayside.

The moderate-size family farmer struggling to survive needs two things: (1) long-run managerial guidance and (2) subsidized credit. These farm families need guidance in adopting the right practices at the right time and in using them effectively once they are adopted. Such families need subsidized credit to compete with their aggressive neighbors, who know how to obtain favorable financial deals, in acquiring and operating modern, productive, but often expensive, physical inputs. Some might argue that government should not be doing these kinds of things. But I do not agree. Providing guidance and special credit to the weak and struggling is one way of making the competitive game tolerable. It is comparable to letting the team with the worst win record in the National Football League draft first in the search for player talent. It is a way of saving a high proportion of the 400,000 and maintaining a high degree of competition in the production of the nation's food supply.

In sum, I am not arguing to get government out of agriculture as a general ideological proposition. I am arguing to get government out of agriculture where it is helping one group of farmers do in another group. I am arguing to keep government in agriculture where it operates to make the competitive game of farming more fair to all concerned, hence, a more acceptable game for all concerned.

Willard W. Cochrane, "The Need to Rethink Agricultural Policy and to Perform Radical Surgery on Commodity Programs in Particular," *Am. J. Agric. Econ.* (December 1985), pp. 1008–1009.

production and marketing environment more equitable for all who are part of the food system, but it is of particular benefit to farmers who cannot afford their own sources of information.

One of the primary goals of USDA's programs has traditionally been to improve the quantity and quality of information on agriculture and its markets that is available to farmers. This information covers a wide spectrum from current market prices and product utilization information to estimates of crop and livestock production in the United States as well as for individual countries around the world. Information on U.S. prices is made more meaningful by the establishment of commodity grades which facilitate reporting prices on a uniform quality basis.

Although USDA data are frequently criticized, they are recognized throughout the world as being the most comprehensive and reliable in the world. The USDA is also recognized as having the most reliable information on the agricultural industry that is available from any source in the United States.

The value of information.   The USDA information policy thrust is rooted in the recognition that:

- Improved information helps everyone involved in the agricultural and food production–marketing–consumption system make more economically rational decisions. For example, information on prices, price trends, and forecasts is crucial to producers and marketing firms in making decisions on what to produce and when to market.
- Improved information makes markets more competitive. One of the basic assumptions of the economic concept of a perfectly functioning market is perfect knowledge by everyone in the market regarding prices, production, costs, and so forth. Absolute perfection cannot be achieved. However, the more reliable the information available to decision makers, the more rational the decisions and the more competitive the market.
- Improved information results in a more equal balance of power among firms in a market. Information is market power. This is probably most widely recognized in the extensive and highly sophisticated information systems that have been developed by the multinational grain companies. These systems bring together all available public as well as privately generated information as a basis for dealing with governments, other market intermediaries, producers, and consumers throughout the world. Highly complete and complex information systems are by no means limited to the grain companies. Every firm that is doing an effective job of purchasing and marketing strives to have more complete information than its competitors or the firms with which it is dealing. Most farmers and smaller businesses, however, do not, as individuals, have the resources to develop or purchase information that even approaches that of the larger firms. The provision for public information bridges that gap and thus results in more balanced bargaining relationships within markets.
- Improved information results in more efficient market coordination.

Information on the quantities of products available and expected to be produced provides signals to decision makers up and down the market channel. Information thus becomes at least a partial substitute for vertical integration.

Information policy issues.   With all its far-reaching beneficial effects, one might think that the marketing information policies of USDA would be relatively uncontroversial. Such is not the case. Five interrelated issues are at the center of these concerns:

- Questions are persistently raised about the *accuracy of USDA data* and their influence on the level of prices. Crop and livestock production estimates have been a major target of this criticism. NASS crop production estimates require a combination of acreage estimates and yield estimates. Once crops are planted, acreage estimates are very accurate. Yield estimates are based primarily on actual statistical sampling and field counts. The basic goal of NASS is to be within 2 percent of actual production. In reality, they are generally within 1 percent of actual production. The human nature of farmers is such that when NASS estimates are high and thus tend to suppress prices, extensive criticism frequently results. Estimates of livestock numbers are more difficult than crop production, but NASS's record of accuracy stands well against the criticism.
- Charges are sometimes made of *political manipulation of numbers* to make the food and agricultural situation look better or worse than the facts would suggest. On the critically important estimates of crop and livestock production numbers, every precaution is taken to see that there is no political influence. A procedure is used whereby once the data have been pulled together by the states, those working on the estimates are literally locked in a room until the final estimate is reached. During the 1973–1974 food crisis, CIA and White House officials were surprised to find that even the secretary of agriculture did not have prior access to the crop production estimates.

    This is not to suggest that all USDA data are completely free of political influence. At times, particularly in the heat of legislative battle or political campaign, numbers do appear to be generated by USDA which are designed to prove a point with little basis in fact. This is particularly true of numbers relating to anticipated expenditures on programs and food price inflation rates. These numbers may be generated by or influenced by the office of the secretary.
- Questions consistently arise regarding the *appropriate division of responsibility* for information generation, analysis, and forecasting between USDA and the private sector. Private firms have been

generating price and production information for years. In commodities such as eggs and red meat, the private-sector quotations from sources such as Urner–Barry and the Yellow Sheet are recognized to be more widely used by the industry than comparable USDA price quotations.

- Computer technology and increased price instability in the 1970s brought on a new wave of private information, analysis, and forecasting services. These profit-oriented firms appear increasingly to be viewing USDA as an effective source of competition for analyzing, forecasting, and putting statistics in a form that could be sold privately at a profit. The result has been increasing advocacy by these interests that USDA handle only data collection, with the private sector handling the analysis, forecasting, and distribution. Moves in this direction, fueled by efforts to control federal spending, would be a sharp departure from persistent efforts by USDA to see that all participants in production and marketing have as nearly equal access to its information and analyses as is possible. It would clearly give larger farmers and agribusiness firms an advantage which would, over time, be reflected in increased concentration of farm production and farm markets.

- Most of the data collected by USDA are obtained voluntarily from individuals and firms. The *increased complexity of agriculture,* integration and size of firms, as well as the proprietary nature of the information they have, make collection of certain types of data, such as prices and production information, more difficult. As a result, increased requirements for mandatory reporting of information have been suggested.[23] There seems little doubt that long-term trends toward a more concentrated agriculture continue to undermine the ability of USDA to collect data voluntarily. Thus, if the quality and quantity of food and agricultural data are to be maintained, more reporting requirements may be necessary. Alternatively, it might be possible to pay a random sample of farmers to provide accurate information, as is frequently done by private surveying firms in the nonfarm sector.

Countervailing Power Policy

Countervailing power *offsets market power with market power.* When market power develops on one side of the market, initiatives frequently develop to build a neutralizing power on the other side of the

---

[23]Kirby Moulton and Daniel I. Padberg, "Mandatory Public Reporting of Market Transactions," in *Marketing Alternatives for Agriculture* (Washington, D.C.: Committee on Agriculture and Forestry, U.S. Senate, April 1976), pp. 28–37.

market. **Countervailing power policy** *is designed to assist producers in balancing the monopsony power of buyers in the markets where producers sell their products.* Countervailing power is important to structure because it provides farmers with a means by which they can form and utilize cooperatives either to provide a marketing and bargaining interface with the corporate agribusiness sector or to integrate forward in competition with corporate agribusiness firms. Since all size and types of farmers are eligible to join cooperatives, smaller farmers can gain some of the advantages enjoyed by both large farmers and integrated corporate firms.

Specific programs designed to accomplish these objectives include the Capper–Volstead Act, marketing orders, agricultural bargaining legislation, and the Packers and Stockyards Act.

Capper–Volstead Act.   *The* **Capper–Volstead Act** *gives producers the right to act together in jointly marketing their products.* Marketing has been interpreted broadly to cover any activity beyond the production level, including joint preparation for market, processing, and pricing. The Act also gives cooperatives the right to form a common marketing agency for the purpose of carrying out the same functions encompassing a market share which would presumably extend to a monopoly.[24] It is still unclear whether cooperatives can control the production of their members. It is clear that without the Capper–Volstead Act, many of the marketing activities currently engaged in by cooperatives would be a violation of either the Sherman Antitrust Act or the Clayton Act provisions restricting mergers.[25]

Although the Capper–Volstead Act gives cooperatives substantial latitude for organizing to exercise countervailing power against buyers, the exemption from antitrust prosecution is not unlimited. Cooperatives do not maintain their exemption where they engage in predatory market conduct to exclude competition.[26] In addition, cooperatives cannot maintain their exemption if they either have nonproducer members[27] or if they conspire with nonproducer corporations.[28]

The Capper–Volstead Act has obviously given producers substantial latitude for offsetting buyer market power. There are, however, only certain commodities for which producers and their cooperatives have taken anything like full advantage of their antitrust exemption. Examples of cooperatives that have acquired sufficient market power to test the limits

[24]*Cape Cod Food Products v. National Cranberry Assn.*, 119 F. Supp. 900 (D. Mass., 1954).

[25]*U.S. v. Borden Co.*, 308 U.S. 188 (1939).

[26]*Maryland and Virginia Milk Products Assn. v. U.S.*, 363 U.S. 459 (1960).

[27]*Case-Swayne Co. Inc. v. Sunkist Growers, Inc.*, 389 U.S. 384 (1967).

[28]*U.S. v. Borden Co.*, 308 U.S. 188 (1939).

of the Capper–Volstead exemption include those in milk, rice, navel oranges, lemons, grape juice, cranberries, walnuts, raisins, and prunes. Among these, only milk, and to a lesser extent, rice and oranges, could be classified as major agricultural commodities.

Cooperatives have been sufficiently successful to be the dominant force influencing prices in the dairy industry. This influence ranges from procurement, processing, and marketing milk and its products to effective organization in obtaining legislation to support milk prices as well as raising prices above the minimum prescribed in federal milk marketing orders. This influence has created sufficient concern to result in several antitrust suits against milk cooperatives for engaging in predatory trade practices and monopolizing markets for milk. In rice, cooperatives have been nearly as effective as in milk, but with considerably less public visibility and with a smaller overall market share. In other words, rice cooperatives have relied more on marketing skill than on raw market and political power tactics that have been typical of some milk cooperatives.

The influence of cooperatives in grain, livestock, and poultry is limited to their role as competitors in the markets where they operate. In these commodities, the balance of market power still lies with the major corporate grain and food marketing firms. Having said this, there is considerable controversy over the potential advantage that the Capper–Volstead Act gives cooperatives over their proprietary competitors.

GENERIC ADVERTISING:
A ZERO-SUM GAME?

Farmers have gotten into the advertising and promotion business in a big way. They advertise milk, beef, grapes, oranges, peaches, cotton, apples, potatoes, and eggs. The total cost is about $110 million and growing. The money is largely collected under check-off programs. When farmers market their products, the government deducts a given amount per unit. A producer group makes the spending decisions. Some of the money is used for market research, but most of it goes for generic advertising. It is generally recognized that brand advertising is more effective, but farmers, USDA, and the Congress do not want to support food and fiber agribusiness firms in their marketing efforts.

USDA initially resisted getting into the advertising business because total demand would not be enhanced. The stomach is only so large, they argued. Therefore, one farm commodity group is just taking market share from another. The winner is Madison Avenue, NFL football players, and media personalities. From the perspective of any commodity, advertising can be justified, but does agriculture as a whole benefit? Probably not. But in America, advertising is like baseball, hot dogs, apple pie, and California fruit.

Cooperative Policy Issues. Issues of cooperative policy evolve largely from public and competitor concerns about cooperatives obtaining and exploiting a truly dominant market position. Specific concerns include:

- An apparent *lack of enforcement* by USDA of the provisions of the Capper–Volstead Act prohibiting undue price enhancement by cooperatives. The undue enhancement provision is viewed by many as the final public interest protection against potential monopolistic cooperative abuse. Concern exists that the USDA has neither formally defined what is meant by the term undue enhancement nor conducted a hearing under the "undue enhancement" provisions. It has, however, conducted several investigations of potential undue enhancement abuses. The secretary of agriculture invariably finds that while, on the one hand, he is charged with promoting cooperatives and the related producer interest, on the other hand he is charged with regulating potential cooperative monopoly price exploitation. One alternative for removing this conflict of interest is to move Capper–Volstead enforcement from USDA to either the Department of Justice or the Federal Trade Commission.[29]

- Substantial concern also exists with the apparent *right of cooperatives to merge* with one another to the extent of obtaining a *dominant market share.* Although some sympathy might exist to curb mergers among cooperatives having a large market share, the court always finds itself caught in the dilemma that if the merger is denied, the farmer-members of the two cooperatives could simply disband and form a single new cooperative.[30] If restrictions are to be placed on marketing cooperative mergers, it will probably have to be done by the Congress. The Congress has not, however, been inclined to further restrain cooperative market power.

- As agriculture continues its trend toward increased scale of production and vertical integration, cooperatives are sometimes being formed by large proprietary agribusiness firms that are also producers of agricultural products. This creates the potential *for large corporations to utilize the Capper–Volstead Act to* **achieve monopolistic objectives.** This issue may once again need to be resolved by the Congress or might be resolved by the courts ruling that large corporate membership is not consistent with the original intent of the Capper–Volstead Act. A recent Supreme Court ruling with regard

[29]An excellent discussion of the undue price enhancement issue is contained in E.V. Jesse, A.C. Johnson, Jr., B.J. Marion, and A.C. Manchester, "Interpreting and Enforcing Section 2 of the Capper–Volstead Act," *Am. J. Agric. Econ.* (August 1982), pp. 431–443.

[30]*Sunkist Growers, Inc., et al. v. Winkler and Smith Citrus Products Co.,* 370 U.S. 19 (1962).

to broilers tended to have this effect when it was held that the contracting growers as opposed to the proprietary integrators were the producers within the meaning of the Capper–Volstead Act.[31]

- As cooperatives continue to grow and acquire market power, questions will arise as to *whether domestic farm programs* **are needed any longer.** These questions have already arisen in rice and milk. In milk, people question whether cooperatives have already acquired sufficient market power to no longer need the assistance of price supports and marketing orders.[32] In rice, the issue is whether the higher price received by cooperative members because of substantial investments in milling and marketing should be considered in computing the average price received by farmers in determining the deficiency payments. Currently, cooperative-generated returns are not considered in calculating the average price received by farmers for rice. Cooperative producers receive the same deficiency payment as independent producers. It could be suggested that if farmers are able to generate higher returns through cooperatives, they should be less reliant on government.

Marketing orders.   **Marketing orders** *provide another mechanism by which producers may initiate programs to regulate the marketing of their commodity to achieve orderly marketing through unified action.*[33] In certain fruits, vegetables, nuts, and in milk, marketing orders can be requested by producers and implemented after a hearing if two-thirds of the producers favor the proposed order. Once approved by producers, an order is binding on all producers.

The order defines the commodity and market area to be regulated. Orders give producers a degree of control over product quality, quantity, or price depending on the specific provisions of the order. Since federal orders are quite different for milk than for fruits and vegetables, each is described separately.

Milk marketing orders set minimum prices that processors must pay for fluid-grade milk. Under marketing orders, milk is priced according to the use processors make of the milk. That is, milk used for fluid purposes is priced at a higher level than milk used for making manufactured products, such as butter, cheese, or ice cream. The higher price results from the more inelastic demand for fluid milk. The result of this

---

[31]*U.S. v. National Broiler Marketing Association,* 98 S. Ct. 2122, Trade Cases, para. 62074 (1978).

[32]Robert Masson and Phillip Eisenstat, "The Pricing Policies and Goals of Federal Milk Order Regulations: Time for Reevaluation," *S.D. Law Rev.* (Spring 1980), pp. 662–697.

[33]This discussion is limited to federal marketing orders. State marketing orders for milk, fruit, vegetables, and nuts have similar provisions but tend to be used mainly in the western and eastern states.

price discrimination on the basis of end use is higher producer returns. Since orders only prescribe minimum prices, cooperatives are free to negotiate premiums over federal milk order prices.

Fruit and vegetable marketing orders rely primarily on control of quality, market flow, and volume management to influence the level and stability of producer returns. Quality control measures specify minimum grades and size of products that may be marketed. Market flow regulations limit the quantities of products that can move into fresh markets on a weekly basis during the heaviest marketing season. Volume management regulations restrict the supplies of storable dried fruits and nuts going into fresh markets through holding supplies in reserve until the next marketing season. The effect is to restrict the quantity a producer can market or to divert excess supplies to alternate markets such as exports (two-price plan). Additional provisions of fruit and vegetable marketing orders may specify varieties of products that may be planted; establish standard packs and containers; and fund research, development, commodity advertising, and promotion.

Marketing Order Issues.   Several marketing order issues have surfaced in recent years. The center of concern in these issues involves the extent to which order provisions operate in the public interest. A related concern is whether orders are really needed to protect producer returns. The major issues include:

- Pricing milk on the basis of use has been attacked by consumer interests for *raising the price of milk above competitive levels* to the detriment of consumers. Without question, consumers pay a higher price for fluid milk as a result of the federal milk order programs.[34] Milk price supports operating without the federal milk order are also considered sufficient by some to raise producer returns and ensure consumers an adequate supply of milk.[35] Milk producer interests suggest that not only was raising producer return the intent of marketing orders but that consumers benefit from the increased stability provided by orders.

- Fruit and vegetable marketing order provisions that limit the supply of products moving to market have similarly been attacked as being *detrimental to consumer interests*. It is argued that grade, flow to market, and volume management regulations all hold edible products off the market, to the detriment of consumers.[36] Those criti-

[34]Roger A. Dahlgran, "Welfare Costs and Interregional Income Transfers due to Regulation of Dairy Markets," *Am. J. Agric. Econ.* (May 1980), pp. 288–299.

[35]Masson and Eisenstat, "Pricing Policies and Goals," pp. 662–697.

[36]Richard Heifner et al., *A Review of Federal Marketing Orders for Fruits, Vegetables and Specialty Crops: Economic Efficiency and Welfare Implications* (Washington, D.C.: AMS, USDA, October 15, 1981).

cal of fruit and vegetable marketing orders do not consider the consumer benefits in terms of uniform product quality over a longer market period sufficient to offset consumer losses in terms of higher prices.

- Fruit and vegetable marketing orders are administered by an administrative committee made up of largely industry interests. While USDA has made efforts to get a public representative appointed to each administrative committee, consumer interests have suggested that two or three *bona fide consumer representatives ought to be required.* Producers are opposed to any consumer involvement in orders.

- It is also suggested that *orders unduly favor cooperatives,* by giving them the right to vote for orders on a bloc basis for all their members. As a result, a cooperative having two-thirds of the producers is in a position to control the order, subject of course, to the discretion of USDA.[37]

Agricultural bargaining.   Providing producers bargaining rights comparable to those enjoyed by organized labor has been the goal of several major agricultural movements. The National Farmers Organization has as its major goal obtaining good faith collective bargaining rights for producers. These efforts have been strongly resisted by the organizations most directly affected, such as fruit and vegetable processors and poultry contractors.

The greatest bargaining benefit for producers is in contract-integrated agriculture, where producers have lost control of many production and marketing decisions. This resulted in the passage of the Michigan Agricultural Marketing and Bargaining Act. This Act gives certified Michigan cooperatives the right to bargain with processors of specified fruits and vegetables on behalf of all producers.

No comparable law exists at the federal level. The closest is the Agricultural Fair Practices Act, which prohibits processors from discriminating against producers because they are members of a cooperative. This law has done little to assist farmers who desire good-faith bargaining rights equivalent to labor.

To be successful in bargaining, the following organizational and product characteristics must exist:

- *The demand for the product involved must be inelastic.* Without an inelastic demand, the percentage decline in the quantity demanded will be greater than the percentage increase in price. The result will

---

[37]Ibid.; see also Robert T. Masson and Phillip M. Eisenstat, "Welfare Impacts of Milk Orders and Antitrust Immunities for Cooperatives," *Am. J. Agric. Econ.* (May 1980), pp. 270–278.

be reduced producer revenue. Since most farm products have an inelastic demand, this condition is normally satisfied.

- *The bargaining group must control a sufficient volume of the product.* The larger the volume of product controlled, the more bargaining power. Generally speaking, at least two-thirds of the production must be controlled to be a significant bargaining force.
- *Unity and discipline must exist within the bargaining group.* Unless the members of the group stick together, the bargaining effort will be lost.
- *There must be recognition that the bargaining group can exercise control.* This recognition must be established at an early stage in the bargaining process. Once a bargaining group fails in establishing recognition, it is much more difficult to negotiate the second time around. Bargaining laws can assist in obtaining recognition for the bargaining group.
- *If successful, the bargaining group must be able to control production.* Producers normally respond to higher prices by increasing output. This normal response must be controlled.
- *The bargaining group must be efficient in performing its functions.* Unless it is efficient, alternative means of production and marketing will be found by the buyers of the product—even to the extent of integrating to produce the product themselves.[38]

Packers and Stockyards Act. In the early 1900s, major concern developed over the potentially dominant position of the major meat packers. In 1910 a Federal Trade Commission (FTC) study of the meat industry concluded that the five largest meat packers were manipulating livestock markets, controlling prices of dressed meat, and extending their control to fish, poultry, and eggs, as well as to fruit, vegetables, and staple groceries.

As a result of this investigation, the Department of Justice brought action against Swift, Armour, Morris, Wilson, and Cudahy for violating the Sherman Act. In 1920, these packers signed a consent decree which prohibited them from:

- Owning public stockyards, public cold storage facilities, or stockyard rail terminals
- Handling or letting others use facilities to handle 114 nonmeat products, including fish, vegetables, fruits, canned goods, and cereals

[38]Leon Garoyan and Eric Thor, "Observations on the Impact of Agricultural Bargaining Cooperatives," *Agricultural Cooperatives and the Public Interest*, N.C. 117, Monogr. 4 (Madison, Wis.: University of Wisconsin, September 1978).

- Handling fresh cream or milk except for sale in processed form
- Operating retail meat markets in the United States

The consent decree has had a major impact on the structure of the meat industry. Its greatest effect has been to encourage the rise of the supermarket chain as a major force in meat marketing. It prevented major packers from being a competitor in retailing meat. In late 1981, the consent decree was dropped. However, its effects on the industry continue to be felt.

The consent decree formed the basis for the passage of the Packers and Stockyards Act (P&S) in 1921. It was in a very real sense designed to prevent the basic abuses discovered in the FTC investigation that led to the consent decree. Specifically, the P&S Act:

- Prohibits unfair, deceptive, or unjustly discriminatory practices
- Prohibits practices that would give particular persons or localities undue competitive advantages
- Prohibits practices that would have the effect of apportioning supplies, manipulating or controlling prices, or restricting competition
- Authorizes the regulation of services and rates at public stockyards
- Provides for honest weights as well as prompt and full pay in marketing livestock and poultry

Much of the initial regulatory emphasis of P&S was on the maintenance of fair competition and reasonable charges in central public markets for livestock. While P&S pursued a policy which was, in effect, designed to maintain the industry structure in its original mold, pronounced structural changes occurred. Increased direct farmer-packer sales reduced the role of public markets, which were a major proportion of P&S regulatory activity. In addition, many new aggressive firms entered the meat packing business. These firms felt less restrained by the provisions of the consent decree. They were more willing to challenge the regulatory authority of P&S at a time when there was structural change occurring in the meat industry, including the development of large-scale feedlots and integrated systems of production and marketing.

In the late 1960s, P&S attempted to get control of structural change in the industry by prohibiting packer ownership of cattle on feed. It was, however, unable to demonstrate adverse effects on competition and eventually dropped legal action. Subsequent investigations into packer joint ventures with feedlots, formula pricing of meat, vertical integration by grain companies, and potential monopoly abuses also ended in a lack of decisive action by P&S.

In the late 1970s, Congressman Neal Smith began actively investigating potential monopoly abuses in the meat industry. After hearings, Smith proposed major regulatory changes, ranging from prohibition of formula pricing of cattle off the Yellow Sheet[39] to placing an absolute 25 percent limit on the market share of livestock purchased by any single packer in any state.

Implicit in the action of Congressman Smith was a concern that P&S has not been sufficiently active in dealing with structural and pricing issues in the meat industry. This point was reemphasized in the late 1980s when four packers gained control of more than 70 percent of the steer and heifer slaughter capacity with no concern being expressed by P&S.[40] Over time, it has become increasingly apparent that USDA's ability and/or will to regulate markets is weak.[41] As a result, the ability of farmers to countervail the power of input and marketing firms is also weak.

Tax Policy

Tax laws have a significant impact on the structure of agriculture. The 1986 Tax Reform Act was designed to reduce the incentives for farms to get larger solely for tax reasons. Available research suggests that it may not have accomplished that objective in crop agriculture, although the incentives for tax-avoidance investments in breeding stock should be materially reduced.

The major changes in tax provisions introduced by the 1986 Tax Reform Act include:

- Lower tax rates and fewer brackets
- Capital gains treated as ordinary income
- Lengthen depreciation schedules
- Limit prepayment of expenses
- Require capitalization of preproductive expenses exceeding two years
- Eliminate income averaging
- Passive investor cannot deduct losses from wages and salaries

While USDA contends that these tax changes help small farms

---

[39]The Yellow Sheet is a private market news service that provides daily quotes on wholesale meat prices. These quotas are used extensively as a basis for pricing meat in the wholesale meat trade.

[40]Burke, "The Big Four."

[41]Ronald D. Knutson, L. Leon Geyer and John W. Helmuth, *Trade Practice Regulation,* Fed. Agric. Market. Prog. Leaf. 8 (College Station, Tex.: Texas Agricultural Extension Service, 1988).

more than large,[42] other research indicates the opposite. Research at Texas A&M and Minnesota indicates:[43]

- Crop farms with more than $40,000 in income will pay less taxes, while those with $40,000 will pay more taxes.
- Taxable incomes for dairy and cow/calf farms increase dramatically. However the percentage is more for small operators than for large operators.
- The ability to defray risk is reduced by the elimination of tax averaging. Farmers who are best at managing risk will have a greater advantage.
- Incentives increase to cash rent because share rent is considered passive investment.
- Incentives for greater labor intensity result from reduced capital write-offs.
- Trend toward a bimodal distribution of farming is accelerated.

Tax policy does influence structure. Tax policies could be constructed to favor moderate-size farms. This would require:

- More progressive property and income taxes
- More restrictions on the ability to transfer estates from one generation to the next

Changes in tax policies that have occurred tend to go in the opposite direction.

Research Policy

It was recognized previously that technological change is one of the factors that has made U.S. agriculture highly productive. One of the side effects of technological advance has been structural change. That is, new technology generally not only shifts the cost curve downward but also shifts it to the right. For example, the self-propelled combine not only reduced the cost of harvesting corn but also made it possible for a farmer to

[42]Gregory D. Hanson and Diane R. Bertelsen, "Tax Reform Impacts on Agricultural Production and Investment Decisions," unpublished paper presented at the American Agricultural Economics Association Annual Meetings, Michigan State University, East Lansing, Mich., August 3, 1987.

[43]Clair J. Nixon and James W. Richardson, "Tax Act Signal to Commercial Farmers: Get Larger or Get Out," and Thomas F. Stinson and Michael D. Boehlje, "Dramatic Tax Rule Changes: Significant but Not Immediate Effects," *Choices* (2nd Quarter 1987), pp. 12–16.

harvest a much larger number of acres. The result of a large number of virtually continuous technological advances has been fewer but larger farms.

In the early 1970s, Ralph Nader's Agriculture Accountability Project became interested in the contribution of public research to the process of technological change. Specifically, this project investigated the extent to which the land-grant university and USDA agricultural research complex emphasized research that primarily benefited large farmers and agribusiness firms. The study concluded:

> America's land grant college complex has wedded itself to an agribusiness vision of automated, vertically integrated and corporatized agriculture. . . . Had the land grant community chosen to put its time, money, its expertise and its technology into the family farm rather than into corporate pockets, then rural America today would be a place where millions could live and work in dignity.[44]

The publication *Hard Tomatoes, Hard Times* was extensively criticized by researchers and officials in the land-grant university system. While the conclusion of the Nader project was obviously overdrawn to make the point, the fact remains that technology is seldom structurally neutral. In fact, question exists whether technology could be made structurally neutral and still realize its benefits in terms of lower costs.

In 1979, Secretary Bergland picked up on the *Hard Tomatoes* theme and an outgrowth was the structure of agriculture project. He questioned the use of federal funds for research projects having the objective of producing large-scale, labor-saving technology.[45] He set up a special task force to investigate the impact of research and extension on the structure. During this period, the Congress earmarked research and extension funds for increased work with small farms and for projects involving direct marketing from farmers to consumers.

The Bergland initiative on research appeared to die with the election of the Reagan administration. It was, however, rekindled by the announcement of joint initiatives between private-sector companies and universities in high-priority genetic engineering research. Questions arose as to whether the primary beneficiaries would be the private-sector firms or the initial farmer adopters of the resulting new technology. The question remains as to whether public research could or should be oriented more toward smaller family farms as suggested by Cochrane and OTA. The long-run cost and competitive implications of such a strategy

[44]Jim Hightower, *Hard Tomatoes, Hard Times* (Cambridge, Mass.: Schenkman Publishing Company, Inc., 1973), pp. 138–139.

[45]Bob Bergland, *The Federal Role in Agricultural Research*, USDA 262–80 (Washington, D.C.: USDA, January 31, 1980).

have not been adequately evaluated. Similarly, the impact of patenting agricultural research discoveries has not received adequate attention. Structure policy has been largely ignored in the farm policy debate because farmers have not put it on the agenda.

THE FUTURE OF STRUCTURE POLICY

Unless public decisions are made on the structure issue soon, there is a distinct possibility that agriculture will have moved so far and decisively toward an integrated industrialized structure that there will be little chance of reversing the trend. This has already happened in broilers, eggs, turkeys, fruits, and vegetables. It is happening in fed beef and hogs. In addition, rising land values can be expected to continue to attract outside capital into agriculture, increasing the relative importance of tenancy in agriculture.

Government policies, although not designed to foster these trends, clearly contribute to them. That is, price and income supports, credit, and tax policies all tend to put the large farmer in a relatively better position to grow and expand than the smaller farmer. The larger the farmer, the more the apparent benefits.

At the same time, it has been seen that there are few policies designed overtly to stem the trend toward agricultural integration and industrialization. Only the antitrust laws appear to have that potential, but even there, not at current relatively low levels of concentration.

Structure will continue to be a policy issue. The trend toward industrialization will adversely affect farmers' ability to convince the Congress of the need for traditional farm programs. The ability of the family farm to survive is in question. Family farm agriculture may be, in the future, limited to part-time farming. Commercial agriculture will, at that time, be primarily integrated, industrialized agriculture. That eventuality is not a pleasant prospect to the believer in Jeffersonian agrarianism and the contribution of family farms to the productive success of American agriculture.

ADDITIONAL READINGS

1. The original Extension Service articles which stirred widespread interest in the structure of agriculture were titled *Who Will Control U.S. Agriculture?* Harold Guither, ed., North Central Reg. Ext. Publ. 32 (Urbana, Ill.: University of Illinois, August 1972).

2. This publication was followed by a series of *Who Will Market Your Milk, Grain, Beef, Cotton and Peanuts?* Ronald D. Knutson, ed., Tex. Agric. Ext.

Serv. Publ. D-1053 to D-1057 (College Station, Tex.: Texas A&M University, March 1978).

3. USDA picked up interest in the structure of agriculture issue in the late 1970s. It published a series of major studies. The most comprehensive is *Structure Issues of American Agriculture,* Agric. Econ. Rep. 434 (Washington, D.C.: ESCS, USDA, November 1979).

4. USDA's most recent report on its structure of agriculture project was *A Time to Choose: Summary Report on the Structure of Agriculture,* by Bob Bergland (Washington, D.C.: USDA, January 1981). When President Reagan took office in January 1981, there was an overt effort to suppress this report and ignore the whole structure of agriculture issue.

5. The OTA report titled *Technology, Public Policy, and the Changing Structure of Agriculture* (Washington, D.C.: U.S. Congress, March 1986) is must reading for anyone interested in the structure issue. OTA initiated the study after it became apparent that USDA, under President Reagan, was not going to pursue the issue.

6. A series of *Marketing Policy* papers is available from Ronald D. Knutson, ed. (College Station, Tex.: Texas Agricultural Extension Service, October 1987).

Part IV

Consumers, Resources, and Agribusiness

American consumers are an ultimate beneficiary of farm policy. They enjoy a plentiful supply of food at relatively low prices. Yet a significant segment of the U.S. population does not have sufficient income to fulfill food, shelter, and health care needs. In addition, questions are being raised continuously regarding the safety and nutrition of the food supply. These issues are not just short-run concerns but encompass the utilization of resources in a long-run context.

The brunt of consumer and related special-interest criticism of U.S. agriculture is not aimed solely at farmers, but also at agribusiness firms who have supplied farmers with more sophisticated, highly productive, and potentially dangerous inputs. In addition, food processors have provided consumers with a host of highly processed, table-ready foods that often contain a host of additives and preservatives—also the subject of increasing health and nutrition questions. Issues of sanitation and the potential for tampering with the food supply continue to haunt the mass distribution-oriented food industry.

The purpose of the next four chapters is to provide an overview of consumer, resource, and agribusiness policies and issues. Chapter 12 reviews policies and issues relating to the price of food. Chapter 13 discusses food safety and nutrition policies and issues. Chapter 14 surfaces the policies and issues involved in resource policy. Although this discussion of resource issues may seem out of place, many of the resource issues have their origin in public interest concerns regarding long-run effects of current policies on the general population. As noted in Chapter 4, the consumer and resource lobbies also are closely aligned as part of what is generally referred to as the public interest lobby.

Having completed an analysis of the impact of agricultural and food policy on farmers and consumers, the remaining group to be analyzed is agribusiness firms. This task is left to the last chapter in Part IV because agribusiness is affected not only by international trade and farm policies but also by consumer and resource policies.

Chapter 12

Food Price Policy

*Inflation has become so bad it has hit
the price of feathers. Even down is up.*

Maurice Speece

Food prices are a major policy concern throughout the world. Because of
political sensitivity of consumers to the price of food, governments sometimes directly control both food prices and farm prices.

While U.S. consumers are not seriously in danger of experiencing
food shortages, concerns about the price of food periodically arise. These
concerns result both from the impact of food prices on expenditures of individual consumers and from the contribution of food prices to the overall
rate of inflation.

At the same time, consumers express concern about food prices,
farmers frequently contend that the government pursues a "cheap food
policy." The purpose of this chapter is to attempt to explain these apparently conflicting perspectives and discuss government options for dealing
with food price issues.

ECONOMIC PERSPECTIVES AND ISSUES

Despite the inherent instability of farm commodity prices, from the end of
World War II until the 1970s, food prices were rarely major considerations in national economic policy. This was due to:

- Food price increases have generally been less than the rate of increase in incomes, resulting in a decline in the share of consumer income spent on food. The proportion of consumer income spent on food declined from 20.0 percent in 1960 to a low of 14.7 percent in 1986 (Fig. 12.1). As long as income increased more rapidly than food prices, consumers generally have had no immediate cause for concern about the price performance of the food system.
- Farm programs and related surplus conditions have generally kept farm prices low and relatively stable. In the 1950s and the 1960s, technological advances increased the level of output and reduced the unit cost of producing food. Price supports were forced lower and remained relatively stable because of these increases in output and efficiency combined with the tendency for government stocks to remain high. Stable to declining farm prices offset food price inflation pressures resulting from inflation and consumer demands for increased convenience. In the 1980s, target prices guaranteed farmers a certain level of return, fostering higher production and lower market prices. The result was further downward pressure on the proportion of income spent on food.

The 1970s were an aberration in the long-run trend toward a lower share of income spent on food. While average annual food price increases of 3.0 percent were the rule during the 1950s and 1960s, food prices rose rapidly after sharp increases in domestic farm product prices occurred in 1972. Food prices rose over 14 percent in 1973 and 1974 and accounted for nearly 50 percent of the overall inflation experienced in the economy dur-

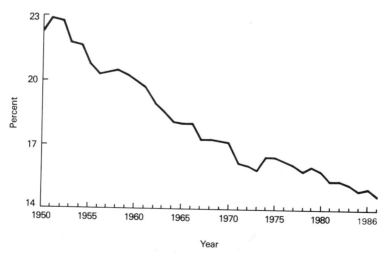

Figure 12.1 Share of consumer income spent on food.

ing the two years (Table 12.1). Food price inflation averaged 8 percent in the 1970s and accounted for an average of 26 percent of the overall inflation for the decade. These comparatively large increases in food prices resulted in only a 0.6 percent increase in the share of income spent on food, from 15.9 percent in 1973 to 16.5 percent in 1974. While food prices were increasing sharply during this world food crisis period, inflation in the rest of the economy was substantially less than food price inflation (6.1 percent in 1973 and 9.8 percent in 1974).

Great concern arose among consumer activists and policymakers over the contribution of food to inflation. President Ford placed an embargo on wheat exports because of the alleged potential bread price of $1 per loaf. Price controls were extended to food despite inevitable adverse consequences for production and prices. Those adverse consequences occurred when cattle producers refrained from marketing during a government-imposed price freeze, which drove beef prices even higher. Broiler chicks were disposed of because integrators concluded that controlled broiler prices and rising feed prices meant that they could not even cover their variable cost of production—an economic shutdown situation.

A lesson from the 1970s was that when food price increases rise to double-digit levels (10 percent or more) and substantially exceed the inflation rate for the rest of the economy, sharp consumer reaction can be anticipated. This reaction occurs even though the average share of income spent on food rises by less than one percentage point.

Three potential reasons for this consumer and policymaker sensitivity to food price increases include:

- Consumers shop for food more frequently and regularly than for any other commodity group. As a result, consumers are more aware of food price levels—they develop a sense of a "fair price." For other commodities purchased less frequently, price changes are not as noticeable, and the concept of a fair or reasonable price is not as clear in the consumers' mind.
- While the average person spends about 15 percent of income on food, poor people spend as much as 40 percent. (Table 12.2). As a result, poorer people tend to be more sensitive to price changes than wealthy persons.
- Food and shelter are two vital necessities of life. Annual consumer spending on each is nearly identical. Because of its overall importance, it is only natural for both consumers and policymakers to react with vigor to food price inflation.

Why Food Prices Increase

Changes in farm commodity prices, marketing costs, and consumer demand combine to cause year-to-year changes in food prices. Certain of

TABLE 12.1   Contribution of Food Prices to Inflation, 1951–1981

Year	Overall Inflation Rate (%)	Food Price Inflation Rate (%)	Contribution of Food Prices to Overall Inflation (percentage points)	Proportion of Overall Inflation Accounted for by Food Prices Inflation[a] (%)
1951	7.9	11.1	2.7	34.2
1952	2.2	1.0	0.4	18.2
1953	0.8	−1.5	0.4	−33.3
1954	0.5	−0.2	−0.1	−16.7
1955	−0.4	−1.4	−0.3	−75.0
1956	1.5	0.7	0.2	13.3
1957	8.6	3.3	0.8	9.3
1958	2.9	4.2	1.0	34.5
1959	0.8	−1.6	−0.4	−33.3
1960	1.5	1.0	0.2	13.3
1961	1.1	1.3	0.3	27.3
1962	1.2	0.9	0.2	16.6
1963	1.3	1.4	0.3	23.1
1964	1.4	1.3	0.3	21.4
1965	1.5	2.2	0.5	33.3
1966	3.2	5.0	1.2	37.5
1967	2.8	0.9	0.2	7.1
1968	4.4	3.6	0.9	20.5
1969	5.7	5.1	1.2	21.1
1970	6.1	5.5	1.3	21.3
1971	4.3	3.0	0.7	16.3
1972	3.4	4.3	1.0	29.4
1973	6.1	14.5	3.5	57.4
1974	9.8	14.4	3.5	35.7
1975	9.1	8.5	2.0	22.3
1976	5.6	3.1	0.8	14.3
1977	6.3	6.3	1.5	23.8
1978	7.8	10.0	1.8	23.1
1979	10.0	10.9	2.0	20.0
1980	13.5	8.6	1.6	11.7
1981	10.4	7.9	1.4	13.9
1982	6.1	4.0	0.7	12.0
1983	3.2	2.1	0.4	12.0
1984	4.3	3.8	0.7	16.2
1985	3.6	2.3	0.4	11.7
1986	1.9	3.2	0.6	30.9
1987	3.5	4.1	0.8	21.5

Source: U.S. Department of Commerce, Bureau of Economic Analysis.

[a]The proportion of overall inflation accounted for by food price inflation is derived by dividing the contribution of food prices to overall inflation by the overall inflation rate.

TABLE 12.2 Proportion of Income Spent on Food by
Level of Family Income, 1973–1974 (Percent)

Annual Family Income Level	Proportion of Total Population with Income Level	Proportion of Income Spent on Food
Under $5000	18.2	38.9
$5000–$8000	14.1	23.0
$8000–$12,000	21.2	18.7
$12,000–$15,000	14.5	15.8
$15,000–$20,000	16.1	14.3
Over $20,000	15.9	10.2

Source: Food Consumption, Prices, and Expenditures: 1960–1980, Stat. Bull. 672 (Washington, D.C.: ERS, USDA, September 1981).

the factors that create fluctuations in commodity prices, such as input costs and trade policies, are controllable to a degree. Those stemming from weather conditions and/or the biological nature of the food production process are much less controllable.

Commodity and retail price variability.   Since 1970 there have been dramatic year-to-year changes in farm commodity prices. Prices nearly doubled from 1970 to 1974 and then remained relatively stable from 1975 to 1977. Commodity prices rose another 34 percent from 1977 through 1980 and then pursued a general downward trend in the 1980s.

Variability in commodity prices is the major factor causing variability in retail food prices. However, retail prices are less variable than commodity prices. That is, in almost all cases the percentage change in retail price is less than the percentage change in the price of the agricultural products used to produce them. This is true for two primary reasons (Fig. 12.2):

- *The value of farm commodities represents only 25 cents of each food dollar spent on food.* The other 75 cents pays for the costs of processing, transporting, and selling. This means that each 4 percent increase (decrease) in commodity prices results in an approximate 1 percent increase (decrease) in consumer food prices if other things remain unchanged.
- *A lag exists between the time commodity price changes are reflected in retail price changes* because of the time involved in transporting, processing, and distributing food products. This time lag is different among commodities. In part, this lag reflects food retailers' pricing practices which reflect the overall trend in prices rather than the price of particular foods at the wholesale level. Thus, when meat prices rise at the farm and packer level, retail margins normally

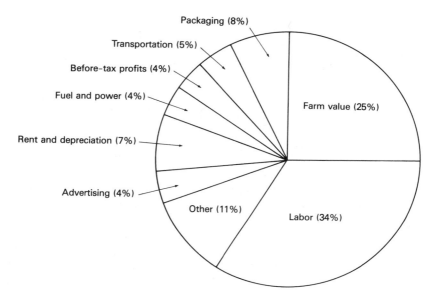

Figure 12.2   What a dollar spent on food paid for in 1986.

tighten. On the other hand, a fall in farm and packer prices results in wider retailer margins.

In the short run, this retailer pricing behavior tends to increase the variability in farm commodity prices. Suppose that beef slaughter is larger than expected. The relative increase in supply will put downward pressure on cattle prices. If retail meat prices fall quickly to reflect the lower raw product cost, consumer meat purchases will increase. *Any stickiness in the retail price decline will cause cattle prices to fall even more because of sluggish demand.*This greater price variability occurs because a farm price reduction due to higher supplies is not reflected to the retail level. As a result, there is no price incentive for consumers to increase purchases. With short-run production being largely predetermined, a glut of supplies develops driving the price down even further.

This stickiness has, from time to time, created sufficient political frustration that the secretary of agriculture has found it expedient to "get on the stump" and "jawbone" retailers to reduce meat prices. In areas such as this, a commonality of the producer and the consumer interest exists in making the market system work better.

Food price increases create news and consumer awareness; food is basic to life, and its purchases are frequent. Fundamentally, it is the variability in food prices, as much as the level of prices, that makes food prices a public concern. This variability results primarily from changes in commodity prices. The potential for price variability is accentuated by weather and world business cycles (macroeconomics) which lead to changes in the supply–demand balance in the United States as well as in the world as a whole.

Marketing costs.   Annual changes in the cost of transporting, processing, and selling domestically produced food products are monitored by the USDA. These data, referred to as the marketing bill, exclude the costs of marketing imported foods and fish, which account for nearly 20 percent of total food expenditures.

The marketing bill has increased each year since World War II. In 1986, the marketing bill was nearly $272 billion, over eight times higher than in 1950. This change, of course, includes the cost of marketing a steadily increasing quantity of food, but there have also been increases in the costs of marketing each unit of food. Associated with such increased unit costs is the fact that consumers have been demanding more convenience foods, involving higher levels of processing. Particularly significant is the increased importance of away-from-home consumption, from 26 percent of the consumers' food dollar in 1960 to 43 percent in 1985. Marketing costs accounted for 84 percent of away-from-home consumption and 70 percent of at-home consumption (Fig. 12.3).

Changes in the relative importance of various cost items in the marketing bill reflect shifts in the types of food consumed and services provided. Changes in the relative importance of the various components of the marketing bill indicate that prices of some marketing inputs are changing more than others and that there have been important changes in the types of foods being consumed.

Labor, packaging, and transportation costs have all increased as a percent of the total marketing bill. The annual percent change in costs of these inputs has tended to exceed the percent change in retail food prices. Labor is the single most important component of consumers food costs, accounting for about 34 percent of the total. Packaging, the second largest nonfarm cost component, accounts for about 7.5 percent of the total marketing bill. Transportation costs account for about 4.5 percent of the total.

The relative size of a cost component has not been a good indicator of its potential policy interest. Profits and advertising are the most controversial components of marketing costs. Together, in 1986, these components accounted for 7.5 percent of consumer expenditures, up from 5.6 percent in 1980. Changes in advertising and food industry profits have frequently been taken as indicators of the need for a concern about the structure of the food industry, particularly in food processing and retail distribution.

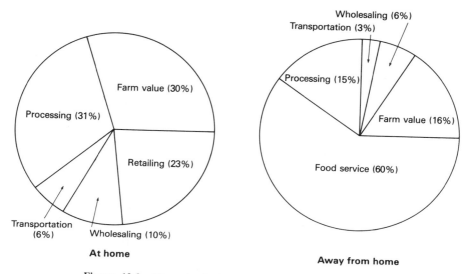

Figure 12.3 Where the food dollar goes at home versus away.

Who Needs the Middleman?

The alleged economic exploitation of farmers and consumers by food industry "middlemen" is perhaps the oldest food policy issue. During the settlement period, farm groups lobbied hard for policies that reduced rail freight rates and increased farmers' relative bargaining power. The interest of the consuming public was first aroused in a major way when it became apparent at the turn of the century that some food firms mislabeled products or used unsanitary processing practices to deceive the public.

Modern-day concerns about the middleman are more subtle. But the public policy issue—economic exploitation—remains the same. The issue has two related aspects: the farmers' share and industry structure.

The farmers' share.   Farmer and consumer interests have, from time to time, argued for policies that would increase the farmers' share of the food dollar. Farmer interests typically contend that their 25 cents of each dollar spent on food is "too small." The implication is drawn that food firms use monopoly power to the disadvantage of farmers, with the result that prices for farm commodities remain low. To dramatize the costs of food marketing, members of the National Farmers Organization sold meat, milk, and eggs directly to consumers at times in the late 1970s at prices approximating their "farm value." The practice ended presumably because the farmers found they could not do it any cheaper.

The fact that farmers receive on average one-fourth of the food expenditure dollar is also used to help support legislation that would raise farm prices. Senator Jesse Helms (R-N.C.), then chairman of the Senate Agriculture Committee, made the following statement as he introduced his version of the Agriculture and Food Act of 1981:

> Consumers have nothing to fear from higher farm prices . . . the cost of labor in food products exceeded the share of the cost that went to farmers for growing the food in the first place.[1]

Those representing consumer interests frequently make use of the "farmer share" statistics as well. For example, they sometimes argue that food processing costs are excessive. Consumer and farmer activists have encouraged programs to promote direct farm-to-consumer marketing. However, while reducing processing costs would increase the farmers' share of the food dollar, it would not necessarily improve prices or profits for farmers. Lower processing costs could simply be passed on to consumers in the form of a lower price. Nor is it certain that food prices would rise any more slowly. Data from USDA show a very close relationship between the farmers' share of each at-home food expenditure dollar and the amount of processing required to bring it to the consumer (Fig. 12.4). Foods that require considerable processing and are bulky (such as bakery products) return a considerably smaller portion to the farmer than foods that require almost no processing (such as eggs). Egg producers with a 1986 farmer's share of 62 percent are no better off than wheat producers with a farmer's share of only 7 percent. *In other words, the importance of the farmers' share tends to be blown way out of proportion. Although it may be possible to reduce the number of middlemen and thereby increase productivity in the marketing sector, the consumer would probably be the primary beneficiary of productivity changes.*

Industry structure.   The declining number of firms in the food marketing industry and their size from time to time surface as a policy issue. It could surface as a central policy issue in the future if trends toward increased concentration continue and/or relative food prices sharply increase. The concern is with the potential exercise of monopoly power by food manufacturers and grocery retailers.

There have been two concerted, rather widely publicized efforts to determine whether monopoly abuses exist in the food industry. In the mid-1960s, a National Commission on Food Marketing conducted a comprehensive study of the food industry, evaluated its competitive nature, and made recommendations for policy changes. The technical study on

---

[1]Statement by Senator Jesse Helms, *Congressional Record—Senate*, S-3484/S-3508 (Washington, D.C.: U.S. Senate, April 7, 1981).

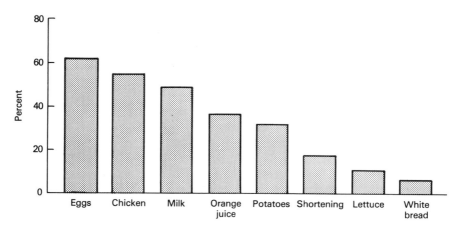

Figure 12.4 Farmers' share of retail food prices, at-home consumption, 1986.

food retailing concluded that although there have been substantial changes in the organization of the industry, "net profit has not contributed to the steadily rising gross margins. . . ."[2] A second study was conducted for the Joint Economic Committee by a land-grant university research group in the mid-1970s. This study was part of a broad congressional examination into the causes of inflation. The study and subsequent related efforts attracted considerable policy attention because of its conclusion that monopoly overcharges "are likely in retail food markets that are dominated by one or two firms and/or where sales are highly concentrated among the largest four firms."[3] Increasingly, this structural characterization is becoming appropriate for the entire food industry. Parker and Connor subsequently concluded that monopoly overcharges in U.S. food manufacturing industries run at least $10 billion but could possibly run as high as $15 billion.[4] This is as much as 25 percent of the value added to food products by food manufacturers. This conclusion was, however, sharply rebutted by O'Rourke, Greig, and Bullock.[5]

The practical net effect of increasing concentration in the food in-

[2]*Organization and Competition in Food Retailing,* Tech. Study 7 (Washington, D.C.: National Commission on Food Marketing, June 1966).

[3]*The Profit and Price Performance of Leading Food Chains 1970–1974* (Washington, D.C.: Joint Economic Committee, April 1977).

[4]Russell C. Parker and John M. Connor, "Estimates of Consumer Loss due to Monopoly in the U.S. Food Manufacturing Industries," *Am. J. Agric. Econ.* (November 1979), p. 639.

[5]A. Desmond O'Rourke and W. Smith Greig, "Estimates of Consumer Loss due to Monopoly in the U.S. Food Manufacturing Industries: Comment," *Am. J. Agric. Econ.* (May 1981), pp. 284–289; and J. Bruce Bullock, "Estimates of Consumer Loss due to Monopoly in U.S. Food Manufacturing Industries: Comment," *Am. J. Agric. Econ.* (May 1981), pp. 290–292.

dustry remains in dispute. The efficiency gains that come from consolidating transportation, processing, and merchandising functions are doubtless substantial. These gains provide most of the incentives for consolidation. Whether they are or ever will be offset by the exercise of monopoly power is unknown. The dynamic nature of the food industry is sufficient to raise serious doubts about the extent of the monopoly pricing that now exists. But farmers, the consuming public, and many economists continue to link farm problems and rising food prices to changes in food industry structure. That presumed linkage alone is sufficient to make structure a continuing food policy issue—particularly with the extensive consolidations which occurred in the food industries in the 1980s.

FOOD PRICE POLICY OPTIONS[6]

Prices serve as the primary rationing device in a market economy. When more is available than people want to purchase at a particular price, the price will fall and more will be consumed. When less is available than people want at the current price, the price will rise and less will be consumed.

If allowed to do so, prices will always rise or fall enough to balance production with consumption. But its functioning has a human effect. When cattle or corn prices fall, farmers see their personal income positions decline. When meat or bread prices rise, consumers see the purchasing power of their incomes decline. Some consumers must make do with less. It is the extent of this human effect that makes price movements in the food system a public policy concern.

Six alternative government programs have been utilized in attempting to directly or indirectly control food price increases:

- Price controls
- Export embargoes
- Reduced import restrictions
- Marketing order controls
- Farm program provisions
- Antitrust restraints

The first five of these six programs were used in the early 1970s as a means of dealing with what were considered to be extraordinarily high rates of inflation combined with high unemployment. Initially, the infla-

---

[6]This section draws on John T. Dunlop and Kenneth J. Fedor, *The Lessons of Wage and Price Controls—The Food Sector* (Cambridge, Mass.: Harvard University Press, 1977).

tion problems were not indigenous to agriculture, but were, instead, general economic problems. However, beginning in 1973, food became a major source of inflationary conditions, with reduced worldwide food production and sharply increased prices. In the 1980s, while food price inflation was not a major concern, government farm programs were a significant factor holding down food prices. In the late 1980s, the need for antitrust restraints applied to the food industry have the potential for being revived.

Price Controls

Historically, price controls have developed under two conditions:

- In times of military conflict, such as during and immediately after World War II, substantial excess demand is evident. Shortages of goods require a method of rationing supplies between domestic needs and war requirements. Under shortage conditions, strong pressures exist to control prices as a means of preventing undue inflation and windfall profits.

- In peacetime, price controls have been imposed during a broad-based inflationary surge and a real decline in wages when there is no other perceived politically acceptable means of bringing these problems under control. Price controls are, under these conditions, generally looked upon as a "quick fix" alternative to the restraint required by more effective longer-term policies such as reduced government spending, restricted monetary growth, and incentives for increased production.

The latter conditions developed in the early 1970s. Total economic output declined during the 1969–1970 recession. The unemployment rate was about 6 percent in 1971, nearly 60 percent higher than in 1966–1969. The consumer price index was rising at a then dramatic 4 percent annual rate. The political importance of these economic woes was heightened by the 1970 presidential election. It was perceived that something had to be done to put things back on course. Price controls were imposed.

President Nixon announced his new economic policy on August 15, 1971. The program was designed to deal with inflation, unemployment, and the growing balance-of-payments deficit. The 90-day freeze on nearly all prices and wages was perhaps the most dramatic for its effect on the average citizen. Retail food prices were frozen, but farm prices were not.

Food prices were, in fact, stable during the freeze. But lower farm commodity prices were the primary reason for the observed food price stability. The reason was not as important as the fact. Food price stability

during the period had an important influence on the popular perception
that the price freeze had been a success.

In November 1971, President Nixon lifted the price freeze and focused on controlling profit margins. Retailers were allowed to pass
through raw material and labor cost increases as long as there was no
increase in profit margins.

After the freeze was lifted, food prices rose at a rate that stood in
stark contrast to the stability experienced during the freeze. In fact, rising farm commodity prices, not larger retailer profit margins, were responsible for the 4.3 percent rise in food prices in 1972. Prices received by
farmers rose 30 percent during the margin control period. This dramatic
price rise was particularly noticeable in the meat sector, highlighting the
important role that commodity prices play in influencing food prices.

Theory of price controls.   Food price controls are relatively ineffective in fighting food price inflation. The principal purpose of such
controls—keeping prices from rising—is itself a cause of their failure. In
a market-based economy price changes are relied on to correct supply and
demand imbalances. High prices both discourage consumption and encourage production. This is particularly true of a competitive industry
where economic forces operate continuously to eliminate excess profits.

Suppose in Fig. 12.5 that the market for meat without price controls
is in equilibrium at price P_1 and quantity Q_1. If income increases because
of a wage increase, the consumer's demand for meat will shift to D_2. That
means that in the aggregate, consumers are willing to purchase more
meat than previously at each price. The first reaction in the market is to
notice that the meat counter is empty sooner. That is, consumers are willing to buy Q_3 pounds of meat at the old price. Noting the shift in demand,

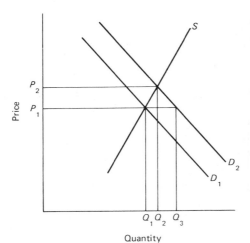

Figure 12.5 Impact of price controls.

the retailer attempts to buy more carcass beef. To do that, given a fixed supply, higher prices must be paid for cattle. Those higher prices are then passed on to consumers. The rising price has two effects. It encourages producers to expand output. But it also discourages consumption resulting in an eventual equilibrium price and quantity, P_2 and Q_2. The result eliminates the "shortage" $(Q_3 - Q_1)$.

The effect of an arbitrary price freeze at P_1 is immediately obvious. Unless the price is allowed to rise, there will be a shortage of meat— consumers will want to purchase more than producers are willing to sell at the frozen price. In that case, some other system must be used to ration the available meat (Q_1). First-come, first-served is a frequently used rationing device. When the meat case is empty, there is no more to sell. Thus, in 1972 on the East and West coasts, lines developed at meat counters, and butcher shops operated with shortened hours—an effect identical to the oil embargo in 1973. Although rising prices used as rationing devices are unpopular, coupons are even more unpopular. More important, neither price controls nor rationing coupons help solve the underlying supply problem. Indeed, using arbitrary price controls and rationing to solve economic problems is like trying to cool the temperature of a warm room by covering the thermometer. *The eventual result is the formation of a black market for the product in which products are sold at or even above the equilibrium price (P_2) to those buyers who have the money to pay for the product.*

Uniqueness of food price controls.   Price controls on food pose even more problems than for most other commodities for two major reasons:

- At the farm level, competitive market forces operate. Only a small profit exists against which the effects of price controls may be cushioned. This contrasts with other industries, where monopolistic profit margins and reduced costs associated with nonprice methods of competition may be used to offset the pressures of price controls. The result of competitive conditions in agriculture is a more immediate and profound response.
- The effects of farmers' response to price controls are frequently lagged or modified by the biological nature of food production. Production cannot be expanded or contracted quickly in response to changes. In fact, price changes in the livestock sector tend to result in short-run production changes that seem perverse. When cattle prices begin to fall relative to the cost of production, producers begin to sell their breeding stock. Such sales reduce their costs but add to current production, which tends to make prices fall even more. In turn, the lower prices intensify the extent of the liquidation. When

prices begin to rise, producers are encouraged to add to the breeding herd, which reduces production and forces prices higher. Actions that discourage rebuilding, such as importing beef, aggravate efforts to bring prices under control.

The food price implications of production cycles were particularly evident during the 1970s. Beef producers, responding to favorable cattle prices, expanded the cattle herd in the late 1960s and early 1970s. The total cattle and calf inventory increased from 109 million head in 1967 to 132 million head in 1975. When grain prices increased rapidly during 1972–1974, cattle production became unprofitable. The freeze on retail meat prices imposed by the Nixon administration only made matters worse for cattlemen. The immediate producer reaction to the price freeze was to hold back on marketing, feeding cattle to a higher weight. The result was shortages at the meat counter. When the freeze was lifted, the larger supply of heavy cattle caused prices to drop abruptly.

Similar effects were felt in other areas of agriculture. As noted previously, poultry producers drowned baby chicks rather than incur the costs of feeding and selling them as broilers at a loss. More hides, fertilizer, and meats were exported because the controls kept domestic prices lower than world prices.

The problems encountered with food price controls have sometimes led to a system of regulations which allows food processors and retailers to pass through price increases at the farm level. However, the detail of and delays involved in approving pass-through of farm level price increases results in suppression of farm prices as well as wholesale and retail prices.

These production/consumption distortions were not unique to the Nixon price control program. They were not a failure of just that particular policy. They were (and are) the predictable and inevitable result of a policy doomed to failure by its inherent approach. In many respects, the only cure for high retail food prices is high farm prices, which result in increased production.

Embargoes

Export embargoes, like price controls, are political solutions to perceived economic problems. Political pressure for export controls in the United States increased abruptly in 1973 with the threat of worldwide food shortages. Preventing shortages and controlling prices required either an increase in supply or a reduction in demand. Short-term increases in supplies were impossible. The only political option available in the short run was to reduce demand by restricting exports.

Export shipments of agricultural products were restricted for purposes of domestic price control three times during the 1970s. The first, in June 1973, was the most extensive and had the greatest effect on prices. The other two, in October 1974 and August 1975, were precautionary in nature and were directed primarily at blocking large sales of grain to the USSR.

Prices fell dramatically after the first embargo was imposed. Soybean prices, for example, fell from their high of about $12.25 per bushel to about $6.25 over a period of about two weeks.[7] This full drop cannot be attributed to the embargo. For one thing, the lack of good information about export sales contributed to the doubling of soybean prices—a price rise that could not have been sustained. Then, too, the 1973 crop was developing nicely and would later become a record 1.6 million bushels—22 percent greater than the 1972 crop.[8] These two factors, improved information about actual exports and the improving crop prospects, undoubtedly contributed in a major way to the lower prices. But farmers blamed the lower prices on the embargo—just as consumers became convinced that the embargoes had done their job.

It is naive to argue that export controls will never again be used to control prices. When commodity exports begin to threaten domestic food security or when grain prices increase so rapidly as to threaten a major liquidation of livestock, it is almost a certainty that ways will be found to reduce demand. An export embargo remains a possible short-run policy option.

Reduced Import Restrictions

It will be recalled from Chapter 6 that two major agricultural commodities—milk and beef—utilize quotas as a means of maintaining domestic prices above world prices. The ability to increase these quotas has been used by the president as a means of price control. Increasing imports, of course, increases supplies available to the domestic market and thus lowers price.

After the price freeze in 1973, domestic production dropped and prices rose. With the potential for shortages, import quotas were lifted for both milk products and beef. Imports of nonfat dry milk, increased from 1.6 million pounds in 1972 to 267 million pounds in 1973, cheese imports from 179 to 230 million pounds, and butter imports from less than 1 million pounds to 43 million pounds.[9] Fresh and frozen beef imports increased 16 percent.[10]

---

[7]*Fat and Oil Situation* (Washington, D.C.: ERS, USDA, December 1975), p. 10.

[8]*Agricultural Statistics* (Washington, D.C.: SRS, USDA, 1974), p. 133.

[9]*Agricultural Statistics* (Washington, D.C.: SRS, USDA, 1977), p. 392.

[10]Ibid, p. 355.

The relaxation of import restrictions—applauded by consumers, food processors, and retailers—was strongly condemned by producers on the grounds that it reduced incentives for domestic production. Interestingly, when U.S. supplies are short, world supplies are also frequently short. Thus even though import restrictions are raised, the supplies may not be readily available, or they are only available because U.S. consumers are able to pay a higher price and bid supplies away from foreign consumers.

In the 1980s, reduced import restraints were suggested as a means of curbing the market power of marketing boards in Canada. Provincial Canadian producer boards had sufficiently restricted output to raise the price of commodities (and producer marketing quotas) to what some considered to be excessively high levels. A relaxation of import restrictions would be an outside source of competition restraining the boards' exercise of monopoly powers.

Marketing Order Controls

It will be recalled from Chapter 10 that marketing orders either directly establish prices (milk) or provide varying degrees of control over the quantity and quality of products that move to marketing (fruits and vegetables). Beginning in 1972, White House agencies such as the Office of Management and Budget, the Council of Economic Advisers, and the Cost of Living Council began to take a great deal of interest in how marketing order decisions of the secretary of agriculture raise commodity prices and thus exacerbate the inflation problem. To prevent this occurrence, these agencies began to monitor closely USDA marketing decisions. Particular emphasis was placed on milk marketing order price increases and flow-to-market regulation for navel oranges and lemons. In fact, White House scrutiny of orders became so intense that changes in order provisions by the secretary required White House approval.

White House interest in orders continued through the 1970s and the 1980s, as indicated by the designation of fruit and vegetable marketing orders as one of the candidates for deregulation by the Reagan administration.[11] Subsequently, policy guidelines were issued by Secretary Block to prevent orders from being used as a means of controlling production and artificially raising prices.

In the late 1980s, concern about the adverse impact of marketing orders on prices and resource misallocation spread from fruits and vegetables to milk. In 1988, the General Accounting Office issued a report

---

[11]Richard Heifner et al., *A Review of Federal Marketing Orders for Fruits, Vegetables and Specialty Crops*, Agric. Econ. Rep. 477 (Washington, D.C.: AMS, USDA, November 1981).

which called for the elimination of milk marketing orders. Orders were charged with unduly raising milk prices in the Northeast and South, lowering prices in the Upper Midwest, and preventing the use of substitute milk forms such as reconstituted milk. Surprisingly, USDA did not contest these charges, but stated that Congress would have to act if policy was to be changed.

Domestic Farm Programs

Farm programs do affect the price of food. Some programs, such as price supports on milk and quotas on sugar imports, raise the price of food. Sugar producers deny this effect by arguing that a reduction in the price of sugar would not result in a reduction in the price of candy bars. Such an argument results from lags in price responsiveness through the marketing channel. Changes in the retail price of candy bars take place in 5-cent increments or in the weight of bars, requiring new production specifications and package labels. Such changes necessarily lag farm price changes. Surely, over time, farm prices and consumer prices are related.

Cheap food policy.   If farm prices and consumer prices were not related, there would be no foundation or purpose to the frequently heard farmer charge that the United States pursues a cheap food policy. A farm policy economist necessarily responds to such a charge with mixed emotions.

A **cheap food policy** *involves the government overtly pursuing policies that hold the price of food below the competitive equilibrium price.* It was seen earlier that the consequence of government setting the price of food below the competitive market equilibrium *and paying farmers that price* is a shortage. Many developing and centrally planned economies pursue this type of cheap food policy.

If the United States pursues a cheap food policy, it is *not* of this variety. Yet the *U.S. farm policy has had the effect of suppressing the price of food.* Target prices cause farmers to expand production and thereby lower the price of food. However, the target price does not result in a shortage. Consumers benefit from target prices by both the lower market price *and* the plentiful food supply. The difference between the U.S. farm policy and the type of cheap food policy that exists in many developing and centrally planned countries is that in the United States the target price protects producer returns.

Consumers at home and abroad receive the benefits of target prices, U.S. taxpayers pay the costs. Thus while U.S. target price policy is frequently referred to as a transfer payment from taxpayers to farmers, it is also a transfer payment from taxpayers to consumers. Remember that taxpayers and consumers are not one and the same. Progressive taxes, such as the income and property tax, sever the link between taxpayers and consumers. Therefore, lower-income people benefit relatively more from the U.S. target price program than do the wealthy. Similarly, lower-income people, along with farmers, would be hurt by the elimination of target prices—taxpayers would be the prime beneficiary.

Grain reserves also affect the price of food and may be considered by some to be part of a U.S. cheap food policy. Yet reserves both raise and lower prices. When reserves are being acquired, farm prices rise. In fact, most publicly held stocks of farm commodities are acquired when government is trying to support (raise) the price. Since reserves become a part of the potential supply, they lower and stabilize price.

Reserves are probably the only means by which government can moderate price increases without potentially severe, adverse impacts on the production decisions of farmers. Even here, however, the timing and method of release become important to determining the nature of the impact. For example, a large quantity of CCC stocks of grain placed on the market just before planting could adversely affect farmers' decisions on what crops to plant as well as the level of fertilizer applications. As in many other public policy decisions, the appearance and timing of the action may be as important as the action itself in determining its effect.

Expensive food policy. Not all U.S. farm programs lower farm prices. Expensive food policies raise the price of food above the competitive market equilibrium price. Price supports on milk and sugar are combined with import controls to raise their prices above the competitive equilibrium. Meat import controls raise prices. Land retirement programs support prices by reducing surpluses. Thus, if the U.S. has a cheap food policy, it is not uniformly pursued.

Some countries overtly pursue an expensive food policy. The most notable examples are Japan and the European Economic Community. Higher food prices are imposed only on their domestic consumers. Such a policy may be sold to consumers on grounds such as food security or preserving a decentralized farm structure (larger number of smaller farms).

Over time, expensive food policies result in surplus production which must either be curbed by production controls, held in reserve, or dumped on the world market. If the surpluses are dumped on the world market, consumers in other countries receive short-run benefits while unprotected farmers in other countries receive lower prices. This effect on world prices is identical to the target price. In either case, the result is a misallocation of resources in the world.

Antitrust Restraints

Antitrust policy was discussed in Chapter 11 as a structure of agriculture policy. It is also a food price policy. The degree of emphasis on antitrust in the food industry has changed dramatically over the past 30 years. In the 1960s, mergers among milk processors and food retailers were severely restricted. In the 1970s, the emphasis in antitrust shifted to hard-core antitrust, such as price fixing and predatory market practices designed to drive competitors out of markets.

In the 1980s, concern about market structure and antitrust almost vanished. Mergers and acquisitions within and among both agricultural input and product markets mushroomed. Market shares for the four largest firms increased sharply. For example, in boxed beef the four largest packers had over 80 percent of the sales nationally. Farm-level purchase of beef cattle was even more highly concentrated in many local or regional markets. Although not as profound, concentration also increased sharply in the seed corn, farm machinery, and poultry business. Such changes in structure could once again make antitrust a focal point for fostering competition and influencing food prices.

A RED HERRING?

To some it may seem ironic that while U.S. consumers spend only 15 percent of their income on food, they are still concerned about food prices. It also appears ironic that while most of this book has been concerned with low farm prices and incomes, high food prices are also an issue.

Such ironies point up the complexity of agriculture and the forces affecting it. They are what make the farm and food policymakers' job so extremely difficult. They also point out the role economists can play in evaluating the trade-offs from various policy options.

Chapter 13

Nutrition, Food Safety, and Food Quality

If the government was as afraid of disturbing the consumer as it is of disturbing business, this would be some democracy.

Frank McKinney Hubbard

While consumer interest in food price and structure issues largely died in the 1980s, concerns about nutrition, diet, food safety, quality, and health continued. These concerns were fostered by a continuing flow of some-times conflicting research results on the relationships between diet and health; the willingness of consumers to buy increasingly highly processed foods; and seemingly increasing occurrences of residues in the food supply, often having a farm input source. This chapter is designed to reflect the dimensions of these concerns and government options for dealing with them. The farm-level effects of increased environmental and food safety regulations are pursued further in Chapter 14.

THE FOOD SAFETY–NUTRITION CONTINUUM

Issues of food safety and nutrition are becoming increasingly intertwined as more information becomes available on the relationships between diet and health. Additives such as salt or sodium nitrite (used to cure bacon, ham, and other processed meats) were once considered completely safe. Now salt has become linked to high blood pressure and sodium nitrite has been tagged as a potential cancer-causing substance.

Even foods themselves, or natural substances within them, are being implicated in specific food safety issues. For example, cholesterol, a naturally occurring substance in animal fat, has become nearly as suspect as a cause of heart disease as salt has as a cause of high blood pressure. Similarly, obesity is being implicated as an unsafe physical condition, suggesting avoiding certain foods and/or restricting food intake—a message that the affected food processors and producers do not want to hear.

Looked at in this context, issues of food safety and nutrition may be viewed as a continuum of health-related food concerns. The one extreme of food-related health concerns would be violent forms of food poisoning such as botulism. In the middle of the continuum would be various additives that are implicated as causes of various health problems, such as cancer or cardiovascular diseases. At the other end of the food-related health concern spectrum would be individual foods or food groups, such as animal fat or sugar, that are suspected of contributing to health problems.

Government regulations may also be viewed as a spectrum of alternatives. At the one extreme, strict federal inspection and banning of certain substances from the food supply would be involved. In the middle, industries might be required to post warning labels or be subject to federal standards of self-regulation, and schools might be required to include in their curriculum nutrition education material pointing out the dangers in certain foodstuffs. The other extreme would involve a hands-off policy where the government has no role. On any individual food safety issue, questions may arise as to where the proper role of government lies on this regulatory spectrum.

FOOD SAFETY

The safety of the food supply has long been considered a responsibility of the federal government. That safe food is an important consumer concern is hardly debatable. But it is also a producer concern—just ask the producers of canned mushrooms or cranberries who have had products withdrawn from the market because of a health threat. Indeed, the meat industry remains the single most effective lobby for continued federal meat and poultry inspection as a means of protecting the integrity of its products.

The perishability of food and its proclivity for carrying bacteria and transmitting disease have been the central public policy concerns with food safety. Perhaps the most feared food safety health risk is botulism (food poisoning). This often fatal disease is caused by a widespread organism that is found in both terrestrial and marine environments. Although feared, its incidence in the United States during the past century has been rare. Of the 688 outbreaks since 1899, 72 percent were traced to home-processed foods.[1]

This remarkable food safety record is partly the result of long-standing and rather strict food safety laws. On January 20, 1879, Congressman Hendrick B. Wright of Pennsylvania introduced in the 45th Congress, H.R. 5916 "for preventing the adulteration of articles of food and drink." In 1904, Upton Sinclair first arrived in Chicago to chronicle the life of immigrant meat packing company workers. His book, *The Jungle,* went beyond the immigrant worker theme to highlight the unsanitary conditions in America's meat packing industry.[2] Shortly after its publication, President Theodore Roosevelt ordered a special report on conditions in the stockyards. The report confirmed Sinclair's account. Before the end of the year (1906), Congress passed a meat inspection law. In the following year, the law was amended and passed as the Meat Inspection Act of 1907; it was not rewritten for 60 years.

In recent years, the issues of food safety and quality have broadened. Consumers now take an active interest in specific program concerns that range from the control of animal feed additives to the passage of laws that require more complete labeling of foods in the grocery store. Public policy interest in such issues has grown as the food system has become more complex. The increase in food product processing makes it impossible for the average consumer to understand fully the physical and chemical properties of the items available for purchase. Some of these properties may be acquired in a very indirect way. For example, since 1966, pesticide use has doubled. Pesticide residues have become a major food safety issue. The commercialized use of animal drugs at low (subtherapeutic) levels did not occur until 1950. From 1960 to 1970, antibiotics used in animal feeds increased sevenfold. Antibiotic residues thus arose as another major food safety issue.

The steady advance of science is raising issues that were unknown even 10 years ago. New scientific approaches are now raising questions about the continued safety of age-old food preparation practices, such as curing pork with sodium nitrite. New technological advances are making it possible to detect the presence of substances at levels of accuracy never before considered.

All these issues can be summarized as an increasing concern in protecting the public's right to know—the right to know that foods are safe

[1]Center for Disease Control, *Botulism in the United States, 1899–1973*, HEW Publ. 77–8279 (Washington, D.C.: HEW, June 1974).

[2]Upton Sinclair, *The Jungle* (New York: Doubleday, Page & Co., 1906) republished by Viking Press, New York, 1946).

and the right to know what packages contain in terms of quality and composition prior to purchase.

Safe Foods

Three distinct sources of contemporary food safety problems can be readily identified:

- **Sanitation** continues to be a significant concern. The center of attention is upon controlling the incidence of botulism, salmonella, and other food poisoning–causing substances. Whereas cases of botulism have become relatively rare, other forms of food poisoning appear to have become more common. For example, in the late 1980s, considerable controversy arose over increasing incidence of salmonella in poultry. Questions also arose regarding the sanitary practices of dairy product processors. The key to avoiding food poisoning is continuous vigilance in sanitation control methods.
- **Farm production practices**, including the use of pesticides, antibiotics, and hormones, have become a major focal point of food safety concerns. Pesticides create concern because of the potential for residues which, if ingested, may cause cancer. Hormones have the same potential. Antibiotics create a concern that continuous use might lead to the development of bacterial mutations that are resistant to antibiotics for which there are no substitutes. In addition, there are concerns that some individuals are highly allergic to specific antibiotics.

  An additional area of concern involves the potential for contaminants entering the food supply and having ultimate adverse health effects through residues. Particular problems have developed where PPB, a fire prevention substance, was accidentally mixed into feed that was subsequently fed to livestock and poultry. The most severe case was encountered in Michigan, where large numbers of dairy cattle and broilers had to be destroyed. Numerous lawsuits resulted from alleged adverse effects on health, particularly among farmers who cared for the affected livestock and poultry.
- **Highly processed foods** have been made more tasty with artificial ingredients, storable with preservatives, convenient to handle, and appealing to look at. The problem is that these properties are instilled in products by substances that have potential harmful effects. Food colorings have been associated with cancer and hyperactivity. Sodium in salt raises blood pressure. Saccharin is a suspected carcinogen. There are also important trade-offs in the use of food additives. For example, while sodium nitrite is a suspected carcinogen,

it is an essential preservative in cured meats to prevent food poisoning such as botulism. Reality suggests that botulism is a more certain killer than the risk of cancer posed by sodium nitrite.

Food Safety Regulation

The safety of the food supply has long been a public policy concern. The first official federal responses came in the late 1800s, but state and local interest in food safety was coincident virtually with the landing of the first settlers.

Three federal agencies today share responsibility for assuring the safety and wholesomeness of the overall food supply. The Food and Drug Administration of the Department of Health and Human Services has the primary responsibility. USDA shares concurrent jurisdiction with the Food and Drug Administration over meat and poultry products. The Environmental Protection Agency has jurisdiction over the use of pesticides that have potential adverse effects on health and safety. Contemporary issues in food safety can be divided into two general categories: food processing and food production.

Food processing. Much time and money continue to be devoted to traditional areas of concern such as sanitation. In the late 1980s, considerable controversy arose as to the need for federal inspectors in meat processing plants and the speed at which poultry processing lines were allowed to run, while still allowing for care in inspection. Milk processors made a major effort to eliminate problems of bacterial contamination. Another focal point of controversy has been the impact of food additives on health and safety. The controlling legislation for food safety is the federal Food, Drug, and Cosmetic Act. This act is designed to protect the public from dangerous and unwholesome products. The original statute was enacted in 1938. It included prohibitions against "any poisonous or deleterious substances in food which may render it injurious to health," but did not include provisions for premarket testing of substances such as food additives, new drugs, new animal drugs, and color additives. Subsequent amendments to this legislation prohibit the addition of substances to food that have not been shown to be safe.

The Food Additive Amendment, enacted in 1958, requires premarket testing of all substances that meet the definition of the term "food additive." The 1958 legislation contains the **Delaney clause,** which was added to the bill as a committee amendment:

> no additive shall be deemed to be safe if found to induce cancer when ingested by man or animal, or if it is found after tests that are appropriate for the evaluation of the safety of food additives, to induce cancer in man or animal. . . .

The procedures for obtaining approval of food additives are also specified in the law. Before an ingredient may be used, it must be the subject of a food additive regulation which establishes a tolerance for its use. The substance in question must be shown to be safe under the conditions of its intended use, and it must be shown to perform effectively its intended function, such as food preservation, when used at intended levels. The Delaney clause dictates that approval cannot be granted if the substance has been shown, through appropriate testing, to induce cancer in man or animal. Subsequent amendments applied the Delaney clause provisions to color additives.

Virtually all classes of food additives have been subject to restrictions and questions regarding the potential for resulting health complications. Preservatives such as sodium nitrite used in curing meat have been implicated as a cause of cancer. Food colorings have been implicated as carcinogens and a cause of hyperactivity in children. Artificial flavorings are suspected carcinogens. The artificial sweetener saccharin has been implicated as a cause of cancer. In addition, salt has been associated with high blood pressure.

Each successive finding or potential association of an additive with a health problem caused major controversy within agricultural groups and related food processors. The sodium nitrite findings were a major scare to the pork and meat packing industries. The saccharin findings had the potential for destroying large segments of the diet food and artificial sweetener industry.

Food production.   The food safety aspects of food production are regulated by the Animal Drug Amendments to the Food, Drug, and Cosmetic Act and the Environmental Pesticide Control Act of 1972, and by the Pesticide Chemical Act of 1954. The animal drug and pesticide regulations have the same intent as Delaney in the sense that cancer-causing pesticides are to be eliminated from the food supply. However, in this case the pesticide is banned only when residues of a carcinogen-causing drug are found in edible portions of plants or animals. The provisions were, for example, applied to prohibiting the use of the growth stimulant DES in beef production and banning the use of the pesticide DDT as well as several other pesticides. They have also been used to require withdrawal of chemicals and drugs from plants and animals several days before harvest or slaughter.

Farmers tend to look at federal requirements for pesticide safety as interference with their freedom and efforts to produce farm products efficiently. They argue correctly that it has become virtually impossible to control certain pests, such as fire ants, without powerful pesticides. Delay and extra costs are incurred by drug and pesticide manufacturers in conducting the tests needed to prove that the safety requirements are

---

REGULATORY IRONY

One of my vivid recollections is of sitting around a table in Washington with a roomful of government regulators. Their purpose was to get the last molecule of diethylstilbestrol out of beef liver, although scientists could not show that anyone had ever been harmed by consuming residues of this feed additive. The air was thick with cigarette smoke (325,000 deaths a year attributable to smoking). After the discussion we adjourned to cocktails (25,000 deaths a year from drunken driving, many of the victims nondrinkers). The inconsistency of regulating others and indulging oneself went unremarked by these people and, so far as I could see, unobserved.

Don Paarlberg, *Farm and Food Policy: Issues of the 1980s* (Lincoln, Nebr.: University of Nebraska Press, 1980), p. 82.

---

met. Without question, banning the use of drugs or chemicals increases the cost of production.[3] As a result, consumers pay higher prices for food that has a greater margin of safety associated with it.

The competitive position of farmers in both domestic and foreign markets is also affected by federal safety regulations. While imports of farm products such as fruit, vegetables, and meats are tested for residues of U.S. banned pesticides or additives, charges continuously arise regarding the disadvantaged position of U.S. farmers competing with foreign producers who are not subject to the same production or processing regulations.

Similarly, in periods of rapid technological change, U.S. food safety regulatory clearance procedures may take considerably longer than those applied in foreign competing countries. The result of this disparity could be the loss of competitive position internationally for particular farm commodities.

Benefits of Regulation

While producers and processors frequently criticize food safety regulations because they impose extra production or processing costs, considerable difficulty is encountered in quantifying the benefits. The value of risk avoidance resulting from regulation lacks precision. Additional difficulty is involved in valuing human life. Many subjective judgments are necessary.

[3]Clark Burbee, William Gallimore, and William T. Boehm, *The Economic Effects of a Prohibition on the Use of Selected Animal Drugs*, Agric. Econ. Rep. 414 (Washington, D.C.: ESCS, USDA, November 1978).

Because of the subjectivity involved in quantifying the value of lives, studies tend to focus on numbers of individuals affected and potential direct costs. For example, a USDA study[4] focused on the benefits of slaughterhouse inspection of carcasses—which receives about two-thirds of the budget for meat and poultry inspection. The benefit calculations were limited to the avoidance of tuberculosis, salmonellosis, and tapeworm. These diseases and parasites typically do not cause noticeable changes in an animal and might, therefore, go undetected without a formal inspection program.

The study concluded that, without inspection, from 2500 to 6500 additional persons would need treatment for tuberculosis each year, of which 150 to 399 would die. Between 50,000 and 100,000 more persons would have a tapeworm problem, and salmonellosis cases would increase by several hundred thousand. The sum of the associated physician and hospital costs plus lost productivity and income could range from $137 million to $605 million. In addition, the abolition of federal inspection programs would probably reduce the exports of U.S. meat. In total, the potential assessment of benefits is several times greater than the program costs of about $300 million per year.

Food Safety Issues and Options[5]

Food safety programs and procedures to implement them raises three major issues and related policy options:

- Tolerance
- Testing
- Labeling

Level of tolerance.   **Tolerance** refers to the amount of a particular substance that is allowed in the food supply and still considered safe and/or wholesome. Zero tolerance means that none of the substance is allowed in the food supply. For most food supply contaminants, some level of tolerance is provided under law. For example, food inspection procedures allow small amounts of insect parts, rodent hair, and so forth in finished products.

The reason for tolerance lies in the impracticality and cost of achieving zero tolerance. The cost of eliminating a substance from the

[4]Tayna Roberts, *National Food Review* (Washington, D.C.: ESCS, USDA, Spring 1980), pp. 25–27.

[5]Thomas L. Sporleder and Carol S. Kramer, "Assessment of Food Safety Programs and Federal Policy Options," in *Federal Agricultural Marketing Programs* (College Station, Tex.: Texas Agricultural Extension Service, 1988).

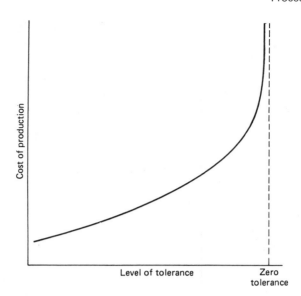

Figure 13.1 Hypothetical cost of achieving zero tolerance.

food supply increases rapidly as the zero tolerance level is approached (Fig. 13.1). This is the case for four reasons:

- There are practical limits on the ability to remove specific substances, particularly when they exist in very small, yet measurable, amounts.
- Many substances that may be carcinogens occur naturally in the food supply in very minute quantities. For example, potatoes contain arsenic; lima beans contain hydrogen cyanide; and spinach and broccoli contain nitrites.[6]
- The development of proven safe substitutes for potential disease causing substances is very costly. Many of the current additives, such as salt or sodium nitrite, are very simple chemically and easy to produce. Finding an acceptable substitute and *proving that it is safe is costly.*
- Detection instruments can now measure parts per trillion. Paarlberg uses the analogy that a part per trillion is like a grain of sugar in an Olympic-size swimming pool.[7] Our ability to measure poten-

[6]Reay Tannahill, *Food in History* (Briarcliff Manor, N.Y.: Stein & Day Publishers, 1973), pp. 379–380.

[7]Don Paarlberg, *Farm and Food Policy: Issues of the 1980s* (Lincoln, Nebr.: University of Nebraska Press, 1980), p. 91.

tially dangerous substances exceeds our ability to eliminate them from the food supply.

Delaney is a *zero-tolerance policy option*. It requires complete elimination of cancer-causing substances from the food supply. Practically, this is impossible. But politically it appears to be impossible to modify Delaney. A vote against Delaney can be charged to be a vote for cancer!

An **acceptable risk criteria** is the practical policy alternative to Delaney. *This alternative would explicitly mandate a systematic risk/ benefit approach to food safety regulation.* It would recognize that most food safety decisions involve some risk to some people. There is no option that gives a true zero risk. It would effectively change the Delaney "Is the product safe?"criterion to "What is the acceptable level of risk and to whom?" With such a change, consumers and decision makers would be more aware of the risks involved in their consumption decisions.

From a practical standpoint, the acceptable risk criteria are being used even on cancer-causing substances. Yet Delaney remains the law!

Testing procedure.   The safety of a particular additive is determined on the basis of feeding large amounts of additives to test animals (mostly rats) over relatively short periods. This procedure is much criticized. For example, when it was determined in the late 1950s that the herbicide aminotriazole was a carcinogen, cranberries were withdrawn from the market. Paarlberg notes that to ingest the same amount of aminotriazole as the test rats, a human being would have to eat 18 tons of cranberries.[8]

In some cases, conflicting conclusions have been reached. The case of the use of sodium nitrite in curing meat is illustrative. In the mid-1970s, a blue ribbon task force of scientists under Secretary Butz concluded that carcinogenic nitrosamines were formed from sodium nitrite in the process of cooking bacon. Secretary Bergland found that the sodium nitrite levels in cured meat could be reduced sufficiently to eliminate nitrosamines from forming while cooking. A study by Newberne then concluded sodium nitrite itself could cause cancer in laboratory rats. Two years later a review of the Newberne study concluded that there was not sufficient evidence in the study to warrant the conclusion that sodium nitrite was a carcinogen. For years, pork has lived under the shadow of this cancer-causing link.

Proof that a substance *causes* cancer or any other disease in humans is exceedingly difficult. The possibilities for human experimentation in testing potentially dangerous substances on a subsection of the popula-

[8]Ibid., p. 93.

tion with larger than normal dosages are severely limited. Yet the animal rights activists object to experimental testing using animals. Putting a substance into use and waiting to see the results also contains many pitfalls. The choice here seems to be the least objectionable of the alternatives.

Safety information and labeling. The private sector could be required to provide more safety information regarding their products leaving consumers the choice of whether to consume the product. For products demonstrated to be potentially dangerous, warning labels could be required. Presumably, different levels of food safety would be available and consumers could choose among them, considering the level of risks involved.

This is the type of approach that has been used on cigarettes and saccharin. Consumption of cigarettes has declined significantly, while saccharin consumers have switched largely to NutraSweet.

The information and labeling approach may not be applicable to all food safety situations. The risks from potentially disease-causing substances are by no means equal. It is unlikely that a labeling system can accurately convey the degree of risks involved in a particular substance. The amount of information required to make an objective decision would be vast.

In certain instances, it may be impossible to effectively translate safety information. For example, in the case of food service operations, it would be impractical to convey information on safety to the customer. Where children are involved, parents would be making food safety decisions on behalf of children which may, in certain instances, be accepted by society, but in other instances, may not be accepted by society. In situations such as school lunches, government would still be making food safety decisions on behalf of individuals.

DIET AND HEALTH

As noted in the beginning of this chapter, the nutrition issue may be viewed as a continuum of the food safety issue. In other words, the health of people is influenced by what they eat. While the effects of poor diet are not as violent and visible as food poisoning, poor diet has been implicated in many of the same diseases as food additives—namely, cancer and cardiovascular diseases. Another dimension of the nutrition and health issue involves the problems of hunger and malnutrition. These issues will be treated after a discussion of diet and health.

Sources of the Diet–Health Problems

The specific nature of the relationship between diet and health is much disputed. Yet it is undisputed that there is a diet–health relationship. Three main sources of the diet-health problem can be identified:

- Eating the wrong foods
- Poor lifestyle
- Obesity

Eating the wrong foods.   Individual choice, custom, food availability, cost, habits, health, geographic location, peer pressure, ease of preparation, age, religion, and ethnic consideration all influence what people eat. Food selection and consumption are related in a complicated way to other aspects of life. For example, the per capita consumption of dairy products among black Americans may be low because some blacks have had difficulty digesting lactose. Teenagers may choose not to participate in the school lunch program in order to spend their lunch hour away from school, because of the quality of the lunch or because they simply prefer to eat "junk food." Highly processed food consumption has increased, in part, because of the working mother and higher preferences placed on leisure time.

Many scientists believe that the American diet is contributing to some of the chronic diseases, such as heart disease and cancer, that afflict people in later life.[9] In addition, they assert that cutting down on fats, calories, sugar, and salt would be positive steps toward reducing heart disease, certain cancers, and strokes. In drawing this conclusion, they cite comprehensive studies such as that of Glueck and Connor;[10] as well as Stamler,[11] which recommend that alteration of dietary practices to reduce saturated fat and cholesterol consumption would be desirable for the public. However, while there appears to be general agreement by a number of scientists that healthy Americans should avoid too much fat, saturated fat, and cholesterol, there is not general agreement on appropriate levels of these components in the diet.[12]

[9]Carole A. Davis et al., *Food*, Home Garden Bull. 228 (Washington, D.C.: SEA, USDA, 1980), p. 3.

[10]C.J. Glueck and W.E. Conner, "Diet–Coronary Heart Disease Relationship Reconnoitered," *Am. J. Clin. Nutr.* (1978), pp. 727–737.

[11]J. Stamler, "Life Styles, Major Risk Factors, Proof and Public Policy," *Circulation* (1978), pp. 3–19.

[12]P.M. Belden and F.J. Cronin, "Dietary Recommendations for Healthy Americans Summarized," *Fam. Econ. Rev.* (1985), pp. 17–27.

TABLE 13.1 Influence of Selected Preventable Factors on Mortality

	Cause of Death[a]				
	Major Cardiovascular-Renal Diseases	Malignant Neoplasms	Accidents: Motor Vehicle and Other	Respiratory Diseases	Diabetes Mellitus
Smoking	VH	VH	L	VH	VL
Diet	VH	VH	VL	VL	VH
Occupational hazards	VL	L	VH	H	VL
Alcohol abuse	L	L	VH	L	L
Drug abuse	VL	VL	H	VL	VL
Radiation hazards	VL	L	VL	VL	VL
Air and water pollution	VL	VL	VL	L	VL
	Number of premature deaths				
In 1973	395,000	90,000	44,000	16,000	24,000
In 2000[b]	595,000	127,000	71,000	33,000	30,000

Source: R. B. Gori and B. J. Richter, "The Macroeconomics of Disease Prevention in the United States," *Science*, Vol. 200 (June 1978), p. 1125. Copyright 1978 by the American Association for the Advancement of Science.
[a]VH, very high (30%); H, high (20 to 30%); M, medium (10 to 20%); L, low (below 5%).
[b]If current trends remain unchanged.

These views are subject to considerable controversy. Dissenting points of view (1) are critical of the use of epidemiological data to draw conclusions on the relation between diet and health,[13] (2) cite studies that contradict the asserted relationships between diet and health,[14] or (3) assert that the relationships are considerably more complex than simply changing diet.[15]

Poor life-styles.   Without question the relationships are more complex than requiring a simple diet–health prescription. Gori and Richter effectively summarized the results of research on the controllable factors in mortality prevention (Table 13.1). Diet is only one of seven factors affecting mortality.

In summarizing the causal relationship for various environmental causes of death, Gori and Richter conclude that the government is devoting too many resources to lower-priority causes such as air and water pol-

[13]Max Kellough, "Comments by a Task Force Member," in *Consensus and Conflict in U.S. Agriculture,* Bruce L. Gardner and James W. Richardson, eds. (College Station, Tex.: Texas A&M University Press, 1979), pp. 194–199.
[14]R. Reiser, "Over-Simplication of Diet: Coronary Heart Disease Relationships and Exogenated Dietary Recommendations," *Am. J. Clin. Nutr.* (1978), pp. 865–875.

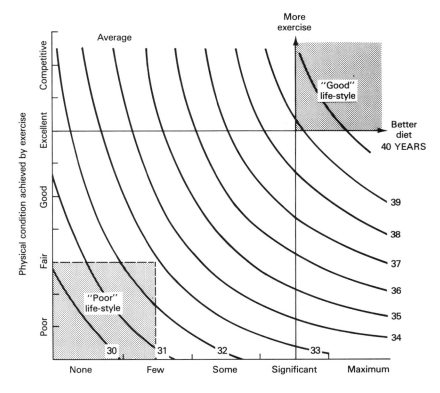

Figure 13.2 Hypothetical relationship between physical condition from exercise, and diet restriction and expected number of years free from chronic disease for a 40-year-old nonsmoking adult.
Source: C. Peter Timmer and Malden C. Nesheim, "Nutrition, Product Quality and Safety," in *Consensus and Conflict in U.S. Agriculture*, Bruce L. Gardner and James W. Richardson, eds. (College Station, Tex.: Texas A&M University Press, 1979), p. 167.

lution to the detriment of making substantial progress on higher-priority causes such as smoking, diet, and alcohol. Yet recent evidence on the extent of water pollution, including pesticide residues, would suggest that all environmental causes may deserve greater attention.

The complexity of relationship between diet and health is probably best illustrated by the relationships suggested in Fig. 13.2, which point out the interactive effects of diet, physical exercise, and smoking on life expectancy. A "good" life-style involves a high level of physical exercise, significant dietary restrictions to maintain low levels of serum cholesterol and total caloric intake, few highly processed foods, and no smoking. With somewhat less exercise and fewer dietary restrictions, the risk of chronic disease increases. These are variables that can be consciously controlled by the individual. The trade-off is one of giving up some of the "pleasures of life" in the short run to live longer.

Obesity.   Obesity, a body weight over 20 percent above the ideal weight, is increasingly becoming recognized as a major health problem.[16] An increasing body of evidence points to the undesirability of the average trend to accumulate weight gradually from age 25 and onward. Public health data suggest that as much as 50 percent of the population is obese.[17]

The principal cause of obesity is overeating, the intake of food in excess of requirements. Available evidence suggests a persistent increase in the extent of obesity. Per capita nutrients available for consumption have increased from 3200 calories in 1947–1949 to 3600 calories in 1987.[18] Although recommended energy intakes vary with age, fewer than 3000 calories generally recommended.[19]

Sources of excess calories are related primarily to excess intake of fats, oils, and caloric sweeteners, all of which have tended to increase in consumption.[20] High fat intake has been associated with increased risk of both heart disease and cancer.[21] Yet total fat intake has also increased by 9 percent from 1967 to 1985.[22] Americans are eating too much of the wrong foods—a factor contributing to health problems.

Nutrition Education and Policy

The key to an improved diet is education. People need to have the information necessary to make intelligent decisions on both what to eat and how much. The key policy issues involve who should provide that information and in what form. Put more directly, what is the role for government in nutrition education?

The USDA has always played a key role in nutrition education. In the federal government, it is designated as the lead agency in the establishment of nutrition education policy. To implement this role, it has established the Human Nutrition Information Service, which operates

[15]Kellough, "Comments by a Task Force Member."

[16]C. Peter Timmer and Malden C. Nesheim, "Nutrition, Product Quality and Safety," in *Consensus and Conflict in U.S. Agriculture,* p. 158.

[17]Susan B. Roberts et al., "Energy Expenditure and Intake in Infants Born to Lean and Overweight Mothers," *N. Engl. J. Med.,* February 25, 1988, p. 461.

[18]B. Marston and N. Roper, "Nutrient Content of the U.S. Food Supply," in *National Food Review* (Washington, D.C.: ERS, USDA, Winter–Spring 1987), p. 19.

[19]F.J. Cronin et al., "Developing a Food Guidance System to Implement the Dietary Guidelines," *J. Nutr. Educ.* (1987), p. 283.

[20]"Food Consumption," in *National Food Review* (Washington, D.C.: ERS, USDA, 1987 Yearbook), p. 4.

[21]Cronin et al., "Developing a Food Guidance System," p. 285.

[22]K. Bunch, "Highlights of 1985 Food Consumption Data," in *National Food Review* (Washington, D.C.: ERS, USDA, Winter–Spring 1987), p. 1

through and with key public and private agencies such as the Extension Service, National Institute of Health, Food and Drug Administration, American Red Cross, American Medical Association, American Heart Association, and the American Dietetic Association.[23]

Nutrition education: prior to 1970.   Prior to 1970, nutrition educational programs were tuned to a generally higher level of physical activity than exists today. *The main message was to eat a variety of the basic food groups.* In the 1940s through much of the 1950s, there were seven basic food groups: green and yellow vegetables; oranges, tomatoes, and grapefruit; potatoes and other vegetables and fruits; milk and milk products; meat, poultry, fish, and eggs; bread, flour, and cereals; and butter and margarine. In the mid-1950s, the basic seven were condensed down to four basic food groups: fruits and vegetables; meat, poultry, fish, and eggs; milk and milk products; and bread and potatoes.

The role of controlling food intake and diet was not emphasized. As traditionally conducted, these programs did not threaten anyone's interests because they were not intended to restrict food consumption behavior.[24] It is interesting to note that neither fat nor sugar was categorized as a food group in either the basic seven or four food groups.

Nutrition education: 1970 and beyond.   The whole approach to nutrition education began to change in the 1970s. A focal point for this change was the formation and activities of the Senate Select Committee on Nutrition and Human Needs. The initial charge of this committee, chaired by George McGovern (Dem.-S.D.) was to define the extent of malnutrition, examine government feeding programs, and make recommendations.[25] Out of the committee's hearings and related activities grew the White House Conference on Food, Nutrition and Health in 1969. The conference did not focus solely on malnutrition but on the broader concept of food and nutrition policy.[26]

The next step in the developing change in nutrition policy was the formation of the National Nutrition Consortium in 1974. The result of its work was an outline of recommendations for a national nutrition policy. The work of the National Nutrition Consortium was debated extensively before the Senate Select Committee on Nutrition and Human Needs. The

[23]Cronin et al., "Developing a Food Guidance System."

[24]Peter Timmer and Malden C. Neisheim, "Nutrition, Product Quality and Safety," in *Consensus and Conflict in U.S. Agriculture,* p. 175.

[25]K. Schlossberg, "Nutrition Policy in the United States," in *Nutrition and National Policy,* B. Winikoff, ed. (Cambridge, Mass.: The MIT Press, 1978), p. 350.

[26]*White House Conference on Food, Nutrition and Health,* Final Report (Washington, D.C.: 1969).

result of the Committee's deliberations was the publication of a set of dietary goals. These **dietary goals** were as follows:

1. To avoid overweight, consume only as much energy (calories) as is expended; if overweight, decrease energy intake and increase energy expenditure.
2. Increase the consumption of complex carbohydrates and naturally occurring sugars from about 28 percent of energy intake to about 48 percent of energy intake.
3. Reduce the consumption of refined and processed sugars by about 45 percent to account for about 10 percent of total energy intake.
4. Reduce overall fat consumption from approximately 40 percent to about 30 percent of energy intake.
5. Reduce saturated fat consumption to account for about 10 percent of total energy intake; and balance that with polyunsaturated and monounsaturated fats, which should account for about 10 percent of energy intake each.
6. Reduce cholesterol consumption to about 300 milligrams a day.
7. Limit the intake of sodium by reducing the intake of salt to about 5 grams a day.[27]

Needless to say, the dietary goals caused great consternation in American agriculture. Livestock producers, dairy farmers, sugar producers, and related agribusiness interests saw the potential for substantially reduced demand and thus lower prices and incomes for their products. This adverse reaction did not discourage either the Congress or the Carter administration from further pursuing the issue. The Congress included in the 1977 farm bill authorization for USDA to be the lead agency in nutrition policy. In doing so, it recognized increasing evidence of a relationship between diet and many of the leading causes of death and health problems. In 1980, USDA and the Department of Health, Education and Welfare (now Health and Human Services) issued a report titled, *Nutrition and Your Health, Dietary Guidelines for Americans*. The **dietary guidelines** were not as specific as the dietary goals:

1. Eat a variety of foods.
2. Maintain ideal weight.
3. Avoid too much fat, saturated fat, and cholesterol.
4. Eat foods with adequate starch and fiber.

[27]*Dietary Goals for the United States*, 2nd ed. (Washington, D.C.: Select Committee on Nutrition and Human Needs, U.S. Senate, December 1977). An earlier version of these goals was published in February 1977. The revision lowered recommendations on carbohydrate intake and raised the recommended salt intake.

5. Avoid too much sugar.

6. Avoid too much sodium.

7. If you drink alcohol, do so in moderation.[28]

Despite their lack of specificity, the guidelines drew a negative reaction at least as strong as the dietary goals. In this case, the reverberations extended through the countryside as employees of the Extension Service began to adopt new educational materials based on the guidelines. These educational materials expanded the four basic food groups to five: fruits and vegetables; bread and cereal; milk and cheese; meat, poultry, fish, and beans; and fats, sweets, and alcohol. *The basic educational message switched from variety to variety and moderation.* No servings of the fats, sweets, and alcohol group are recommended.[29] Serving sizes were reduced throughout, with less meat used in the menus and recipes.

When the new educational approach was taken to the country by extension nutrition specialists, it was not unusual for farm groups, particularly cattlemen and dairymen, to question them and their administrators regarding the use of the guidelines and related educational materials. Some educational programs were stopped—at least temporarily. Timmer and Nesheim put the controversy in the following perspective: "When nutritional educators begin to mount programs aimed at reducing the intake of foods thought to be associated with major public health problems such as coronary heart disease, cancer, and diabetes, then opposition and widespread controversy erupted quickly."[30]

More fuel was added to the diet–health, nutrition education controversy in 1982 when a National Academy of Sciences scientific advisory committee found that foods such as fats and smoked foods appear to be linked to certain types of cancer. The committee recommended reduced salt and smoked cured food intake, reduced fat intake, increased fruit, vegetable, and whole grain cereal consumption, and alcohol consumption in moderation. The National Cattlemen's Association called the panel's findings "inconclusive and premature."[31]

Politicians, however, had difficulty arguing against the moderation message. Even the Reagan administration, which had made a campaign issue out of the dietary goals, the guidelines, and Carol Foreman, did not repudiate them. In 1982, Secretary of Agriculture Block appointed a committee of scientists to review the dietary guidelines published in 1980. In

---

[28]*Nutrition and Your Health, Dietary Guidelines for Americans* (Washington, D.C.: USDA, HEW, 1980).

[29]Davis et al., *Food.*

[30]Timmer and Nesheim, "Nutrition, Product Quality and Safety," p. 175.

[31]Bart Schorr, "Certain Foods May Increase Cancer Risk Committee Says, Urging Changes in Diet," *The Wall Street Journal* (New York), June 17, 1982, p. 4, col. 2.

their 1985 report, the committee recommended only minor changes in the dietary guidelines and some clarifying statements in the accompanying text.[32] The second edition of the dietary guidelines forms the basis for federal dietary guidance policy.[33]

This example of public policy teaches an extremely important lesson. *Despite much controversy surrounding the dietary goals and guidelines, the scientific base of their content, combined with the persistence of their professional advocates, allowed them to survive and gain general acceptance.* Clearly, the guidelines are still controversial, but they are based in science and have become increasingly supported by research.

Effects of the guidelines.   From their inception in the mid-1970s, the guidelines do appear to be having some impact on American food consumption habits. Studies of American consumers indicate that a health trend is becoming part of the American life-style. Most Americans (87 percent) know that their choice of foods has long-term effects on health, including heart problems, weight gain, cholesterol buildup, high blood pressure, diabetes, and cancer. Up to two-thirds of the respondents knew that salt was associated with high blood pressure, eggs were associated with cholesterol, and fats contributed to heart disease.[34]

Some improvements in diets have been observed. Consumption of nutritious foods such as lowfat milk, yogurt, fresh fruit, fresh vegetables, chicken, and fish are up. Yet so is the consumption of fat and sugar.[35] Average cholesterol intake exceeds 450 mg per day, while the guidelines recommend 300 mg per day.[36]

Federal information and education designed to improve diet–health relationships will continue. The controversy surrounding these recommendations will also continue. The effects of changing consumption patterns will be felt by farmers initially in the prices they receive and subsequently in production.

HUNGER IN AMERICA

Hunger may be defined as the sustained failure to consume nutrients in sufficient quantity and in the proper proportion to sustain normal body functions. Hunger in America became a major issue in the mid-1960s.

[32]*Report of the Dietary Guidelines Advisory Committee on the Dietary Guidelines for Americans,* Admin. Rep. 100 (Washington, D.C.: USDA, 1985).

[33]*Nutrition and Your Health: Dietary Guidelines for Americans,* 2nd ed., Home Garden Bull. 232 (Washington, D.C.: USDA, HEW, 1985).

[34]A.E. Sloan, "Educating a Nutrition-Wise Public," *J. Nutr. Educ.* (1987), p. 303.

[35]"Food Consumption", p. 3.

[36]Cronin et al., "Developing a Food Guidance System," p. 286; Donald H. Dunn, "Curbing Killer Cholesterol," *Bus. Week,* October 26, 1987, p. 122.

The National Advisory Commission on Rural Poverty was created to study, evaluate, and make recommendations on means of removing poverty in America. Its report, *The People Left Behind,* focused increased attention on the problems of the poor—only one of which is hunger.[37] This and subsequent studies identified hunger in America as a major national problem and concern.

A late-1960 USDA study found that one-fifth of the households in the United States had "poor" diets. Thirty-six percent of the low-income households were found to subsist on poor diets by the same study. A team of medical doctors made on-site visits in several poor counties and shocked the nation by its conclusion that people in 280 counties were living in such distressed conditions "as to warrant a Presidential declaration naming them as hunger areas."[38]

In the late 1960s and early 1970s, the elimination of hunger and poverty in America became a major policy goal. A plethora of programs was established as part of President Johnson's Great Society plan. Many of these—including the food stamp; women, infant, children; free or subsidized lunch; and expanded nutrition programs—emphasized food assistance and education.

In the 1970s, the hunger problem appeared to dissipate as the economy expanded and the Great Society programs were implemented. A 1979 study by the Field Foundation, an organization dedicated to the elimination of hunger, comes to about the same conclusion. "Our first and overwhelming impression is that there are far fewer grossly malnourished people in this country today than there were ten years ago . . . tremendous progress has been made."[39]

In the 1980s, the hunger problem reappeared, not with the vigor of the 1950s and 60s, but nonetheless serious. As the unemployment rate increased from 5.8 percent in 1979 to 9.7 percent in 1982, the poverty rate increased from 11.7 percent to 15.0 percent, respectively. However, the Reagan administration held the line on food stamp expenditures and actually cut them in calendar year 1982 (Fig. 13.3). Poverty rates remained above 14 percent through 1985.

In reaction to this deteriorating situation, a Physicians' Task Force on Hunger in America was appointed. The Physicians' Task Force concluded that of 35 million people in poverty, 20 million go hungry.[40]

[37]National Advisory Commission on Rural Poverty, *The People Left Behind* (Washington, D.C.: 1967).

[38]Citizens Board of Inquiry into Hunger and Malnutrition in the United States, *Hunger USA* (Boston: Beacon Press, 1968).

[39]Nick Kotz, *Hunger in America: The Federal Response* (New York: The Field Foundation, April 1979).

[40]J. L. Brown, "Physicians Task Force on Hunger in America," in *Poverty and Hunger in America,* Serial 99-4 (Washington, D.C.: Committee on Ways and Means, U.S. House of Representatives, April 30, 1985), p. 11.

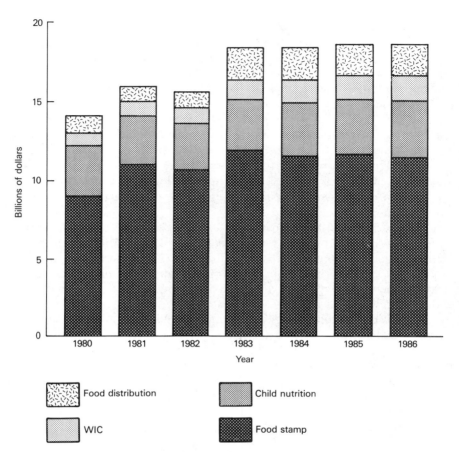

Figure 13.3 Federal expenditures on the food programs.
Source: Economic Research Service, *National Food Review* (Washington, D.C.: USDA, various issues).

Causes of Hunger

How is it possible for hunger to be a problem in a food-rich nation? Most public policy discussions on that topic focus on three factors:

• Lack of resources
• Lack of access
• Lack of knowledge

Lack of resources.   The American food system is market-oriented. The available foods, like other goods and services, are rationed in the market to those with the resources to purchase them. To put it simply, it is frequently argued that a large portion of the population does not earn enough to purchase nutritionally adequate diets.

Data for 1987 on the distribution of income indicate that those families having the lowest one-fifth of the U.S. income distribution would spend over 35 percent of their income on food based on a low-cost nutritious diet prepared entirely at home. For a moderate-cost nutritious diet, over 45 percent of income would be spent on food. The lower one-fifth of the black population would spend about two-thirds of its income on food for the low-cost diet. This obviously is the center of the hunger problem.

How to deal with the hunger aspects of unequal income distribution has been a matter of public debate. Many believe that a *lack of income indicates a lack of initiative.* Others argue that *access to food is a basic human right, not something to be "earned."* The Rome World Food Conference in 1974 and subsequently the U.S. Congress passed such "right to food" resolutions. Policy solutions usually fall somewhere between these two views.

Lack of access.   Even if sufficient income is available, consumers must have access to food in order to avoid malnutrition. Natural disasters, like floods or earthquakes, can cause hunger if food supply lines are cut off. Lack of access can, however, also be a problem for those living in remote areas, such as on Indian reservations. It has also been identified as a problem in the city ghettos, among the elderly, and for some children.

The question of access to food has been at the center of many food policy debates. Congressional inquiries from time to time have focused attention on the exodus of grocery stores from the inner city. The issue was hotly debated when the food stamp program replaced the direct government distribution of surplus foods.

Lack of knowledge.   Educational level has been identified as one of the most important factors influencing food choice. Data from the Household Food Consumption Surveys indicate that, on average, the highly educated spend more and buy a better mix of food per person. After a thorough analysis of the data, one researcher concluded: "Regardless of the amount of money spent per person for food, among households with less education, there was a larger proportion with poor diets . . . the percent of poor diets increased as education decreased."[41]

---

[41]T. K. Meyers, "Can a Case Be Made for Nutrition Education?" address at the Third International Congress, Food Science and Technology, Washington, D.C.; August 9, 1970. For more recent confirmation of the relation between education and nutrition, see Jean-Paul Chaves and K. O. Keplinger, "Impact of Domestic Food Programs on Nutrient Intake of Low Income Persons in the United States," *South J. Agric. Econ.* (July 1983), pp. 155–162.

This factor, too, has been at the center of public policy debates about food. Nutrition education programs in particular have been widely supported because the data are so convincing. But, as noted previously, there is considerable disagreement over the content of the nutrition message and how it is to be delivered.

Food Assistance Policy and Program Alternatives

Like the commodity programs, the national commitment to eliminate hunger is an outgrowth of the Great Depression. The early food assistance programs were designed to dispose of surpluses—they were producer-oriented. Beginning in the 1960s, the emphasis shifted from farm income support to the elimination of domestic hunger and improvements in nutritional health within the general population and among target groups such as school children and pregnant women. While the program emphasis is very likely to shift some over time, the policy emphasis on improving nutrition is likely to continue. The focal point of the debate centers around the options of no food assistance, food distribution, food stamps, and welfare reform.

No federal public assistance.   *The free market distributes food and all other goods and services on the basis of ability to pay.* Those with adequate incomes are able to make the needed purchases. Those with less income are not capable of purchasing as much. The poor become dependent on their families and on private organizations such as churches and the Salvation Army for assistance and care. Families of the poor are also frequently poor. Dependence on private organizations does not spread the burden of unemployment and low pay over the general public.

It is precisely this result that has led over time to the development of public food assistance programs. Markets allocate food based on the ability to pay; the nutritional needs of people depend primarily on biological factors. Private relief operates on a highly imperfect basis.

Publicly financed food assistance programs have generally lacked the support of free-market advocates. They have argued that such programs tend to reward the lazy and unproductive. There is an element of truth in that charge. However, certain members of all societies have limited resources through little or no fault of their own, at least for a time. Examples include the involuntarily unemployed (the steel worker whose plant is closed down because its technology is obsolete), those physically or mentally unable to work, the elderly, and children.

Adequate nutrition is critical to breaking the cycle of poverty. Neither adults nor children are able to perform up to their physical or mental capabilities when they do not receive nutritionally adequate diets. An adequate and balanced distribution of the food supply has also been an important element in political stability in almost all organized societies. For all these reasons, it is difficult to provide even a single example of a country that relies exclusively on free-market allocation of food.

Food distribution programs.   The Federal Surplus Relief Corporation (FSRC) was organized in October 1933. It had two primary purposes:

- To relieve the national economic emergency in agriculture by expanding markets for farm products
- To relieve the hardship and suffering caused by unemployment through purchasing, handling, storing, and processing surplus agricultural commodities

This government agency, in cooperation with the Agricultural Adjustment Administration, purchased surplus agricultural commodities for direct distribution to the unemployed and their families.

In 1935, the FSRC became the Federal Surplus Commodities Corporation. The name change reflected a change in program emphasis from general help for the unemployed to specific help for the farm sector through surplus disposal and the encouragement of domestic consumption. This change in program thrust was accompanied by an amendment to the Agricultural Adjustment Act of 1933 that for 30 years would serve as the cornerstone for funding food assistance programs—Section 32.

Section 32 appropriated 30 percent of the gross receipts from duties collected under the customs laws (tariffs) for exclusive use by the secretary of agriculture to encourage exports and the domestic consumption of "surplus" commodities. Surplus food distribution programs were developed which provided commodities such as butter, cheese, flour, cornmeal, and dry beans directly to the poor and to school lunch programs.

The most serious problem with direct food distribution was that there was no choice on the specific commodities received. As a result, waste was noticeable. In addition, there were complaints that donated foods were displacing regular market purchases. By the late 1930s, the need for a new system was clear.

Food stamps.   A novel food stamp idea grew from this dissatisfaction with direct food distribution. The plan generated substantial food industry support because it involved the use of commercial trade channels for surplus food distribution. Needy families would be authorized to purchase orange stamps approximately equal to their average food expenditures. These stamps could then be used to purchase, at regular prices, any type of food. For each dollar of orange stamps purchased, households would receive 50 cents worth of blue bonus stamps. Blue stamps would be used only for those foods declared in surplus by the secretary of agriculture.

The food stamp plan actually had no statutory authority of its own but was rationalized as a surplus disposal method under Section 32. This fact stands as a constant reminder of the wide-ranging flexibility to make policy used by the executive branch during the Roosevelt administration.

The early food stamp plan received widespread support. Both the Democratic and Republican party platforms called for continuation of the program in 1940. The food distribution industry supported the program with enthusiasm. In the years that followed, the program was put into effect in nearly half of the counties in the country. These counties contained almost two-thirds of the population of the United States according to the 1940 census.

Secretary of Agriculture Claude Wickard ended the program in March 1943, by stating that the conditions which had brought it into existence—unmarketable food surpluses and widespread unemployment—no longer existed. The program ended largely without fanfare; the nation was preoccupied with war. But the seeds had been sown for later development of a nationwide food assistance effort based primarily on human need rather than on farm income support.

Food Assistance Program Expansion.   After World War II, food assistance programs once again emphasized direct distribution of commodities that were in surplus. Section 32 provided a continuing source of funding. But in a land of abundance, some still went without adequate food.

President John Kennedy, in his first executive order, issued a command to expand domestic food distribution. The executive order did not mention food stamps. But in early February 1961, he announced that food stamp pilot programs were to be initiated. This decision was to become the forerunner of the food stamp program, which was made part of permanent legislation in 1964.

Child nutrition programs were also expanded early in the decade. In 1961 the National School Lunch Act was amended to include authorizations for special assistance cash subsidies to the school lunch programs. The school breakfast program and broader nutrition aid for children from needy families were initiated in 1966.

Rapid expansion of food assistance efforts took place during the 1970s. This expansion was an outgrowth of a national effort to overcome poverty, which was given considerable importance by the widely publicized study entitled *Hunger USA*.[42] The expansion of food assistance programs had the following characteristics:

• Total food assistance spending increased from $1 billion in 1969 to nearly $19 billion in 1983 and then leveled out.

[42]Citizens Board of Inquiry, *Hunger USA*.

- The number of persons receiving some sort of food assistance tripled.
- Targeted programs for pregnant women and infant children, the elderly, and children in day care centers, among others, were established.
- The primary emphasis shifted from essentially surplus disposal to mostly income supplement and improving the nutritional health of the nation's low-income people, yet surplus disposal still has a role.

The Modern Food Stamp Program.   Since the early 1970s, the food stamp program (FSP) has been America's primary food assistance program. In the 1980s, FSP expenditures accounted for nearly 60 percent of all food assistance spending.

The food stamp program, like its predecessor, was designed to provide low-income households with the food-buying income necessary to purchase more nutritious diets through regular market channels. The total value of the monthly food stamp allotment is based on three factors: food costs, income, and family size. The basic guide used to allocate food stamps is that households should not have to spend more than 30 percent of their income to purchase a nutritionally adequate diet. Suppose, for example, that a family of four earns $750 per month and that USDA calculates that a low-cost nutritious diet (referred to as the thrifty food plan) would cost that household about $70 per week ($280 per month). That household would receive about $55 per month in food stamps ($750 × 0.30 = $225; $280 − $225 = $55). A household that earns no income would receive the cost of the thrifty food plan (published monthly by USDA) less 1 percent. The 1 percent deduction was added in 1982 as part of the Omnibus Budget Reconciliation Act.

In 1986, participation in the food stamp program averaged just over 19 million in people—down from over 20 million in the early 1980s. Benefits per recipient averaged about $46 per month.

The food stamp program has been much debated. The issues that form the basis for the controversy related primarily to the values and beliefs of the American middle class. Regardless of the evidence, many Americans are unwilling to believe that as many as 1 in 10 needs or deserves public food assistance. A list of the questions most frequently debated would include:

- **How should program eligibility be determined?** (Who deserves assistance?) Most people accept the fact of poverty in America. Whether all households with less than a poverty income deserve food assistance is another matter. Some suggest that work should be a condition for receiving stamps. But many recipients cannot work because they have to care for their children.

- **How much assistance is adequate?** The thrifty food plan, based on recommended daily allowances (RDA), serves as the basis for how much assistance should be provided. This plan is the least costly of four family food plans developed by USDA. It specifies the quantity of foods in 15 different food groups that families with different-age children might be expected to use to meet the recommended dietary allowances.[43]

- **Should food stamps be available to strikers?** In 1980, the Congress limited the eligibility of strikers for food stamps. Those who chose to strike, apparently, were considered to have voluntarily put themselves in a low-income position. In 1988, the U.S. Supreme Court ruled that such limitations were within the power of the Congress and not a denial of equal treatment under law.

- **Should food stamps be used to purchase items other than nutritious foods?** Most persons defend with a vengeance their right to make product purchases without government interference. Still, the most frequent criticisms of the food stamp program are that recipient households are seen purchasing foods that others cannot afford and that money that would have been spent on food is used to purchase cigarettes and liquor instead of more nutritious food items. The available data on food stamp use do not support those criticisms, but such evidence has not reduced the popularity of the claims.[44]

- **Do food stamp recipients have better nutrition?** In terms of the nutrients that the recipients are most likely to be deficient in, food stamps have been found to result in a statistically significant, but small, improvement in nutrition.[45] However, there is also evidence that as income increases, the effectiveness of food stamps in improving nutrition diminishes to zero. Food stamp recipients having a college education spend no more on food than nonrecipients having comparable education and income.[46] How can this be if they

[43]Interestingly, the thrifty food plan was developed by USDA on court order after a finding that its predecessor, the economy food plan, did not provide sufficient daily allowances to maintain adequate diets and did not discriminate sufficiently among the sexes and ages of family members.

[44]Sylvia Lane, "Poverty, Food Selection and Human Nutrition," in *Agricultural-Food Policy Review,* AFPR-2 (Washington, D.C.: ESCS, USDA, September 1978), pp. 39–44; and Sylvia Lane, "Food Distribution and Food Stamp Program Effects on Nutritional Achievement of Low Income Households in Kern County, California," *Program Evaluation: Completed Studies* (Washington, D.C.: FNS, USDA, April 1977).

[45]Chavas and Keplinger, "Impact of Domestic Food Programs," p. 162; J. Allen and K. Godson, "Food Consumption and Nutritional Status of Low Income Households," in *National Food Review* (Washington, D.C.: ERS, USDA, Spring 1985), pp. 27–31.

[46]Jean-Paul Chaves and M. L. Young, "Effects of the Food Stamp Program on Food Consumption in the Southern United States," *South J. Agric. Econ.* (July 1982), p. 136.

are on food stamps? *These recipients simply use food stamps in place of income that would have been spent on food. Food stamps thus free up income that can be used for nonfood purposes. In other words, giving food stamps, as opposed to giving cash, does not mean that either more food will be purchased or that the nutrition of the recipients will be improved.* Therefore, it is extremely difficult to restrict the use of food stamps or the use of the income freed up by food stamps.

- **Do food stamps benefit farmers?**   To the extent that food stamps increase consumption, farmers benefit from food stamps. Research results suggest that increases in consumption average 40 to 50 cents for each dollar of food stamp expenditures.[47] Most of increased consumption would go to producers of cereal grains, beef, pork, dairy products, and poultry.

These conclusions lead to mixed emotions about the merits of the food stamp program as opposed to straight cash welfare payments. While farmers benefit, they also question whether welfare programs foster a lack of individual initiative. Perhaps the greatest farmer benefit from food programs is not the increased consumption but the ability to bargain politically (horse trade) for farm programs. As noted previously, farm bills are also food bills. This reality brings the farmer and urban interests together.

School lunch programs.   Surplus disposal activities of the Federal Surplus Commodities Corporation, together with appropriated monies from Section 32, also helped give rise to federal child-feeding programs. At first, surplus commodities were disposed of using schools as the distribution points. This led to the spread of school lunch programs nationwide. In 1937 more than 3800 schools received commodities for lunch programs serving 342,000 children daily. Five years later 79,000 schools were serving surplus commodities to 5.3 million children.[48] But as with the food stamp plan, food donations dropped sharply from 1942 to 1944, raising serious questions about the long-term stability of the school meal programs.

Domestic food assistance to the nation's school children was formally established when the National School Lunch Act was passed in 1946. As stated in the authorizing legislation, the objectives of the National School Lunch Program (NSLP) were to "safeguard the health and

[47]Chaves and Keplinger, "Impact of Domestic Food Programs;" Chaves and Young, "Effects of the Food Stamp Program;"Allen and Godson, "Food Consumption and Nutritional Status;" and William T. Boehm and Paul E. Nelson, "Food Expenditure Consequences of Welfare Reform," *Agricultural-Food Policy Review*, AFPR-2 (Washington, D.C.: ESCS, USDA, September 1978), p. 48.

[48]*Agricultural Statistics* (Washington, D.C.: USDA, 1952), p. 392.

well-being of the Nation's children and to encourage the domestic consumption of nutritious agricultural commodities and other food." To do this, the federal government encouraged and assisted public and nonprofit private schools of high school grade and under to serve well-balanced lunches to children. This assistance has, over the years, included the following:

- A basic cash and donated food subsidy for all lunches; children from low-income families receive an added subsidy. Initially, the emphasis was on foods purchased under Section 32, but over time, cash subsidies became more important.
- Cash subsidies for school breakfast provided mostly to children of lower-income families at reduced prices.
- Funds to partially reimburse states for undertaking the added administrative activities.
- Funds to help schools acquire food service equipment (discontinued in 1981).
- Funds for nutrition education programs and special development projects.

From 1947 to 1981, federal expenditures for the National School Lunch Program increased from less than $100 million to about $4.6 billion (cash and commodities) and then leveled out.[49] Over time, the federal government has been paying for an increasingly larger share of the total cost of the program. In addition, an increasing share of school lunches has been either free or at a reduced price. Free and reduced-price lunches are factors that have sharply increased the cost of the school lunch program. In 1986, out of 24 million participants in the school lunch program, about 50 percent received either free or reduced-price lunches.[50] In 1982, major cuts in the school lunch program was proposed by the Reagan administration. The stated objective of these cuts was to reduce subsidies to medium- and high-income families. These efforts only resulted in stable school lunch expenditures throughout the 1980s.

The overall attitude toward the school lunch program appears to be considerably more favorable than that toward the food stamp program. Yet several issues exist:

- Pressure continues from producer interests to utilize the program as a surplus disposal program. School lunch accounts for over 4 percent of the demand for milk. During the mid-1980s, school lunch was

[49]Ibid.; and *Agricultural Statistics*, 1986, p. 499.

[50]M. Matsumoto, "Recent Trends in Domestic Food Programs," in *National Food Review* (Washington, D.C.: ERS, USDA, Winter–Spring 1987), p. 24.

used as an outlet for surplus cheese and beef purchased to reduce the price depressing effect of the dairy termination program. Schools resist pressures to use the program for surplus disposal, which dictates what they serve in lunches. Many would rather receive all cash with the flexibility to buy whatever foods meet the specifications of their dietitians.

- The minimum nutrient requirements for the program have been specified by the USDA. These requirements have always been controversial and politically sensitive. A 1981 cost-cutting move to get ketchup classified as a serving of vegetable in the school lunch program was one of the factors resulting in the dismissal of the head of USDA's food assistance programs.

- The quality of lunches varies widely. Since the 1970s, an effort has been made to serve a larger proportion of foods that children like to eat, such as the "All-American Meal" of hamburger, French fries, tomatoes, lettuce, and milk. However, meal quality still remains highly variable.

- The extent of the federal subsidy became a major issue in the early 1980s as the Reagan administration attempted to reduce costs. Shifting a higher proportion of the costs to the children raised questions as to how many would drop out of the program and thus receive inadequate nutrition. Since the evidence clearly indicates that school lunch improves nutrition,[51] support for the program has been particularly strong.

Women, infant, children program.   The Women, Infant, Children Supplemental Food Program (WIC) is targeted toward mothers with children who are already participants in other welfare programs. *WIC integrates health care, nutrition education, food distribution and food stamps into a comprehensive health and nutrition program.* In the nutrition program emphasis is placed on providing high-quality protein to pregnant and nursing mothers and young children.

WIC has been demonstrated to be one of the most successful food assistance programs.[52] A North Carolina study found increased birthweight of babies, reduced incidence of anemia, and improved nutrient intake by the participants.[53] A Harvard University study estimated that up to $3 in

[51]David W. Price, Donald A. West, Genevieve E. Scheier, and Dorothy Z. Price, "Food Delivery Programs and Other Factors Affecting Nutrient Intake of Children," *Am. J. Agric. Econ.* (November 1978), pp. 609–618.

[52]Carol Tucker Foreman, "Human Nutrition and Food Policy," in *Agricultural-Food Policy Review,* p 19.

[53]Benjamin Sexauer, "Food Programs and Nutritional Intake: What Evidence," in *Agricultural-Food Policy Review,* p. 41.

hospital costs are saved for every $1 spent on the prenatal component of
WIC.[54] Chavas and Keplinger list crucial factors that contribute to the
WIC program's success in improving nutrition:

- Precise targeting to pregnant and breast-feeding women, and in-
  fants and children under 4 years old
- Showing evidence of nutritional deficiency
- Providing selected food items in addition to food stamps
- Combining nutrition education with food assistance

WIC does not have as good an image as its record of meeting its objectives would imply. The reason probably lies in the notion that the program fosters unwed mothers and a welfare-dependent life-style.

Welfare reform.   Major questions about the form of public assistance have been raised in the 1970s and 1980s. As the food programs
grew in number and cost, so did the number of critics. Welfare rights advocates argued for fewer restrictions on expenditures—for programs that
could allow recipients to make purchase decisions like other citizens.
Taxpayers complained that the programs were too costly, too complicated, and not sufficiently restrictive. Welfare reform became a national
political issue in the early 1970s.

The food assistance programs were a major part of the welfare reform proposals. Several proposals were made to cash-out all programs of
special assistance for one cash payment. That is, the basic notion is that
all welfare programs would be consolidated into a single cash assistance
program. School lunch assistance would also be in the form of cash as opposed to the combination of cash and commodities.

Welfare reform raises at least three important policy issues for agriculture:

- *A simple cash transfer system is less effective in enhancing farm income than programs that target the aid to food purchases directly.*
  When people are given the choice, the tendency is to spend 10 to 20
  cents out of each additional dollar on food. If the food aid is direct,
  there is less choice. Farmers gain more for each dollar's worth of
  food aid, although the gain is not as great as sometimes suggested.
- *Targeted food assistance programs are more efficient in improving
  the nutritional status of the recipient.* Taxpayers concerned about the
  nutritional status of the poor are able to assure themselves of increased food intake if the programs restrict the recipients' choice.
  Cash-out debates in the Congress almost always include discussions

[54]Michael Reese et al., "Life Below the Poverty Line," *Newsweek*, April 5, 1982, p. 25.

that focus on whether children of the poor would really be helped if adult recipients used the cash to purchase alcohol and gamble. That is largely an uncontrollable issue unless food programs are to be highly targeted and controlled as in the case of WIC.

• *Food assistance programs have generally been part of major farm legislation and appropriations.* They provide a reason for urban congressmen to vote for farm programs and for rural congressmen to vote for welfare programs. Urban support for traditional farm programs could be considerably reduced without food assistance programs.

There is far from unanimous agreement on the political significance of moving the food assistance programs out of USDA. One point of view suggests a transfer of food assistance out of USDA because appropriations for food assistance programs are competitive with farm program appropriations. Others argue that to remove those programs from USDA would leave the department as a farm advocacy organization with a very small budget, which would ultimately erode the broad base of support required for USDA to remain a separate cabinet-level department.

When the welfare reform issue is ultimately seriously considered by the Congress, the position of the agriculture establishment will be most interesting. Each organization will have to evaluate not only the impact on its membership but also the impact on its effectiveness as an organization. The perceptiveness of farm organization leaders in weighing these impacts could ultimately also affect their positions within the organizations!

THE PERVASIVENESS OF FOOD POLICY ISSUES

Everyone can and does get excited about food policy—farmers, processors, retailers, consumers, and policymakers. Everyone must decide what foods to consume and in what quantity they should be consumed. No one debates this point. The crucial question is the role that government should play in attempting to influence what people eat. This is an issue that will not go away. It will be around long after farm programs are abandoned—if that ever happens!

ADDITIONAL READINGS

1. The best current source of information on food policy issues and programs is the *National Food Review,* a publication issued three times a year by ERS, USDA, Washington, D.C.

2. A series of articles in *Agricultural-Food Policy Review,* AFPR-2 (Washington, D.C.: ESCS, USDA, September 1978), provides a good review of the issues in food assistance programs.

3. One of the most comprehensive statements on food safety policy was given by Carol Foreman before the Agricultural Outlook Committee on Agriculture, U.S. House of Representatives, on September 16, 1980.

4. F. J. Cronin et al., "Developing a Food Guidance System to Supplement Dietary Guidelines," *J. Nutr. Educ.* (1987), pp. 281–301, is an excellent article on the technical development of the second edition of the dietary goals and guidelines.

Chapter 14

Resource Problems and Policies

Ecologists believe that a bird in the bush is worth two in the hand.

Stanley C. Pearson

From the time of the founding of the American republic until only recently, the nation's natural resources base, including its land, forests, water, minerals, oil, and gas, was viewed as being virtually unlimited. The development and growth of the national economy was seen as being closely linked to the use of those resources. National policy was and to a large extent still is directed at obtaining the rapid development and use of the resource base. This policy has been pursued primarily through economic incentives—making the resources widely available for use at relatively low prices. It is a policy that is now under question.

Resource development and utilization occurred rapidly as the nation's population grew. The frontier was closed after the first hundred years; an energy crisis occurred before the end of the second hundred years; and availability problems became visible with water and other resources. A serious concern emerged in the 1970s over the despoliation of the environment, occurring in part because of the manner of use of the natural resources. In the 1980s, the focal point of concern became the interrelated problems of soil erosion and water quality. This interrelationship results from the interaction of soil erosion and modern farming practices, involving the use of chemicals and commercial fertilizer, that leads

to the degradation in the quality of the water supply—including both surface water and groundwater.

THE ISSUE OF LIMITED RESOURCES

From a perhaps overly simplistic perspective, there are two basic types of
resources—renewable and nonrenewable. **Nonrenewable resources**
have a *limited supply in the relevant decision time frame.* For example,
some underground aquifers have a limited supply in that they do not recharge or do so only very slowly. Once water is used from such aquifers, it
is gone. In other words, there is only a given stock of nonrenewable resources.

    Renewable resources *are capable of being replenished.* They are,
in essence, a flow resource while nonrenewable resources are a stock resource. The water in the Mississippi River might be viewed as a renewable resource in that it is continuously regenerated.

    In reality, it may be argued that all resources are nonrenewable in
that once used, they will never be the same. At least the cost of restoring
the resource to its original state is either prohibitively high or the time it
takes for restoration is so long that it is not the same.

    The existence of nonrenewable resources places an inordinate bur-
den of responsibility on a society and its policymakers for the welfare of
future generations. *Use of a nonrenewable resource means that some future society is inevitably denied access to the resource.* In response, it
might be argued that the role of technological change is one of overcoming constraints of nonrenewable resources. Such an argument, however,
is not very satisfying to the parent whose child is dying of cancer apparently caused by a chemical residue in the water supply.

    *The issue of limited resources is not only one of absolute supply limits
but also degradation in the quality of resources.* Despite surpluses, substantial concern continues to exist over the supply of the essential agricultural inputs: land, energy, and water.[1] The focal points of supply concerns are on the conversion of cropland to nonagricultural uses, loss of
soil due to erosion, increased energy costs, and the availability of water
for irrigation. Concerns about the quality of resources center on water
quality, soil erosion, and the potential for climatic change.

    Increased visibility of these concerns has put resource policy on the
agenda of policymakers. Resource issues are largely public interest issues. They can either be antagonists to farmers or sometimes become part
of a coalition needed to enact a farm bill and achieve other policy objectives—as happened in the 1985 farm bill.

    [1]Sandra S. Batie and Robert G. Healy, "The Future of American Agriculture," *Sci.
Am.* (February 1983), pp. 45–53.

THE LAND RESOURCE

A major concern of the federal government in the early years of the nation was getting the vast land areas settled. Land was made available either free or at very little cost to those who were willing to farm it. The population grew rapidly and settlement was soon achieved. Land use patterns were firmly established by the beginning of the twentieth century. The quantity of land in farms has since remained a relatively stable 1.1 billion acres.

Several attitudes about land have proved instrumental in determining the resource policies pursued for over 200 years. From a tradition traced to the values and beliefs of the nation's European ancestors, the American immigrants viewed land ownership as an absolute right. Private property rights are thus particularly strong with regard to sale and use of land. Because of great advancements in crop yields, substitutes, in effect, have been developed for cropland. This has influenced the value placed on conserving the land base. That is, with the ability to substitute inputs for land, conservation of land has been viewed as less important.

When population pressures intensified, the demand for homes, recreation, roads, services, and food increased while the quality of the environment declined. Questions began to arise which almost inherently conflict with traditional property rights.

- What are the rights of the individual for using the land as opposed to the rights of the society to determine the manner in which the land is to be used?
- How well is the market for resources working in protecting the quality of resources in comparison with the demands of society?
- To what degree should land use policies be tailored to needs of particular areas by state and/or local governments versus more uniform federal policies?
- What assurance is there that future generations will have an adequate supply of resources to satisfy their food needs?

Basic to all these concerns is having enough land to provide adequate amounts of food for the American people. Questions remain on the nature of priorities for using land resources to feed people in other countries.[2] Any evidence of depleting the land resource base through irreversible loss or through prodigal use that depletes its inherent productivity or despoils the environment has become a cause for public concern. The land resource problem thus relates directly to:

[2]Lauren Soth, "The Grain Export Boom: Should It Be Tamed," *Foreign Affairs* (1981), pp. 896–912.

- The size and productivity of the land base
- Whether the land base is being depleted through wind and water erosion
- The nature of agricultural–nonagricultural competition for land

The Land Base

The total land area of the United States is estimated to be 2.264 billion acres. Only 20.8 percent of this is cropland (Table 14.1). Another 25.9 percent is pasture and rangeland. Thus about 45 percent of the total U.S. land area is used for agricultural purposes.

The 472 million acres classified as cropland represent all land in the crop rotation rather than the acreage used directly in crop production. Part of the cropland base is used for crops, part for pasture, and part is idle in any given year. In 1980, the land used for crops was 380 million acres, 80 percent of the cropland base. The 87 million acres not cropped could be cropped, and some fraction of the grassland pasture and range could be converted into cropland. However, all the land that is not now cropped but potentially could be is presumably less productive and more subject to erosion than that now cultivated. The conversion of this land will occur only when it is economically feasible for farmers to do so. This happens when prices and the net returns per acre are sufficient to repay the investment required for development.

Although the size of the land base expands with increases in real farm prices and incomes, there are clearly limits to this expansion within the range of relevant prices. These limits make it particularly important that the quality of the agricultural land base be maintained.

Soil Conservation

The degradation of the land through erosion by wind and water is one of the more widely recognized but least understood of the problems of

TABLE 14.1   United States Land Use Patterns

Use	Acres (millions)	Percent of Total
Cropland	472	20.8
Permanent grassland, pasture, and range	587	25.9
Forest land	703	31.1
Urban transportation, defense, recreation, and other special uses	151	6.7
Miscellaneous other land	351	15.5
Total	2264	100.0

Source: 1981 Handbook of Agricultural Charts, AH-592 (Washington, D.C.: ERS, USDA, October 1981), p. 3.

agriculture. Some effects of erosion are readily apparent to the public. The dust bowl of the 1930s led to a substantial and continuing federal policy to encourage soil conservation. The Soil Erosion Service was formed in the early 1930s as a temporary agency of the Department of the Interior. In 1935, in the wake of the Dust Bowl disaster, it was renamed the Soil Conservation Service and made a permanent part of USDA. It was augmented in 1937 by a system of conservation districts which now govern, through locally elected boards, soil and water conservation policies in nearly every county of the United States.

The major soil conservation concern involved whether farming practices are slowly but persistently exhausting soil resources, thereby making future food supplies uncertain. Ironically, even with the long history of concern about soil erosion, there were no reliable estimates of the extent and severity of the erosion of the nation's agricultural land prior to 1977. The Soil Conservation Service in that year completed a national resource inventory of the soil and water conservation problems.

Sheet and rill erosion by water, the generally uniform removal of a thin layer of the soil surface, is the most prevalent form of erosion on agricultural land. Total sheet and rill erosion in 1977 was estimated at 4.044 billion tons of soil, the equivalent of 2,247,000 acre-feet. Wind erosion in the Great Plains amounted to 1.462 billion tons, 812,000 acre-feet. Gully erosion totaled 298.3 billion tons, 165,700 acre-feet.[3]

Erosion is not uniformly distributed. Over one-half of all agricultural land erosion occurs on cropland, one-third occurs on rangeland, and the remainder occurs on pasture and forestland. Erosion occurs at relatively low rates on most agricultural land. That is, less than 5 tons per acre annually is lost on two-thirds of the cropland. Rates in excess of 10 tons annually per acre are found on 17 percent of the cropland acreage.[4] As would be expected, most of the erosion occurs on land used to grow row crops and small grains. This happens because the soil is stirred by plowing, and only partial vegetative cover leaves much of the soil surface exposed to wind and rain. The average annual erosion rate on land used for row crops and small grains is 8 tons per acre. The bulk of soil erosion is, therefore, on land producing cotton, sorghum, soybeans, corn, and wheat that is fallowed (Table 14.2).

Most soils have a capacity to regenerate 2 to 5 tons of topsoil per acre annually. If the erosion does not exceed the rate of regeneration, the soil resource is maintained. Most soils can, therefore, incur some erosion without significant adverse impacts on crop productivity, although the runoff associated with water erosion may have severely adverse environ-

[3]Soil Conservation Service, "Soil Erosion," unpublished paper (Washington, D.C.: USDA, 1981). An acre-foot is an acre of land 1 foot deep.
[4]Ibid.

TABLE 14.2 Average Annual Erosion Rate by Crop

Crop	Average Annual Erosion Rate (tons/acre)
Cotton	19.9
Sorghum	12.6
Soybeans	8.2
Corn	7.6
Wheat/fallow	6.5

Source: Clayton Ogg and Arnold Miller, *Minimizing Erosion on Cultivated Land: Concentration of Erosion Problems and the Effectiveness of Conservation Practices* (Washington, D.C.: ESS, USDA, April 1981).

mental effects—particularly in terms of water quality (see below). A soil tolerance loss of 5 tons per acre has come to be accepted as the threshold at which erosion becomes excessive.[5] When this standard is applied to the available information on erosion soil loss, the problem is seen to be relatively concentrated—that is, the most severe erosion occurs on a small proportion of the acreage (Table 14.3). Water erosion is concentrated in Iowa, Missouri, Tennessee, Kentucky, and the Southeast, while wind erosion is extensive in the High Plains region of Texas, Colorado, and Kansas.[6]

An important consideration is that the erosion problem became more severe over time. While Iowa soil losses decreased from 21.1 tons per acre in 1949 to 14.1 tons in 1957, it rose to 17.2 tons in 1974.[7] Various economic influences, including the expansion of foreign markets, have encouraged farmers to plant crops such as corn and soybeans year after year and from fence to fence—frequently at the expense of shelter belts and windbreaks. These market incentives have also contributed to a trend toward greater specialization on many farms. Midwest farmers, for example, market their crops directly rather than feeding them to hogs and cattle. This reduced the organic matter available to the soil. It also reduced the need for pastureland or such crops as alfalfa, which tend to retard erosion by providing constant ground cover.

From the few indicators available, progress was made in reducing erosion in the 1950s and 1960s. This was the period when active soil conservation programs were combined with acreage diversion programs which were devoted to hay crops and pasture. However, during the 1970s most observers agree that the erosion problem increased.[8]

[5]Sandra S. Batie, *Information Needs for the Formulation of a Soil Conservation Policy* (Washington, D.C.: Conservation Foundation, October 22, 1981).

[6]Batie and Healy, "The Future of American Agriculture."

[7]Ibid., p. 48.

[8]Batie, *Information Needs.*

TABLE 14.3 Combined Sheet, Rill, and Wind Erosion on Land Used
for Row Crops and Small Grains (including Fallow), 1977

Rate of Erosion (tons/acre)	Acres (millions)	Percent of Total	Excess Erosion[a] (millions)	Percent of Total
0–4.9	203.2	60.2	0	0
5–9.9	67.2	19.9	133.5	8.5
10–14.9	25.0	7.4	180.4	11.4
15–19.9	13.2	3.9	162.1	10.3
20–24.9	7.6	2.2	131.3	8.3
25 and over	21.3	6.4	967.7	61.5
Total	337.5	100.0	1574.9	100.0

Sources: Compiled from National Resource Inventory Data, USDA, SCS, 1978, and
reported in Clayton Ogg and Arnold Miller, *Minimizing Erosion on Cultivated Land:
Concentration of Erosion Problems and the Effectiveness of Conservation Practices* (Washington, D.C.: ESS, USDA, April 1981).
[a]Erosion of over 5 tons/acre.

Soil Erosion Technology

The traditional topographic methods of erosion control are contour
plowing and terracing. These methods are designed to reduce the velocity
of water running downhill and increase the absorption of water into the
soil. Such methods have been the mainstay of soil conservation techniques. However, they are often not equal to the conservation problems
that modern farming creates. Constructing the most modern and effective type of terrace, the parallel tile outlet, which involves drainage
through underground tile, cost $250 to $300 per acre in 1980.[9] Some
farms might require several hundred acres of terraces to bring the erosion problem under control. Even the most conservation-minded farmers
have difficulty justifying the long-term investment terracing requires, especially at prevailing rates of interest.

Minimum tillage, zero tillage, or conservation tillage have recently
emerged as perhaps the most promising means for widespread erosion
control. Since the greater part of erosion damage is done as raindrops
strike the ground, erosion can be significantly reduced by leaving the
field covered with crop residue. This can be accomplished by tillage methods such as chisel plowing, which is already fairly well accepted in the
Corn Belt. Unlike the conventional moldboard plow, which turns over all
the soil in a field, the chisel plow cultivates in strips, leaving one-third to
one-half of the previous crop's residue undisturbed.

Zero tillage, of course, does not disturb the residue at all. By not

[9]J. F. Timmons and O. M. Amos, *Economics of Soil Erosion Control with Application
to T-Values,* Iowa Agric. Exp. Stn. J. Pap. J-1 625 (Ames; Iowa: Iowa State University,
1979), p. 55.

plowing, erosion can be reduced as much as 90 percent. Although savings in fuel consumption can be realized from zero tillage, weed control is a serious problem. The moldboard plow kills weeds by burying them. Without plowing, more herbicides are required for effective weed control, increasing chemical cost by $10 to $15 per acre in 1980 and risking groundwater contamination.[10]

The Persistence of the Soil Erosion Problem

Technical solutions to the problems of soil erosion exist. *The major problem is economics. In the short run, conservation simply does not pay.* Even in the long run, the economic benefits to a farmer engaging in soil-conserving practices are questionable.

To illustrate, an Iowa study indicates that if a farmer invested in a combination of soil conservation practices that reduces annual soil losses from 20 tons to 4 tons per acre annually, he would receive a negative return of $67.90 per acre over the life of the conservation practice. Further investment to reduce erosion losses to zero tons per acre produces a negative return of $258.35 per acre.[11] Other studies for other farming areas show similar results. One of the main reasons excessive erosion continues is simply that many conservation practices do not pay for themselves in terms of their impact on production.

Whether soil conservation pays is influenced by whether degradation of the soil resource (productivity losses) gets reflected in land prices. If soil erosion discernibly affects the soil's productivity, the price offered for eroded or eroding land should be reduced accordingly. If so, there would seem to be no need for public programs to reduce soil erosion. The market would offer sufficient incentive for the problem to be self-correcting. Yet many observers suspect that the market may undervalue the adverse effect of erosion. A persuasive reason for this is that the market gives less weight than society to maintenance of productivity of the land as a hedge against future demand for food and fiber. The evidence on this point is admittedly scant, but what there is presents no evidence that present erosion effects on future productivity enter into land prices.[12]

Libby explains the erosion control strategies of farmers in the following terms.

> Farmers have many motives influencing their behavior. They have a sense of responsibility for the land. . . . They acknowledge the community responsibility. . . . But farmers respond to economic incentives of price and cost.

[10]Ibid.

[11]Ibid.

[12]R. B. Held and M. Clawson, *Soil Conservation in Perspective* (Baltimore: The Johns Hopkins University Press, 1965).

. . . Primary attention must be given to economic incentives that affect the relative attractiveness of conservation.[13]

The soil conservation problem thus ends up to be one of **externalities**. *That is, society puts a higher value on conservation than either the market or the individual.* The result is predictable, a persistent soil erosion problem that will probably intensify. If the problem is to be solved, it would appear that government assistance is needed to solve it.

Conservation Policy to the Present

USDA and the Environmental Protection Agency have responsibility for programs designed to reduce soil erosion. USDA programs are conducted through Soil Conservation Service (SCS). This agency, through its local Soil Conservation Districts, works jointly with the Extension Service to provide technical assistance to farmers on the technology of soil conservation. In addition, it provides subsidies to farmers for engaging in soil-conserving practices such as the construction of terraces. From 1935 to 1982, USDA has made outlays of more than $22 billion for cost-sharing subsidies, technical assistance, resource management, loans, research, and education. SCS has an annual budget in excess of $250 million.[14]

This magnitude of financial support should have gone a long way toward the development of an effective soil conservation program. Part of the problem is that the term "conservation" itself has taken on a political meaning broader than its literal meaning. This is seen in the following definition by the SCS itself:

Soil conservation is the application on the land of all necessary measures in proper combination to build up and maintain soil productivity for efficient abundant production on a sustained basis. Soil conservation, therefore, means protecting the land against all forms of soil deterioration, rebuilding eroded and depleted soils, conserving moisture for plant use, proper drainage and irrigation where needed, and other measures which contribute to maximum practical yields and farm and ranch income—all at the same time.[15]

Such a definition has been used to justify spending appropriations on a wide variety of functions, some of which may actually contribute to erosion and soil depletion. For example, SCS monies have been exten-

[13]Lawrence W. Libby, "Developing Agricultural Policy to Achieve Lower Rates of Erosion on Fragile Lands," unpublished paper (East Lansing, Mich.: Michigan State University, 1986), p. 5.

[14]Information obtained from USDA, Soil Conservation Service, 1982.

[15]Robert M. Salter (Washington, D.C.: SCS, USDA, December 17, 1952), p. 1.

sively utilized to construct drainage systems, which, in fact, facilitate the runoff of soil and water.[16] They have also been used to provide subsidies for the purchase of agricultural lime, which made production possible on soils that were inherently erosion prone. In addition, the benefits of cost-sharing programs were widely dispersed among soils having different erosion characteristics. Less than 19 percent of the soil conservation practices installed have been placed on the highly eroding lands. Over one-half of the cost-sharing practices have been placed on lands with erosion rates of less than 5 tons per acre per year.[17]

There are many reasons for this use of soil conservation monies. First are the political pressures—members of Congress who control the program fundings are influential in determining where the funds are spent. Also, the agencies need the popular support of farmers and thus have considerable incentive to spread program benefits widely. Further, a lack of data on the nature and extent of the erosion problem has limited the agency's abilities to focus assistance on the farms with the most severe problems, even if program managers had attempted to pursue this approach.

In the mid-1970s, Congress expressed its concern about the impact of soil erosion on water quality by enacting into law the federal Water Pollution Control Act. This act mandated control over nonpoint sources of pollution by the Environmental Protection Agency. Soil erosion is a nonpoint source of pollution in the sense that there is no identifiable single source such as the dumping of untreated chemicals from a refinery.

The Water Pollution Control Act was designed to remove soil sedimentation from the water by 1985. The problem, however, is much more complex than just a regulatory mandate. Measuring the quantity of pollutants from a particular farm is virtually impossible. Even if it were possible, many farmers could not afford to employ satisfactory erosion control techniques. Enforcement could thus put many farmers out of business.

As questions regarding the extent of erosion increased, the Congress enacted the Soil and Water Resources Conservation Act (RCA) in 1977. The act required USDA to (1) appraise, on a continuing basis, the soil, water, and related resources of the nation; (2) develop a program for furthering the conservation, protection, and enhancement of these resources; and (3) annually evaluate program performance in achieving conservation objectives. A National Lands Survey was conducted to fulfill the requirements of the 1977 act until the 1985 farm bill when three significant actions were taken:

[16]Earl O. Heady, *Agricultural Policy under Economic Development* (Ames, Iowa: Iowa State University Press, 1962), pp. 558–560.

[17]USDA, *National Summary Evaluation of the Agricultural Conservation Program: Phase I* (Washington, D.C.: ASCS, USDA, 1981).

- The **Conservation Reserve Program** (CRP) was established to remove 45 million acres of highly erosive land from production for a 10-year period. Participation is voluntary, with landowners submitting competitive bids for land to be included in the reserve. Land eligible for the CRP is cropland unsuitable for farming or eroding faster than three times the natural rate of soil formation. Once a bid is accepted, the landowner may not cultivate the land for commercial purposes. The government pays an annual rent plus half of the cost of establishing grass, legumes, or trees. In order for a farmer to afford to participate in CRP, the rental rate paid by the government must be greater than the farmer can earn from the land by cropping plus the cost of establishing and keeping up the cover crop. Grazing is not allowed except in emergencies. In order to limit the adverse impacts of reduced production on rural communities and agribusiness, no more than 30 percent of the cropland in any county can be placed in CRP.

- **Soil conservation cross compliance** required that all highly erosive land have an approved conservation plan that reduced excessive erosion by January 1, 1990. While not receiving extensive debate in the 1985 farm bill deliberation, this provision may have been its most important soil conservation action. It has been suggested that the provision was not the product of congressional deliberation, but resulted from the initiative of public interest groups in combination with congressional staff.

- **Sodbuster** and **swampbuster** provisions, which, respectively, prohibit fragile grasslands or wetland brought into production after January 1, 1986, from receiving farm program benefits. These provisions were designed to curb the incentives for farmland conversion provided by the benefits of farm programs.

The 1985 farm bill obviously made significant strides in reducing soil erosion. In the process, progress was also made to improve water quality, another major resource problem discussed in this chapter.

FARMLAND RETENTION AND PRESERVATION

Will Rogers once said of land, "they make so little of it nowadays,"[18] presaging the present concern over the loss of agricultural land to nonagricultural uses. Following World War II, the patterns of life and the patterns of land use in this country changed dramatically. The population, which before the war had been largely distributed in the cities and

[18]Charles R. Frink and James G. Horsfall, "The Farm Problem," in *The Farm and the City: Rivals or Allies*, A. M. Woodruff and Charles R. Frink, eds. (Englewood Cliffs, N.J.: Prentice-Hall, Inc., 1980), p. 81.

on the farms, moved in massive number to the suburbs. Single-family dwellings on what appears to have been ever larger lot sizes housed an increasing number of American families. Industries decentralized as a massive road-building program increased the ease of transportation.

This trend continued throughout the 1960s and much of the 1970s, abetted by government actions responding to the ever-growing political power of the suburbs. Road building, mortgage guarantees, subsidies and tax deduction for single-family dwellings, tax-exempt municipal bonding, utility rate structures, and other forms of government influence accelerated the changes throughout the postwar period. Government tax policies have also encouraged conversion to nonfarm uses. When all land is taxed on the basis of its market, as opposed to its use value, agricultural land that is near urban centers frequently takes on a market value, and thus a tax rate, that makes farming less attractive.

By the beginning of the 1980s, opposing forces developed that made the future less predictable:

- The end of the postwar baby boom, working women, gasoline shortages, rising energy prices, inflation, and high interest rates created new interest in central city restoration and development.
- A countervailing trend may be developing toward the purchase of land by the wealthy for second homes and for retirement homes in rural areas. Such land may be used at so much less than its agricultural productive capacity that it might legitimately be considered a nonagricultural use. The difference from other nonagricultural uses is that this land has greater potential for being converted back to agricultural use.
- Most states changed the tax base for agricultural land to its use value as opposed to its market value. This change in policy was designed to reduce the incentive for conversion to nonagricultural uses.

As a result of these trends, there has emerged a rather widespread concern about the consequences of continuous loss of agricultural land. Thus the issue of preservation of agricultural land has emerged as an increasingly important component of food and agricultural policy. This issue has received much attention in the eastern and western United States, where urban and recreational uses of land have encroached upon agricultural uses, with a resulting need expressed by some individuals and interest groups to channel growth and development.

Dimensions of the Problem

Estimates of the rate at which farmland was being converted to nonfarm use ranged from 1 million to 5 million acres per year. The Soil

Conservation Service has estimated that nonagricultural uses are actually preempting 3 million acres per year, but "leapfrogging" and "scattershot" development are isolating another 2 million acres.[19] Cotner found that cropland acreage is falling an average of 1.4 million acres per year. This study indicates that 1.3 million acres are added to the cropland base each year, while 2.2 million acres are converted from cropland to grass and trees, and 0.5 million acres are lost to urbanization, reservoirs, highways, and other uses.[20] This total loss of 2.7 million acres (0.5 + 2.2 million), against the 1.3 million acres of new cropland developed each year, led to an estimate of an annual net loss of 1.4 million cropland acres.

The Resources Conservation Act required predictions on future agricultural land losses. The most optimistic prediction from this source was 1 million acres each year.[21] USDA and the Council on Environmental Quality commissioned a National Agricultural Lands Study that reported generally higher levels of losses.[22]

The wide range in estimates and predictions reveals an uncertainty of the data. The widely differing interpretations have been exasperating to many who are seriously concerned about the problem. The situation has been characterized as "reminiscent of the problem of the half-blind man in a very dark room trying to locate a black cat that was not there."[23]

Luzar and Batie described the farmland retention issue as being amorphous.[24] At the national level the issue is as described above—a concern about adequate supplies of food and fiber. At the local level the issue subsumes a number of related land use issues with different constituencies and competing agencies. For example, in the Northeast the issue is **farmland preservation**—*preventing conversion to nonagricultural uses.* In other regions, the issue is one of **farmland retention**—*keeping farmland actively in cultivation until an orderly transfer occurs to higher-valued uses.*

The land that is sought to be preserved or maintained in agricultural use varies from "prime farmland" to quaint images of "rural America." Prime farmland is often the first chosen to be developed because of the low cost of development. Preservation of the images of rural America

[19]A. M. Woodruff and C. R. Frink, "Introduction," in *The Farm and the City*, p. 3.

[20]Melvin L. Cotner, *Land Use Policy and Agriculture: A National Perspective*, ERS-630 (Washington, D.C.: ERS, USDA, August 1976).

[21]Woodruff and Frink, "Introduction."

[22]USDA, *National Agricultural Lands Study: Summary Report* (Washington, D.C.: USDA, 1981).

[23]Woodruff and Frink, "Introduction," p. 4.

[24]E. Jane Luzar and Sandra S. Batie, *Improving Land Use Policy Analysis in the Southeast: Lessons from Virginia's Agricultural and Forestry District Act* (Mississippi State, Miss.: Southern Rural Development Center, April 1986), p. 14.

as amenities, for example, places a high value on maintaining smaller family dairy farms or roadside markets.

Preservation motives involve issues of the desired structure of agriculture as discussed in Chapter 10. If the goal of preservation or retention is to maintain agriculture as a healthy component of the economy, preference may be given to larger commercially oriented operations or even industrial farms. If, on the other hand, the goal relates to maintaining rural ambiance, preference may be given to a smaller family farm structure.

Cultural issues such as the maintenance of ethnic communities might also be involved in the preservation policy decisions. Increasingly, the issue of farmland retention involves protection of the natural environment designed to maintain water quality and wildlife habitat or control soil erosions.

Sifting through this image of policy objectives and goals, Gardner has identified the following potential benefits that society may desire to gain from farmland preservation or retention policies:

- Maintain food and fiber productive capacity.
- Maintain a healthy local agricultural economy.
- Maintain environmental amenities associated with open space.
- Maintain a sound, orderly, and efficient urban development strategy.[25]

Success in developing land use policy is very dependent on care and consensus in the specification of goals. As in any well-designed policy, clear distinctions need to be made between objectives and the exact relationship of policies to objectives.

Farmland Retention and Preservation Options[26]

Options for retention and preservation inherently involve issues of the level of government at which action is taken and the substance of the regulation itself. While considerable political energy has been spent to develop a national farmland retention policy, the product of this action has been described as symbolic but ineffectual.[27] The 1981 Farmland Protection Policy Act was signed into law to reduce the effect of federal activities on the conversion of farmland. The act provides a framework for

[25]B. D. Gardner, "The Economics of Agricultural Land Preservation," *Am. J. Agric. Econ.*, (1977), pp. 1026–1036.

[26]This section draws heavily on the work of Luzar and Batie, *Improving Land Use Policy in the Southeast*, pp. 23–42.

[27]Ibid., p. 27.

USDA to develop criteria for the identification of the effects of federal programs and agencies on the availability of farmland. It then requires that all agencies (except defense) evaluate and propose revisions in rules, procedures, and programs to reduce adverse impacts on farmland availability. For example, a federally funded highway might be rerouted to avoid consumption of prime farmland. While enacted with good intentions, such impact analyses are frequently better at keeping bureaucrats employed than at effectuating policy. The thrust of meaningful policy development, therefore, is transferred to the state and local level, where six main options are employed to influence agricultural land use.

Agricultural zoning laws *provide exclusive zoning of land for farming in 22 states.* The main purpose of agricultural zoning appears to be the preservation of open space. The most frequent use of this technique is in the Northeast, where there is relatively intense competition among nonagricultural uses of farmland. While agricultural zoning is a low-cost option to the public, farmland can be reduced in value by agricultural zoning because of limitations on its development potential. Wisconsin blends tax incentives with zoning to offset at least a portion of the resulting land value reduction.

Purchase of development rights *involves public action to compensate farmland owners for benefits of development separate and distinct from the farm value of land.* This leaves the landowner the right to use the land for agricultural purposes, while transferring the development rights to the local or state government.

About a dozen states authorized the purchase of development rights. While compensating farmland owners for income forgone from development, the purchase of development rights is costly. For example, King County, Washington was projected to pay $240 million for development rights on 30,000 acres ($8000 per acre).

Right-to-farm laws *protect farmers against legal actions taken against accepted agricultural practices.* These politically popular laws (with farmers) protect farmers from nuisance lawsuits which might otherwise drive them from agricultural pursuits. For example, a hog farm might be protected against an air pollution suit. Critics charge that such laws have little potential for achieving specific land use objectives and constitute a license to pollute.[28] Public costs are low.

Preferential assessment of agricultural land *requires that land for property tax be assessed on the basis of its agricultural use value rather than its market value.* In its pure form, no penalty is associated with conversion to nonfarm uses, although deferred taxation in cases where development takes place, or restrictions on development, may be included in preferential taxation contracts. The theory is that without a property tax

[28]Ibid., p. 35.

break, farmers located near a city may not be able to afford to farm and may be prematurely forced to sell their land to developers. However, experience suggests that differential assessment is more of an income transfer to landowners than a mechanism for retaining land in agriculture. This is because the income from development forgone by a landowner generally is greater than the tax saving, therefore not effectively discouraging development.

Agricultural districts *designate specific areas of land for long-term agricultural use.* Membership in the district is voluntary and is linked to differential assessment and/or protection from nuisance ordinances. Pioneered by New York, agricultural districts are used by about 12 states. Districts are effective only if there is a substantial economic incentive to attract participation; districts are formed in most regions; and the contract is over a sufficiently long period. The cost of agricultural districts is the revenue forgone from differential assessment.

THE WATER RESOURCE

Water, it has been argued, is the most critical natural resource to agriculture.[29] Whereas substitutes for energy and land exist in the form of technology, there are no good substitutes for water. Agriculture is the largest single use of water resources. It is estimated that 83 percent of the water consumed is used in farming.[30] *The* **water problem,** *therefore, is largely an agricultural problem.*

Irrigation has been a critical factor in the ability of the world to feed an ever-expanding population. Irrigation has expanded to the point where, in the late 1980s, it covered 18 percent of the world's cropland and provided one-third of the world's food.[31] Irrigation is at least equally important in the United States with the share of the value of food production from irrigated land approaching 50 percent.

Because of its importance and limited supply, water has become an important agricultural policy issue. There are three major dimensions to this issue:

- **Water supply development** is not a new issue for the arid and semiarid parts of the United States, where extensive irrigation sys-

[29]G. W. Thomas, "Water: Critical and Evasive Resource on Semiarid Lands," in *Water and Water Policy in World Food Supplies*, W. R. Jordan, ed. (College Station, Tex.: Texas A&M University, 1987), pp. 81–90.

[30]W. L. Brown, "New Technology Related to Water Policy—Plants," in *Water and Water Policy*, p. 37.

[31]W. R. Rangeley, "Irrigation and Drainage in the World," in *Water and Water Policy*, p. 30.

tems have been built with public funds. Some of the most highly industrialized agricultural production systems (and largest farms) have been built utilizing publicly financed water supplies.

- The **allocation of water supplies** has been an age-old policy issue. In some areas of the West where population has grown rapidly, and in areas such as the Great Plains where underground water supplies are not rapidly regenerated, the problem has become one of allocation of limited water supplies. Although this is not a new problem, questions have arisen as to whether prevailing water rights policies are sufficient to deal with the developing pressures.

- **Water quality** has become the major issue of the 1990s. In the 1970s, significant action was taken to improve the quality of water from identifiable sources (*point pollution*). In the 1980s, attention began to shift to *nonpoint pollution*, such as erosion and runoff from farmland. In the 1990s, the focal point of concern is contaminants of the water supply, where agricultural chemicals are a potential significant source of contamination.

Water Development

Up to the 1970s, the major thrust of federal water policy was on development of alternative sources of water. Although environmental concerns slowed federal clearance procedures for many individual projects, **development** *continues to be a major policy thrust.* Yet the answer to an increasingly tight water supply has, more often than not, been drawing on limited supplies of groundwater.

The large-scale projects to provide water for agricultural development of the West began in the early 1900s with passage of the Reclamation Act in 1902 and creation of the Bureau of Reclamation (now the Water and Power Resources Service) in the Department of the Interior. Some 12 million acres of cropland (an area roughly twice the size of New Jersey) have been added to the nation's cropland base through irrigation projects in the eight decades since the establishment of the Water and Power Resource Service.[32] Many more projects are under construction or in the backlog of approved but yet unstarted projects. The federal government annually spends $5 billion on water-related planning, construction, maintenance, and grant and loan programs.[33] The federal government typically pays 80 to 90 percent of the cost of water projects, with states paying the remainder. The recipients of the water are usually obligated for less than 20 percent of the investment in structures and conveyance systems, including interest on the investment over the repayment period.

[32]Department of Interior data.

[33]Carter, *Water Policy*, p. 2.

As surface water demand has reached near full development, increased pressure has been placed on groundwater supplies. However, even here the withdrawal rates now frequently exceed the replenishment rates, and the water table drops as a result.

With use requirements increasing each year, the size of the underground water supply and how long it will last are becoming the vital questions of the day. This is especially true for one of the largest of these underground sources, the Ogallala aquifer, which lies under eight Great Plains states, including Texas, New Mexico, Colorado, Kansas, Oklahoma, Nebraska, and to a lesser extent, South Dakota and Wyoming (Fig. 14.1). The Ogallala supplies water for approximately 14.3 million acres and is tapped by more than 150,000 irrigation wells. This aquifer nurtures 25 percent of the nation's irrigated farmland, on which 12 percent of the nation's corn, cotton, sorghum, and wheat and one-half of beef cattle are produced.[34] Bagley estimated that more than 40 percent of High Plains personal income is attributable to groundwater irrigation.[35] Nearly half of the available water has been utilized, and recharge rates are only a fraction of the annual withdrawal. Future use potential appears to range up to 75 years, but many wells go dry each year, requiring conversion back to dryland production.

Development of existing water sources will continue to be a major thrust of federal water policy, particularly in regions of the country, such as the East and Midwest, where substantial potential exists to capture and utilize surface water runoff more effectively. In the Plains, discussion frequently arises concerning the need for extremely large-scale water projects designed to offset reduced availability of groundwater in large areas served by nonregenerating sources such as the Ogallala aquifer. Such proposals include diverting water either from the Ozarks region of the Mississippi watershed or from the northern Rocky Mountains. Water projects of this type could involve outlays of over $20 billion.

A major change in federal spending priorities would be required if such large-scale water projects were to be undertaken. Equally important, however, is the controversial nature of water diversion programs from states such as Arkansas to states such as Texas, which are clearly outside natural watershed flows. The potential clearly exists for greatly increasing both the cost and the availability of water to areas where it has previously been a free good. Questions will undoubtedly also be

[34]Chris Szechenyi, "The Thirsty Plains Drain a Dwindling Water Table," *Kansas City Times* (Kansas City, Mo.), May 13, 1981.

[35]E. S. Bagley, "Economic Impact of Groundwater Depletion in Western Kansas," unpublished manuscript (Manhattan, Kans.: Department of Economics, Kansas State University, 1971).

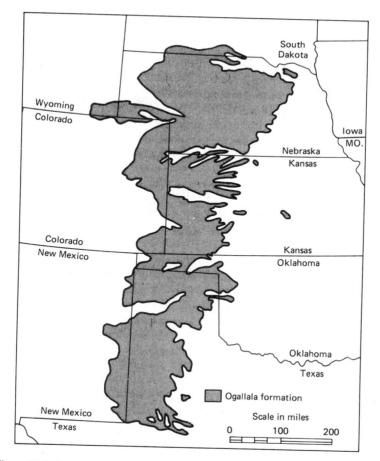

Figure 14.1 Region covered by the Ogallala formation.
Source: Harry L. Manges, "Hydrologic Considerations for the High Plains Area of Kansas," in *Ground Water Quality and Quantity Issues* (Washington, D.C.: Committee on Agriculture, July 23, 1981), p. 74.

raised as to whether federal tax dollars should be spent on water projects where the benefits are clearly regional in scope. On the other hand, without extensive water development, all consumers will experience increased food prices resulting from reduced food production in the region served by the Ogallala aquifer.

Although further development of available water supplies will help, it is probably not the complete answer to the nation's water problems. Other alternatives designed to increase the efficiency of water use will be required.

Water Allocation and Use[36]

Water allocation involves issues of how limited water supplies are allocated among competing uses. The key element in allocation decisions has been the legal rights to the available water supply. Over time, increasing concern has arisen over the need for water conservation measures, including the pricing of water. Policies regarding water allocation and use can be classified in six categories:

- The **riparian doctrine** holds that owners of land whose land borders on a water course or water body have rights to the use of water, rights that cannot be lost by nonuse, and rights that require reasonable use. Reasonable use is based on the concept of sharing so as not to have an unreasonable impact on others. The riparian doctrine tends to be used in areas of the eastern United States where water is relatively plentiful.
- Most western states rely on the **prior-appropriation doctrine**, where rights are based upon *first in time, first in use*. In other words, water rights are ranked based on the order of appropriation by users. When there is not enough water to fill all appropriations (users), the last appropriators are the first to be curtailed. Interestingly, appropriative rights can be lost through nonuse—thus tending to encourage use of a limited water supply.
- **Administrative permit systems** require a showing of reasonable beneficial use for construction of wells, dams, or reservoirs. Reasonable beneficial use is defined as use of water in such quantity as is necessary for economic and efficient utilization in a manner consistent with the public interest. Permits are for a specified period, such as up to 20 years.
- **Reasonable use rights** are often applied to groundwater, which may or may not include a concept of sharing, referred to as *correlative rights*. In other words, in some states landowners can pump as much as is reasonable (needed) without consideration of the effect on others. In other cases, the effects on the supplies of others are relevant considerations in the quantity used.
- **Conservation** of available water supplies has become an increasingly recognized means of making the available supply of water go further. The days when water can be treated as a free good are in the past. A farmer can no longer afford to run irrigation pumps until

[36]This section relies heavily on the work of Sandra S. Batie, "Water Law in the Southeast," in *Emerging Issues in Water Management and Policy*, Sandra S. Batie and J. Paxton Marshall, eds. (Mississippi State, Miss.: Southern Rural Development Center, 1983), pp. 1–14.

water runs out the end of the field. Farmers recognizing this fact are looking for means of conserving the available water supply. University scientists, equipment manufacturers, and seed, chemical, and fertilizer companies are seeking new technologies and management systems for reducing irrigation levels. Short-season varieties, drought-resistant varieties, drip irrigation, crop rotation, and optimum as opposed to maximum yields are all part of the new water-conservation-oriented terminology. The changes required are not as simple as adjusting one input level; they generally require totally new management systems. That is, reduced water use also suggests the need for different plant varieties, as well as reduced fertilizer and chemical use.

Developing these new technologies and management systems involves large investments by the public sector or the private sector or both. The willingness to make these investments will have considerable impact on the effectiveness of water conservation strategies in dealing with water problems. It will also determine the need to impose more stringent allocation and pricing alternatives.

· **Pricing water** in a market context could be used as a means of allocating available water supplies. But price seldom, if ever, is used exclusively to ration the available water supplies. If price were used exclusively to allocate supplies, farmers would likely be losers. Consumers and industries, having a degree of power to pass through the cost to consumers, could almost inevitably pay a higher price for water.

Pricing is frequently used to pay some share of the cost of water from irrigation projects (public or private). Public projects are frequently highly subsidized by the government (federal and/or state). In California, for example, water is generally priced at approximately one-third of its cost.[37] Since California agricultural products compete with those produced in other regions, pricing is a very controversial issue. Yet even in other regions, increased irrigation costs, associated with higher energy prices, added an important pricing dimension to water that encouraged conservation.

Water Quality

Federal policy regarding water quality is governed by the Clean Water Act of 1972, which virtually rewrote previous, largely ineffective, policies. Yet despite the change in policy about two decades ago, deterio-

---

[37]*The United States Department of the Interior's Proposed Rules for Enforcement of the Reclamation Act of 1902*, ESCS-04 (Washington, D.C.: ESCS, USDA, 1978), p. i.

rating water quality continues to be a major concern as the issue of the 1990s.

Contamination of both surface and groundwaters by toxic chemicals, mutagens, and carcinogens is fully as important an issue as depletion of water resources. The Colorado River, whose water is used to irrigate 2 million acres of prime farmland, is slowly becoming more saline. In the course of its flow from its headwaters in Colorado to the Mexican border, the river's salt content increases from about 50 mg per liter to more than 800 mg per liter—well above the EPA maximum for safe drinking water.[38]

Groundwater contamination has been found in almost every state in which it has been studied—and groundwater is the sole source of supply for more than half of Americans. Data from Iowa indicate that as much as 50 percent of the chemical and nitrogen fertilizer applied may by lost into groundwater and surface water.[39] Toxic chemical runoff having its origin in agricultural pest control has become a major health concern in highly productive farmland areas stretching from Iowa to California.

The Clean Water Act and related legislation implementing its provisions made substantial progress in reducing pollution by construction of waste treatment facilities. It set the stage for subsequent initiatives in agriculture by beginning research and planning for the control of agricultural or other nonpoint sources of water pollution.

The Clean Water Act was designed primarily to deal with surface water. Policy regarding the quality of groundwater has centered on point sources of contamination such as superfund programs designed to clean up the worst sites. No comprehensive policy for dealing with groundwater quality existed up to the late 1980s.[40]

Four basic alternatives exist for dealing with issues on nonpoint pollution of water originating in agriculture:

- **Retiring farmland** *from production reduces pollution of water.* This policy has been pursued by targeting the retirement of 40 million acres of highly erosive farmland under the 1985 farm bill conservation reserve program (CRP). Further retirements of highly erosive land have been proposed. In addition, the soil conservation compliance provisions of the 1985 farm bill will aid water quality by reducing water erosion.

[38]Brown, "New Technology Related to Water Policy," p. 38.

[39]Ibid.

[40]Roy Carriker, "Public Policy Options and Alternatives: Federal, State and Local Perspectives," in *Water Quality: Agriculture and Community Concerns in the South* (Mississippi State, Miss.: Southern Rural Development Center, May 1986), pp. 85–91.

- **Land retirement programs** *such as CRP could be* **extended to lands** *where the soil structure is particularly* **subject to seepage** *of agricultural chemicals through the soil structure into either ground-water or runoff.* Such a proposal was made by Senator Dole during the 1988 presidential campaign and will undoubtedly receive further consideration, assuming that agricultural excess capacity continues.

- **Research designed to reduce water requirements** *of plants or increase the efficiency of irrigation holds the potential for reducing runoff and seepage of agricultural contaminants.*[41] Even greater potential may lie in the products of biotechnology, which hold the potential for engineering substitutes for toxic agricultural chemicals, including commercial nitrogen fertilizer.

- **Regulation of applications of chemicals** *to cropland could become a more important factor in controlling farmland pollution.* EPA currently evaluates chemicals for their healthy, safety, and environmental aspects. Greater weight could be given to assessing and managing the risks associated with agricultural chemicals in terms of their effects on water quality.

ENDANGERED SPECIES

Some seemingly innocuous resource laws can potentially have a major impact on agriculture. One such law is the Endangered Species Act. Originally enacted in 1973 and applied largely to preserving predators of livestock, this act has been successfully strengthened by six amendments, with ever-increasing potential adverse effects on the use of chemicals in agriculture. The Endangered Species Act may be the strongest environmental regulation that exists.

The purpose of the act is to provide a means whereby the ecosystems upon which endangered species and threatened species depend may be conserved. To achieve this objective, the act mandates that all federal agencies *shall* seek to conserve endangered and threatened species. All agencies (including EPA, USDA, FDA, etc.) are required to consult with the Secretary of Interior (Fish and Wildlife Service) on *any program* that may have environmental impacts. Violations of the act carry both civil and criminal penalties.

Until the 1982 amendments requiring agency consultation, USDA and EPA largely ignored the Endangered Species Act. Now, if any federal

[41]Brown, "New Technology Related to Water Policy," p. 37–41.

program adversely affects an endangered species, it must make reasonable and prudent adjustments in the program to eliminate that adversity. Species are listed as endangered upon complaint, after survey, and required public rule making and notification procedures. Either plants or animals may be endangered. Some insects, such as certain butterflies, have been listed as endangered.

The potential impacts on agriculture can easily be illustrated. Assume that a mussel found in streams is listed as endangered. Assume also that the mussel is adversely affected by a pesticide or herbicide used on rice. The use of that chemical could be banned on any land whose runoff feeds into the stream where the mussel is found. Alternatively, a herbicide may be prohibited in any area where an endangered plant is found. Note also that particular weeds may be endangered, the Texas bitter weed being a case in point.

Interestingly, the Endangered Species Act is absolute in that economic considerations in determining an appropriate remedy are not relevant. Only the best biological data can be considered.

THE ENERGY RESOURCE

Prior to 1973, energy was abundant and inexpensive. The use patterns for energy reflected these conditions; economic incentives for conservation were minimal. The production system was heavily influenced by the abundance of relatively cheap energy. U.S. agriculture became heavily dependent on inexpensive energy used to produce fuel, petrochemical fertilizers, and pesticides. U.S. production technology, machinery, and farming systems became geared to low-cost fossil fuels.

The energy situation changed abruptly in the 1970s with the formation of OPEC and subsequent interruption of energy movements internationally. Abrupt increases in energy prices had important impacts on agriculture both in terms of its use and in looking to agriculture as a potential supplier of energy. While the energy crisis of the 1970s was relatively short lived, it had some pronounced impacts on agriculture of longer-term significance.

It has been estimated that 4 percent of total energy consumption in North America is used for agricultural production.[42] Two-thirds of the energy is used in farm machinery, while nearly 30 percent is used for the production of commercial fertilizer. Total energy consumption by the food system is less than 20 percent. With developing countries striving to

[42]L. V. Faidley, "Energy for World Agriculture: Water Implications," in *Water and Water Policy*, p. 264.

catch up technologically, their agricultural energy consumption is expanding more rapidly than that of developed countries.

The energy shortage of the 1970s had two major impacts on agriculture:

- It created an economic conscience regarding the use of energy in production. Energy could no longer be treated as an inexpensive, readily available input. Farmers were forced to seriously evaluate the cost of pumping irrigation water, the price of fertilizer, and the amount of tillage needed for efficient production. During the 1980s farm crisis, cost reduction became a key to farm survival. Energy conservation surpassed all predictions. During this period of adjustment, energy-related agribusiness firms, such as fertilizer and farm machinery manufacturers, cooperatives, and other farm supply businesses, scaled back the scope of their operations.[43]

- Agriculture was looked to as a potential alternative source of energy. As part of the alternative fuels policy, substantial subsidies were provided for the construction of ethanol production facilities, and tax subsidies were provided for gasohol—a 10 percent ethanol, 90 percent gasoline mixture. These subsidies were highly popular with farmers because the production of 2.6 gallons of ethanol requires about a bushel of corn. If 10 percent of U.S. gasoline consumption were to come from ethanol, nearly 4 billion bushels of corn would be required—half the U.S. crop. For some corn farmers, the alternative fuels market looks better than the export market.[44]

The alternative fuels market must be looked at very realistically from an economic perspective. Gasohol required substantial subsidies to make its price competitive with gasoline. These subsidies of 90 cents or more per gallon were in the form of exemptions from federal and/or state taxes. Even with these subsidies, gasohol, as a general rule, failed to meet the market test. Sales did not rise to expectations, and policymakers became frustrated over tax revenues forgone because of the subsidies.

In the 1980s, ethanol production and use was given a boost by a decision to phase out the use of lead as a means of increasing the octane level of gasoline. Ethanol provided a clean and low-cost alternative octane booster. As a result, commercial demand for ethanol has continued to

---

[43]This is not to imply that energy prices were the only factor adversely affecting these firms. High interest rates and extensive retirement of farmland were also important. For further discussion, see Chapters 8 and 15.

[44]See Chapter 15 for the interrelationships among alternative fuels policy, sugar policy, and EC corn glutin trade policy.

grow. Despite this strong commercial demand, pressure existed for subsidies designed to keep corn costs to ethanol manufacturers low. The desire of ethanol (and sugar) manufacturers for low corn costs provides a rationale for maintaining a target price program which keeps corn prices relatively low.

Although there is extensive discussion of agriculture's potential to play an important role in an alternative fuels policy, the outlook is not particularly promising. An energy expert has made the following short-run outlook concerning alternative fuels:

> Thus OPEC has 1½ times the capability of the United States to produce. With this tremendous OPEC production "overhang" in a free-trading international economy, the difference associated with capital-investment needs is conclusive in competitiveness. Alternative energy technologies requiring large capital investments . . . have no chance for widespread application under these conditions.[45]

The longer-run outlook for alternative fuels depends on the combination of the technological change in energy, world population growth, and income growth in developing countries. Interestingly, these are the same basic factors that affect agriculture's long-run outlook.

THE LABOR RESOURCE

Students of agricultural economics have traditionally been taught that the major agriculture production inputs are land, labor, capital, and management.[46] Even so, the labor resource in farming has received scant attention. Through most of the development of U.S. agriculture, the labor on the vast majority of farms has been supplied by the farm operator and his family. This is still true but is also changing. The proportion of farm work being performed by hired workers has grown steadily, to 35 percent of total farm labor in 1980.[47] Operator and family labor, including the operator's management input, have traditionally been a residual claimant to income, receiving a return only after expenses for other inputs have been paid.

Labor in addition to that of the operator and family is required on larger farms and on farms specializing in the production of labor-

[45]F. S. Patton, "Global Energy Perspectives, 1985," in *Water and Water Policy*, p. 262.

[46]The resource, water, is noticeably absent.

[47]Leslie Whitener Smith and Robert Coltrane, *Hired Farmworkers: Background and Trends for the Eighties*, Rural Dev. Res. Rep. 32 (Washington, D.C.: ERS, USDA, September 1981), p. 3.

intensive crops such as fruits and vegetables. Requirements increase substantially at planting and harvesting seasons. Such labor has usually been available and at relatively low prices. This, too, is changing as farming becomes more highly mechanized and less manual labor is involved.

The Hired Work Force

The most recent information about the hired farm work force comes from a 1979 survey. At that time, there were 2.7 million people 14 years old and older in the hired farm work force. This was an increase of about 200,000 workers from the low point reached in 1970 (Table 14.4). Hired farm labor is a diverse group, ranging from the full-time, year-round worker charged with the responsibility for much of the farm operation, to the migrant worker relegated to the most undesirable jobs on the farm. The hired farm labor force in 1979 was characterized by Pollack as follows (Table 14.4):

- They were predominantly young, white, and male. 75 percent of all hired farm workers were white, 12 percent were Hispanic, and 13 percent were black and other minorities; only 22 percent of the workers were female.
- The median age was 23.4 years. Fifty-seven percent were less than 25 years old.

TABLE 14.4   Hired Farm Workers, by Numbers of Days Worked, 1945–1985 (Percent)

Year	Total Number (thousands)	Days of Hired Farmwork during the Year				
		Less Than 25	25–74	75–149	150–249	250 or More
1945	3212	39	26	11	8	17
1951	3274	34	28	12	9	17
1956	3575	42	26	11	9	12
1960	3693	41	24	13	11	12
1965	3128	40	26	13	9	12
1970	2488	44	25	12	7	12
1975	2638	45	21	12	9	13
1979	2652	34	25	12	13	16
1983	2595	37	19	15	15	13
1985	2522	37	20	11	14	18

Source: Susan L. Pollack, *The Hired Farm Working Force of 1979*, AER-473 (Washington, D.C.: ERS, USDA, August 1981). Updated from Susan L. Pollack, *The Hired Farm Working Force of 1983*, AER-554 (Washington, D.C.: ERS, USDA, June 1986).

- Hired farm workers had lower educational levels than the total population, and the majority of workers were not heads of household; 44 percent did not continue schooling beyond the eighth grade.
- More farm workers resided in the southern and north central regions; most were nonfarm residents.
- The earnings of hired farm workers are among the lowest of all occupational groups. Average annual earnings were only $4185 from both farm and nonfarm employment. Regular workers earned $4995 for 200 days of work. Year-round workers earned $7646 for 310 days of work.
- The majority of hired farm workers worked fewer than 150 days at farm work. Regular and year-round workers were 29 percent of the work force, but contributed 73 percent of the total days worked.
- Only about 8 percent of the workers are migrant laborers.[48]

These statistics suggest that as the labor issues continue to emerge, the general policy thrust will probably be focused on ways to make agricultural employment competitive, not just to maintain a labor force that is available because it has no better alternative. It is likely that to raise labor productivity, the thrust will be to move away from highly casual labor patterns to more employment stability. This is because worker training and accumulative experience are necessary to raise productivity, and employers will need to retain employees longer to recoup investments made in developing these work skills.

To retain workers in a more stable form of employment, the quality of work they do will have to be upgraded. Advancement opportunities, better workers, and better employers will be an accepted goal of all policymakers.[49]

Major Labor Issues

Until the 1970s, labor was seldom a major issue in agricultural policy. This is perhaps because of a lack of a widespread and active agricultural labor market. The few exceptions were the plight of black sharecroppers in the South, the extension of the minimum wage to agriculture, and the organized use of foreign labor. In the future, three issues are likely to dominate the use of farm labor:

- The need to increase the minimum wage

[48]Susan L. Pollack, *The Hired Farm Working Force of 1979*, AER-473 (Washington, D.C.: ERS, USDA, August 1981).

[49]Kenneth L. Deavers, paper presented to the Annual Meeting of the National Council of Agricultural Employers, Orlando, Fla., February 3, 1981.

- The right to organize
- The use of illegal aliens

Minimum wage.   A 1966 amendment to the Fair Labor Standards Act extended the minimum wage to labor employed on farms that used more than 50 man-days during any calendar quarter of the preceding calendar year. A man-day was defined as any day in which a worker performs at least 1 hour of agricultural work. Until 1978, the minimum wage for farm labor was maintained at a lower level than for nonfarm labor. Agriculture is not required to pay time and a half for overtime.

From 1978 through 1981, the minimum wage was increased from $2.65 per hour to $3.35. Further increases in the minimum wage were being debated in the late 1980s. The basic rationale for increasing the minimum wage relates to the fact that most of the people who are below the minimum wage earn poverty-level incomes. Many of the hired farm workers have low incomes and low skills. Farmers justify paying low wages by either suggesting that they are paying the going wage or what the workers are worth.[50] The result is the creation of a cycle of low wages, low skills, and low education. The minimum wage is also viewed by organized labor as a base from which they can bargain for higher contract terms.

Farm interests have traditionally suggested that increases in the minimum wage result in greater incentives to mechanize, use chemical weed controls, and related technologies. The result, they suggest, is more unemployment. There is a substantial quantity of research which supports this theory of substitution. This research generally shows that with all other variables held constant, for every 10 percent increase in the wage rate, the employment of hired farm labor would be expected to decline about 2 percent in the short run (1 to 2 years) and 10 to 30 percent in the long run (5 to 10 years).[51] Thus, although substitution possibilities tend to be limited in the short run, over time, incentives exist for the development and adoption of a wide range of new technologies which reduce labor requirements.

Right to organize.   The National Labor Relations Act (NLRA) is the basic federal statute that gives employees the right to organize and bargain collectively with employers, who are required to bargain in good faith. It prescribes unfair labor practices on the part of both unions and

[50]Joseph D. Coffey, "National Labor Relations Legislation," *Am. J. Agric. Econ.* (December 1969), p. 1072.

[51]Ibid., p. 1067; Theodore P. Lianos, "Impact of Minimum Wages upon the Level and Composition of Agricultural Employment," *Am. J. Agric. Econ.* (August 1972), pp. 480–481; and Edward W. Tyrchniewicz and G. Edward Schuh, "Econometric Analysis of the Agricultural Labor Market," *Am. J. Agric. Econ.* (November 1969), p. 777.

employers. It created the National Labor Relations Board (NLRB) to administer the act. Agricultural laborers are explicitly excluded from the definition of the term "employee" and are not subject to the National Labor Relations Act.

Most farm labor is unorganized. The major exception is the United Farm Workers, organized in the West by Cesar Chavez. Farmers have generally reacted negatively to the unionization activities of farm labor. This is particularly true of the American Farm Bureau Federation, which has been a consistent opponent to giving farm workers the right to organize. Farmers' objections result primarily from:

- The impact of higher wages on their cost of production, with an inability to pass through those higher costs in the short run.
- The potential for strikes at harvest, with the effect of destroying a farmer's source of income. This potential is particularly likely with perishable crops, where a strike at harvest would be the most effective union bargaining tool.
- The secondary boycott tactic, where coercive pressure is exerted on a third party, such as a grocery chain, not to handle products of farmers who are opposed to unionization. Such coercive pressure may include organized action of members not to buy groceries from noncooperating chains, encouraging other union members to do likewise, or making a general plea to consumers to buy only union products.

Support for hired farm workers has been considerably broader than the organizations themselves. The California movement has received widespread support from church groups, student groups, civil rights groups, urban politicians, and organized labor. Even in agriculture, the National Farmers Union has been much more conciliatory in its attitude toward organized farm labor. It apparently believes that if all other laborers are given the right to organize and demand higher wages, farmers are in a better position to bargain for higher prices, either through the political process or through the marketplace.

The following policy alternatives are available for giving farm workers the right to organize.

Extend Present Provisions of the NLRA to Agricultural Workers.   This would bring agriculture under the same collective bargaining law, regulations, and court decisions as other industries. It would prohibit the secondary boycott. It would give the NLRB the authority to decide appropriate bargaining units, access to farms for organizing, minimum size of farm operation covered, type of petitioning for elections, and balloting procedures. It would supersede all state laws. It would not prevent strikes during critical periods of growing or harvesting.

Enact Special National Labor Relations Legislation for Agriculture. Such legislation could consider the unique problems of agriculture in terms of preventing losses due to strikes, compulsory arbitration, and the issue of secret ballots. Compulsory arbitration has been sought by farmers to allow an important third party to decide how a labor dispute should be settled. The decision of the arbitrator would then be binding on both parties. Organized labor has strongly opposed compulsory arbitration procedures. Even if such special legislation were enacted, many of the rulings already made under NLRA would likely be applied to the interpretation of the agriculture act.

Enact Special State Legislation for Agriculture. The California law could probably be the model for any such legislation. The basic purposes of the California law are to encourage and protect the right of farm workers to organize, to select representatives for the purpose of bargaining, and to prohibit employers from interfering with those rights. The California Act created a five-member Agricultural Labor Relations Board, which makes the ultimate rulings on the validity of elections and constitutes a court of appeals for unfair labor practices cases. Although secondary boycotts are prohibited by the California law, this does not extend to the passing out of leaflets, picketing, or labeling products sold in supermarkets to draw attention to a dispute.

Interpretations of the California law by the courts would probably be considered in interpreting similar legislation in other states. The most controversial ruling of the California Board was one that gave unions the right to have access to farms for the purpose of conducting organizing efforts.

Michigan and Ohio have each established a commission that supervises private treaty arrangements and dispute settlements between growers' associations, processors/packers, and labor organizations.

Each of these alternatives runs into many of the same consequences as discussed in the case of the minimum wage. That is, higher wages and, in this case, the threat of labor problems encourage mechanization and may lead to higher food prices. On the positive side, unionization may be a means to reduce poverty, break the cycle of low wages that attract low productivity, and improve the health and education level of hired farm laborers.

Illegal aliens. Prior to the enactment of the Immigration Reform and Control Act of 1986, it was estimated that there were over 3 million illegal aliens living in the United States. About 350,000 of these were believed to be employed in agriculture. Most of these were concentrated in the western and southwestern United States.

The Immigration Reform Act took major steps to deal with the illegal alien issues:

- Provision was made for illegals who have been continuous U.S. residents since January 1, 1982, to obtain temporary and, later, permanent residency status. Three million illegals were expected to register. Over time, the desired result was to integrate persons who have been living in the United States into the American melting pot.
- It became illegal for employers, including farmers, to hire illegal aliens. Employers are required to verify that the employees are legally employed by the employee's attesting that he or she is legal to be employed and has produced a social security number with a driver's license. Criminal penalties exist for repeat violations.
- Special agricultural worker status was granted to illegal aliens who have performed agricultural services for perishable crops on a temporary basis (90 to 365 days) since before May 1, 1986, but are not permanent U.S. residents. Perishable is defined to include essentially all crops except cotton. These workers may also apply for temporary status and, later, permanent status.
- A streamlined program was established for hiring temporary foreign residents if recruitment efforts of U.S. residents fail and if the prevailing wage structure is not affected.

If effectively enforced, the Immigration Reform Act could result in short or intermediate term shortages in agricultural labor—particularly for perishable products. The number of legal temporary workers is likely to sharply increase, depending on the interpretation of allowed entrants. The reduced supply should result in higher wages and benefits for agricultural markets. There will also be increased pressure to adopt laborsaving technology.

Disputes over the rights of farm laborers to organize, the level of the minimum wage, as well as the employment of foreign laborers, will continue. Yet their complexion will change as agriculture continues to industrialize and moves into a higher-technology era. In this era, the proportion of hired farm labor as a share of farm employment will continue to increase.

The level of skill required of farm labor will also increase. More professional farm managers will be employed. Farm labor will have to be more adept at running computers and increasingly complex farm machinery, and at performing embryo transfers, injecting somatotropin, and adjusting the combination of inputs to the more complex products of biotechnology. In other words, farm labor will require more than just back-breaking work, but also a higher level of skill—after requiring higher levels of education.

In this process of change, farm labor issues will parallel those developing in the remainder of the economy. This should not be surprising as agriculture becomes more like the remainder of the economy.

THE SCIENCE AND TECHNOLOGY RESOURCE

Throughout this chapter, the changing mix of resources used in agriculture has been noted. Labor and land are relatively less important resources; water, capital, and management are more important. The major factors changing the mix of resources in agriculture have been science and technology.

The U.S. system of research and development for agriculture has been highly lauded and copied in many countries of the world. That system has three major components: federal research stations, agricultural experiment stations in each state's land-grant university, and the cooperative federal–state extension service. The rapid rate of productivity growth in the U.S. farm sector is frequently cited as the tangible results of that system.[52] The total input bundle used in food and fiber production today is not vastly different from that used in 1920. Yet the output resulting from the use of that amount of resources is today more than double that obtained in 1920 (Table 14.5). This greater output is the result of technology—of scientific research and its application in the form of hybrid corn, chemical fertilizers, chemical pest control, improved cultural practices, irrigation, and the like. The impact of these technological advances can be shown in the carrying capacity of the land for people. Carrying capacity is obtained by dividing the yield in pounds per acre of crops by the consumption of food in pounds per capita. Today, about 1 acre is required to feed one person, compared to 2 acres in 1950 and 3 acres in 1910. Private-sector research is generally more highly applied ith a pri-

TABLE 14.5 Indices of Input Use, Output, and Productivity
(1967 = 100) in Agriculture 1920–1980

Year	All Inputs	Total Output	Productivity (All Inputs)
1920	95	42	44
1930	98	43	44
1940	97	50	51
1950	101	62	61
1960	98	76	77
1970	97	84	87
1980	103	104	101

Source: Economic Indicators of the Farm Sector: Production and Efficiency Statistics (Washington, D.C.: ERS, USDA, January 1982), p. 77. Updated from *Economic Indicators of the Farm Sector: Farm Sector Review*, 1986 (Washington, D.C.: ERS, USDA, January 1988).

[52]V. Ruttan, *Agricultural Research Policy* (Minneapolis, Minn.: University of Minnesota Press, 1982).

AGRICULTURAL TECHNOLOGY: YOU CANNOT PUT THE GENIE BACK IN THE BOTTLE

The economic malaise in parts of U.S. agriculture in recent years has caused some agriculturists to question the benefits of continued development and diffusion of technology. One view is that investments in research leading to further technological advance should be curtailed because there are agricultural surpluses. Another view is that research should be reoriented toward reducing costs rather than increasing output. A third would limit transfer of technology to foreign countries. All are fallacious arguments.

Reducing investments in research would have little effect on near-term rates of growth of productivity, output, or surpluses. It could, however, have serious negative effects a decade or more into the future on productivity, production costs, and our competitiveness in world markets. Agricultural research cannot be turned on and off like a spigot. It requires continuity of investment over a long period. Furthermore, to attribute current economic surpluses to research and technology alone is to ignore the many other contributing factors—rigid, poorly constructed farm policies, economic policies that constrain demand in domestic and foreign markets, protectionist policies in foreign countries that limit or prevent access of U.S. farm products, for example.

The suggestion that research should concentrate on technologies that reduce per unit costs of production rather than output is a non sequitur. Given the competitive nature of agriculture, techonology that reduces per unit costs will, in all likelihood, stimulate agricultural output relatively quickly.

The concern about transfer of U.S.-generated agricultural technolgy to foreign countries arises from the contention that such transfers erode our competitive position in world markets. Even if we chose to limit transfer of technology, there would be practical problems in "keeping the genie in the U.S. bottle" in an interdependent world with rapid, easy communication across national boundaries. If it is neither practical nor desirable to limit foreign transfer of technology, what can be done to ensure that U.S. agriculture benefits as fully as possible from U.S.-generated technology?

Perhaps the most important strategy is to ensure a balance between basic research to create new knowledge and applied research to ensure that technology is developed, adapted, and transmitted as fully and quickly as possible for commercial use in U.S. agriculture. As the pace of science quickens and its results become ever more broadly diffused globally, we may need to modify current methods of transferring technology from the public to the private sector. The anticipated flow of biotechnology lends some urgency to reexamination of public–private relationships for transfer of that technology from the laboratory to the field. Rather than attempting to "bottle up the genie," we should seek the most effective means of applying its power.

Kenneth R. Farrell, *Calif. Agric.* (March–April 1988), p. 2.

with a primary emphasis on development and commercial application of the more basic results of public research. Private research accounts for over 50 percent of all U.S. agricultural research.[53]

Public support for agricultural research and extension activities increased modestly from the enactment of the Hatch Act in 1887, which established state—federal research ties, through World War II. Sharp increases in appropriations occurred from the mid-1940s through the mid-1960s. At that point, the total scientific resource commitment to agriculture leveled out.[54]

Federal involvement in agricultural research and technology has a mixed rationale:

- *Initially, it was designed to benefit farmers by increasing their productivity and solving their problems as they arose.* Those who benefited most were the farmers who adopted the product of science first. Their costs fell as output increased. Increased output, however, reduced price, and, with an inelastic demand, farm income fell. Those farmers who were last to adopt were worse off and eventually forced out of agriculture.

- *Agribusiness benefited from the increased proportion of farm costs spent on purchased inputs.* A continuous flow of new technologies into agriculture provided the opportunity for agribusiness to capitalize on public-sector research discoveries.

- *The ultimate beneficiary of public research was the consumer, who received an abundant supply of food with a decreasing proportion of income spent on food.* This occurred simultaneously with the release of labor from food production, which was then available to other sectors of the economy for the production of goods and services that contributed to a steadily rising standard of living.

- *In the longer run, research has a primary goal of sustaining the base of natural resources to assure a continuing supply of food for future generations.* Over time, this goal has become increasingly important as questions have arisen regarding the world food supply, resource availability, and environmental problems.

As farmers have increased the scale of their operation, as farm income has approached and sometimes exceeded nonfarm income, and as pressures to reduce government spending have increased, questions have arisen regarding the need for large public research commitments to agriculture. These questions have particularly been raised by the Office of

[53]Office of Technology Assessment, *Technology, Public Policy, and the Changing Structure of Agriculture* (Washington, D.C.: U.S. Congress, March 1986), p. 256.

[54]Office of Technology Assessment, *U.S. Food and Agricultural Research Assessment Report* (Washington, D.C.: U.S. Congress, June 1981).

Management and Budget (OMB) as they attempt to establish spending priorities. OMB has argued that much of the research and development could be advantageously left to the private sector and supported by farmers through a check-off program. In a check-off program, each farmer is assessed a small amount per unit of product marketed.[55]

Added impetus for increased private-sector agricultural research support has come from investments by private firms in primarily research-oriented functions such as genetic engineering, nitrogen fixation, and increasing photosynthetic efficiency. Increased incentives for these investments have resulted from the granting of patents for the products of agricultural research. In the 1970s, the Congress authorized the granting of patents to developers of new plant varieties. In 1980, the U.S. Supreme Court extended patent rights to new life forms. When combined with the ability to copyright computer software, virtually all discoveries of university and private-sector research became patent or copyright protected. Patent and copyrights held by universities are regularly sold or leased to private-sector firms for development and exploitation.

In this new research environment, the questions raised by Hightower in *Hard Tomatoes, Hard Times* regarding the relationship of agribusiness and land-grant universities became even more relevant. An increased proportion of private-sector support for research would mean *higher prices for the products of agricultural research*—whether new plant varieties or computer software. Similarly, greater credence is added to OMB concerns about who should pay for the agricultural research. In the new research environment, primary emphasis would be expected to be placed on those types of research holding the greatest potential for earning the greatest returns from either farmers or consumers. Societal goals for research, such as soil conservation and environmental impacts, would receive less emphasis. Real food prices would be expected to continue to fall as the pace of technological change accelerates.

DEALING WITH FUTURE RESOURCE PROBLEMS

Public policies designed to conserve these resources cannot be expected to be particularly popular with farmers because of their tendency to regulate resource use and because they tell farmers how to farm. Sacrifice of freedom appears to be inevitable as increased government involvement in resource use occurs.

Major questions concern the role of the market versus regulation in solving resource problems. Government can either act to enhance market

[55]Check-off programs currently exist for cotton, milk, and a number of other products. However, most of the revenue from these programs goes for advertising.

forces, by actions such as decreasing subsidies, or resort to regulation of resource use as a means of avoiding shortages and preserving resources for future generations.

ADDITIONAL READINGS

1. A. M. Woodruff and Charles R. Rink, *The Farm and City: Rivals or Allies* (Englewood Cliffs, N.J.: Prentice-Hall, Inc., 1980), provides a good discussion of a number of contemporary issues in the resource policy.

2. The book *Water and Water Policy in World Food Supplies*, W. R. Jordan, ed. (College Station, Tex.: Texas A&M University, 1987) provides an excellent compilation of articles on water resource issues.

3. The OTA study *Technology, Public Policy, and the Changing Structure of Agriculture* (Washington, D.C.: U.S. Congress, March 1986) provides a comprehensive study of the potential consequences of rapid technological change on research policy and resource use.

4. Maurice M. Kelso has an excellent article that discusses the urgency of addressing resource issues titled "Values, Beliefs and Myths in Natural Resource Policy Making," in *Increasing Understanding of Public Problems and Policies—1987* (Chicago: Farm Foundation, January 1988).

Chapter 15

Impact of Agricultural and Food Policy on Agribusiness

> *The business of government is to keep government out of business—that is, unless business needs government aid.*
>
> Will Rogers

Agribusiness *as used in this chapter refers to those firms whose main business relates to providing food and fiber, but which are not primarily involved in production.* Agribusiness includes input suppliers such as agricultural lenders, fertilizer manufacturers and dealers, feed manufacturers, as well as plant and animal breeders, seed companies and dealers. Agribusiness also includes firms that transport, market, handle, process, distribute, wholesale, retail, and serve food—in essence, from the farm gate through the supermarket and/or fast-food outlet. Firms integrated into production are part of agribusiness. Thus, Tysons, the largest broiler producer and processor, is treated here as being an agribusiness firm (as opposed to a farmer) because of the importance of its input supply, processing, and marketing activities.

Most of the discussion in this book has related to the impact of agricultural and food policies on farmers, consumers, and taxpayers. Yet the farm value is only 25 percent of the retail price paid for food by consumers. The rest goes to the middleman. In addition, it was observed in Chapter 9 that production expenses account for about three-fourths of cash receipts, leaving 7 percent to the farmer and 18 percent for purchased inputs. However, only 13 of the 18 percent goes to agribusiness, with the remainder being paid for other cash expenses, such as taxes, hired labor,

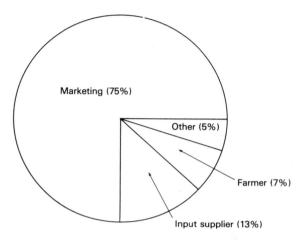

Figure 15.1 Relative importance of agribusiness in food and fiber production and marketing, 1985.

and rental payments. The bottom line is that 88 percent (75 percent plus 13 percent) of the consumers' food dollars goes to the agribusiness sector (Fig 15.1). From Chapter 8 it may be recalled that agribusiness employment totals 18.6 million jobs.

Because of their prominence in agriculture, agribusiness firms are profoundly influenced by agricultural and food policy. This is evidenced by the sophisticated network agribusiness firms have developed to influence farm and food policy decisions as discussed in Chapter 4. Despite the importance of policy on agribusiness, little is written on the topic. Yet a large share of the readers of this book are likely to be or become agribusiness employees.

Every agribusiness firm needs to have the ability to assess the impact of policy changes on its operations. This chapter is designed to provide insight into the nature of potential impacts of farm and food policy on agribusiness as well as some theoretical or analytical approaches to addressing the policy issues confronting business. The chapter first discusses the major agribusiness segments; then the policy goals of agribusiness are specified. Subsequently, impacts are examined in terms of the main policy categories such as price and income policy, stocks policy, and so forth. Case examples are regularly utilized to make particular points.

AGRIBUSINESS SEGMENTS

While a reasonably common set of policy goals can be specified for agribusiness, the emphasis or priority that these goals receive varies. As a result, it is desirable to first define the agribusiness segments that are important from a policy perspective. For this purpose, five major agribusiness segments can be identified.

- **Input manufacturers** are the industrial firms that develop and manufacture the inputs used by farmers in the production of farm products. They often hold patents or copyrights on these inputs. Many of these firms are not exclusively dependent on agriculture for their sales, but are multiproduct and even multinational petroleum, chemical, pharmaceutical, or machinery companies. These firms' most direct contact with agricultural and food policy probably relates to food safety and resource issues, such as residues, endangered species, water quality, and soil erosion. However, the demand for their products is directly affected by farm programs that influence production.
- **Input suppliers** are the wholesale and retail distributors of farm supplies. One distinguishing feature among input suppliers is whether they are owned by farmers (predominantly as cooperatives) or by nonfarm investors. Farmer-owned input suppliers tend to be more sensitive to the needs and policy goals of farmers. Thus, while investor-owned fertilizer dealers often express strong vocal political opposition to production controls, cooperative fertilizer dealers simply bear the agony of reduced sales.
- **Integrated agribusiness** is directly involved in input supply, sometimes manufacturing, farm production, marketing, and sometimes processing. Nonfarm-investor-owned companies such as Cargill, ConAgra, and Tysons, as well as some cooperatives, such as Sunkist, Welch, and Sunsweet, have the characteristics of integrated agribusiness. As contrasted with most farmers, integrated agribusinesses recognize the importance of controlling the production–marketing channel to their success. Their attitudes toward government tend to be influenced by the extent to which they can control or manage the policy tools. For example, while broiler integrators are highly opposed to government involvement, fresh fruit and vegetable integrators (particularly cooperatives) embrace marketing orders as a control tool.
- **Market intermediaries** cover a wide range of firms and functions that facilitate the sale of and/or physically handle farm products without changing its form. Market intermediaries profit from volume and from price variation. For example, futures market brokers do not do much business when prices are resting on loan rates. Similarly, Cargill and Continental grain suffer when export volume is curtailed by high loan rates. In other words, market intermediaries are strong free-market advocates. They cover a wide range in size, from multinationals to independent auction market operators.

- **Food processors and marketers** hold the franchise on the products thao consumers buy. Included are the processors, manufacturers, wholesalers, retailers, and fast-food operators. Their most direct contact is with consumers. Their greatest policy interest, therefore, is in food policy, although farm and resource policy are also an important concern.

AGRIBUSINESS POLICY GOALS

The diversity of agribusiness is more apparent than the diversity of agriculture. Yet the business dimension of their operations makes agribusiness firms more inclined than farmers to have a common set of farm and food policy goals. In other words, agribusiness firms are more likely to approach policy issues from a strictly business perspective. This is because business goals and economics take precedence over value differences that tend to divide farmers and farm organizations. The following policy goals have been suggested for the agribusiness sector:[1]

- There is a desire for an *abundant supply of farm products that is readily available.* Agribusiness profits from volume. This is more typical of commodities than it is of branded products; although even on branded inputs and food, product volume is a key to profit. Therefore, policies that reduce volume tend to be opposed by agribusiness.
- Agribusiness favors programs that *expand domestic and international markets.* Examples include foreign market development, check-off programs, foreign food aid, cooperator programs, food stamps, school lunch, and even export subsidies. It prefers programs that utilize commercial markets as opposed to government donation (food aid) programs. Farmers, on the other hand, prefer donation programs because more commodity is moved per dollar of government expenditures.
- Agribusiness firms desire to *minimize restrictions on their operations.* Programs that interfere with their marketing strategies are opposed. Firms want to maximize latitude for decision making. Government regulations either reduce the firms' flexibility in making decisions or impose extra costs, and often they do both.
- Agribusiness firms prefer supply and demand *responsive markets.* In effect, this is saying that they prefer instability. Most large agribusiness firms have a sufficiently good intelligence system that they

[1]T.A. Stucker, J.B. Penn, and R.D. Knutson. "Agricultural-Food Policymaking: Process and Participants," in *Agricultural-Food Policy Review*, AFPR-1 (Washington, D.C.: ERS, USDA, January 1977), pp. 1–11.

are able to anticipate change, take advantage of it, hedge against it, or adjust to it. This is particularly true of market intermediaries and integrated agribusiness firms. It is less true of input manufacturers and input suppliers.

- Like other bureaucratic institutions, agribusiness *resists change*. Although agribusiness is as a general rule opposed to regulation, they sometimes oppose deregulation. This is particularly true of "mature" industries that utilize regulation to protect against decline and change. Milk processors oppose doing away with milk marketing orders because of uncertainty over what the market would be like without regulation.

Agribusiness goals are not completely consistent. Preferring instability and resisting change are hardly consistent! Yet policy goals are seldom consistent. There are trade-offs. Priorities have to be set. Compromises have to be reached.

From these goals alone, an agribusiness policy agenda could be written. *It would be a market-oriented agenda with relatively low levels of government involvement.* But the world is not all that simple. Some of the conflicts will become apparent in the discussion that follows.

POLICY IMPACTS ON AGRIBUSINESS

Discussions of agribusiness policy impacts could be approached in several different ways. For example, five agribusiness segments could be discussed separately. However, on many, if not most, issues agribusiness takes much the same policy position. The discussion that follows is in terms of policy area with illustrative case examples in each area to indicate the complexity of the issues.

Trade Policy

Agribusiness firms tend to be free-trade oriented. They tend to be strong supporters of the MTN and GATT. They are strongly opposed to any policies that would have government more involved in commodity trading. The reasons for this opposition are obvious:

- Free-trade policies expand trade volume. Exports and imports expand because market prices decline as trade channels are opened. Commodity profits depend on volume and profits are probably easier to gain with lower price levels.
- Less government involvement leaves more functions to be per-

formed by agribusiness. This is the case both on the seller (exporter) *and* buyer (importer) sides of the market.

- Free-trade policies reduce the market power of both producers. Therefore, relatively speaking, the agribusiness middlemen are given more market power.
- Free-trade increases price variability, thus allowing market intermediaries to generate higher returns due to hedging, price analysis, market information, and forecasting activities.

Where government is involved, agribusiness desires to be heavily influencing the implementation decisions. Being able to make a decision for government may be more profitable and predictable than the free market. The key then becomes one of staying in a position of control, insider knowledge or heavy influence to profit from government decisions.

Multilateral trade negotiations.   Trade negotiations and GATT are often criticized for being ineffective. Quite clearly, trade negotiations and GATT procedures have been more effective for the industrial sector than for agriculture. Yet despite GATT's weaknesses, there have been many gains to producers and agribusiness from trade negotiations. Perhaps the most significant gain has been in the soybean trade with the European Economic Community and Japan.

In the 1960–1961 Dillon Round of the MTN, the United States and the European Economic Community agreed not to impose any duties on soybeans and soybean meal for two reasons:

- The European Economic Community was, and still is, highly deficient in vegetable proteins for balancing livestock and poultry feed rations. To a lesser extent, it was deficient in vegetable oils as well.
- With the formation of the European Economic Community in the late 1950s and the establishment of the Common Agricultural Policy (CAP), which utilizes the variable levy as its main protective tool, the community was under heavy pressure to show a degree of good faith toward the MTN and GATT.

This EC soybean concession has had tremendous long-term value to U.S. farmers and agribusiness firms. EC soybean imports have mushroomed as the poultry and hog industries have expanded. In addition, the importance of soybeans in balancing rations has become more apparent.

The European Economic Community imports soybeans both as whole beans and as soybean meal (Fig. 15.2). EC meal imports have grown consistently since 1970, while soybean imports decreased some-

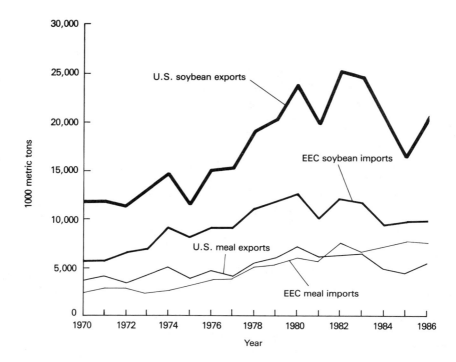

Figure 15.2 Trend in imports of soybeans and soybean meal by the EEC and in total U.S. exports, 1970–1986.

what after 1980. This decline partially reflects increased competition from Brazil in the world soybean market. Brazil is primarily an exporter of meal as opposed to whole beans.

The benefits of the EC exclusion of the variable levy is very apparent when the trend in EC soybean imports is compared to its coarse grain imports. In coarse grain imports, where the European Economic Community maintains a variable levy, the trend is decidedly negative. In the absence of a variable levy, the trend in soybean imports is clearly positive (Fig. 15.3).

The Dillon Round decision on soybeans is not without controversy. EC farmers blame soybean imports for displacing homegrown grains, reducing the consumption of olive oil, and increasing butter surpluses—a by-product of whole bean imports is soybean oil, which is used as a cooking oil and to make margarine. In the mid-1980s, the European Economic Community threatened to place a tax on vegetable oil as a means of partially imposing a duty on soybeans. The United States strongly objected, with the effect of at least delaying the EC action.

In separate MTN action, Japan has reduced its 13 percent duty on

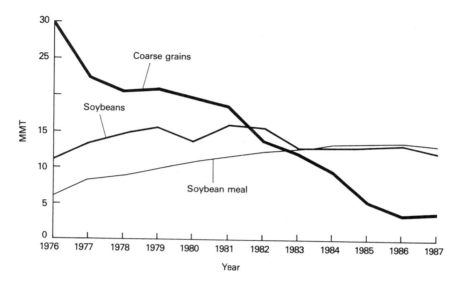

Figure 15.3 Trend in EEC soybean, soybean meal, and coarse grain imports, 1976–1988.

soybeans to zero. There is probably no better testimonial on the importance of trade negotiations to agribusiness and farmers than the soybean experience. In the late 1980s, soybean exports to the European Economic Community totaled approximately $4 billion—10 percent of all U.S. agricultural exports.

Cartels and Marketing Boards

Agribusiness firms, led by the multinational grain companies, are strongly opposed to marketing boards. This opposition is so strong that it extends to attempting to prevent producer educational materials on marketing boards from being produced, distributed, and utilized.[2] The reasons are well explained by Schmitz:[3]

- *The establishment of a marketing board would greatly reduce the role of the private grain firms and the multinational grain companies* that currently dominate U.S. grain export sales and handling.

[2]Mike Turner et al., *Who Will Market Your Grain*, D-1057 (College Station; Tex.: Texas Agricultural Extension Service, March 1978) was the target of an agribusiness attempt to limit the use of marketing board educational materials.

[3]Andrew Schmitz et al., *Grain Export Cartels* (Cambridge, Mass.: Ballinger Publishing Co., 1981), pp. 38–48.

These companies buy grain directly from U.S. farmers or from farmer-owned cooperatives, arrange for transportation to ports, maintain extensive port-handling facilities, make sales directly to foreign customers, arrange for ocean freight, and handle international financial transactions. Under a marketing board system, these multinational companies could buy grain only from the board. In addition, a large proportion of board sales would be government to government. Thus the grain companies would become *strictly handlers* performing largely transportation-related functions— often referred to as the logistics of the grain trade. Similarly, the role of smaller private grain companies and grain cooperatives would change dramatically. They would operate as storage agents for the board. They could not buy grain from farmers—that would be the responsibility of the board.

- *The objectives of the marketing board and the private companies would directly conflict*, as illustrated in Fig. 15.4. If the marketing board acts as a producer monopolist, it equates its marginal revenue with marginal cost (supply) producing quantity Q_b, selling at price P_b. On the other hand, a grain company with monopoly power in the seller's market and monopsony power in the producer market will equate its marginal outlay for grain (MO) with its marginal revenue

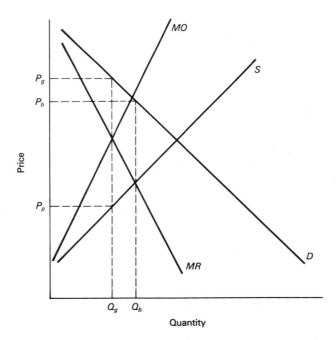

Figure 15.4 Objectives of marketing board and private companies conflict.

(MR), buying quantity Q_g, paying price P_p, and selling at price P_g. In other words, the grain companies will desire to buy a smaller quantity, pay producers a lower price, and sell at a higher price than a producer-oriented marketing board.

• *The business of grain market intermediaries would decline.* The need for and role of the futures market under a marketing board would be highly uncertain. With all grain purchased by the marketing board and with producers paid the average price generated by the board, there would be little need for hedging at either the producer or grain handler level. The volume of hedged trading would, thereby, be reduced. Under these circumstances, the role and/or justification for the futures market is uncertain. Since the futures market is, in effect, a central pricing point or price discovery mechanism for the international grain market, a new world pricing point could be required.

• *The producer marketing system would be radically changed.* There would be no producer marketing decision because marketing would be through the board. Storage decisions would likewise be at the discretion of the board. As indicated previously, cooperatives performing storage functions would become agents of the board.

Price and Income Supports

It is often asserted that no one benefits from high price supports other than producers. Similarly, it is often asserted that farm programs are mainly designed for crop producers and that livestock producers enjoy few benefits. Such generalizations lose points on exams. The following are two interesting cases where agribusiness becomes a major beneficiary of crop policies. They also illustrate that the secondary effects of policy may be as important as the primary effects.

Sugar policy.   Historically, the United States has been a net importer of sugar. U.S. sugar production has been maintained by setting a high support price and restricting imports sufficiently to achieve the support price level. However, this sugar policy has provided the umbrella for the development of a corn sweetener industry which has substantially reduced sugar consumption.

The 1985 farm bill effectively set the sugar price support at $0.21 per pound, while high-fructose corn sweeteners (HFCS) has traditionally been priced about 30 percent lower, at about $0.15 per pound. HFCS is a nearly perfect substitute in some sugar uses. As a result, sugar consumption has persistently declined while HFCS consumption has persistently increased (Fig. 15.5). In 1987, HFCS had captured about 53 percent of the U.S. sweetener market.

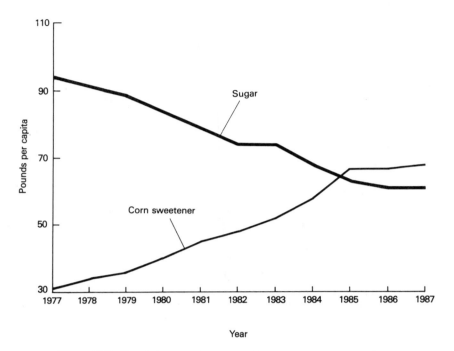

Figure 15.5 Trends in per capita sugar and corn sweetener consumption.

Interestingly, U.S. sugar producers have not been the ones hurt by this policy because their price has been supported. The lower sugar consumption comes largely at the expense of developing countries that export raw sugar to the United States. To maintain the sugar price at $0.21 per pound, import quotas have been gradually reduced (Fig. 15.6). The world sugar price has been in the $0.05 to $0.09 per pound range during the 1980s, so the United States is a preferred market to developing countries with its support price.

U.S. sugar policy has had four fascinating effects on agribusiness:

- Sugar policy in combination with ethanol subsidies has built a corn sweetener industry involving major agribusiness firms with sales of about $1.5 billion in 1987. Without U.S. sugar policy, the modern corn sweetener industry would not exist.
- Noncaloric sweeteners have also enjoyed an umbrella of price protection. While it may be argued that people consume noncaloric sweeteners for reasons other than price, high sugar price supports have enabled competitive pricing of products such as diet soft drinks.
- Sugar refiners that process imported raw sugar have been going out of business.

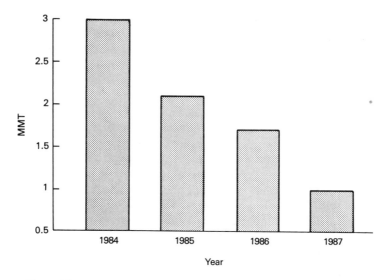

Figure 15.6 The sugar price support is constantly reducing the import quota.

- Imports of sugar-containing products have become a major competitive problem for U.S. processors of products such as candy. Candy companies that operate both in the United States and in countries such as Canada, which does not support the price of sugar, have had a substantial competitive advantage.

For the same reasons that corn sweetener interests support high sugar price supports, corn interests would fight against either a lowering of the support price or a conversion of the sugar program to a target price program. Either action would make sugar more price competitive with HFCS. The corn sweetener lobby, therefore, has become a prime advocate for the sugar program.

Price support loan.   The conditions under which the price support loan constitutes a floor price for commodities was discussed in Chapter 10. In general, the loan rate is a floor price. When the government stands ready to accept forfeited commodities at the support price, all producers are eligible for the loan (participate in the program), and commodities are not released by USDA using other means, such as the PIK certificates. It stands to reason that if these conditions are fulfilled, agribusiness firms cannot attract commodities out of the hands of producers or the government unless they are willing to pay the loan rate plus accumulated interest costs. Commodities may not, therefore, be available for export by the market intermediaries at the competitive prices.

Even if the loan rate is below the world market price, price-supported commodities may not be available for export. Farmers' marketing decisions are influenced by expectations and risk. With no downside price risk (they can always forfeit at the loan rate), if farmers foresee a reasonable chance that the market might rise above the loan rate, they will tend to hold commodities off the market. This behavior also has an adverse impact on exporters. Therefore, the security of the loan itself can cause farmers not to make commodities available and, thereby, drive up the market price or deny the market the volume needed to satisfy demand at competitive prices. *It may be concluded that the loan rate does not have to be above the world market price for exports to be reduced.*

The effect of the loan program on producer behavior is an integral part of the residual supplier problem. The loan program puts market intermediaries, who are primarily dependent on exports of U.S. commodities in a very difficult competitive position. On the other hand, multinational companies are not in as difficult a competitive position because they can trade the commodities of other countries, although their sources of supply may also be limited by the prevalence of state trading arrangements.

One alternative for encouraging marketing of products under loan without incurring large increases in government costs is to convert the nonrecourse loan to a recourse loan.[4] While still providing the farmer credit at harvest, a recourse loan would remove the price floor. In addition, whereas interest is not charged on nonrecourse loans where the commodity is forfeited, it would be charged under a recourse loan since there is no forfeiture. A recourse loan would also be different in that deficiency payments would not be made under a recourse loan when the market price falls below the loan rate. Recourse loans have been proposed, but farmers logically prefer the nonrecourse loan. Yet, U.S. agribusiness exporters are disadvantaged by the nonrecourse policy.

Target Price Policy

Agribusiness is opposed to farm subsidies. If this is the case, *target prices are an exception to the rule.* While high loan rates arguably benefit input suppliers (farmers buy more inputs), exporters are hurt. In the long run, all agribusiness segments are hurt by high loan rates because production controls generally result. On the other hand, *target prices benefit all agribusiness segments*:

- Exporters like target prices because they encourage production. Target prices also lead to more competitive prices, unless the world market price is below the loan rate.

[4]Another option involves the use of PIK certificates, which will be discussed subsequently as a stocks policy issue.

- Domestic processors prefer target prices because they are more likely to be able to sell finished products at prices that are competitive with imports. For example, with the target price and the marketing loan, cotton exports have not only been stimulated, but domestic mills also have been placed in a competitive position to sell cotton fabrics at prices competitive with imported fabrics and synthetic fibers.
- Livestock and poultry integrators like target prices because they result in low feed prices. Lower feed prices have a markedly increased impact on the interest of poultry producers in farm policy. For years, the National Broiler Council had either opposed government involvement in agriculture or had taken no position. In 1987, realizing the lower feed prices that result from the target price program, the National Broiler Council voted to support the 1985 farm bill, which embodied large direct payments to feed grain farmers.
- Input manufacturers and suppliers favor target prices because farmers' expected returns are raised. Higher target prices mean that it is profitable to apply more fertilizer and utilize farm machinery more intensively. The net effect is increased sales as long as target prices are not so high that production restrictions become so large that they override the benefits of target prices.

The appeal of target prices presents an interesting problem for an administration that is trying to garner support for MTN policies designed to promote free trade. An elimination of subsidies by the United States as proposed by the Reagan administration in the opening round of the MTN would require a concession to eliminate target prices. The main beneficiary of reduced target prices is taxpayers in terms of reduced government costs—not agribusiness and not producers. As indicated in Chapter 7, the root of protectionism is domestic farm programs.

Stocks Policy

One of the most complex and politically sensitive tasks of the government is that of managing commodity stocks. How stocks are managed has a tremendous impact on price levels, price variability, commodity availability, and, therefore, upon firm purchase, storage, and marketing decisions. Illustrations include the problem of releasing CCC stocks, holding stocks in forms other than commodities, and the management of public and private dairy stocks.

Releasing CCC stocks.   One of the secretary of agriculture's most difficult decisions involves the release of government stocks. Charges of manipulation of prices and cheap food abound when the agriculture secretary places CCC stocks on the market and, thereby, suppresses commodity prices. A classic example occurred in 1987 after USDA made an agreement with the Soviet Union and China to buy at competitive prices. To make commodities available to U.S. exporting companies without substantial increases in the market price, PIK certificates were used as subsidies to exporters of wheat to the Soviet Union. In addition, the secretary took two actions:

- He established an auction market for CCC owned wheat whereby the USDA would redeem certificates for wheat at a price that it deemed necessary to secure the Russian business. The bidders were companies (presumably mostly exporters).
- Upon finding that there was not a sufficient surplus of PIK certificates, he made 100 percent of the deficiency payments for wheat and barley in generic PIK certificates. In the past, PIK certificates had only been used for half of the payments.

The farm organization lobby became irate at these actions, which, by releasing commodities from CCC stocks, had the effect of suppressing producer prices while directly benefiting only a small number of exporters. Farm state congressmen cited wheat market prices dropping as much as $0.39 per bushel from a market price of about $2.50. Prior to the USDA action there were widespread predictions that the market price of wheat would need to rise sufficiently to cover interest on the CCC loan and thereby encourage farmers to release sufficient grain to sell the Soviets and Chinese. Chairman Glickman, of the House Wheat, Soybean, and Feed Grains Subcommittee, charged that by this action, the USDA was acting like a "grain board."

No doubt there has been an increasing tendency toward USDA intervention in grain markets since at least 1970. This intervention has not always been on behalf of producers. The 1987 action on behalf of exporters to get commodities released from CCC stocks is but one example.[5]

Holding stocks in other forms.   Government stocks depress market prices even when they are not released. The larger the stocks, the more depressed the price, up to the point where the price simply rests on the loan rate. Why then does the government hold stocks in the form of commodities? Instead, why not hold them in the form of cash or land?

The money stock idea arose during the world food crisis in the early 1970s. It was observed that the cost of storing commodities in strategic locations is so high that it would be cheaper to give countries needing commodities cash to buy grain as opposed to food aid. Yet if a country's

[5]For other examples, see Morgan, *Merchants of Grain*.

ability to buy is enhanced, when supplies are short the market price is driven up even higher. The higher price tends to encourage production in future periods, which is offset somewhat by the more unstable price. In other words, *commodity stocks foster long-run supply and price stability, while a money reserve fosters instability.* Agribusiness firms would do better, in relative terms, under a money stocks policy because they are better able than most farmers to manage risk.

Holding land out of production can also be viewed as a stocks policy. However, it has different effects than holding either commodity or money stocks. Stocks of land held out of production do not influence prices in the short run. In the long run, however, land reserves affect prices because of their potential for being put back into production. For agribusiness, land held in reserve is a two-edged sword—it reduces input sales and reduces volume of product marketed and/or stored.

Managing dairy stocks.   Government involvement in stocks has a marked impact on agribusiness inventory management policies. In many respects, under current farm programs the government has become the inventory manager. But such an answer is too simple. Money is made and lost over changes in the value of inventories. Government policy therefore becomes important from the perspective of who holds the inventories during periods of changing prices.

Dairy price supports provide an excellent illustration of how the private and public sectors interact in holding stocks. The government stands ready to purchase any manufactured dairy products (butter, cheese, and nonfat dry milk) offered to it at the support price. Government stocks can be bought by private firms at 10 percent over the support price. Manufactured dairy products purchased by the government are produced continuously. However, more milk is produced in the spring than in the fall. Milk prices may rise above the support level in the fall when milk supplies are short and often fall to the support level in the spring.

In the late winter and/or early spring, there is incentive for the private sector not to hold stocks of manufactured products. In the fall, however, inventories tend to increase in value as long as government stocks are not overly large. If a processor sells to the government in the spring, not anticipating a large price increase in the fall, substantial profit opportunities are forgone. If private stocks are held in the spring and the price increase does not materialize in the fall, losses are incurred, at least in terms of storage and inventory holding costs.

Of course, the greatest opportunities for gain are when price support levels are increasing, at which time there are strong incentives to hold private stocks. On the other hand, an anticipated price support reduction signals heavy sales to the government and lower private sector stocks. Similarly, potential inventory value changes explain why cooperatives that process manufactured dairy products (butter, nonfat dry milk, and cheese) prefer the USDA assessing (taxing) producers to pay for the cost of the government purchasing and storing these commodities as contrasted with a price support reduction. These examples not only serve to illustrate government policy impacts on private-sector inventory management decisions, but also the importance of being able to elevate the interaction of supply, demand, and government policy decisions as they affect commodity prices.

Production Controls

The impact of government on agribusiness, perhaps, can be seen even more clearly in cases where public decisions are made to control production. Input manufacturers, input suppliers, and market intermediaries experience almost immediate effects on their operations, with impacts often extending to the economic viability of rural communities. The 1980s provide an excellent environment to evaluate and, to a certain extent, quantify these impacts. Examples from land retirement and the dairy termination programs are used to illustrate the complexity of the effects of production control policies.

Land retirement programs. It will be recalled that throughout the 1970s there were strong incentives to expand production. Most of the land that was retired by government programs in the 1960s (other than that planted to trees) was put back into production in the 1970s. The decline in exports during the early 1980s, combined with ever-increasing production, led to the potential for a large accumulation of government stocks. To forestall this development, large quantities of land were removed from production (Fig. 15.7). The government implemented the original Payment-In-Kind (PIK) program, which removed a record 83 million acres of land from production. Farm input sales, most of which were already in inventory, plummeted. For example, while from 1974 to 1981, fertilizer sales increased at an annual rate of 7.7 percent, in the period 1981–1985, they *declined* at a rate of 5.6 percent.[6] Fertilizer employee numbers declined at a rate of 5.5 percent annually and capital expenditures declined 16.2 percent annually. In farm machinery, tractor sales increased by 15.2 percent annually from 1974 to 1981 but decreased by 15.3 percent from 1981 to 1985.[7] Farmer cooperatives, such as Farmland Industries, went through years of downsizing as sales of fertilizer, petroleum and other farm supplies declined (Fig. 15.8). For machinery dealers such as Inter-

[6]Stan Daberkow, *Agricultural Input Industry Indicators in 1974–85*, Agric. Inf. Bull. 534 (Washington, D.C.: ERS, USDA, November 1987).

[7]Ibid., p. 13.

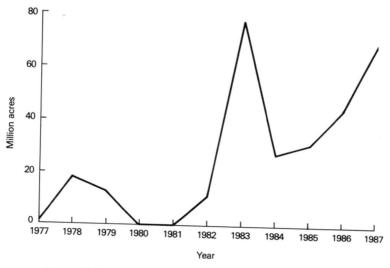

Figure 15.7 Quantities of land removed from production, 1977-87.

national Harvester, PIK was the straw that broke the camel's back, as tractor sales declined during subsequent years (Fig. 15.9).

The impact of particular government programs and economic forces on agribusiness during the 1980s, as contrasted with the 1960s, is very interesting. Recall that in the 1960s the prevailing policy tools were acreage allotments and price supports (there were no target prices). In the

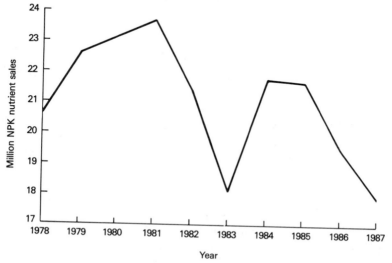

Figure 15.8 Fertilizer sales declined in response to increased land retired, during the 1980s.

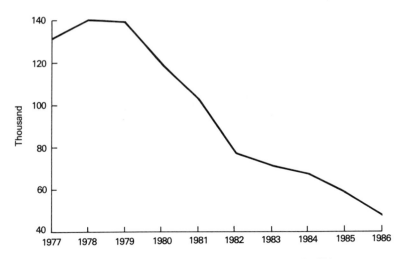

Figure 15.9 Tractor sales, over 40 horsepower, 1977–1986.

presence of only allotments and price supports, a cutback in acreage had two economic effects:

- It reduced the quantity of land to be farmed, thus tending to reduce input sales.
- It had the potential for increasing commodity prices, thus tending to increase input sales.

The effects are seen more clearly in Fig. 15.10. The marginal value product (*MVP*) curve represents the demand for fertilizers per acre of corn produced. *MVP* is the marginal product (the extra corn production resulting from an additional unit of fertilizer applied) times the price of corn.

Recognizing the existence of diminishing returns, removing land from production in the 1960s reduced the marginal product of land as land is farmed more intensely. This shifts the *MVP* curve to the left from MVP_1 to MVP_2 (Fig. 15.10). This has the effect of reducing the quantity of fertilizer demanded from Q_1 to Q_2 at fertilizer price P_f. If P_1 is greater than either the support price, production controls increase the price of corn from P_1 to P_2 which shifts the fertilizer demand curve back to the right from MVP_2 to MVP_3.[*] The result of the higher corn price is to increase fertilizer demand from Q_2 to Q_3. The net effect is a small reduction

---

[*]This analysis assumes that the price support level is sufficiently low that the price of corn rises above the support level.

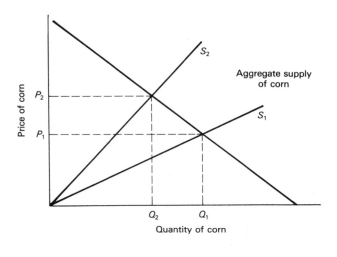

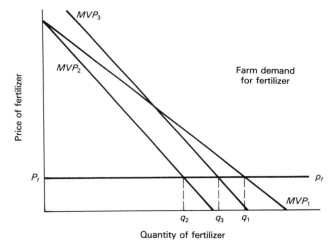

Figure 15.10   Effect of production controls on the supply of corn and on the demand for fertilizer with price supports.

in the quantity of fertilizer demanded from Q_1 to Q_3. Throughout the 1960s, these opposing forces operated with no great harm to the farm input industries. In fact, input demand grew as the proportion of purchased inputs used by farmers increased (see Fig. 9.10).

In the 1980s, taking the same amount of land out of production had a much more adverse impact upon agribusiness. The reason lies in a change in farm policy—the substitution of target prices for support prices. With the target price programs, any increases in producer prices that resulted from the large production cutbacks simply meant less government payments, not higher incomes (returns) to crop producers! The difference in economic effect of price support versus target price policy is more clearly illustrated in Fig. 15.10. With the target price set substantially above the now-higher market price (P_1), removing land from production is not compensated for by an increase in producer returns. Therefore, while the shift in fertilizer demand occurs from MVP_1 to MVP_2, there is *no compensating shift* to MVP_3 due to the increased market price *because the target price, not the market price, drives production decisions.*[9]

Dairy termination program.   The indirect impacts of farm programs are often unanticipated and can become highly controversial. One of the best illustrations has been the impact of dairy programs on the beef industry. For years, the beef industry had little or no interest in domestic farm policy related to other commodities. The basic attitude of cattlemen tended to be that of "give us our beef import quotas and leave us alone." This was the case at least until the dairy diversion program of 1983 and the dairy termination program of 1986.

The impact of dairy programs upon the beef industry results from about 15 percent of the beef and 25 percent of the hamburger meat being by-products of the dairy industry. Both the dairy diversion and termination programs had substantial impact on beef supplies because they were explicitly designed to reduce cow numbers. Termination meant more beef in the supermarket during dairy herd liquidation.

From an economic perspective, the impact of these programs on beef prices is relatively easy to analyze.[10] For example, the dairy termination program bought dairymen out of production and required that their herds, composed of about 1.5 million head of cows, heifers, calves, and bulls, be slaughtered. Slaughter requirements were divided into three six-month periods selected by the dairy farmers whose bids were accepted by the government. Economic theory suggests that participating farmers would tend to slaughter at either the beginning or the end of the period. Farmers who were not covering their variable costs of production would tend to:

- Sign up in the first slaughter period.
- Slaughter at the beginning of the period.

[9]This analysis assumes that no decoupling policies and no effective payment limits exist. A good exercise involves explaining why!

[10]To some economists this analysis may be viewed as being overly simplistic. It is presented as an illustration of a general approach rather than a definitive answer to a relatively complex issue. For example, all red meat and even poultry might be considered in analyzing price impacts. The illustration is not designed to discourage more complete approaches which would be expected to be utilized by agribusiness firms.

Of 1.5 million dairy animals signed up for the program, 832,000 were to be slaughtered in the first period. Utilizing the expectation that 52 percent would go to market in the first two months of the first period, it was estimated that 63 million pounds of beef would be added to the supply. This was 5.6 percent of the total expected beef slaughter based on past experience and outlook information. With a beef price elasticity of demand of -0.31 at the farm level, a 5.6 percent increase in supply would be expected to lead to an 18 percent decline in the price of fed cattle by the following formula:

$$\frac{\% \text{ increase in supply}}{\text{elasticity of demand}} = \% \text{ change in price}$$

$$\frac{5.6}{-0.31} = -18$$

A portion of the downward price pressure created by increased beef supplies was offset by mandated purchases of 400 million pounds of red meat by USDA for school lunch, export, and military commissaries located outside the United States. If these meat purchases were spread equally throughout the 17-month slaughter period, the quantity demanded would increase by 1.6 percent per month. This would reduce the expected price decline by 5 percent (1.6/.31), to 13 percent during the first two months of the program.

The result of the actual drop in price, which was very close to that estimated above, was a law suit by livestock producers designed to force increased purchases of beef by USDA to regulate the flow of cattle to slaughter. As a result of this law suit, USDA purchases were increased, although only minor steps were taken to redistribute slaughter.

Without question, the indirect impacts of dairy programs on livestock sharply escalated cattlemen's interest in domestic farm program issues. The subsequent Harkin bill proposal to more than double the price support level for feed grains and milk, as well as impose mandatory production controls, led to the conclusion that beef prices would fall by over 23 percent if the resulting increased slaughter of 2 million were spread over a six-month period.[11]

The dairy termination program had both positive and negative impacts on agribusiness. Meat packers slaughtering dairy animals were deluged with business, utilizing facilities to capacity. Similarly, the business of market intermediaries (brokers, auction markets, and cow jockeys) increased sharply. Milk cooperatives and processors located in milk-deficit regions having heavy participation in either the diversion or

[11]Ronald D. Knutson et al., *Policy Alternatives for Modifying the 1985 Farm Bill* (College Station, Tex.: Texas A&M University, 1987), p. 75.

termination program scrambled for milk supplies. Intermarket movement of milk supplies increased sharply to meet local market needs. Milk
cooperatives having commitments to supply the full milk needs of large
processors (full supply contracts) were particularly hard pressed to meet
their commitments.

Structure and Resource Policy

From settlement of the frontiers to the present, government has attempted to influence the structure of agriculture and facilitate technological progress. The agribusiness impacts of these policies are often overlooked. Examples are presented from cooperative and patent policy.

Cooperative policy.   Cooperatives not only enjoy the benefits of
certain antitrust exemptions, they also have the privilege under the price
support program of taking out commodity loans on behalf of their member producers. Referred to as Form G lending authority, cooperatives can
utilize this privilege if they have pooling contracts with their members.
Under such a contract the producer commits to market through the cooperative. The cooperative normally takes out the CCC loan as soon as the
commodity is received from the member and provides the producer an advance which may be some percentage of the loan rate. The cooperative is
free to market the commodity just like the producer and must pay off the
loan as soon as the commodity is sold. The producer receives the pool or
average price whenever the pool is settled.

The advantages to cooperatives from Form G lending authority include:

- The commodity is controlled by the cooperative from the time it is
  received. The cooperative is free to sell the commodity in domestic or
  foreign markets whenever it is advantageous.
- The CCC loan interest rate may be less than the market rate.
- The cooperative enjoys the nonrecourse loan forfeiture privileges if
  the market price does not rise above the loan rate—just like the
  farmer.

Form G lending authority has been used extensively by rice and cotton cooperatives, which were the original recipients of the privilege. Cooperatives are much stronger in these commodities than is typical of
grain cooperatives. When in the mid-1970s, Form G lending authority
was extended to grain cooperatives, the multinational grain companies
were sufficiently upset to challenge the USDA's authority in court. The
multinationals apparently feared that cooperatives' relative market position would become stronger in grain. However, this has never material-

ized. There are three alternative explanations for cooperatives' lack of success in exploiting Form G lending authority in grain to the advantage of producers:

- Grain farmers hold the right to market their grain independently more dearly than do rice and cotton producers.
- Management of grain cooperatives does not have the same level of marketing talent as does that of rice and cotton cooperatives. As a result, they would be unable to generate higher average levels of producer returns.
- Multinational grain companies have so many other advantages, such as being able to buy and sell the grains of countries throughout the world, that grain cooperatives were unable to compete.

Reality indicates that each of these factors probably plays a role in grain cooperatives' relative lack of use of Form G lending authority.

Research and patent policy. Publicly sponsored research has been a tradition in U.S. agriculture extending to the creation of the land-grant universities in each state. These universities, with a prime responsibility for agricultural research and technology transfer, are a driving force behind the progressiveness of American agriculture.

Agribusiness has been a primary beneficiary of agricultural research in the following ways:

- Input manufacturers have converted the products of agricultural research into new varieties, chemicals, and machinery. Agricultural extension has encouraged the adoption of this new technology whenever it proved advantageous.
- Food processors and marketers have enjoyed the benefits of higher-quality, lower-priced farm products.
- Input manufacturers and market intermediaries have been more competitive in foreign markets, where both the inputs and the farm products have been sold.

In the 1980s, patent rights were extended to the products of biotechnology. This expansion of patent rights allows input manufacturers and food processors to capture an increased share of the benefits from agricultural research and could change the structure of farming.[12] The benefits of patents are obvious in terms of higher profits (monopoly rents) for inputs

[12]Universities also gain from the extension of patent rights to biotechnology because they receive increased private-sector support from agribusiness and generally hold the patents with rights being sold to an input manufacturer or food processor.

or products having patent rights. In addition, clearly superior patented inputs or products might be used as a lever for gaining increased control of a commodity through contract or ownership integration. Commodities having the benefits of patent rights might be effectively converted into branded food products. Such structural changes could become the focal point of future controversy regarding the structure of agriculture.

Food Policy

The impact of food and demand expansion programs on agribusiness is often overlooked. Yet whole industries have been built to serve the food needs created by programs such as school lunch. The food stamp program has a decidedly different impact on food processors and marketers than have commodity distribution programs. In addition, domestic and international generic advertising and promotion programs create demand surges with direct agribusiness benefits.

School lunch.   USDA is the largest purchaser of prepared foods in America through its school lunch program. Schools serve 24.3 million people each day. All of these meals are, in varying degrees, subsidized by USDA. Arguably, the school lunch program fostered the food service sector of the food industry and contributed significantly to the development of the fast-food business.

Food processor and marketer impacts are materially different depending on whether schools' food needs are subsidized by giving the schools commodities or cash. If schools are given commodities, USDA makes the decision on what is bought. In addition, commodity purchases are from national companies as opposed to local business. Schools have much more flexibility when they buy commodities themselves. Local processors and marketers often get the business. In addition, more value-added foods are generally purchased by schools. That is, while USDA has a tendency to buy a standard product such as whole carcass turkeys or dried beans, schools buy turkey breasts or canned beans. USDA aims for having the greatest impact on producer prices, while schools buy for convenience.

School lunch also influences what people eat. Without school lunch, children would carry their own lunches, made up largely of bread, luncheon meat, peanut butter, jelly, cheese, fresh fruit, and soft drinks. School lunch fosters the consumption of vastly increased quantities of dairy products (particularly milk and processed cheese), hamburgers, canned peaches, canned pears, beans, canned tomatoes, hams, macaroni, potatoes, fats, oils, eggs, turkeys, and hot dogs. Spillover effects obviously exist on what the population eats.[13]

[13]Students can readily identify with and discuss how school lunch influenced what they ate in high school and their current attitudes toward certain foods.

Food stamps versus commodity distribution.   One of the historic controversies in USDA food programs is whether to distribute food stamps or commodities. The major difference between the two systems is in its food processor and marketer impacts. Commodity distribution bypasses food retailers. In addition, different food processors may supply USDA's commodity purchase programs than sell to food retailers. Secondary impacts of commodity distribution programs may extend to other commodities. For example, if butter is distributed, margarine sales are adversely affected.

Because commodity distribution programs displace commercial sales, food retailers have been ardent advocates of food stamps. Food stamps not only allow the poor to purchase more food, but also allow the purchase of more value-added products. The major beneficiaries of food stamps, therefore, are the food retailers and processors that produce branded, value-added products.

Advertising and Promotion

In 1986, USDA spent about $300 million on domestic and international advertising and promotion programs.[14] While producers provided the vast majority of these funds through check-off programs, agribusiness was a major beneficiary.

The prime objective of advertising and promotion programs is to expand demand. This has the short-run effect of raising prices and the longer-run effect of expanding supplies. Agribusiness benefits from the short-run price increasing impact as much as farmers—maybe more. When demand is expanding, it is easier for food processors and marketers to pass on price increases. Profits, therefore, tend to be stronger. Some of the most profitable years for dairy processing plants were in the mid-1980s, when demand for dairy products was rising while the milk price support was being reduced. The reason lies in the fact that the combined effects of increased advertising financed by a milk producer check-off program and reduced milk prices. Interestingly the reduced milk price effects on consumption served to provide the illusion that the advertising program was considerably more effective than it really was.

Similarly, market intermediaries benefit from international demand expansion activities. Cooperator programs help teach potential foreign buyers how most effectively to utilize U.S. agricultural products. This responsibility would otherwise fall largely on the exporter. Benefits are realized by both the farmer in terms of expanded demand, and by market intermediaries in terms of increased volume of product handled

[14]Ronald W. Ward, Walter J. Armbruster, and Stanley R. Thompson, *Generic Advertising, Research and Promotion Programs* (College Station, Tex.: Texas Agricultural Extension Service, November 1987).

at reduced costs. The precise magnitude of these benefits is difficult to quantify, but with over $25 billion in exports it is not unreasonable to anticipate agribusiness benefits that exceed the producer contributions!

AGRIBUSINESS INVOLVEMENT IN POLICY

Agribusiness involvement in policy is both offensive and defensive. Defensive involvement is designed to prevent adverse impacts on a firm's costs, volume, and profits. Offensive involvement is designed to capture a share of the benefits of government assistance that may be enacted primarily to help farmers and/or consumers. Little, if any, attention has been given to the distribution of costs and benefits. However, judging from the proliferation of agribusiness lobbying, the payoffs must be substantial from both offensive and defensive lobbying.

It can also be observed that relatively few farm or food programs are enacted that have a consistently negative impact on agribusiness. If proposed, such potentially negative programs are swiftly defeated. Witness the fate of the Harkin mandatory supply control bill. If enacted, programs having a negative impact on agribusiness are generally of short duration or are modified to materially reduce the impact. These realities attest to the sophistication and power of agribusiness lobbying.

Chapter 16

National Agricultural and Food Policy

> *Our task is not to fix the blame for the past,*
> *but to fix the course for the future.*
>
> John F. Kennedy

The establishment of a consistent national agricultural and food policy involves the development of a set of overall policy goals as well as a consistent set of policies and programs to achieve those goals. Agricultural and food policy is seldom formulated in a manner that explicitly recognizes the interrelationships between agriculture and the rest of the economy. The result is a myriad of policy inconsistencies and conflicting actions: the use of food as a tool of diplomacy conflicts with USDA efforts to expand markets; the efforts to develop markets conflict with soil and water conservation objectives; prices are controlled when increased production is needed; price and income supports are raised in the face of surplus production; and research to increase productivity goes on when surpluses are large and growing.

The Congress, the president, and state and local governments regularly take action to solve a particular problem without recognizing that the actions may create even more severe problems or exacerbate the existing ones. This happens for several reasons:

- The overall set of policy goals is seldom specified. If specified, insufficient attention is given to establishing priorities among the many goals as a means of resolving conflict.

- The focus of attention in government is frequently very short run—solve the problem at hand, without regard for the effect on the achievement of other goals. Farm policy debates are frequently so protracted that only policy crises are able to attract sufficient attention for resolution.[1]
- The political reality of the desire to be reelected frequently overrides other goals of the policymakers.
- The causal relationships and interrelationships among and between policy variables and goals are frequently little understood (or overtly misunderstood) by the policymakers.
- Each interest group tends to seek a solution to its problem without consideration for the effect on the achievement of other policy goals.
- All interest groups are not equally represented in the process of policy formulation. Since the American political process is largely an adversarial process, those interests that are best represented have an inherent advantage in achieving their goals.

The result is that the American system is not geared to consider broad policy goals and priorities. Nor is policy itself made in a manner that considers broad policy goals. Policy evolves over time and gradually moves toward a point of greater consistency. The biggest conflicts develop in a time of transition, such as in the 1970s, when the supply–demand balance began to tighten, resource limitations became more apparent, consumer concerns intensified, and efforts to control the growth of government increased. Even so, there has been recognition of the need for a more comprehensive and consistent national policy framework for food and agriculture.[2]

DEVELOPING A NATIONAL AGRICULTURAL AND FOOD POLICY

Lee suggests four steps in developing a national agricultural and food policy:

- *Agreement on an overall policy goal or objective.* A deliberate statement of what agricultural and food policy seeks to accomplish must be expressed in terms of an overall goal. All other goals are subsidi-

[1]William T. Boehm, "Agricultural Policy: Some Hard Choices Ahead," *South. J. Agric. Econ.* (July 1981), pp. 1–9.

[2]T.A. Stucker, J.B. Penn, and R.D. Knutson, "Agricultural-Food Policymaking: Process and Participants," in *Agricultural-Food Policy Review*, AFPR-1 (Washington, D.C.: ERS, USDA, January 1977), pp. 1–11.

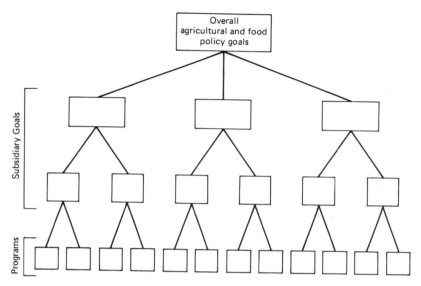

Figure 16.1   Hierarchy of policy goals.

ary to this overall goal. Choosing this goal becomes absolutely critical to the ultimate resolution of any conflicts that exist or might develop. Several alternative overall goals will be discussed
subsequently.

- *Specification of subsidiary goals.* For each of the major policy
  areas—international, domestic farm, food, and resource policy—this
  book has specified an array of policy goals. These goals need to be
  reevaluated in light of the overall goal. Additional goals may need
  to be established for relatively new policy areas, such as resource or
  structure policy.
- *Establishment of an order of priority among the subsidiary goals.*
  The subsidiary goals need to be directly related to the overall policy
  goal or objective as a hierarchy of goals (Fig. 16.1). Where a particular subsidiary goal fits in the hierarchy is critically important to the
  emphasis it receives in the overall policy package.
- *Development of programs to realize the subsidiary goals and, in turn,
  the overall goal.* Such programs must not only recognize the subsidiary goal but also its place in the hierarchy of goals.[3]

[3]John E. Lee, "Food and Agricultural Policy: A Suggested Approach," in *Agricultural-Food Policy Review*, AFPR-4 (Washington, D.C.: ESS, USDA, April 1981), pp.
136–148.

ALTERNATIVE NATIONAL GOALS AND OBJECTIVES

The overall agricultural and food policy goals have a critical impact not only on the hierarchy of goals but also on the specific programs designed to achieve these goals. More important, it appears that a shift in the overall goal or objective may have occurred in the late 1970s and early 1980s. For example, from the 1940s through much of the 1960s, the overall goal of agricultural and food policy was to raise farm incomes to the level of nonfarm incomes. In the late 1960s or early 1970s, the overall goal began to change and the hierarchy of goals started to shift. This shift was caused by several factors, including a rise in farm income relative to nonfarm income, the expansion of markets through exports, and a decrease in rural representation in the Congress due to reapportionment.

In the 1980s, the goal of farm policy appeared to shift back in the direction of maintaining farm prices and incomes. A number of alternative goals had, however, evolved and were being promoted by various interest groups.

- Assuring an adequate supply of food and well-being for the world's population
- Improving the nutritional status of the American population and ensuring the safety of the food supply
- Maintaining a high level of farm prices and incomes to provide farmers with income stability over the long term
- Maintaining a structure of predominantly moderate-size farms
- Eliminating domestic farm programs and establishing a world free-trade environment
- Maintaining agricultural and food policies that contribute to overall economic and foreign policy objectives

Each of these overall goals implies a substantially different mix and hierarchy of subsidiary goals and programs to carry it out, thus warranting further elaboration.

Supply Assurance

The assurance of an adequate supply of food requires programs designed primarily to expand production and see that food is available where and when it is needed. The primary concern is to feed people adequately throughout the world. The implication is quite clearly a right of every person to an adequate supply of food. The policy is, therefore, global as opposed to purely domestic in orientation.

The hierarchy of subsidiary goals consistent with the overall supply assurance goal places emphasis on international programs to expand food production and domestic and international food assistance programs, as well as the preservation of resources for future generations. No preference is given to production at home versus production abroad. Emphasis is placed, instead, on producing products wherever they can be produced at the lowest cost.

Programs consistent with the supply assurance objective include world and individual country food reserves, international price stabilization and enhancement programs, increased research and development assistance, food distribution programs, and soil and water conservation programs. Domestic farm programs would take a back seat to international agricultural programs. Emphasis in these programs would be on maintaining farm price and income stability from a worldwide perspective.

Support for the supply assurance objective would come primarily from church groups, international organizations, and conservation groups.

Improved Nutrition

In the mid-1970s, when farm incomes were relatively favorable, consumer concerns shifted. Improved nutrition and food safety came into a position of prominence as the overall policy goal. The person most closely associated with this effort was Carol Foreman, then assistant secretary for food and consumer services in USDA. Foreman outlined the following steps in the development of a national agricultural and food policy:

1. Determine nutritional needs for optimal growth, performance, and well-being. This required increased research into the nutrients essential for good health as well as the relation of diet to disease and related health problems.
2. Clarify the U.S. role in feeding the world, including the role of food reserves, food assistance, exports, embargoes, and technical assistance. The inclusion of this step results in similarities with the supply assurance objective.
3. Stimulate and sustain production of those commodities that are needed to meet nutritional needs. This would require a reassessment of those commodities that are supported and promoted in line with nutrition and trade needs. Beef would likely receive less support, fruits and vegetables more.
4. Assure availability of food at reasonable prices by fostering an efficient and competitive marketing system. This requires antitrust policies and regulation of excessive advertising and packaging.

5. Assure a safe, high-quality food supply. This, in the view of Foreman, requires more than just regulation of additives and manufacturing processes. It also includes regulating the quantity of fat and salt in food.

6. Assure an adequate diet to those who cannot afford it. This includes provision for expanded nutrition education so that people are better able to assess what they should be eating at lowest cost.[4]

In a nutshell, the Foreman proposal placed nutrition first in the policy development process. All other goals were subsidiary. Many farm interests charged that during the Foreman years in USDA, nutrition-oriented policies had, in fact, taken over the department. Consumer groups, nutritionists, and the medical profession continue as the main proponents of the nutrition goal.

High Farm Prices and Incomes

Many in agriculture would like to see a return to the high price and income policies that characterized the 1940s and 1950s. Agriculture, they contend, is still the backbone of the nation, and the government has a responsibility to assure the health and well-being of farmers, even if it means high food prices, reduced exports, and high government costs.

Maintaining high commodity prices and incomes requires a highly controlled agriculture. Production control programs would be required to curb production. High commodity price supports and production controls would limit exports largely to those that are subsidized. Improved nutrition would clearly be a lower-level goal, if it existed at all. Similarly, international development assistance programs would be clearly subsidiary to direct food assistance and two-price export plans. Farm organizations and related rural interests would be the main proponents of the goal of high farm prices and income.

Maintaining Moderate-Size Farms

Although many farm advocates think otherwise, there is no assurance that a high farm price and income policy will maintain moderate size. Rather, it may simply fuel inflation in land prices, encourage outside investment in agriculture, and encourage larger farms to expand by purchasing smaller farms at an even more rapid pace (economic cannibalism).

Recognizing the potential for higher prices and incomes resulting in

[4]Carol Tucker Foreman, "Toward a U.S. Food Policy," in *1978 Food and Agricultural Outlook* (Washington, D.C.: Committee on Agriculture, Nutrition, and Forestry, U.S. Senate, December 19, 1977), pp. 10–20.

fewer, rather than more, farms, OTA did an extensive analysis of the public policy requirements for the survival of moderate-size farms.[5] It was determined that virtually all agricultural programs would need to be biased in favor of moderate-sized farms to assure their survival. Such programs would include the exclusion of large farms from income support, directing public research toward overcoming the economies of size and management, and providing public marketing services solely to the benefit of moderate-size farms. Price supports could not be utilized, because benefits could not be targeted for moderate-size farms. Advocates of such policies include public interest groups such as church groups. Interestingly, the major farm organizations generally have not been supportive of such policies presumably because their directors tend to be managers of large farm operations—most of which are family farms.

Free Trade

In preparation for the Uruguay Round of GATT negotiations, the Reagan administration set forth a negotiating position of eliminating all forms of domestic subsidies to farmers by year 2000. This position recognized the previously stated reality that domestic farm subsidies are the basic cause of barriers to trade. In addition to eliminating domestic farm programs, free trade implies the elimination of all import and export barriers to trade in all countries. Trade still would not truly be free, in that barriers such as state traders or exchange-rate distortions could still exist. However, free-trade advocates assert that the general welfare would be enhanced. Such advocates include export- and import-oriented businesses, many economists, and export-oriented policymakers.

Economic and Foreign Policy Consistency

As noted in Chapter 8, monetary and fiscal policy have a direct impact on agriculture. In addition, agriculture and food policy can be directed in a manner where its primary goal would be to serve economic and foreign policy objectives. There is, in fact, increasing evidence that in the 1970s and early 1980s, broader economic and foreign policy goals were a primary motivating force behind agricultural and food policy. Examples of economic- and foreign-policy-motivated actions included the imposition of the Soviet grain embargo in 1979, sanctions imposed during the Polish crisis in 1982, spending ceilings placed on farm and food stamp programs, and limitations placed on the use of marketing orders for purposes of controlling production.

[5]Office of Technology Assessment, *Technology, Public Policy, and the Changing Structure of Agriculture* (Washington, D.C.: U.S. Congress, March 1986).

A continuation of such trends might suggest that over time agricultural and food policy would simply become a subset of general economic and foreign policy. If this happens, domestic farm programs such as target prices would probably vanish, and CCC commodity loans and other farm lending programs would be blended into other government lending policies, such as those of the Small Business Administration. The food stamp program would become a part of general welfare policy. Land-grant universities would cease to have a special USDA-supported mission in agricultural research and extension functions. The functions of USDA could, in fact, be distributed among various federal agencies, such as the departments of Health and Human Services, Commerce, Interior, and State; the National Science Foundation; and the Small Business Administration. Whether free trade exists would depend on general economic and foreign policy decisions.

CONCLUDING REMARKS

The future of agricultural policy is about as difficult to predict as the future of agriculture itself. Although changes in policy are frequently slow to occur, progressive change is evident. Agriculture and food problems are moving targets. Surpluses and low prices are sometimes interrupted by deficits and high prices. Economic booms are interrupted by recessions and unemployment. Agricultural and food policy goals shift as priorities change.

The basic volatility of agriculture and the importance of food to the survival of humankind complicate the problems of farmers, consumers, and policymakers in arriving at a mutually acceptable agricultural and food policy. This initially requires an understanding of the policy options, their consequences, and their interrelationships. Secondarily, it requires a willingness on the part of those affected by agricultural and food policy to recognize each other's interests and seek compromise solutions. This is not an easy task, but it is as important to agriculture as food is to life itself.

Index